DUMP

RECIEV-
ING HOME

FARM

WATERMELON CORNER ↘

HWY--80

BLVD

CAMPUS

WILLOWS

BUCKNER

ROCK-
BOTTOM

BULL
POND

BLVD

EVAN'S
STORE

FORNEY RD.

RAILROAD SIDING

URBANDALE

PLEASENT GROVE

Buckner Memoirs:

The Orphan Chronicles

The Buckner Alumni Association

Book Project Committee:
Bobbi Richardson Batchelder, Vernon Horsley
Leston Lee McNeil, Jerre Graves Simmons

Jerre Graves Simmons, Editor

Contents

Foreword

When R. C. Buckner died in 1919, one writer wrote that the greatest monument "Father" Buckner left behind was the thousands of fine young men and women who stood as a testimony to the work of Buckner Orphans Home. Since Father Buckner began the work of Buckner Orphans Home in 1879, the greatest testimony of this work has been the people whose lives have been touched.

Buckner has always been about people. That is unique among "institutions." When we tell the Buckner story, we tell stories about people. When we talk about the difference Buckner makes in our world, we talk about changed lives. When we talk about success, we are not referring to a financial bottom line, but to individuals who are now living full and meaningful lives.

So it is fitting that those whose lives have been directly affected by Buckner would add their voice to this story. This book is a recollection—a memoir of these "children," many of whom are now fifty years removed from their Buckner days. And while they are adults, their memories are those of children. As you read these memories, you will find yourself laughing at some stories and crying at others.

Today, as it was 100 years ago, these alumni and former residents stand as the greatest monument to the ministry of Buckner. They are a reminder that we are engaged in a work that is eternal rather than temporal. What greater joy can there be than the joy found in changing a life forever? Here then, are their stories.

Kenneth L. Hall, President,
Buckner Baptist Benevolences
Summer 2000

Prologue

Building on the Past

*"Am I not engaged in the highest work known
to men and angels?"*

— R. C. Buckner

Dr. Robert Cooke Buckner, a Baptist pastor from Tennessee, was the motivating force behind the establishment of Buckner Orphans Home. During the annual meeting of the Deacons Convention in Paris, Texas, in 1877, a resolution was passed to begin an orphans home as soon as $2,000 could be raised. Dr. Buckner was named fund raising agent by his peers.

Two days later, Dr. Buckner collected his first funds—$27—when he passed his hat among fellow brethren visiting under an oak tree; the first dollar was his own. By the end of 1879, he had $1,200, which he supplemented with a personal bank note. With a state charter in hand, he rented a small cottage in East Dallas in December 1879 to care for the first three orphan children.

In 1880, forty-four acres were purchased six miles east of Dallas, where Buckner Children's Home still operates today. Gradually adding land and property, the Home owned more than 500 acres by the turn of the century. Buckner is the fifth oldest organization in Dallas.

Father Buckner, as he was affectionately called, was also heavily involved in community and state affairs. In 1877, he founded the first high school in North Texas for African Americans. He was instrumental in establishing the Dallas Humane Society and served as its president. He founded Children's Hospital in Dallas in 1894, and he was one of the driving forces behind the opening of Baptist Memorial Sanitarium (now Baylor Healthcare System), serving as president of the Board from 1904-1908.

In Baptist life, Dr. Buckner was president of the Baptist General Convention of Texas longer than any individual past or present, from 1894-1913, and he founded the Baptist Women's Missionary Training School in 1904.

In 1914, at the age of eighty-one, Father Buckner and the trustees affiliated the home with the BGCT, as long as the charter would be adhered to—that the Home be operated to benefit the needy. The Convention accepted the responsibility and elected a twenty-seven-member board of trustees.

Father Buckner died on April 9, 1919, 40 years to the day after the first charter was filed. At his death, one writer wrote of R. C. Buckner: "Of some men great in the councils of their country, leaders in state craft or on the battlefield, heroic monuments remind us. But the finest monument this good man left behind is the monument of living men and women who, under his Christian care while girls and boys, have grown up into the estate of splendid citizenship, of sturdy manhood and sweet womanhood; having become living assets in that great ledger of both assets and liabilities we call humankind. An undying memorial to how well this good man wrought the Buckner Orphans Home remains. As sparkling and sustaining as dew upon the grass, so were his good deeds."

Since his death, the foundations which he established have been wisely built upon and managed to expand into a multi-faceted ministry offering a wide array of services, while never losing sight of the original intent of R. C. Buckner.

Today, Buckner is one of the largest private socialcare agencies of its kind in the nation. Under the leadership of Dr. Kenneth L. Hall, the organization's fifth president, Buckner is a vastly diversified ministry dedicated to the restoration, care and healing of children, families and senior adults.

Buckner Children and Family Services helps children, individuals and families in sixteen cities and towns across Texas. While keeping with the traditional residential placement for children in several areas, Buckner has also created new and innovative ways of offering prevention and intervention for at-risk children and families.

Seeing the need to provide a service to senior adults, Dr. Buckner became one of the first to provide care for the aging by establishing cottage homes adjacent to the orphans home. The first residents of the cottages were disabled aged Civil War veterans and their wives, including a crippled Confederate veteran who had served the Orphans Home as a dentist.

In September 1954, the Mary E. Trew Home for the Aged was opened on Samuell Blvd. Within a short time, Buckner Retirement Services became known as a leading provider of quality care for senior adults, and today has facilities, in-home services and community programs in seven Texas cities, with facilities in one other city nearing completion.

Also growing from R.C. Buckner's commitment to care for "not one, but all orphaned children," Buckner Adoption and Maternity Services has seen thousands of children adopted by loving Christian families. In 1996, Buckner International Services, a subsidiary program of Buckner Adoption, began work in Russia and Romania, providing humanitarian support and international adoption.

Through the expansion of programs and services in 1998, Buckner enhanced its ability to successfully fulfill its mission statement. In doing so, Buckner continues its tradition of "building a brighter future . . ." for those we serve.

SCOTT COLLINS
Director of Communications
Buckner Benevolences

Acknowledgments

To the other members of the Book Project Committee, without whom there would have been no beginning or ending: to Bobbi Richardson Batchelder, whom we credit as The Initiator of the Project; and to Vernon Horsley and Leston Lee McNeil, the two public relations experts and supporters par excellence, the entire Alumni Association owes the most profound thanks for your contributions to the project.

To the Buckner Home Alumni Association and the Board of Directors, whose endorsement of our Book Project gave us the courage to proceed with our plans, thanks again and again.

To Bob Stokes, who earlier attempted to do this very thing, who graciously left us his legacy of manuscripts and whose spirit inspired our own tenacity, we acknowledge our debt.

To the contributors to the book, thank you for trusting your manuscripts and pictures to us and, indeed, for your financial support when it was needed.

To those who helped with errands, identifications of pictures and people, research and helpful suggestions—usually needed at the last minute—especially Bill Simmons, Ruby Dobbs, David Reynolds, Dessie and Wayne Hamrick, Helen Swift, Ken Norman, and Sally Bingham; to you all, our extreme gratitude.

To our friends and relatives who listened for so long to all our stories about getting the book ready for publication and finally obligingly ordered copies for themselves, we applaud the constancy of your friendship.

To Pat Williams, Executive Assistant to the President of Buckner Benevolences, who fortuitously lent her expertise in proofreading our manuscript, a special thank you for all your assistance.

To Ed Eakin and his staff at Eakin Press, who seem to be blest with endless patience with the inexperienced, thank you for your indefatigable kindness.

Finally, we owe the greatest debt, which we can never repay, to Scott Collins of Buckner Benevolences, who faithfully took the time to give our project needed direction, found a publisher for us and every time we faltered, with his sage counsel, set us on the right path again. His stalwart and continued support of our project made our perseverance possible to the very end.

Introduction

Those of us who grew up at Buckner Orphans Home discovered as we grew older how much we loved that red brick campus that for over 120 years remained a beacon on a hill in East Dallas County. Year after year we returned there for Homecoming. After we learned the time had come when those buildings would have to be torn down to make way for a different kind of caring for homeless children, we were prompted to preserve our heritage and memories.

J. B. Cranfill and J. L. Walker have produced a biography of our founder, *R. C. Buckner's Life of Faith and Works*. Dr. Karen Bullock has written a history of the Home, its administration and the growth of Buckner Benevolences in her book, *Homeward Bound: The Heart and Heritage of Buckner*. Buckner Benevolences even produced *Home Sweet Home*, a picture book history of the buildings on the campus. But that campus was crowded for many years with children whose activities made every brick and board, every road and sidewalk, every tree, flower and blade of grass resound to the tenor of their lives. While those lives were rigidly structured, we were not all alike. But we are alike in wanting to preserve the memories of our days as orphans.

The entire story of Buckner will not be told until the children who grew up there also have their say. Memory is not an exact science; it is subjective and personal. However, the reader will find in these pages, as one alumni put it, "the truth as we remember it," even if some experiences are older than five decades. Our stories are from people who graduated from the high school or left the home in the 30s through the 70s. Every decade brought some changes, but when the Buckner campus became ringed about with heavily populated surroundings and shopping malls, it was no longer possible for the orphans to lead the protected and secluded life that had been a hallmark of our nurturing and education. At the same time our society began to turn its vision from institutional care for children to saving and reuniting their families. Therefore Buckner's ministry changed.

Like all children we were often both kind and cruel, happy and sad, creative and passive, cooperative and rebellious, and in this book we tell all—not just stories that show us in a saintly light.

Assembling the records of the laughter and tears of our adventures as Father Buckner's Orphans has been a labor of love. The thread of gratitude to our supporters, especially Texas Baptists, the Buckner family and the Home staff runs through every page. The love for those individuals who cared for us so relentlessly twenty-four hours a day, seven days a week for so many years is overwhelmingly apparent. As we celebrate our youth, lived together, we wish also that those who gave so unselfishly of themselves to the shaping of our lives, could read what we have written. We probably never thought to say thank you to them, but we honor their memory and the memory of the friends who became our families as we shared the orphan experience.

We came to Buckner because our homes and families had been destroyed by overwhelming disasters: illness, desertion or deaths that left us helpless. At Buckner we found food and shelter, an education, faith in God, friends and above all stability. It was as if a hand reached down, plucked us from dire circumstances and carried us away to prepare us for a better life than we had even imagined possible.

We knew the rest of the world led lives very different from ours; we felt true happiness was somewhere in the future and not available to orphans. Happiness would come when we were "away from here" living in the real world. What we did not know was how precious in retrospect the memories of those early times would become to us.

Our lives at Buckner made it possible for us to have skills to fulfill the dreams that we dared not dream for ourselves. We want to record here for history that our adult lives stand as testimony that the dream Father Buckner had for orphan children to become productive citizens, was not an impossible dream. This book is dedicated to those who supported us, the Buckner family, the staff, the orphans themselves, friends, teachers, caretakers, and all those who wrote their stories and shared these memories. In addition, we owe a great debt of gratitude to Buckner Benevolences, especially Dr. Ken Hall, Neal Knighton and Scott Collins, who lent their support and expertise to our endeavors and made this publication possible.

Here in their own voices are the memoirs of five decades of those children whom Buckner salvaged from hopelessness.

Jerre Graves Simmons, Editor

The Thirties

"Let the little children come to me, and don't prevent them for of such is the kingdom of heaven." Matthew 19:14 (RSI)

Miss Leona Moore, c '30s

by David M. Wells

For several years beginning in 1928, Miss Leona Moore taught art and writing (as it was then called) to the fifth, sixth and seventh grades at Buckner Home Academy, located on the campus of Buckner Orphans Home, a few miles east of Dallas, Texas.

She subsequently served as Dean of Girls at the Home, where she became known as "Ononi" (O-no'-nee) to the generation of children who were at Buckner in that era. These "Home Kids," as they always refer to themselves, grew to love this gentle but fun-loving woman who had learned and practiced the art of communicating with young people a full generation before that word had such an important connotation placed upon it.

In the doggerel following, the author attempts to recapture through nostalgia those things—now many years gone—which Miss Moore meant to him and to all Home kids who have been privileged to know and love her.

OUR TEACHER

She came to us at Buckner in '28
From Oklahoma, which I think is out of state,
To teach art and writing in the Old Grammar
    School,
Where Miss Neal, the principal, held iron rule.
She introduced us to the method called Palmer,
Those push-pulls and ovals can bring a kid trauma.

Though I tried and tried in my miserable scrawl,
I never got a paper hung up on the wall.
And when it come to line and form,
I'm afraid they were rendered nothing but harm.
As for perspective, I learned to face it;
I never drew a line that I didn't erase it.
But they say it's the cunning who win the race;
If the paper is thin enough, you can always trace.
If it hadn't been for the Mona Lisa
I'd never have learned "I-talion," like "Pizza."
There were Bonheur, Homer and their artist
    friends,
And what's his name who painted "Harp of the
    Winds"?
Remember that Indian in a cave roasting corn?
I thought in the Tribe Ta-os he was born.
Well, the Indian moved from the cave to a house
And I learned he wasn't a Ta-os, but a Toos.
From Miss Durham, Miss Washburn, you and
    Miss Neal,
We learned our school work and we know it still;
It's been a long time since we climbed those stairs,
And we've traded those old desks for easy chairs.
Remember the laundry and the old school court?
Buckner's changing so you'd think starboard was
    port.
True, art and penmanship aren't keystones of life,
But she brought us much more in this vale of
    strife:
To smile, to sing, to laugh, to love—
Those gifts through her were ours from above.
Over forty long years still glistens a treasure
Of love so deep that one cannot measure.
Now my thoughts turn serious, and they're hard
    to rhyme.
This orphan can sense it's quitting time,

So the rest of my tribute won't be in verse.
I intend it for the better. (It couldn't be worse.)

Her life is like a loaf of bread cast upon the waters. This loaf was not leavened with the usual agent, but rather it was leavened with a love for children. This love benefited all children, but it was found to be most beneficial to orphan children. And she come upon a whole sea of orphan children and cast her loaf upon that sea. And verily, there returned to her a special love from those orphan children. And their love is so bounteous that it never ceases. And it shall never cease. God bless Leona Moore!

It had to be Leona Moore

by Bob Stokes

"He got stuck in the mud and had to push-pull . . . push-pull . . . push-pull . . . push-pull . . . push-pull and swing!

"You circle around . . . around . . . around . . . around . . . around and pig-tail."

During the decade of the 30s, if you remember hearing the above instructions, you were bound to be in Miss Leona Moore's penmanship class.

Many of the students attending Buckner Home Academy during that era, learned the basics of good penmanship by the formation of W's and O's, as well as the correct formation of all capitals and lower letters of the alphabet, under her instructions.

This beautiful, rotund lady's favorite expression for mischievousness was: "If you don't stop, I'm going to pinch your head off and throw it in your face!"

Estes C. Wright, '33

A LIFE TO BE LIVED

As we journey through life here on this planet called earth, we encounter continual changes and challenging situations under which we must live. Some of these can be very difficult; others, very good. Some few individuals find a peaceful, happy life from birth to the grave, but this is not the normal path we tread.

I look back on my days at Buckner Orphans Home as a period of difficult change, but I am very thankful for that time. It filled a great need in my life and the lives of my two younger sisters, Eura and Rena.

We arrived at BOH in late January 1927. In the seven preceding years we had lost our mother of TB, our grandfather with whom we had lived for five years, of pneumonia; and our father of a ruptured appendix. When he died, he had only been remarried for two years—during which time we had been living with him. At the time of his death, he had been working for the Ford Assembly Plant in East Dallas.

At a local Baptist Church, he sang in the choir and was a member of a male quartet, which went to the Buckner Orphanage once to sing. He was quite impressed with what he saw and heard. That night after he returned home, he remarked to his wife that if anything happened to him, he would like for us to be sent to Buckner Orphans Home.

Believe it or not, within a few months he had died, and we were at BOH. I won't say those weren't hard days. I cried myself to sleep many nights, and I struggled with a lot of emotion and bitterness.

My sisters were across campus, even in the same dormitory, but they were assigned different beds on different floors and didn't see that much of each other. With different classes and assignments, we saw very little of each other at school. There was an approved custom that allowed boys and girls, if they had no work assignments during that time, to stand outside the exit doors of Manna Hall and talk to each other after the evening meal. This was a tremendous help to new children on the campus. My two sisters and I looked forward to this time every evening, especially during that adjustment period. Being the big brother, I had to fight my emotions and try to encourage them all the time. If we got mail, which wasn't often, it was usually addressed to me and I shared that with them. I had the advantage of seeing it first, so I was usually able to get my emotions somewhat under control before they saw it.

I struggled with a lot of things during those early months. My school work suffered and my grades showed it. My interest in any play activity died. I sat around and watched kids play, but I wasn't interested in participating. I'll confess that I was at a low ebb.

I will ever be grateful to a teacher, whose name I can't remember now, who stopped me once at the end of a school day and asked if she could talk to me a few minutes. We talked for quite a while. She asked questions about my life and what I was going through. She could see that I was in turmoil. We began to talk about the Lord, how He loved and wanted to help us and about His death on the cross to take our sins and to redeem us. That day she led me to trust the Lord Jesus as my Lord and Savior. That became a vital relationship that has lived within me ever since. My life changed. My struggle and emotions began to ease up. My interest in things began to come to life. My grades improved.

I didn't have all the answers at once but my life returned, and I have praised God ever since for what He has done in my life.

Others may have stories that are similar, or different or more dramatic, but I felt that I needed to put my story into written form. I trust that it may help someone along life's way.

I want to say God has given me a wonderful life, including my life at Buckner Orphans Home. I want to thank Him and all those who have contributed along the way.

College days during the Depression years were another time when financial needs were a struggle, but God answered many prayers. I have a degree in Electrical Engineering from New Mexico State University and have worked in power distribution, underwater sound research, electronics and sound fields.

For thirty-five years I had the privilege and responsibility for electronics and sound engineering work with the Moody Institute of Science under the umbrella of the Moody Bible Institute. Dr. Irwin Moon was the man who had the vision of blending the Bible and Science to reach the unreached of the world.

During my college years, God brought into my life my wonderful wife, Sigrid Evelyn Gustafson. We have been married for fifty-nine years and have five children, sixteen grandchildren and three great-grandchildren.

We are both in our eighties and enjoying reasonably good health at this time. What more can a man ask of life?

FALL PECAN HARVEST

Through the years at Buckner Orphans Home, some of us older boys liked to go to the woods west of the campus when we had free time. One year we noticed people picking up pecans around where they were picnicking. Further investigation revealed pecans still hanging in the burs on several large trees.

We liked pecans and began trying to figure the best way to get them from the trees before the black crows and squirrels harvested them. We tried hitting the limbs with pieces of branches but found them too short, too brittle or too heavy. Finally, my eyes sighted a patch of yard cane down by the creek. I took my knife from my pocket, cut a straight pole about ten feet long and stripped its entire length of leaves. The result was a light, tough pole, excellent for flailing the pecans. I was soon up in the tree and pecans were hitting the ground.

Holding on to a firm branch above my head with my left hand and using the pole with my right hand, I stood on larger branches at the point where they grew into the trunk of the tree. The boys on the ground picked up the pecans as they fell. Although there were several trees in the area, and a harvest season lasted no longer than three week-ends, we always got our full share for each year.

The secret of our success was our ability to flail the nuts from the trees before they fell from the burs naturally.

I think we must have harvested well over a hundred pounds for each of the three years that we worked during our high school days.

We sold most of the nuts for spending money for our annual trip to the Texas State Fair in October of each year.

FOOTBALL IN THE EARLY THIRTIES

In 1932 our football practice field was self-laid-out in the northwest corner of the boys' play area. A goal post stood at the south end of the field only. This placement was designed to keep kicked balls off the road at the north end of the field as we practiced.

Our uniforms were "hand me downs" from various sources and we wore whatever fit. This included helmets and shoes. We seldom had more than three or four balls; consequently, we guarded them very carefully.

The team was selected from about eighteen to twenty boys. Our school in those days probably averaged about fifty to fifty-five boys in high school and a number of those were not interested in football or had assigned duties that did not allow them to participate. To practice, we broke the squad into sections for different drills, both offense and defense.

We practiced about four to five days per week after school. The principal was our coach, but often he could not be with us after school, and the team captain had to lead the drills.

The coach selected the first team players for each position and this group played both offense and defense for the whole game unless a player was injured. Then a substitute took his place until he could return to the game. We had few injuries in most games.

Another unique situation was that we had no home games. We always played our games at the other teams' home fields because we had no stadium and no home supporting crowd to finance the game.

We played in a league of other small high schools, mostly from farming communities, and there was an agreement for this arrangement. I do not remember the names of all the schools we played, but we held our own pretty well with most of them though we were usually outnumbered and outweighed by the others. We usually had crowd support in most games we played.

We did pretty well for the season and came to the final game tied with Irving, a small community between Dallas and Fort Worth. We played on even terms for most of the game, but toward the end, their team blocked a punt, covered the ball in the end zone for a touchdown and won the game, 7-0.

We were disappointed but still felt we had had a good season. It was an enjoyable experience for my last year in Buckner Home.

James W. Cook, '34

by Bob Stokes

James Cook came to BOH from Ranger, Texas, in 1926 with six brothers and one sister when he was only eleven years old. Both parents were deceased.

He embarked on an Army career soon after leaving BOH in 1934. After twenty-four years in the service he retired with the rank of Major. Still young and energetic, he began a second career as

Budget Director of the University of California at Sacramento.

Retired from the university after seventeen years, he had forty-one total years of work well done. It was time to devote himself completely to his lovely wife, his four children and the grand-children.

Woodrow "Square Can" Sears, '34

ROCK SHOOTER: WEAPON OF CHOICE

One of the most desirable things for the younger boys at Buckner during the 20s and 30s was to make their own rock-shooter! It was quite a simple procedure.

The boy had to find a suitable forked tree limb or a piece of flat wood, shaped to fit a small hand, and place a "V" cut in the upper ends. Then attach two rubber bands cut from an auto innertube to the stock at one end and to the leather pouch or sling at the other. Then place a rock or marble in the pouch and hold it with thumb and forefinger while extending the stock forward, stretching the rubber bands. By releasing the fingers—zoom—the rock could find its mark rather accurately up to twelve or fifteen yards. Some of our shots were accurate at further distances with this weapon! Generally, the targets were glass bottles, tin cans, wasp nests and stray dogs! Also birds!

Even though the rock-shooters were against the rules of the Home, the boys continued to make them and spend many hours enjoying their homemade weapons.

Raymond "Pig" Monday, '35

by Bob Stokes

In the early 1920s three children from Pampa, Texas, were placed in Buckner Orphans Home: Mildred, Dean, and Raymond Monday. For some reason Raymond was nicknamed "Pig." Pig graduated in 1935 and returned to Pampa to look for a job when Texas was just beginning to recover from the depression. He walked the streets and scanned the local newspaper for possible openings.

Finally, he noticed an ad for a radio announcer on the local radio station and applied for the job. The station manager was so impressed, he hired Raymond immediately. Raymond was elated, loved the radio job and soon knew that he wanted to pursue broadcasting as a profession.

Shortly after the Japanese attack on Pearl Harbor and the beginning of WW II, I was in my room at Howard Payne College, listening to the news over KBWD in Brownwood, Texas. After the news cast was over, the announcer said, "Your announcer has been Ray Monday." Since that name was familiar to me, I called the station and asked to speak with the announcer.

The operator asked me to hold for a moment. Then I heard, "Hello, this is Ray Monday."

I said, "Oh, yeah, could this be Pig Monday?"

The reply came, "Oh, my goodness, you must be from Buckner." After I told him who I was, we met for coffee and reminiscing. It was a great day because neither of us had known that the other was in Brownwood.

After WW II, I got a job as recreation technician at the VA Hospital in Waco, Texas. Once again I was listening to WACO radio and heard the announcer remark, "This is Ray Monday speaking." Yes, and how ironic. Again it was Pig Monday. What a coincidence to meet again via radio.

Raymond bad been in the Armed Forces Radio Service and spent some time on the job in Paris, France. While in Paris, Raymond met and fell in love with a pretty French girl. He brought her to Waco, where they were married, and, according to reports, he spent his life in radio.

David Wells, '35

At Buckner Children's Home (formerly Buckner Orphans Home) it is currently the custom at Christmas time for all of the children to visit in the homes of their "sponsors," meaning people who share their households with one or more of Buckner's present students.

So for about three days, including Christmas Eve and Christmas Day, the Buckner Campus is deserted and silent.

But like Dickens' Ghost of Christmas Past, we—you and I, old friend—can relate to a time forty Christmases gone, a time when those same deserted and silent buildings were aglow with the sights and sounds of Christmas.

Old friend, you and I know Buckner's children will have another enjoyable Christmas this year with their kind and generous friends. But I am just not certain that their memories four decades from now will be so clear and so sweet as the memories we share of that long ago and far away.

CHRISTMAS AT BUCKNER
(1930)

When Miss Vallie called matrons to the
  Commissary,
You knew you were heading for the Season so
  Merry.

The matron chose for you some wonderful things
Then tied them together on a long piece of
  string.
And at the string's end was a black stocking—
  filled
With candy, nuts, and fruit; boy, how you thrilled!

If you always bathed and combed your hair
  straight,
You might be the lucky one to get roller skates.
A status symbol for all the other kids to see
Was that cord around your neck to hold the
  skate key.
The best skates of all were Union Hardware;
If you got that kind, you were floating on air.
Even if the sidewalks had many cracks,
Oft in my fancy I want to go back.
I wonder if I could still "walk the chain"
Around the lamp posts and back again?

A bicycle once came for Big Peggy O'Neal
And all were envious of this great deal.
But then for Peggy came a cruel blow—
"All the kids get to ride it," ruled Brother Joe.
As you might guess, this raised so much static
Brother Joe put the bike in the High School
  Attic.

Christmas Day brought that wonderful meal,
And you again discovered that celery was for real.
On those supperless days, the kids were left
  guessing
How much to save of the turkey and dressing.
Though you stuffed and stuffed, it's most
  surprising
How hungry a boy gets 'ere the next morning's
  rising.
Holiday—no school—just play, play, play;
Some wished it would stay forever this way.
And before Christmas Cheer had faded away,

Came yet another feast—Father Buckner's
   Birthday;
Plus a bag box of brittle for each and every kid,
And you always saved the pretty lid.
But Christmas was gone when in the attic you
   were put
With a brick, a nail and a pile of "hicker" nuts.

That was Christmas at Buckner; has it been
   forty years?
You're right, my friend: those really are tears.
They're partly from nostalgia, and partly from
   joy;
I've always been lucky—I was a Buckner Home
   boy.

Emma (Atkinson) Laird, '36

by Erin Ferguson, Emma's granddaughter

FOND MEMORIES

There are many fond memories Emma Laird
Atkinson holds of Buckner Orphanage, founded
by Father Buckner, and after his death run by Hal
and Joe Buckner.

One night, in the girl's dormitory, Crouch
Hall, discussion began between a group of girls
about their favorite fruit. One of them, Catherine
Reynolds, claimed proudly that her favorite fruit
was apples. She went on to add that she could
probably eat a dozen apples at one sitting. Her
friends, of course, took her up on the claim.
Twelve good-size apples were purchased from the
general store the next day. By suppertime that
night, every soul within a mile knew that the girl
would eat (or try to eat) the apples instead of the
usual meal.

The children all filed in, sang a song, prayed
over the food, and sat. Silence reigned. Throughout the room, the sound of apples crunching
could be heard. Half, one, then two apples disappeared. Finally, Miss Mamie told the matron,
Miss Crow, to get that girl out of the room so that
all the children could eat!

The distraction eliminated, the orphanage
ran on as usual with one exception. Later that
night, after the Manna Hall had been cleared, the
girl finished her apple feast. The prize she
received was a small cake. She cut a large hunk
out of the cake, ate it, then went to bed.

During the night, the children listened for

sounds of painful death. They never came, and the
victorious girl never let on to any signs of bellyache.
A happy ending— for everyone but the apples.

Sometimes, after a rain, the Buckner
Orphans would engage in more daring stunts
than apple eating contests. Namely, they would
take a block of soap down to the old concrete
banister and, soaping their bellies, they would
take a joy ride down the wet concrete. Some went
head first; some, feet first. It's odd how the criti-
cally acclaimed imagination of children today
can't find such a dangerous after-storm activity
with just a bar of soap and a wet banister.

Then there was the memorable year when
Emma Laird took a salesmanship class at school.
The teacher told the class, "If you go out and look
straight up at the sky for long enough, pretty
soon a group of passers by will gather around and
look up into the air. If enough people tell a person that they look sick, they will go to bed and
call the doctor." That was the wrong move. Soon,
the girls in the dorm decided to play a truly evil
trick on the matron, Miss Crow.

The next day, each member of the girl's
dorm made a comment about her health, such as:
"Miss Crow, you don't look well. Are you ill?"

"Miss Crow, you look so pale!"

"Miss Crow, don't you think you should be in
bed?" Before the morning was over, the unfortunate woman took the day off and went home to
bed. And then there was the attic. Every building
at Buckner had either a basement or an attic with
creepy tales told about it. Buckner's legendary
"house of horror" was the attic where stories were
told of bloody footprints and the like. One night,
a girl in the dorm dreamt that she wet her bed,
took her sheets down to the basement to wash
them and hung them up to dry in the attic. Now,
this dream would not be worth recording except
that, when the girl woke, she was halfway down
the attic stairs.

Then there was Christmas. In South Texas,
where Mrs. Atkinson lives now, there is little or no
snow, even in late winter, certainly not around
Christmas time. So she looks back with a special
fondness to the Christmases spent in Buckner
when snow coated the ground almost every year.
The older children would wake up at 4:00 A.M., go
outside and stand under the street lights to sing
carols.

After the little children got up, they would go
into the school auditorium to get their "strings,"

little cloth bags with goodies inside. The children made treats from their Christmas fruit and clean snow. The auditorium and stage were ornamented beautifully. What better Christmas could a child ask for?

Then there was the matter of the Fair to consider. On Fair day all the Buckner children would trundle down to the Fair Grounds with free passes and whatever money they had. (The boys would pick cotton during the summertime to earn money.) Mrs. Atkinson, in her wilder youth, rode all the scary rides, INCLUDING the ones that went upside down.

There is so much more to tell about Buckner Orphanage, about field trips and graduations and best friends, far more than can be recorded here. However, I hope that more stories are told and look forward to reading them.

Howard L. Myers, '36

A.K.A. Tom Brown

ANOTHER WASP STORY

In the late 20s and early 30s, I was in on lots of "wasp fights" but the story of this one was told to me by Mr. Duck Elliott many years later when we both lived in Tucson, Arizona.

The wooded area southwest of Buckner, called White Rock because of the white chalk formations along the little stream running through it, usually had many, many, wasp nests in the spring. Buckner boys would often sally forth, armed with sling shots and a cluster of brush for swatters, and proceed to demolish as many of these "Indian Wasp" colonies as possible.

On this particular trip, "Tater" Pethoud and a half-dozen Buckner Boys, after shooting down several nests, and out-running the angry wasps, arrived at one of the several swimming holes so dear to our hearts. Tater cautioned the group not to disturb any nests close to where they would be swimming sans clothing. However, it was Tater himself who, climbing a tree overhanging the water, discovered a well hidden wasp nest. "Hey, you guys, watch this! I'm gonna jump, snatch this nest down with me and drown the Indian Wasps!"

Carefully gauging his trajectory via wasp nest, he carefully jumped into the water. Holding the severed nest at arm's length, Tater, wasps, and

nest plunged into the water. The other boys, playing it safe, scrambled onto the bank to watch.

Alas! Things didn't go as Tater planned! Most of the wasps left the nest on the way down, and lost no time in attacking Tater before he hit the water. Even the ones staying on the nest didn't drown! The waxy coating on their bodies allowed them to pop up like corks. These, after jiggling their wings a bit, joined in the attack. Tater would duck under and swim as far as he could, only to find those wasps waiting for him as he surfaced. His yells were matched with loud laughter from those watching from the bank.

Flinging water like a windmill to distract the wasps a bit, Tater reached the bank. Now here the wasps found some other nude bodies to attend to, and the watchers' laughing quickly turned into yelling, as they hastily grabbed up clothes, slingshots and brush "swatters" to make a fighting retreat from the area.

The story quickly spread as Tater made a visit to Bethshan to have his many stings looked after, and all who heard it vowed never to attempt to drown any of those wasps again!

I THINK I HEARD SOMETHING CRACK

One time, around early November, 1933, I had a very frightening experience in a Buckner field gang, engaged in stripping a cotton field southeast of the water tower. There were at least twenty boys in the group with Mikey Hawthorne as our "straw boss."

We were making that last "pick" of the field, pulling that last bit of cotton, hulls and all, and throwing them into a large wagon. The wagon, with wide tread wheels, did not have mules hitched to it. We boys served as the motive power. When it needed moving, we clustered around it, and pushed.

I happened to be just ahead of the left side rear wheel for my spot to push. While the wagon rolled slowly forward, my right foot got caught by the rear wheel behind me. Before I knew what had happened, that wide tread had crawled up my right leg, slamming me to the ground.

It so happened that my position was such that the other boys did not see what had happened. Those ahead, didn't look back, and those on the other side, behind the wagon, couldn't see me. I was so surprised by that wheel crawling up my leg that I didn't even cry out. So the wheel slowly crawled up my right leg, across my back and exited across my left shoulder, just missing my head. The wide tread of the wagon, plus the soft earth I was being pressed down in, plus, I am sure some Divine Intervention, prevented me from being hurt. Luckily for me, very little load was in the wagon so far.

The boys in the rear of the wagon first spotted what had happened. Their startled yells brought Mikey Hawthorne running to see what had happened. As he helped me to my feet, he asked anxiously, "Hey, Tom, are you all right?"

Well, I WAS just fine, but knowing I would not get off that hot dusty work party if I told the straw boss that, I blurted out the first thing I could think of: "Well, I think I heard something crack!"

The roar of laughter from that group of boys, could surely be heard clear up to the Manna Hall! Why they found that remark so darn funny I still do not know!

That remark did get me off that work party, however, for Mikey told me to get over to Bethshan and have them check me out. It's true that for months, I had to listen to the jeers from Buckner boys of all ages: "Hey, Tom, did you really hear something CRACK?"

Donald C. Cook, '37

by Bob Stokes

Donald C. Cook, from Ranger, Texas, entered BOH at the age of seven. He lettered in football and basketball in 1936 and 1937, graduated in 1937 and attended North Texas State Teachers College in Denton, Texas. Donald joined the U.S. Air Force and became a pilot. While in the Air Force and stationed in the Philippines, he received his BA Degree from the University of the Philippines.

He retired from the Air Force after twenty-two years with the rank of Major, but returned as a civilian civil service employee for the Air Force and remained another twenty years. He accumulated a grand total of forty-two years of dedicated service.

At this writing he lives in retirement with his wife in San Antonio, Texas.

Nell (Kolb) Grover, '38

BEFORE BUCKNER

I was born December 13, 1919, in San Antonio, Texas, the last of four children. My mother had lost one daughter to diphtheria in 1917. An older sister, a brother, who was deaf, and I were left. My father disappeared, never to return, two months before I was born. Soon after, my mother, who had been working in a hospital for tubercular patients, contracted tuberculosis, and we went to live with my mother's parents on a farm east of Gonzales, Texas. My sister and I attended a one-room schoolhouse three miles from the farm. We rode 'Ole Roan through all kinds of weather and loved it! My grandparents died within a year of each other, followed by my mother just before I was seven years old. My brother was attending the School For the Deaf in Austin, Texas, but my sister and I were sent to Chicago to live with my mother's sister and her family.

Within a year my sister was returned to Texas, for our aunt was convinced that she had contracted TB. We soon learned that this was a mistake, and a friendly couple sent my sister to school. The following year my aunt and her family took a vacation to Mississippi to visit friends; in fact, one of them was the lady for whom my mother had named me. Without explanation, my aunt put me on a bus bound for Gonzales, Texas. I was dressed in a white dress with red dots and was carrying my doll. I was eight years old and so proud that I could remember where my uncle's printing office was located. He was totally unprepared when I marched in, another mouth to feed in the middle of the Depression! I lived with his family until the following summer in 1931 when he was able to get me accepted at Buckner Orphans Home.

AT BUCKNER

I'm thinking in retrospect that in spite of the Depression, the thirties were a new beginning for Buckner Orphans Home. Not long after I arrived, work began on the much needed new buildings. This was possible because of the good-hearted interest of the Baptist people of Texas.

The "new" Manna Hall was one of the first new buildings. We no longer had to pluck chickens in that old kitchen and mop floors with cut-up pieces of old quilts, we had a new kitchen and dinning room. However, it was in the old Manna Hall where I met the wrath of Mamie Daudelin. She really "put me in my place" for pointing out where my spot in line as a waitress would be to pick up food for my table. I was vindicated later, however, by being assigned to wait on the senior boys' table at which Jimmie Mills, Thomas Bearden and Bob Stokes were seated. They were members of our winning football team of 1937!

The new hospital was built, followed by the middle girls' building, the senior girls' building and later our Sunbeam Home for the little ones. I had worked in the old nursery when Jimmie Sherrell was a baby there. Later, I worked in the new hospital, cooking for a time until they could get a real cook—I was about thirteen! I also helped take care of the patients when it was tonsil removal time. One favorite job I had was working in the commissary opening the boxes of clothing that came in from the good Baptists of Texas. At that time Thomas Bearden worked in the bakery, but I'm afraid he never noticed me!

We lived from day to day—doing the best we could at our assigned jobs, our school work and trying to survive the long dull summers. In the thirties the swimming pool, located in the high school, was closed, never to open again. I remember swimming only one summer. Years later an outdoor pool was built.

I loved to sing. In fact, Ethel Reid and I used to sit on the curb in front of the senior girls' building and sing—switching harmony mid song—for anyone who cared to listen. Later I was pleased to be chosen to sing in a trio with Dorcas Sanders, and Clarine Marsh. We got to go to several churches and once to a music competition at Baylor University. We didn't win but we had fun.

I also sang in the Home Choir on Sundays and will never forget the mural scene someone painted in the Baptistry. I suppose it will be destroyed when the Chapel is torn down.

We were big on football, having a great team that featured among others, James Mills, Thomas Bearden and Bob Stokes.

In the fall of 1937, we felt that since we had a winning football team, we should have a pep squad to lead the fans and encourage enthusiasm for the team. So Ethel Reid, Dorcas Sanders and I were selected as leaders.

Since we had never even seen a cheerleader perform, we followed Miss Leona Moore's in-

structions and hoped we did not look ridiculous doing so.

We had no money for uniforms, but no problem; we went to the commissary to see what we could find. Even though in those days girls were not into wearing slacks, we got boys' white cotton pants and dyed them purple. We also dyed white shirts gold, and then added purple ties. We were all set!

As yet we had no football yells, but we did have a school song, thanks to Leona Moore and Grace Stamps Mills. With the cooperation of a lot of people, we quickly worked up a few yells and were ready to go!

I remember a very tragic incident when I was working in the laundry. We were inserting sheets into the big mangle, and Marie Lucille Wood Hauck somehow got her left hand caught in the mangle. It was a minute before we could get the machine stopped, and by that time she had lost half of three middle fingers on that hand. Marie Lucille was in my class, and we were always so proud of the way she never let her accident keep her from playing the piano. She played for our songs before meals in the Manna Hall and wherever else she was needed.

AFTER BUCKNER

When I graduated in May 1938, it was decided that I would return to my uncle's home in Gonzales. Leona (Ononie) Moore drove me to the bus station in Dallas. We both cried when I boarded the bus. I thought it would be the last time I would see her, but I had delightful contact with Ononie for many years to come. I boarded the bus for Gonzales, and as we left Luling, Texas, I was the only passenger left on the bus. Well, it didn't take the bus driver long to introduce me to my first pass, nor did it take me long to see to it that he realized his mistake!

My uncle met me at the bus station. My aunt and her son ran a flower shop, and I was soon learning to make funeral wreaths and corsages as well as cooking for the family. I also worked in a Five and Dime Store and typed for a law office and the County Court House. This was all good experience, I realized later.

In the summer of 1941, an uncle and aunt came through our town on vacation and invited me to come live with them and go to their local

Secretarial/Radio College. Their children were gone and I did not hesitate!

So I took a bus for Port Arthur and was soon enrolled in Radio College. The government was asking women to get involved as it sure looked like we would be in the war and men would be called, of course. Even so, I was the only girl enrolled and made a little money teaching typing to the fellows who needed it to record code as they received it. In August of 1942, I accepted a position as a broadcast engineer with KARK, Arkansas' only NBC Station at the time. I worked ten hours a day and seven days a week for four years all during World War II!

I later married Leland Kolb, an ex-Marine Pilot, and we came to California in August 1946. Lee enrolled in Berkeley, graduating in January 1949. Our son, Richard Leland, was born that spring. Soon after, Lee went to work for Chrysler Corporation and was with them for almost thirty years. We were transferred to Oregon for twelve years, and in 1954, our daughter, Merry Gaye, was born. We were transferred back to San Mateo, California, in December of 1967. By this time our son, Rick, was in the Army and spent his year in Vietnam. With many of our prayers, he came home safely. Both children eventually married and live not far from us. Rick has one son and Merry has a son and daughter, our beautiful grandchildren!

Irene (Chick) Marsh, '38

by Bob Stokes

BLOOMER BLOOPERS

A young, pretty little girl at Buckner loved dill pickles tremendously. It was her chore to serve food to the girls waiting on the tables in Manna Hall. One day during a brief interlude, she proceeded to the pantry where Miss Mamie kept the dill pickle barrel. Considering her intentions, she realized she would have to make a fast trip while Miss Mamie was detained with other matters. As she was returning to her station, she passed Miss Mamie, who stopped her, asking if she had been into the pickles.

"Oh, no, Miss Mamie!" she assured her, but with the aroma of pickles so strong as she passed by, Miss Mamie could not help noticing; so she raised the girl's dress and shook a bloomer leg. Of course out fell a pickle. She then shook the other bloomer leg and out fell another pickle. This humiliated this little girl completely. She was also disconsolate at having lost her pickles.

In 1992 my brother Frank and I visited Irene Marsh (Chick) in Big Springs, Texas. She finally told this true story on herself. But she says this experience never has lessened her love for dill pickles, still one of her favorite foods.

After graduating from Buckner, Irene attended Howard Payne College at Brownwood. Being such a fun-loving girl and friendly to everyone, she was honored by the student body with the nickname of "D-O-P-E-Y."

Bob Stokes, '38

OUR ADMISSION TO BUCKNER HOME

It was on a June morning in 1928, that a younger brother, an older sister and I arose from a night's sleep and were taken to Buckner Orphans Home. Brother Joe Buckner had just dispatched permission for the Stokes children (the three youngest) to be admitted on arrival. The Receiving Home had just been completed and was ready for admissions.

My younger brother, Frank, was seven; I was nine; my sister, eleven. We three younger children were being taken care of by a neighbor couple, Ted and Helen Coleman, at Athens, Texas. Two other older sisters and an older brother remained in Athens to look out for the property that our dad had left at his death.

Minnie, our oldest sister, was married and lived not far from the Colmans. Lea, our next oldest sister, stayed with Minnie and her husband for a short time until an Uncle took her to O'Donnell, Texas. Earl, our oldest brother, was soon married.

Our mother had died of pneumonia about five years previously. Then our father, weakened with depression and working long hours at carpentry and share-cropping, died unexpectedly at age forty-seven. Our father's death left his children in a dilemma. Thanks to Buckner Home, that dilemma was solved. We were then, and still are, most grateful that we were accepted in our time of peril.

As we left Athens, just Mr. Coleman and the three of us, we headed toward Dallas. After we had just passed Seagoville, to our right we saw the road sign indicating Buckner Boulevard. Still the scenery was mostly hay fields, oat patches, corn fields, and scrub mesquite bushes. Occasionally we saw a clump of old post oak trees and very few houses. As we approached the next intersection coming out of Dallas, we saw the sign for Scyene Road. To the left on both sides of Scyene Road were two graveyards. (One was to hold the bullet-riddled bodies of Bonnie Parker and Clyde Barrow in a few years.)

As we progressed down a hill from that point and leveled off over a track crossing, there was Military Parkway. The rail crossing was the track for the interurban that ran from Dallas to Mesquite.

After another quarter mile, we saw a railroad crossing near the Forney Road intersection. On the left was a small country store and filling station, known as Evans Store. That's where we orphans later spent our pennies when money was given to us by relatives or friends. From this point, we could easily see the sprawling Buckner campus. The road led straight forward to the fence surrounding the Home. Then it veered left to the front and on to East Pike. We turned right on East Pike, passed the electrical sub-station, passed Dick Porter's residence, turned left at the old Buckner Bakery and proceeded to the new Receiving Home.

Mrs. Dena Saddler welcomed us to our new home. Bertha, Frank and I were greatly impressed with the large buildings and new surroundings. Mrs. Sadler showed us our sleeping facilities, lockers, bathrooms, etc. She informed us that a doctor and nurse would be by the next day to check on our health and give us the necessary inoculations. That was our introduction to Buckner Orphans Home!

THE STOKES FAMILY AFTERWARDS

Bertha graduated from Buckner High in 1936. She was soon married to Roy Bremer, a paint foreman for the Mayo Clinic in Rochester, Minnesota. They raised two children.

Robert left in 1938 and attended Howard Payne College on an athletic scholarship. He won numerous honors at Buckner in football, track and basketball, and in 1937 played as All-Star in the Onion Bowl in Garland, Texas. He won eight events in county, district and regional track meets in 1936, the first year BOH became a participant in the Texas Interscholastic League Athletic Program. He repeated the same honors in '37 and '38 and was selected as All-County in football and basketball for those two years.

In 1939 he was the first freshman to ever be Hi-Point-Man in Howard Payne and Texas Conference history. He won first place in all three weight events, shot put, discus and javelin. In football he was chosen All-Conference in '41 and '42. Also MVP in '41 and '42. Finally he was selected Little-All-American in 1942 and placed in Howard Payne University's Sports Hall Of Fame in 1987.

He received a B.A. Degree in Physical Education, entered the Navy and became a Physical Fitness Instructor. As a Navy participant, Robert was Hi-Point-Man in the Texas Relays Track meet held in Austin, Texas, in 1945. He also won shot put, discus and javelin at the Oklahoma AAU track meet the same year.

He received an honorable discharge from the Navy as Chief Specialist (A) (AA) on December 12, 1945, and was hired as athletic technician at the Veterans Administration Hospital in Waco in 1946. Two years later he transferred to the VA Hospital in New Orleans as Recreation Director and remained there until his retirement in 1980. Counting his military and VA service Robert had almost thirty-eight years of government service.

After retirement he and his wife, Grace, lived in New Orleans. They had two daughters, one son and three beautiful grandchildren.

DONALD WASN'T HEAVY

Surely most of you have heard or read the story as told by Father Flanagan of Boys Town in Omaha, Nebraska. It is the story of two brothers who entered the premises of Boys Town Orphanage, searching for a home, care, and love. The older brother, whose clothes and shoes were all tattered, was carrying his shoeless, shirtless brother on his back. He was asked, "Isn't your load too heavy?"

The lad replied, "No, he ain't heavy, Father. He's my brother!"

In the thirties there is a similar brotherly

love story to be told of Buckner Orphans Home. During the long, hot summer of 1932, Shorty Collins, farm supervisor, assigned one of his tractor drivers to plow some new farm land that used to be the Buckner Cemetery. It was just below The Willows, located about 600 yards back of the commissary. He also directed two other boys to ride the disc-plow for added weight to help keep the discs in the sun-parched ground.

After driving the initial trip around the field, Shorty turned the Farm-all Tractor over to the driver to continue the plowing. First, he cautioned the driver to keep a close watch on the riders because of the rough terrain, and then left to supervise other details.

After some hours of plowing, the driver saw one rider's legs slip through the center core of the plow and become lodged between two sharp discs. The driver was able to stop immediately. His quick reaction to the situation prevented a more serious accident. However, when the rider's legs were removed from the entanglement, he complained of pain in his right ankle. He was unable to put any touch-down-weight on his foot.

Being greatly concerned, the driver immediately took the injured boy on his back and carried him about a mile to the hospital. The x-rays indicated the right ankle was broken. It was put in a plaster cast, and the boy was given crutches for about six weeks. Shortly thereafter, the young lad was back, as active as ever!

You may ask, "Who were these three young farmers?" The tractor driver was James Cook. The injured boy was Donald Cook, the tractor driver's brother. The other young plow rider was the writer of this story.

ATHLETICS, A DISCIPLINE TOOL AT BUCKNER: A CELEBRATION OF DEAN TAYLOR AND HIS BOYS

In the early thirties the entire nation was in a Depression. The financial and economic conditions had deteriorated to the point that people were restless and fearful of the future. The children at Buckner were caught up in the same frustration, and there were discipline problems brought on by the uncertainty of the time.

The older boys were trying to organize adapted athletic activities to channel the younger boys' excess energies. But without the necessary facilities, equipment and backing, it was a frus-

trating situation. For touch football, the boys used stuffed stockings. For baseball, there weren't enough gloves to field a complete team. Some field positions had to be played without gloves. The young boys played basketball with anything that would bounce, including tennis balls. In track, the participants would run in tennis shoes or bare-foot. The athletic facilities were minimal. The football and track fields were full of "pock holes" and "sand-burrs," as was the baseball field. Basketball practice was held on an outside clay court, but in inclement weather the team practiced in the attic of McElroy Hall.

The boys in the high school grades had a football team but were without the direction of an experienced coach. The 1934 team was directed by Mr. G. G. Dickey, Superintendent of the School. The team was not in a league and so selected their opponents from independent teams around the county. Many times the football players were unable to practice because of their work details on campus; thus, the team did not have sufficient practice and discipline to play consistent football in an interscholastic league district.

In the spring of 1935, Gordon S. Taylor, a Howard Payne College graduate, was hired as Dean of Boys and history teacher. He had played football and had previous experience working with and teaching young men at a Baptist Academy in San Marcos, Texas. He used his coaching skills to instill good sportsmanship and fair play in the boys through their activities.

After working a short time at Buckner, Mr. Taylor confided to his wife, Ruth, that he was quite sure he knew what the children needed. "They need a well organized, competitive athletic program." He felt the boys and girls were too confined and needed contact, athletically and scholastically, with other children in the community. He was skeptical as to whether or not he would be able to convince Brother Hal that an athletic program would be helpful.

Mr. Taylor called Brother Hal the next morning and requested a conference with him at his earliest convenience. "Sure, Brother Taylor, come on over to the office!"

Thoroughly convinced that he was right in his evaluation, Mr. Taylor went to the office and presented his idea. He told Brother Hal, "These orphan children need to compete against other schools and other children in the community. They want to prove to themselves and others that they are not inferior just because they are deprived of one or both of their natural parents."

"Oh, Brother Taylor, you are so convincing in your logic, but the Baptist people of Texas are supporting us at great sacrifice, and I don't think they would approve of our spending money on athletic programs and equipment in these depressed times."

There were some moments of silence, and then Brother Hal looked up across the desk at Gordon Taylor and said, "I trust you are right; I can't turn the children down. Let me see your plans and costs."

To field athletic teams in boys' football, basketball, track, and girls' basketball, there was an estimated cost of about $600, a very large sum in those days. This also included fielding a boys' grammar school soft-ball team. Regular baseball was eliminated from consideration because of the popularity of soft-ball in 1935.

After a few moments of discussion, Brother Hal gave approval to the program with an admonition that winning was not to be emphasized too strongly. Brother Hal sincerely felt that a winning athletic program would not help the Orphans Home. Mr. Taylor, of course, felt otherwise and was anxious to prove it!

Gordon Taylor left the office that day with numerous added responsibilities and not a penny in additional pay. Henceforth, he was not only Dean of Boys and teacher, but also coach.

Mr. G. G. Dickey and Coach Taylor began implementing the program immediately. A request was submitted to the Texas Interscholastic League County Program, but the submission was too late to be included in the 1935 schedule. Both the boys and girls' applications were approved to start the 1936 season in the 10-B County League.

After an inventory of the old football equipment, Coach Taylor bought additional equipment to dress out about thirty to thirty-five players. The new blue and gold uniforms were not the best or highest priced equipment, but the Buckner Hornets were as proud as peacocks of their new uniforms.

The 1935 football team played as an independent and scheduled on an open-date basis. With no records available for the 1935 season, the win/loss record is unknown. Even Coach Taylor didn't remember the specific statistics but felt certain that the Hornets won more games than they lost that year.

Brother Joe Buckner, managing the Home at the time, promised to give the team a dollar bill for the first win of the '35 season. That promised "buck" was presented to Coach Taylor after the Hornets beat the Gophers of Grand Prairie by the score of about 26 to 6. The Hornets pulled a sideline hide-out play on Grand Prairie in the first quarter of play. This play, which is now illegal, plus the famed Buckner spread formation kept the Gophers rattled for the rest of the game!

Brother Joe was in attendance that day. His presence left a genuinely warm feeling with the team and showed Coach Taylor that the athletic program had his backing.

Coach Taylor framed the dollar bill and hung it on the wall near the administrative offices below the chapel, and it is known to have remained there for many years. In fact, the memento may still be in the trophy case at the Home.

Coach Taylor stressed basic football fundamentals during the 1935 season. He drilled the team in proper techniques, in blocking, tackling, catch, carrying the ball, and insisted on hustle, hustle, hustle! Coach placed importance on team play, good physical conditioning and sportsmanship.

After the 1935 season, Coach Taylor called his football players together and gave them his assessment. "We had some wins this year and we had some losses, but that is only a part of the record. This year each of you has consistently improved from game to game. You have learned that your opponents were not superior to you as you had imagined. Just remember, they put their pants on one-leg-at-a-time just as you do! Next year if you continue to improve, continue to hustle and play as a team, winning will take care of itself. You have learned that winning is more fun than the alternative, and in another year or two the Buckner Hornets will be top of the pack in district 10-B.

"We want to especially thank the girls' Pep Squad who contributed greatly to the fighting spirit of our team this year. We commend them for their spirited backing and ask for their continued support next year."

Entering the Interscholastic League District 10-B in 1936, the Buckner Hornets played Garland, Irving, Mesquite, Grand Prairie, Richardson, Carrollton, and Lancaster. To round out the schedule, Buckner played two Dallas City League B Teams.

Even with no official records for verification

of the wins and losses that year, it is understood to have been a losing season. However, Coach Taylor recalls that it was a learning season for the Hornets and a good number of experienced lettermen would be returning the next year. The Irving Tigers won the 10-B District in 1936.

Buckner's real loss during 1936 was not on the athletic field, but it was the sudden death of Brother Joe Buckner. He died of a heart attack shortly after suffering a cerebral hemorrhage at his home on the campus. It was truly a sad day for all the children at the Home. Brother Joe had given himself to all!

In 1937, just the second year after being admitted into the Interscholastic League District 10-B schedule, Buckner won the District Championship by defeating Irving's Tigers, the previous year's champs, 19 to 0. The Orphans garnered their title a game and a half ahead of runner-up, Garland Owls. The only losses in 1937 were to two non-district opponents, Denton Demonstration School and their strongest Bi-district opponent, Diamond Hill.

The team lost a squeaker to Denton by the score of 7 to 6, and their loss to Diamond Hill was 31 to 13. The Buckner Hornets scored 238 points in 1937 to their opponents' 58. It was touted by the district coaches that the Buckner lads had an awesome running and passing attack that year. Coach Taylor was selected as Coach of the Year in 1937 in District 10-B.

One of Buckner's loyal fans, Ruth Taylor, the coach's wife, pulled a sneaker during the 1937 football season! She became perturbed at the Dallas newspapers because of the coverage they were not giving BOH athletics. Mrs. Taylor visited the newspapers and made her feelings known. She told them that it was ironic that they gave the Masonic Orphans Home of Fort Worth more publicity than they did Dallas' own Buckner Orphans Home. She left the offices of the newspapers she had visited that day expecting more fairness in their publicity.

Coach Taylor was unaware at that time of his wife's visit to the papers. Later, he said it evidently did some good because the papers called and wanted to come out, get an interview and take pictures of the team.

The 1938 football season rolled around, and Buckner was once again favored to win their football district title. Coach Taylor and his team upheld the preseason prediction and won their

district for the second consecutive year without a defeat in district play. The only blemish on the Hornets' record was their defeat by Diamond Hill of Fort Worth in the Bi-district Playoff for the second straight year.

By this time Buckner was not only becoming dominant in football, but also in basketball and track. At the end of the '39 season, Coach Taylor's athletes had won two district football championships, three basketball championships and two track championships. This was quite an accomplishment, considering that Buckner had only been competing in district competition since the 1936 season.

But with the athletic accomplishments, the Baptist supporters all over the state of Texas were beginning to insist that Buckner consider providing the necessary athletic facilities on the campus.

Under the leadership of Mr. Paul Danna, President of the Board of Trustees, the board approved construction of a cinder track, football field, basketball gymnasium, and an outdoor swimming pool. Locations for the facilities were made and work began without delay. Brother Hal had become a real big fan of Buckner athletics and followed the teams as often as he could. Coach Taylor had proven to Brother Hal and the Board of Trustees that athletics were beneficial for the children and the Home.

The teams continued to win awards and honors, and the 1940 team gained the 14-A District title for the third time in four years. They won the Bi-district by playing Handley to a tie of 6 to 6, winning the skirmish on first downs, 13 to 5. This put them in the regional playoffs against Mart, the champs of Districts 11-A and 12-A. They lost the game by a single point, 13 to 12 on a questionable pass interference call on a Mart conversion try. After assessing the penalty against Buckner, the Mart Panthers made good their second try by kicking the extra point. It was the final game for both teams since the regional title was the highest stake in Class A football at the time. According to the Buckner Hornet, the Home's news publication; Dizzy and Paul Dean, St. Louis Cardinals' baseball pitchers, were in attendance at this game. When they were acknowledged by the game announcer, they stood up and waved at the players and those in the stands. A thrilling moment for athletic fans!

From 1941 through 1945 there were ravages of war going on in Europe. Reports of battles won and lost continued to head-line the newspapers all over America. (Coach Taylor's son, Gordon Stewart Taylor, Jr., declared "missing in action" in 1944, was later a prisoner of war in Stalag #1 Prison Camp near the Baltic Sea and finally liberated by the Russian forces under the command of Marshall Zukov.) There were 380 Buckner boys who served their country honorably in the military forces. Seventeen of them sacrificed their lives!

Athletic teams continued at Buckner during the war years. The team members were smaller, younger, and less experienced because of the draft and volunteer induction, but they continued to win their share of football, basketball and track honors.

At the end of the 1945-46 year, the Home lost its first athletic coach. Dean Taylor returned to his alma mater, Howard Payne, as Dean of Men and Professor of Psychology. A young man by the name of M. C. Greenwood took over the athletic program at Buckner.

In summary, the athletic facilities had been completed, and they were second-to-none in the Dallas Country League. Many of Coach Taylor's athletes had won individual and team honors at the high school level. Some attended college on athletic scholarships; some under his influence attended on academic scholarships. One even became an All-American!

CATCH THE ONE BEHIND . . . NAAAAAH!

Glen James, a resident at BOH in the late 20s and early 30s, had an older sister who worked as a clerk at Titches Department Store. Glen hitchhiked into Dallas one time during the summer to visit his sister. After the visit Glen's sister gave him enough money to return to Buckner by bus. Glenn, not knowing much about city buses, went out on East Grand Avenue and waited for the "Sunshine Bus." Soon the bus pulled up and stopped. The bus driver opened the door and told Glen that his bus was full and for him to catch the next one behind. Glen misunderstood and simply proceeded to the outside rear of the bus and then climbed onto the luggage rack ladder. He held on for dear life as the bus began to roll faster and faster

As the bus approached the hill at Grove Hill Cemetery, Glen got up enough nerve to glance back and saw another Sunshine Bus following about a quarter mile behind. Then it dawned on

him that the driver had meant that he was to take that bus instead of catching onto the outside ladder.

Sure enough when he got to the Buckner stop, the driver didn't even slow down. On and on and on he went, and Glen couldn't get off because the bus didn't stop until it got to Mesquite. He was so embarrassed at his misunderstanding that he mingled around with the departing passengers until the bus left. Only then did he hit the road walking back to the Orphans Home. He said he arrived back as the sun was coming up the next morning!

"The only good thing about it," Glen said, "was I still had my bus money, but, oh, my feet were sore. I never told my sister about the incident either. In fact, I waited years to tell anyone."

I LEARNED IT WAS FURNITURE POLISH

In 1931 when I was twelve years old, I performed duties for Brother Joe and Miss Sadie Buckner at their residence on campus. I generally kept the lawns mowed, flower beds tilled, shrubbery clipped and did other such chores requested by Miss Sadie. On this particular day Miss Sadie asked me to run down to the commissary and ask Mr. Porter (commissary supervisor) for two loaves of bread and some liquid veneer. Having only two items, I didn't think I would have any trouble remembering, so I didn't concentrate on memorizing the list.

Well, by the time I had walked the 200 yards to the Commissary, I had forgotten one of the items that Miss Sadie had requested. As I walked into Mr. Porter's office he asked, "What does Miss Sadie want today?" I said, "Miss Sadie wants two loaves of bread and—and—she wants—oh, gosh, I've forgotten at the moment, but it sounds like liquid manure!"

Well, with that, Mr. Porter almost fell from his desk laughing loudly. He remarked, "Bob, go out there and raise up 'Ole Blue's tail, and you can get all the liquid manure you will need."

After all his laughter, Mr. Porter asked Jimmie Mills (his assistant) to go down and get Bob a bottle of FURNITURE POLISH.

With chagrin, I sheepishly left the office and delivered the order to Miss Sadie. But I didn't tell her about my forgetfulness and the remarks of Mr. Porter. 'Ole Blue was a female mule used to pull the Commissary's hack that made deliveries to (old) Manna Hall and supplies to the various buildings. Many people will remember 'Ole Blue. But, thanks to Mr. Porter, Miss Sadie won't remember Blue's "liquid manure."

THIS WASN'T HUMOROUS
UNTIL AFTERWARD

McElroy building housed junior residents, boys ages seven through fourteen. The preteens weren't assigned duties other than cleaning (sweeping and mopping) their rooms, making their own beds, keeping lockers clean and orderly, and dusting radiators.

In inclement weather the matrons would run us all to the attic to get us out of our rooms and out of their hair. From the third floor to the attic there were two sections of stairs. From the mid point of the stairs to the attic door was a 10-inch-wide bannister that all the kids loved to slide down, rear end first, when leaving the attic

Some cruel prankster got a nail and tacked it into the lower end of the bannister. The first two or three boys got only their pants ripped in the crotch. One little guy got his scrotum damaged and the matron put a towel diaper on him and sent him to the Hospital for repairs. The doctor surgically repaired the damage, kept him in bed a few days and returned him to McElroy dormitory

The episode caused two things. Everyone became more cautious about sliding down the bannister for a little while, and the poor little guy got a new nick-name.

OH, THE INNOCENCE OF LEVI PAYNE

In 1937 our Junior High School class was taking English literature. Miss Norman was our teacher and on one particular day we were reviewing "The Lady of the Lake." Each student was required to stand in front of the class and read aloud in rotation three pages from the book. Levi Payne and I had a seat near the end of the rotation. Sitting behind him, I had been pulling Levi's shirt tail out of his trousers. Finally when he tucked his shirt tail in, in preparation to stand before the class, he got hold of his brightly colored shorts instead of his trousers. Knowing what was going to happen soon, I stopped pestering him. His shorts were showing about four inches above his belt line outside his trousers, and we were all extremely modest about showing our underwear in those days.

The closer the time came for his turn to read, the more my "tickle-box" became uncontrollable. Then the climactic moment arrived; Levi strolled up to the front of the class and turned around near the teacher's desk, facing the class and within four feet of Miss Norman's desk. At that point the teacher knew why my laughter was so intense. Naturally the class eventually saw Levi's underwear showing and joined in the laughter. Miss Norman demanded that I remain after class.

Soon the school bell rang to dismiss the class. It was time for me to face the music. I believe to this day if Miss Norman had had a gun, I would not have been here today to tell this story; she would have shot me dead for destroying the atmosphere of her literature class. But after about five minutes of her glaring at me with sparks in her eyes, she burst out laughing and said, "Get out of here, Bob Stokes!" The rest of the year, when we met in the hallways or away from the English classroom, we always had a real pleasant chuckle for one another.

LeRoy Bell, '39
by Bob Stokes

Leroy Bell came to BOH in January of 1931 from Denison, Texas. He was eleven-years-old. He also had two brothers, Charles and James, but both parents were dead. Leroy lettered in football in 1938 and 1939. He enlisted in the Army Air Corps and served six years, reaching the grade of Staff Sergeant.

He then lived in San Antonio and the lower Rio Grande Valley, where he retired after thirty years with the American Oil Company. He is married and has two daughters and two grandsons.

Leroy says he is enjoying retirement, playing lots of golf and, with his wife, serving as Volunteer Missionaries in a large medical center and resort ministries in Raymondville, Texas.

Edna Mae (Evans) Davis, '39

MEMORIES OF BUCKNER

My three sisters and I went to live at Buckner Orphans Home on June 2, 1930. We all stayed there until we graduated from high school. Many of the buildings were built during the 30s.

One of my most vivid memories is of the Manna Hall. The old dining room was near the old girls' building, separated by a cement court. The floor of Manna Hall was cement and very hard to keep clean. Since Miss Mamie always insisted that the floor be clean enough to eat off of, we worked hard to keep it that way.

I remember on Friday evenings we soaked all the greasy spots with a thick paste of soap and water so we could scrub them on Saturday morning—it really worked too. I remember one rainy night when all of us 700 plus kids were in Manna Hall for the evening meal. We had pans placed under all the spots where the roof was leaking. Suddenly, Brother Hal Buckner came in the door with rain running off his rainwear. He called us to attention with a very important announcement. He had been away for several days trying to raise money for a new Manna Hall and wanted us to know, as soon as he got home, that he now had the money so that we would soon have a new place to eat. Instead of our cheering, he had us all stand and sing "Praise God From Whom All Blessings Flow."

Before long, we were eating in the beautiful, new Manna Hall, where everything was convenient, and the floor came shiny clean with a single mopping. We made tennis courts in the old building, and Miss Leona Moore taught us girls to play the game.

Since I spent years in the old girls' building, I have many good memories of it, but a few are not so good. We had large rooms with about 30 beds in each, with one matron in charge. Many of the matrons were "old maids." They cared for all of us with very few problems (so it seemed). All the bathroom facilities were in the basement and even those kids on the third floor had to share that basement facility. The first large room had lots of basins. You went through that room into the next room where the toilets were, and then to the next room where the bathtubs were. Most of the basement area was a large room where we all played. It was warm in the winter and cool in the summer. There was a dark corner where we lay on the cool floor and took naps on long hot summer days. We always made our own fun. One of our favorites was seeing who could walk the farthest on her hands with her feet up in the air.

When we Davis kids went to Buckner, our youngest sister, Thelma, was only five but would be six before school started, so she didn't have to go to the nursery. She was in the dormitory with other girls her age, with Miss Bernice Orr as the matron. Thelma remembers that each night Miss Orr would take turns putting two of the girls on her lap. She would rock them and talk to them about how much they were loved. I remember how we envied the girls because Miss Orr brought them gifts, sometimes purple plums, after she had taken a day off and gone to Dallas. Her kindness is remarkable because we have very little memory of other matrons demonstrating affection.

I have another memory which wasn't funny then, but is now as I recall it: On Christmas Eve, it was too late to go caroling after we got our "Strings" and returned to our rooms, so one year Miss Leona Moore said all who wanted to could get up about 4:00 A.M. (regularly we got up at 5:00 on Christmas morning) and go caroling around the other buildings. I joined all the other hardy souls. The air was cold, but above freezing.

When we went to the older boys' building, Charlie Wells, Bob Stokes, and some others on the second floor, opened their windows. They told us that one boy was sick and wanted us to come closer so he could hear us sing. We didn't trust the boys, but they kept insisting, so some girls went closer. The boys then poured water on them. We all went unhappily to our rooms, where those who were wet changed into dry clothes. Unkindly enough, the boys said we had sounded like we needed a drink! I don't remember anyone volunteering to carol for them after that.

Father R. C. Buckner and wife, Vienna Long Buckner.

Statue of Father Buckner with Edna Mae Reynolds

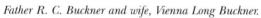

Old Girls' Building

Old Manna Hall

Colonel R. C. Buckner and his father, Brother Hal Buckner

*Mrs. Hal F. Buckner with daughter-in-law,
Sara Frances (Mrs. Robert Cooke) Buckner.*

Charles, LeRoy, and James Bell at the Receiving Home, 1929.

Brittany Daniel with Sarah Haley in front of the Old Nursery, c. 1930.

The boys working with the wagon: Zack Ward, Benny Ford, Howard Baumgarden; (back) Paul Ford, Henry Curl.

Sunbeam Home Children

Melodeers Trio: Nell Kolb, Clarine Marsh, Dorothy Sanders, 1938

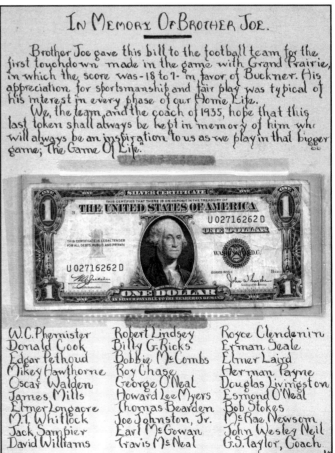

Brother Joe Buckner's gift to the football team, 1935.
(Framed in honor of his support)

Annie V and Jane Marie Arrant, c 30s.

Ruby Longacre, pianist; Margaret Rouse, director of the trio

Beloved art teacher, Leona Moore; Exes celebrate her birthday.

The Class of 1939: 1st Row: Lucia Rogers, Clara Dodson, Mary Ella Clough, Dorothy Porter, Edna Mae Davis, Mary Lou Price, Frances Wimberly, Minnie Lee Brown; 2nd Row: Margaret Beauchamp, Billie Bert Weeks, Jackie Adkins, Maxine Sherrell, Florene Stamps, Zelma Harrell, Billy Ricks; 3rd Row: James Heidelberg, Douglas Wells, Waldo Davis, LeRoy Bell, Thomas Bearden, Bill Johnson, Elmer Morris; 4th Row: J. D. Satterfield, Travis McNeil, Howard McKee, Bennie Ford, Chester Longacre.

Ruby Davis and Mary Lou Price embrace the sign.

Laurine, Corrine, Thelma, and Edna Mae Davis near Crouch Hall, 1936.

The Forties

*"He reached down from heaven and took me out of my great trials.
He rescued me from deep waters. He delivered me. . . ."*

Psalms 18:16-17, RSI

Robert Dewberry, c '40s

by Fay Dewberry Luker

Like so many other Buckner boys during the war years, Bob did not graduate with his class, but left early to join the Navy and fight for his country. When he returned for the Fiftieth Reunion of his sister's class of '44, he brought the house down with laughter when it became his turn to tell about his life at Buckner, saying, "I was in the class of 44. I was in the class of 43, and the class of 42, and. . . ."

Coxswain Robert Dewberry was aboard an attack transport during the battle for Guadalcanal. His orders were to pilot a landing craft to rescue the Marines penned down on the island. They were under heavy fire, and he and his craft also were exposed to the fire of that fierce battle. Again and again he followed his orders and returned to remove troops until night made it impossible to continue.

The next day at dawn he went back to do his duty, but the craft that he had been using was missing. He thought at first that the Japanese had come in and stolen his boat, but eventually found where it had sunk during the night. Because it had had so many shell holes from enemy fire, it could no longer stay afloat.

The South Pacific Area Commander awarded Robert a citation for his brave actions under formidable circumstances.

Robert is now retired from the U.S. Post Office and lives in Dallas.

In addition to Robert, all three of the other Dewberry brothers, Herbert, Clyde Lee and Steward, served their country with distinction during World War II.

Thomas Van Pelt, c '40s

by Leston Lee McNeil

MEMORIES OF MY BEST FRIEND

The day I moved from the Old Nursery to the Little Boys' Building, a matron walked with me, helping me carry my meager belongings to the Little Boys' Building. Once there she turned me over to a new matron, who took me to the room I was assigned, showed me my bed, placed my things into one of the clothes closets, and departed.

There were a few kids around; in fact, five others in my room, but not one said a word to me or even seemed to notice that there was a "new" kid moving in. So, I began to think wistfully of the friends I had left behind in the Old Nursery.

When the new matron blew the whistle for us to line up to march to our evening meal—with the tallest kid up front and the smallest in the rear—I realized I was the shortest kid and would be last in line. As I shyly approached the line, I was surprised to hear someone say, "Hi," in a very friendly manner. I looked up and there, just in front of me in line, was a blond haired kid with a big smile on his face. That hello was the beginning of a

24

long friendship. I soon found out that Thomas Van Pelt was his name, he had a brother named Frederick, and they had come to Buckner from Uvalde, Texas.

From that first hello in the chow line in 1932, until June, 1943, Thomas and I were inseparable. We lived in the same room, or at least on the same floor as we progressed through Buckner's routine moves from the Nursery to the Little Boys' Building, on to other buildings, and finally all the way to the Senior Boys' Building. We went to school, played football, went swimming, hunting, and "bumming" together. We were two of about five or six boys who were always together.

I remember when Thomas got knocked out cold while practicing football; he was the first person I ever saw out cold. He recovered to engage in many other adventures. Once the two of us planned and executed a raid on Blue Beard's Chamber in the Commissary. We did not get to enjoy our booty, but the raid itself was exciting. He, Frederick, and I swam a lot. We all three learned to swim in that old mud hole, Bull Pond, even built ourselves a boat—about twelve feet long—from lumber liberated from one of the many Buckner construction sites. After getting the boat all nailed together, we picked up asphalt from the highway to use as tar to make the boat leakproof. Then we melted the asphalt in a bucket over an open fire. With a real show of ingenuity, Thomas wrapped a stick with a wad of cloth for a swab to put the tar onto the boat. He did a masterful job of applying the tar until he was almost through. We got careless, and that swab of hot tar ended up stuck to the inside of my arm at the elbow. It made one heck of a scar that stayed for a long time.

Thomas was smart. He might not have had the best grades in school, as he seemed to be always thinking of things other than school, but when it came to figuring things out, how to get into or out of something, he had few peers. He was the best artist I have ever known. He could sit down for a few minutes with a pencil and paper and come up with a great sketch of a cowboy on a bucking bronco, with the horse and man in perfect proportion. Even after he went into the United States Navy, he would include sketches in his letters to me.

With two others, we slipped off from the campus in June of 1943 to go into Dallas to join the Navy. At the time we were only seventeen and

between our Junior and Senior years of High School.

As things worked out, Thomas was inducted into the Navy, but I was turned down because of my eyes. I was told to get myself some glasses and come back, but I never did. I heard from Thomas regularly from the time he went into the Navy until I graduated from Buckner in May 1944. By that time he had been in the Navy almost a year and already visited a lot of places neither of us had ever expected to see. I got one picture from Hawaii and some from other overseas ports. Unfortunately, after I left Buckner and moved to California, we rarely corresponded, and in 1945 we lost contact altogether. All I knew was that he was stationed on the USS *WASP.* I never heard from him again, and it was with great sorrow that I learned of his death.

I guess it is safe to say that Thomas was my very best friend ever. We spent ten happy years of our lives growing up together at Buckner, and I loved every one of them. He was full of mischief, with imaginative ideas for having fun and exploring Buckner's perimeters and beyond. We had planned, ever since we were twelve, to get ourselves a ranch to live on someday. I think we were both serious about the idea, and I do believe if he had not been killed in the war, we would have done just that.

Bryan B. Duckworth, '40

by Bob Stokes

Mrs. Duckworth, Bryan's mother, and her six children entered BOH in 1934. She was fortunate to find employment at the old nursery, located at the west end of the high school building. Bryan graduated from Buckner in the class of 1940. He then attended Howard Payne College for a semester. By the time war broke out in 1941, he had accumulated enough hours to be classified a sophomore.

Then Uncle Sam called and he joined the Navy. He spent almost four years in the Navy and was discharged as an Aviation Storekeeper, 1/C in 1946. Still determined to get his college education, he enrolled at North Texas State Teachers College in Denton, where he received his Bachelor of Business Administration with a major in accounting.

After working in accounting for a few years, Bryan decided he needed more variety and became involved in personnel administration, where he remained for twenty years, never working long enough for one firm to be able to retire.

Over the years Bryan says he has owned ranches, farms, and even a Purina Feed Store in Houston for thirteen years. He is presently (1993) President of the Nacodoches County Board of Realtors.

Avocationally, Bryan loves to play golf and plays it as often as possible. He owns a sailboat and says it is also a great hobby. Then too, so is flying. In 1983 he received his private pilot's license and loves soaring with the eagles.

Bryan was married in 1948 to a pretty little lady from Mart, Texas. They have three sons. One lives in Nacodoches, one in Tomball, and one in Seguin. Rightfully Bryan and his wife brag about their five beautiful grandchildren.

Leroy Gafford, '40

by Bob Stokes

Leroy was placed in Buckner Orphans Home in 1925 when he was only about sixteen months old. With him came his three older brothers, Cecil; eleven, Clarence; nine and Raymond; five. Both parents were deceased.

Years later the Gafford boys realized just how grateful they were to have been placed in Buckner. Leroy finished Buckner High School in 1940 and went to the National Youth Administration at Burnet, Texas, for about a year.

In January of 1942, he joined the Army Air Corps at Duncan Field, Texas. His brother Cecil had already served three years and reenlisted in the Air Corps about the same time.

Shortly the unit with the two brothers in it was called up, and sent to India for duty in March of 1942. After approximately three years, they were returned to the U.S. in 1945, and Leroy was given his discharge.

Still desiring to get further education, Leroy started his freshman year at the University of Texas. While attending UT, he joined the ROTC and received his Second Lieutenant's commission upon graduating in 1950.

By this time the Korean War had started, and he was called back into the Army and sent to

Germany for thirty-eight months of duty. Again he returned to the States and was discharged for a second time.

While Leroy was in the active Army Reserve program, he graduated from the U.S. Army Command and General Staff College at Fort Leavenworth, Kansas, in 1970. Then he enrolled in the U.S. Army Industrial War College and graduated from it in 1973.

Reverting back to his civilian work ethic, he worked for Nalco Chemical Company selling oil treatment chemicals, and was sent to Odessa, Texas for his duty station.

After seventeen years with Nalco, he had the opportunity to return to the Dallas area with Universal Oil Products, selling water treating processes for the commercial and industrial heating and cooling systems. He remained with UOP for ten years before going into business for himself, selling water treating chemicals and apartment supplies.

Leroy retired in 1985 but stayed in the Army Reserve Program, and after thirty-four years of combined active and reserve time, he retired with the rank of Colonel.

He now (1993) lives in Arlington, Texas, with his wife, Rosemary. His brother, Clarence, died of a heart attack while waiting with his brother, Cecil, to play a round of golf in San Antonio in 1981. Cecil retired from Southwestern Bell Telephone and is in a nursing home in San Antonio.

Louise (O'Connor) Malone, '40

MEMORIES OF THE MANNA HALL

Because we gathered there three times a day for every day of our lives at Buckner, some of our most striking memories are of the Manna Hall, our dining room. It was so named, according to tradition, by Brother Hal, "Because our bread is from Heaven as truly as was that of the children of Israel." The first Manna Hall had been finished in 1913, but the final one was completed in 1937. That is the one that I remember.

Eclairs were our special treat on Thursday nights when I was growing up at Buckner. Miss Mamie, the supervisor, captained her Manna Hall ship with a sharp eye, firm commands and a quick hand. When we were helping in the kitchen, we could sometimes grab a quick goodie in the pantry, or hide behind a pillar to gulp down a stolen bite of something, but we never got away with an extra eclair. They were carefully counted and Miss Mamie guarded them personally. I have wonderful, tantalizing memories of those Thursday suppers!

Ruby (Dobbs) Davis, '41

MEMORIES OF BUCKNER

When we were young, the land between Crouch Hall (the girls' dorm) and Freeland (the boys' building), where the Maris Center is now located, was called, "No Man's Land." Girls and boys, in the night hours, met each other out there amongst some cedar trees. One night I thought it would be fun to slip out of the dorm (I didn't have a boy friend to meet.) and go out there to see what it was like outdoors after everyone else was in bed. I got outside the door and just couldn't go any further, so made my way back into the building, and up the stairs to my room. I think the kids in the past called that being "chicken." It was the closest I ever got to breaking that rule.

The boys living at Buckner had fun going rabbit hunting. They would spread out in a line, about five to ten feet apart. With sticks large enough for weapons in their hands, they'd start walking across the farmlands to disturb the cotton-tails and the jack rabbits from their abode. Having done so, they'd chase them, and when they were close enough, club the rabbits with their weapons. Some of the farmers didn't seem to like this, but could not do much about it, for there was always a field full of boys. The guys would almost always come up with a big rabbit haul. Miss Mamie would take the rabbits, cook them, then give them to the boys to eat. The older girls waited on the boys' tables, but did not get any of the rabbits to eat. I have often wondered just how good those rabbits tasted.

I still have memories of the old Junior Girls' Building, which is gone now. It was a two-story building with a big veranda on the front. We used to sit out there for hours at a time or sometimes we would run all around it, inside and outside. The showers for bathing were located in the basement of the building. This basement had very poor lighting with dark corners, and we had to go

there in the darkest of night to take a shower—spooky—you bet! The dorms had rooms with about twelve to fifteen beds in them. The head matron would call us into her office at about five in the morning if she thought we might have done something we shouldn't have. On one occasion, Rubye Louise Arrant booed Miss Deal, a matron, for something while the table waitresses stood waiting in line to go into Manna Hall. As Miss Deal looked over the girls, Rubye said to me, "Oh, my God, she knows my people, and she will surely tell them what I've done."

I was standing in front of Rubye, and Miss Deal couldn't see her, so I said to her, "Don't worry, she thinks it was me."

Sure enough at 5:00 A.M. the next morning, I was called into her office. Miss Alexander, the head matron, wanted to know why I had booed Miss Deal. I told her it wasn't me; then she said, "Well, you know who did it." I told her I knew, but was not going to tell her. You guessed it! I got a whipping, but at least Rubye's people never did know about her misbehavior.

Sometimes the senior girls would invite the younger girls over to spend Saturdays with them. They would let us go through their jewelry and keepsakes, look at pictures, and do whatever we thought we'd like to do. They called us, "Little Sis." The ones I remember were: Myrtle Bolton, Dorcas Sanders and Roberta Howard—I still have a picture where Roberta wrote on the back, "To my Little Sis." The only person I have run across, besides me, who remembers this happening is Thelma Davis Houston, for she also was invited over to the senior girl's building.

Mary Elizabeth Pollard and I "had Store Room" (our work assignment), located in the Manna Hall. Miss Mamie, the dietitian, would often save cookies for her son, and had a certain place she would put them for safe keeping. Once Mary Elizabeth, the commissary boys and I got into the cookies and ate them. Of course Miss Mamie missed the cookies. I had gone to the balcony for something, and while I was gone, she asked Mary Elizabeth about the cookies. She denied knowing anything about them. (You couldn't get away with lying to Miss Mamie.) When I returned, Miss Mamie asked me about the cookies. Not knowing she had already asked Mary Elizabeth, I told her the truth: that Mary Elizabeth, the commissary boys, and I had eaten them. Wouldn't you know that Miss Mamie slapped the fire out of Mary Elizabeth for not telling her the truth?

We had very little money, getting what we had from ironing the teachers' and matrons' clothes. Sometimes the people visiting the Home, whom we guided through the dorms, would give us money. When the time came that we could spend the money, we would walk about a mile to a little county store called Evans Grocery, near the railroad tracks. Guess what we would buy? A sour pickle was most often our choice, and to us they really tasted good.

While we lived in the Junior Girls' Building, some of the kids got "itch." It would appear between the fingers and in various other places on the hands. We usually played games on the concrete slab, where the old Manna Hall building once sat, next to the girls' dorm. The girls who were fortunate enough not to get the itch wouldn't hold hands with the ones that had it because they were afraid they would catch it. A good nickname branded on them was, "Itchy."

Oh, yes, I remember very well how we enjoyed Brother Joe Buckner coming to the girls' area; sitting under the trees, and talking to us. Brother Joe had come all the way to Stamford, Texas, to see Euna Fay, my sister, and me when the WMU at First Baptist Church in Haskell, Texas, was trying to get us into Buckner. We actually had lived in Haskell, but after our mother died, we went to Stamford where my older sister lived at that time.

When I was a senior, I roomed with a girl named Louise Rushing, a very good friend of mine. As best I can remember, all the lights were to be turned off at nine at night. Once a cricket came into our room, and you have never heard of such noises as all the chirping sounds it made. It finally got to Louise, so she jumped out of bed, and after getting a shoe, began her chase. She went all over the room hitting here and there. I can't say if she hit it or not, but it finally stopped singing or was scared away. Still and all she may have squashed it.

Once upon a time Angie Nell Hudson (Laird now) and some other girls were sitting on a bed. She was telling a story, and I reached over and put her hand up above her shoulder. She didn't even notice, just kept on talking. After awhile she realized she was holding her hand straight up, but that someone else had put it in that position, and wanted to know who had done that. Believe

it or not, she didn't beat me up for that when she found out I was the guilty one.

I also remember some rather good times at Buckner! We played basketball, volleyball, baseball, and sang in choirs. I remember once we organized a Mexican singing group and dressed in Mexican costumes. We felt very "showbiz." I have never forgotten B. B. (Big Brother) McKinney, coming to Buckner, teaching, and leading us in hymns. The children would just sing their hearts out for him. I always enjoyed Church, Sunday School, and BYPU. I also, enjoyed riding in the back of a large truck, with the Pep Squad, while going to and from football games the boys played. We yelled like mad for the Buckner Hornets in the trucks and at the games.

Talking about Buckner is like talking about my children, grandchildren, and my one great grandchild. I have no trouble talking about these things, just trouble stopping when I do get started.

Earl B. Dobbs, '44

LIVING AT BUCKNER

Living at Buckner Orphans Home, I had a number of jobs assigned to me. Probably when I was either a junior or senior, I worked in what was called the Commissary. This was the place where all the goods, like clothing, foodstuff (eggs, canned vegetables, jams, jellies, turkeys, chickens, etc.), bedding (quilts, sheets, pillow cases) were stored. Also bread was made there, and ice in one hundred pound blocks. The milk from the diary was processed there. Oddly enough, this was also the place where the children came for their haircuts.

Eggs given to the home (I think, in twelve dozen cases), were stored there in the cold storage vault. Over a period of time the eggs would become rather old, and would have to be candled (a procedure to determine their condition, good or bad). Candling was done by holding an egg between the eye and a light to examine it. We had a box, about six inches tall and about a foot or so long, with holes a little smaller than an egg cut out in the top side, and with each hole padded. A light bulb was placed in the box. This chore needed to be done, one egg at a time when there was a full vault of eggs. Two or three men from outside the Buckner family would come do the candling. I just happened to be selected to help these men by bringing the eggs to them, and after they finished the procedure, placing the eggs back in the proper place. This doesn't sound so bad, but the catch was the vault was awfully cold; probably forty to fifty degrees or less. Those of us who helped would put on all the clothes we could find, yet after staying in the cold storage vault for a period of time, we would just freeze. What a relief it was when those men decided to take a break for coffee or lunch. I guess that is why my back still gets so cold to this day. More than likely, most of the kids from Buckner never knew this frosty examination of the eggs was happening, but they surely ate good eggs as a result of it.

While in the Buckner family, I had a number of jobs; cleaning dormitories, working in what was called the Field Gang, or working in the Commissary, but I never worked with the Dairy Bunch. While working in the commissary, I had the additional job of cutting the boys' hair. Looking back and trying to remember, I believe the way I learned was through Mr. Bill Porter, the man in authority over the commissary. I believe he kinda liked me for some reason, and he told me just to get those electric clippers, start on one side and go around the entire head. I think I finally got pretty good at it through time. I had some of those guys (more popular) who wanted their hair cut a particular way, or with side burns, and I successfully managed that. The problem was those little kids who would scramble and twist and wiggle and would not sit still at all. The only way I could get their attention and get the job done, was by giving them a hit on the head with the scissors. That seemed to quiet them down. I have asked some of the boys if they remembered my cutting their hair. They said yes, but did not mention the hit on the head, for which I am grateful. I hope they don't remember that.

When going overseas, during WW II, I was selected to cut hair on the ship, but don't remember any complaints. I still have that skill, and a set of tools, so together my wife and I cut my hair to this day. I hope the younger kids from that time don't remember my discipline, for I'm not sure it was the proper thing to do. It would be called cruelty these days.

Paul Pace, '41
by Bob Stokes

Paul's life at BOH started on September 24, 1934, along with his two brothers, Charley Wayne and Tommy; and their only sister, Christine. This was after the death of their mother in August of 1933.

During their early years the Pace family had been through deep and troubled waters, and they were profoundly grateful to the Orphans Home for taking them in their time of need.

Paul graduated from Buckner High School on January 17, 1941. Soon after leaving the Home, he married his Buckner sweetheart, Frances Davis; the sister of Waldo and Nadine Davis who also were living at the Home.

Today (1993) Paul and Frances, fifty-two years later, look around themselves in Huntsville, Alabama, and see three beautiful daughters, six beautiful grandchildren and two beautiful great grandchildren. Paul and Frances acknowledge that they are richly blest.

During WW II, Paul spent nineteen months in the Navy. While in the service he was afforded the opportunity to learn the basic functions of IBM equipment. He began as a key-punch operator and admits that one little simple job started him on a career that would later open doors through which he walked and communicated with top leaders throughout the U.S. and half-way around the world in Vietnam. He held computer related managerial positions with the U.S. Navy, General Services Administration (GSA), Strategic Air Command (SAC), Marshal Space Center and with the Army in Vietnam. He was Director of the General Services Administration Computer Center in Huntsville when he retired.

Besides his computer business, Paul had another compelling desire tugging on his heart and soul. That was to be a minister. He prepared himself and became an ordained, minister in December of 1953. After taking early retirement on June 1, 1972, Paul had the chance to become a full time Baptist Minister.

He has pastored churches in Alabama and held evangelistic revivals over the years in Alabama, Tennessee, Arkansas, and Kentucky. Reverend Paul Pace says one of his most difficult tasks came when he was called to Dallas and Emory, Texas, to conduct the funeral services for his best

Buckner friend, Billy Harting, who now rests in the Grove Hill Cemetery about two miles from the Home.

Joe Frank Wood, '41

by Bob Stokes

THE FIRST BUCKNER ATHLETE TO WIN STATE

Joe Frank Wood was born August 26, 1921, in Rotan, Texas. There were four children in the family. He had an older sister, Marie; a twin sister, Virginia; and a younger brother, Raymond. They were placed in Buckner in 1925. Their mother passed away at the young age of twenty-six. Their father was killed in an auto accident about a year later while on his way to visit his children.

Joe loved to go rabbit hunting as did many of the boys at Buckner. It was good recreation, which turned out especially good for Joe because while chasing rabbits he learned running skills and physical endurance that eventually permitted him to get a college education on a track scholarship.

In 1940, his junior year in high school, he made the football team as left halfback and the team went on to win the District and Bi-district, but was defeated by Mart, Texas, for the regional finals. This was the highest plateau that Buckner had met in their football standings.

He went out for track in the spring and run the 880. Joe ran his first district meet and won the 880 in a record breaking time of 2:06 and asked Coach Taylor if he could run the mile in a practice meet. The coach agreed. He ran the mile in a practice meet in Dallas in 4:47. Coach Gordon Taylor was so impressed he told Joe to concentrate on running the mile from then on. In the Bi-district Meet the following week at S.M.U, he ran 4:47, setting a Bi-district record and tying the State record. Joe missed the regional meet because of illness, but by virtue of his having the fastest time in Bi-district, the Texas Interscholastic League permitted Joe to participate in the State meet. His arch rival, Jerry Thompson, had won the Regional Meet while Joe had been ill. Joe was determined to avenge himself at the State Meet. Sure enough Joe came through the winner in 4:37. His arch-rival came in fifth place.

After the State Meet, Coach Taylor's Buckner Miler was invited to run in the Southwestern AAU Meet in Denton and won the Junior College division on a Monday night; time, 4:26:6. The following night Joe ran in the senior division and won in 4:26:4.

In 1941, Joe's senior year at Buckner, he wanted to play football again with the Hornets, but Coach Taylor refused to allow him to play. He told Joe that he had the potential of obtaining his college education from his track achievements, and he should not jeopardize this chance by getting hurt in football. It was a bitter pill for Joe, but he conceded to the wise thinking of his coach and continued to stay in good physical condition.

Because of all of Joe's track records, compiled at Buckner, he was contacted by Jock Sportsman, Track Coach at NTSTC in Denton, offering him a track scholarship. Joe accepted the offer and enrolled in the fall term. During his freshman year, Joe participated in several track meets and won the mile in all of them, including the Lone Star Conference. There was great competition, but Joe prevailed.

The U.S. entered WW II on December 7, 1941, and he enlisted in the Navy for military service and spent most of his four years in the South Pacific.

After the war, he returned to continue his education at NTSTC. However, since all the new coaches around did not remember him, he was informed that all the athletic scholarships had been given and if he desired to return on a full-pay basis, he could. Needless to say, Joe was mighty devastated.

Later that evening Joe returned to Dallas and spoke long distance to Gordon Taylor, who by this time was Dean of Men at Howard Payne College. Mr. Taylor spoke with Cap Shelton, track coach at HPC. Cap immediately told Mr. Taylor to call Joe and tell him to come on down to Brownwood; he would be given a full scholarship on Dean Taylor's recommendation.

For the next three years, he attended HPC and continued to be most successful in track. He won the mile track event each of the next three years in the Texas Conference. He graduated HPC with a B.S. Degree in 1949.

Ironically, he got his first coaching job only a few miles from Buckner at Mesquite High School, where he was head-track coach and assistant football coach for twelve years. During his tenure, his track teams won 8 of 12 district titles. Many of his track athletes won in the State Meet. While coaching at Mesquite, Joe continued his education at SMU and received a Masters Degree in School Administration.

Eventually he elected to become a High School Principal in Edgewood, Texas, and remained for eleven years before retiring in 1985.

Joe and his wife Margaret (the former Margaret Hall of Buckner) live on a forty-acre property near Edgewood. Joe, who remains very active in his church and community, is the first Buckner athlete (track) to win State and was awarded the Distinguished Buckner Alumnus Award in 1990.

Theda Greathouse, '42

THUMBS UP

Class Poem of 1942

Thumbs up to the fact that we're leaving;
To be sad would never do.
For that would only be deceiving
The "spirit of '42."

They say if you laugh, you'll have company;
If you cry, you'll cry alone.
So laughing and crying we'll carry
The joys and tears we have known.

For the time that a youth is more likely
To strike gold in the rugged and wild,
Is when he is too young to marry, and
Too old to be known as a child.

So hats off to bygone immortals;
Their task is forgotten and through.
Thumbs up to the open portals,
And these, the graduates of '42.

Marcus Larry Seale, Jr., '42

Professional name: Larry Buchanan

When we came to the Home, there were six of us. I was the youngest. Then, going up the ladder was my brother, Ermin Earl Seale; sisters, Alma, Mozelle, Audra, and Blanche.

Then, one by one, the older siblings started to graduate and go out into the world of commerce and other relationships. Finally, there was my last big brother, Earl, leaving. I shifted from foot to foot, embarrassed when he come over to our building to say goodbye. I suddenly felt all

alone. Earl started to leave and I couldn't hide a little boy's tears.

"What's the matter Bud? We'll all be only seven miles away."

I blurted out, "I lost my sisters, now I'm losing my only brother!"

As we spoke the siren wailed, calling the kids to dinner—the noon day meal in those days.

Earl pointed to the long lines forming the march to Manna Hall.

"You're wrong little brother. You haven't lost us, and you've gained three hundred brothers and sisters."

By the time I got in line for Manna Hall, I was smiling.

Owen Major Thomas, '43

BUCKNER MEMORIES

My first encounter at Buckner was April 1936, when I was twelve. When I arrived at Buckner, the Receiving Home was quarantined because of illness. There was no place for this orphan to go.

So, because of the goodness of Brother Hal Buckner, who incidentally had interviewed and accepted me into the Home family at my sister's home in San Antonio, I was taken into his home for my two-week observation time before being placed in a dorm on campus. While in the home of the Buckners, I got to know the family intimately, which consisted of Hal, his wife; Miss Bertha, their daughter; Jo Buckner Stewart Shurette, and her son; Hal Stewart. Hal and I were the same age, and both of us were baptized by Brother Hal later on. I think I had a unique experience. I don't believe that any other orphan ever lived with the family.

One of the memories I have of Miss Bertha is her saying what nice manners I had. Manners such as saying thank you, asking to be excused from the table, using the right silver, etc. These had been taught me by my sister before I left her home. These remarks really impressed me.

Having had this contact with the family, I felt comfortable in approaching Brother Hal with my needs while I lived on the campus. It was through this support that I was able to ask him if I could study piano—no boy had ever studied piano before. He agreed that I could study piano and use the piano in the school auditorium to practice on Sunday afternoons. Eventually, other boys also studied piano.

This ultimately led me to my life work, teaching music in public schools, accompanying vocalists, and being a director of music for various churches and groups.

While I was studying at Baylor University, Brother Hal died, and I was asked to come and serve as an honorary pall bearer. I was pleased to do this. Years later, when Miss Bertha passed away, Miss Jo called and asked me to come to play the piano during the "viewing" at their home. Many of my experiences were like those other kids had, but I felt this was a little different, since I had had such a close contact with the Buckner family.

While at the home, I was able to accompany for the Boys' Chorus. One of my favorite instructors was Helen Hutchins, who really challenged me to develop my musical talents. I also played for church services in the chapel. Another highlight was being able to play for B. B. McKinney, a great Southern Baptist musician, who came and led the music in revivals at the Home. Many of the kids of the late 30s remember my playing at the Manna Hall as they marched in for meals.

Like most of the other kids, I had jobs of every kind from the dairy to laundry delivery, gardener, dorm cleaner, etc. I enjoyed the watermelon feeds in the summer after we surreptitiously "removed" the melons from the trucks as they stopped at the signal on Highway 80. I also enjoyed camps with Dean Gordon Taylor and the boys at Lake Dallas.

One of my athletic highlights was playing football under Coach Taylor (third string tackle), and I actually played two minutes in the final game with Garland High School. That was the end of my athletic career.

Overall, I wouldn't trade my experience at the Home for anything. We received a good education and good training with an excellent religious "upbringing." I feel I have truly been blessed. Without Buckner, I may not have had the opportunities I had.

FROM HIS WIFE, RUTHMARY

[For the nominating committee for Alumnus of the Year, Ed.]

Owen graduated from Buckner in June of 1943, and signed up for the Navy. In September he was sent to boot camp in Coeur D'Alene, Idaho. In November, he was sent to San Francisco to the Naval Overseas Freight Terminal. He was a Storekeeper at that office until May of 1946 when he was sent to the Naval Supply Depot in Oakland. He says they called themselves the Market Street Commandos. Actually, they didn't do any fighting, or at least he didn't, so I guess they weren't really commandos and can't think of any great war stories to tell. Their job was to keep the supplies going out, and I guess they did a good job of that.

After he got out of the Navy, the stories get better. Maybe I should back up to San Francisco. He always attended First Baptist Church, played the piano for some of their services and for the Sunday night fellowship for the young people, called "Fireside." We had lots of servicemen go through the church, and it had a very active program for the men and women. We had several WACs and WAVEs and one Marine girl.

Later he left San Francisco, went four years to Baylor, got his teaching credentials in music and then taught one year in Hillsboro before we were married. In 1951 we came to Sonoma where he taught the rest of his thirty-three years.

After work hours, he has always had a church choir. In addition, he directed a group of women called the Kenwood Carolers and a community group, the Sonorna Community Chorus, for several years. He now directs and plays for a men's double quartet, the Silver Foxes. For the past four years he has directed the Sonoma Cantata Choir, which he started, for a Christmas and Easter Cantata, doing two performances for each season.

Owen also played for a Junior College vocal class for four years; for the past ten years he has played at one rest home every week for an hour and at another one once a month for their birthday parties.

I must not forget to mention the monthly hymn sings that the churches have. We play the organ and piano for them. There are about six different denominations that get together for these. This is where the Cantata Choir began.

Most of the churches are small and don't have enough people to do a decent musical alone.

Other than music, he has supervised the government food surplus give-away for the past five years. Before that, he helped in getting the food to the distribution point. He has done many other things, but as you know music is his most loved occupation. Need I say all of these are volunteer positions, and the pay is nothing, except the satisfaction he derives.

Herbert Ray White, '43

by Vernon Horsley

THE MISSING KEY

I worked part time in the bakery and commissary during my senior year. Since I didn't have many classes, I'd go to the bakery to help out in my spare time. Mr. Porter was in charge of the commissary, and once he gave me his key and asked me to go get coffee.

I was delighted to do so. On my way to the commissary, I took the key by the bakery and stuck it into a piece of the soft dough that was being prepared for the day's bread, and put the dough on top of the oven where it could dry out and make a mold for me.

Since I worked in the bakery and the commissary, I soon got an opportunity to go to town for supplies. I purchased a blank key, brought it home and using my dough mold and a file, shaped it; hoping that it would fit the lock to the commissary. I was successful and able to sneak into the commissary to get clothes for myself whenever I needed them. However, someone else evidently noticed I was wearing nice clothes all the time and drew their own conclusions.

I had hidden the key on a ledge inside in my locker at the dorm. One day it was missing! I didn't know what to do. All I knew was that somebody else had it, and the more people who had keys, the more danger I was in. I was scared that Gordon Taylor himself had found it. I knew that if so, in a few days I would be called in for punishment.

However, I thought more realistically, some other kid probably had it. I set out to try to find it, but all of a sudden, the key was back in its place! It had been stolen from my room and then replaced. Someone else must have made a copy. I

checked the list to see which other boys had gone to town to pick up groceries. The only one on the list for that day was Nathan Castle, so I figured he must have stolen it from my room to make his own copy.

Eventually I found that three copies had been made. Nathan Castle, Lee McNeil and Billy Ray Clark had copies. I knew because they also sported many new clothes.

One night my friend, Thomas Van Pelt, and I decided that we had to get all the copies of the key back. First, we went to Nathan's room and finally found his in a secret compartment in his billfold. We found Lee McNeil's in his locker in about the same place as I had hidden mine, but we couldn't find Billy Ray Clark's. We had a dilemma. We decided it had to be in the gym where Billy Ray worked.

Now Thomas also worked in the gym with Billy Ray, so that night we let ourselves into the gym with Thomas' key and searched everywhere, even under the bleachers, until we found it hidden where the equipment was stored. We had to pick the lock of the storage compartment on top of the grill to find Billy Ray's key, but that was no trouble for a Buckner boy!

We got all three keys back and never said a word about it. We just sat at the Top of The Hill and watched the boys blame each other and argue about them. The truth is that I don't remember what I did with mine. I might finally have just thrown it away. I had had all the fun with it that seemed possible by that time.

I just wish now I'd kept it so I could show it around at Homecoming!

Ruth (Procopio) Ashley, '44

When I left Buckner Orphans Home in 1944, I lived with a minister and his wife in Dallas and worked for my room and board. I took care of their twelve-year-old daughter and attended business college for a year. My twin brother, Ralph George Ashley, who was in the Marine Corps, paid my tuition. After a year I got a job in an insurance company and made plans for moving out on my own. I was on the job for a month when I received a telegram from the Marine Corps in San Diego, California. They informed me that Ralph had been killed in a motorcycle accident. I flew to San Diego to attend his funeral. He is buried at the Golden Gate Cemetery in San Francisco, California.

I decided to stay in San Diego, got a job, met Joseph Procopio in July 1945 and became engaged on my twenty-first birthday. After he was discharged from the Navy, we were married and bought a home in Syracuse. After four years, Joe decided to go back into the Navy, a very smart move. We sold the house and moved many times.

Our last duty station was San Diego, California—full cycle, since that is where we had met. No one would rent to us with our five boys, so we bought a house in Imperial Beach, California. Two months later, Joe was sent overseas for six months. He finally retired from the Navy after twenty-two years and got a job with the San Diego Unified School District. I studied cake decorating for five years and started my own decorating business in our home. I ran the business for twenty years and decorated all of our five sons' wedding cakes and many more. I still decorate cakes for family and friends just for the fun of it. It keeps me busy and in practice. I also do ceramics and crochet.

Joe retired from the School District after nineteen years. We took a two month trip across country in our oldest son's new motor home. It was a beautiful trip visiting relatives and friends.

When all our sons left the nest, we moved to Arkansas for four years, but always came back to Imperial Beach for the holidays.

On our fourth and last trip to California, I lost Joe, my husband of forty-five years. I'm glad it happened there instead of in Arkansas. All my sons and their families were present to help me through the grief,

I moved back to Imperial Beach, California, for two years, and lived with my son, Patrick, in our old house until I moved into a beautiful Senior Citizen Apartment. I love it. In fact, of all the places I've been, I love California the best.

Joseph H. "Jake" Corbett, '44

I entered the U.S. Army Air Force in June of 1944, and was discharged in November, 1945.

I attended Howard Payne University in 1946, and graduated with a B.A. in July of 1948. I be-

gan attending the University of Texas Medical School in September, 1948, and graduated with an M.D. Degree in June of 1952. At that time I interned at the Fort Worth County Hospital.

I married Marie Shamans in Brownwood on April 4, 1947. We have three children, John, Lisa and James. We also have three grandchildren, Jason Corbett, Tiffany Corbett and Nikolai Marie Tucker.

I served as Flight Surgeon in the U.S.A. Air Force from 1953 to 1955 at Randolph Air Force Base and Clovis Air Force Base, New Mexico. I was discharged as Captain in July of 1955.

Since then, I have practiced Family Medicine in Waco, Texas. We live on a working cattle ranch and have over one hundred mama cows.

Patsy (McLemore) Corbett, '44

Several miles from the campus, Buckner owned some wooded property with a large cabin on it. Each summer we had a Fourth of July Barbecue there, and sometimes during the summer a group could spend the afternoon just exploring the woods and enjoying being off campus.

When we were seniors, we had an overnight camping trip. It was a special time for us girls, and the only time I remember that we were allowed to wear shorts! Everyone took their cameras to take pictures to remember this last time together. Feeling rather bold and risque, Fay Dewberry and Doris Ridge decided to pose in just their underwear.

Everything went OK until the pictures were developed. Fay was "waiting on" one of the big boys' tables in Manna Hall, and while she was in the kitchen, the mail was put at her plate. The boys saw the envelope of pictures, opened it and passed them around to everyone. Sure was exciting!

Actually, I was the one who took the pictures. Don't know why I was not in a picture—must have had a hole in my underwear!

After graduation from Buckner, I could summarize my life in only four words—wife, mother, grandmother and housewife!

As a wife, I have been married forty-eight years, seven months and twenty-three days—and not one time have I thought about a divorce. However, I have thought about murder several times.

I married Eugene McLemore when he was only eighteen years old, weighed 167 pounds and was in Uncle Sam's Army. He is now sixty-six years old, weighs 245 pounds and is the smartest man I have ever known.

I consider myself a good wife because after all, I am the one who fattened him up and I am the one who taught him everything he knows! If you don't believe me—just ask me—don't ask HIM! All in all, we've had a good life and hope to celebrate that golden fiftieth together.

I have a daughter and a son. As a grandmother, I have been blessed with one grandson and twin granddaughters.

As a housewife—it seems I've been one practically all my life—beginning at Buckner when I learned to sweep and mop at the age of nine. At age sixty-seven, I'm still sweeping and mopping!

My biggest accomplishment in life is being a Christian. I was baptized by Brother Hal at Buckner on May 1, 1939. I was immersed with my twin brother, Lee, and my younger sister, Edna. As a child of twelve, I can remember how big and beautiful the baptistry seemed. And how amazed I was, when I returned to visit years later to see how small it actually is—but it remains beautiful in my memories!

I have always given Buckner credit for my Christian teachings, strong faith, my happy childhood, and for wonderful friends who have remained loyal to Buckner and each other for over FIFTY YEARS! Thank you, Buckner.

Fay (Luker) Dewberry, '44

THE BEGINNING

For me it started in December 1935. Four of my five brothers and I were driven from Quanah, Texas, to Buckner Orphans Home by Mr. Coker and his daughter from our church. We were taken to the Receiving Home, run by Dena Saddler and her husband, and kept there for a period of time to see that we had no communicable diseases to pass on to the larger body of Buckner children. The structure of the Receiving Home made quite an impression on me. The big rooms, wide halls, high ceilings, some tile floors and the rich, dark wood made the building look like a mansion to me. The food was good and the Saddlers were very nice to all of us. I would not have minded

staying there till our Mother came for us. For at that time, I was sure she would; Mother had been sent to a TB Sanatorium.

By the time school started after the Christmas break, we were able to go to the dormitories and start to school. I was nine years old and in the fourth grade. Living in a dormitory with lots of girls was a new experience for me, who had no sisters. The building had three floors and the older girls lived on the upper floor. The younger girls lived on the middle floor, and the lower floor; a partial basement with daylight windows, was an activities area.

THE QUILTS AND CLEANING

When we were living in the big old frame building, each room housed twenty to thirty girls. Each bed was made up of quilts that we "tore apart" each Saturday morning. Does anyone remember that the Baptist ladies of Texas quilted for us all those quilts which we used as mattresses? We shook every quilt, folded and replaced it on the springs—one layer at a time, forming a mattress. The better you got at abutting one edge with another, the better mattress you had for the week. Our bottom sheet went to the laundry every week, and the top sheet became our bottom sheet for the next week. Thus we only had to launder half as many sheets! We had no pillows.

We were responsible for mopping the floor around our beds. (We had wooden boxes at the foot of the bed for clothes and "stuff.") After the mopping, we cleaned the large double hung windows at the end of the room. I liked to do the outside. I'd sit in the window, knees held by the window and fall back and down till my head touched the outside building, then swing back up. In between playing, I managed to clean the windows too!

THE MANNA HALL

When we went to eat at the Manna Hall, we formed lines on the lower floor of our building and marched into Manna Hall, according to our age group and size. Largest went first, smallest last. At that time the Manna Hall was across a courtyard from our dormitory. In the summer we lined up in the courtyard. Neither of these buildings are now standing. They were replaced with buildings of fireproof construction. As a senior, I lived on the same site in an almost new building.

The girls' buildings were on the south side of the circle drive, and the boys' buildings were on the north. As we marched into Manna Hall, someone played the piano and a group of the older kids stood by the piano and sang a hymn. One of the matrons asked a blessing. After that, bedlam broke out. Can you picture 600 or so children talking and moving silverware at the same time? I always looked over at the boys as they came into Manna Hall to get a glimpse of my brothers. My youngest brother, Clyde Lee, was easy to spot for he was the smallest boy in line for several years. He never grew to five foot three, which was as tall as I grew.

SCHOOL AND PUNISHMENT

I enjoyed school. I cannot say why because I never made very good grades. My best friends though were very studious. I enjoyed games and reading. Spelling was always my worst subject, and I'm sure my classmates were not particularly good at spelling either. Years later a classmate friend wrote in a letter that she and her husband had purchased a new "coop." They had actually purchased a new "coupe."

I was not an easy child to push into a mold; consequently, I got into a lot of trouble. The usual punishments were working in the yard, "sitting on the wall," or being campused and denied any privilege of leaving our circumscribed, fenced area.

I do not ever remember "sitting" alone. There were several of us that always seemed to get into trouble together. One of the following was always with me: Wanda Johnson, Alma Ruth Wells, and Evelyn Culbertson. One of the all time memorable "sittings" I had was one summer afternoon. There were four or five girls "sitting." We were "set out," several beds apart, in a long dormitory room. We could not see each other and were to be silent and reflect on our sin. During that particular "sit," I asked the matron's permission to go to the rest room. She told me I should have gone before I came to "sit." She left her room and was gone for a long time. Perhaps she was giving me time, but I took matters into my own hands, so to speak. The floor was quite uneven and the moisture ran away from me. I was allowed to mop the floor and clean myself only after my "sitting" was over. Until something else silly came along to laugh about, all the girls giggled about that.

Another punishment was going to bed early. This seemed to be more or less for twelve or thirteen-year-olds. Of course I got to go to bed early lots of times. I also worked outside as punishment until I began to like it. I decided that the best thing I could do was learn to like my punishments, and then maybe they would be changed. As seniors, some friends and I were forced to dig a rose bed, of which we all eventually became very proud.

In my opinion, there were ladies who worked at Buckner to have a place to raise their children, and then there were those whose life was a bare bones existence because they were not trained to do anything else except take care of children. But in addition, there were a few who really tried to make a difference in the lives of the kids. There was one matron in the boys' dormitory who was the mother of a friend and classmate. We all loved her. We loved our teachers too. There were some ladies who had been brought up in church and were idealistic. These ladies really stood out and were well liked and remembered with love and affection. There were also kind ladies and men who were in charge of our work regimen. We gave our affection to them.

WORK

My first job was to dust the parlor. Now I do not remember how often I did this. But, this job assignment was a real plum. The furniture was heavy Victorian and dark, so it really needed dusting. There also was a mirror in the parlor where I enjoyed peeking at myself. The other girls teased me that I was always primping and I'm sure it was true. This was a new experience for me because there is no earlier memory of a mirror in my life. My grandfather's mirror, which he shaved by, had been too high for me.

When I was tall enough to iron at an ironing board, my job was to press clothes in the laundry. As with everything else, I was not alone. There were girls of all ages and sizes ironing. There were ladies who operated pressers, washers, tumblers and mangles. My first experiences were ironing little kids' clothes. As I became larger and more proficient, I ironed larger children's clothes. We were given our batch of clothes sprinkled, wrapped and ready to go when we showed up after school or after quiet time in the summer.

We also worked in the Manna Hall. My first job for Miss Mamie was mopping the floor. There were heavy benches on each side of large tables. It took two of us little girls to move the benches. The hardest part of this job was to sit close on the benches and wait with other mop girls, but not talk nor giggle. Then when the larger girls had washed, dried and replaced the dishes for the next meal, they waited for Miss Mamie to give her approval on their jobs and let them go. When they were gone we were able to clean the floor. As with the tables, clean was not clean until we had the approval of Miss Mamie, a tough taskmaster who required total compliance. I know of no girl who came away from her duty without verbal or physical abuse. Miss Mamie herself had grown up at Buckner. She married and had a family before she returned to Buckner to rule over the kitchen and Manna Hall. I do not know who her mentor was, but she must have also been a strong personality. At a later date I waited on tables, and another time I got up at four o'clock in the morning to go to the kitchen and eye the potatoes for the day's meals. The potatoes were first put into a large tumbler that took off their skins. Then several of us kids sat together with a pan of potatoes to eye.

Occasionally, we stirred the hot chocolate. This pot was accessed by a stepstool and the chocolate was stirred with a long wooden board similar to an oar. After each meal, we went to the kitchen and cleaned all the cooking equipment. This was called "having kitchen." One or two times I "had balcony." Now this job was for one or two girls at a time and was considered a plum job. Part of our duty was to come in after school and fold "cup towels" so they would be ready after the meals. We passed these out, one to a table, for the girls to use to dry dishes. The balcony was where guest groups came to eat, and we waited on those people and cleaned up after them. We tended "cakes" that church groups sent to the Home. Naturally this was my favorite duty. Not even Miss Mamie could tell when one slice of a cake was gone.

Our matrons had about thirty children each they cared for. This must have been a big job. Besides checking our rooms for cleanliness, our beds to see they were made each day in "show" condition, they also had to check our closets that were opened up so visitors could feel proud of the Buckner children they were contributing to. At night the matrons checked to see that we were studying or reading our daily Bible readings.

There were baths to oversee, hair washings and medicine distribution. We'd get ready for bed at night and the matron would call out that the medicine closet was open. It was usually kept locked, but at night before we went to bed, anyone with a sniffle or other problem was treated. I had allergies but was treated for a cold off and on all the time I lived at Buckner. There was a common medication—Sal Hepatica, aspirin and something else (can't remember what) that when mixed with water fizzed up your nose and was not too unpleasant to drink.

CLOTHES, HAIR AND THE WORKERS

Several times during the years, the matrons went to the commissary to select clothing for each of us to wear. There were always changes to be made as we grew taller or wider or wore out what we had. Color and style had very little place in our wardrobe. If it fit us we wore it! Of course we traded items if it was to our advantage. After the large old building with so many girls crowded into a room, the new buildings we moved into were luxurious. We had real mattresses. The floors were cement and easy to clean. Two rooms of four girls shared each bath, but there were four lavatories, three commodes, one tub and one shower. We managed very well with no more than eight girls sharing use.

There was one time though that I had a roommate who would not bathe. This became very offensive, and we lured her to the tub one day after school and bathed her, clothes and all. This was not the conduct our matron expected of us; consequently, we got new room assignments. This turned out to be a very lucky change for me.

As I got older, I discovered a talent. I liked to "fix" hair. I could roll hair, comb it out and make nearly anyone look good. In those days we used bobby pins to curl our hair. They made tight curls. Joyce Work didn't use bobby pins; her mother taught her to curl her hair on rags. She had long pretty hair, and the ends didn't split like the rest of ours did. Sarah Haley had as much hair as I did, and it was as curly as mine. Doris Ridge had thin hair which was real easy to roll.

Our schools were on the campus. We were taught the same subjects that were taught in public schools across Texas. We had some very good teachers and some not so good. As far as I know, there was only one teacher fired during the eight years I lived at Buckner. This teacher/principal was very hard on the boys. In the school where he went after leaving Buckner, one of the boys at the next school stabbed him in the stomach. My brother, Bob, remembers being punished several times by this man.

Most of the time, our worst punishment in school was just being forced to do the same thing over and over again. Some of the teachers stayed on campus during the summer and taught Bible School. They kind of acted like camp directors for summer activities too.

MR. PENNY

On Saturday nights we always had a picture show. These movies were the gift of a Mr. Penny who owned The Odd Penny Cafe in downtown Dallas, close to the Continental Bus Station. It was a wonderful thing for someone to do for us. I'm sure it was a sacrifice for Mr. Penny. Anyone who ran a demanding business and then gave up his Saturday night to provide entertainment for a bunch of orphans must have been a very good man.

Today I do not see as many first run movies as I did then. As we left the auditorium after a movie, we acted out parts of the show. For a week we'd play the Do You Remember? game of acting out further parts of the last picture show. One would last us a whole week. If it was really slapstick or really funny, we would reenact the show for months. Sometimes a particular line would stay with us for years. Love you, Mr. Penny!

MISCHIEF

One spring day in high school, I had the maniacal idea of putting a thumb tack in the seat of someone at each class period. As we moved from one class to another, it became more of a challenge to find an unsuspecting victim. After being duped once each victim learned to check before they sat at every class. At the change between the last two classes, one of the teachers held me up in the hall, asking about a project we were working on in her class. As I approached home room, Miss Range told me to hurry because I was holding up the class. Needless to say, I hurried. Miss Range stayed outside in the hall for a few minutes. I quickly sat at my regular desk on the front row where I got the point of a dozen thumb tacks! I remember it as spring because my dress was quite thin and also because that is the time the sap rises.

When we cooked something in Home Economics Class, we could call some friend in to eat our efforts. Doris and I had teamed up on a mock cherry pie. When Miss Walker had tasted it and given us a good grade, we called in friends to share the pie. While we were eating it, one of the boys asked who had washed the cranberries. Doris said Fay and Fay said Doris at the same time. We finished eating it anyway, even though we all understood that no one had washed those cranberries.

Not every person at Buckner had a nickname, but in our Class of '44, there was Billy Ray "Little Pickle Barrel" Clark, Joseph Herbert "Jake" Corbett, Katherine "Kit" Kirby, Edna Mae "Foxie" Reynolds, Ella Mae "Cotton" Taylor, Barbara Louise "Babs" Waller, Joe Weldon "Ike" Rushing, Doris "Charlie" Ridge and yours truly, Vannie Fay "Raisin Toe" Dewberry.

I remember how I got my nickname. One summer afternoon some of us decided to move a super size table. We had already learned that if we turned it over top side on the floor, we could move it better. However, this time it landed on my big toe! I had a super size big toe all that summer and the next. When it got well, people forgot about it and went on to something else. But I made the mistake of telling Tom Luker about my nickname after we were married, and he reminds me of it still.

SINGING

Psalms 100:1 says, "Make a joyful noise unto the Lord, all ye lands." Well, we called what we did singing, and as long as I can remember we sang. We sang all the popular music we heard on the radio, in the movies and also we sang hymns. Of the hymns, we were partial to the ones written by B. B. McKinney. He often came to Buckner to lead us in singing while I lived there. He told us the B. B. in his name was for "Big Brother" to us. We just ate that up, and considered him to be our brother!

AFTER BUCKNER

I can not believe how anxious I was to leave Buckner Home back in 1944. After looking forward to leaving for so long, I was finally on my way. I had a job at A. Harris & Company in the credit department and lived with my mother and sister-in-law. They worked nights and I worked days. I was alone for the first time in my life, and I could not believe a "grown" woman could be so lonesome. I missed my classmates, the crowds of kids and the order of life at Buckner.

That fall, Texas Tech seemed like such a large place. I lived with an aunt and uncle. They treated me just like one of their own children, but I was moody and out of place. After one semester, I went back to Dallas and got a job at the Community Chest with an aunt (only six years older then me) and her family. We were more like sisters than aunt and niece.

After a year or two, I signed on to sell magazines. A crew was going all over and I wanted to see some of the country. We worked all the nearby states, went as far north and west as Seattle and then down the coast to Southern California. When we again reached Dallas, I'd seen enough of the country and got a job with the telephone company, where I worked off and on for twenty-three years until retirement in 1982.

I married Tom Luker in 1950. We lived in a lot of different places: Shreveport, Louisiana, Oklahoma City, Overland Park, Kansas, as well as Dallas. When we moved back from Kansas, we built a house on a farm we had south of Terrell in Kaufman County, Texas.

Farming was a new experience, not at all like the hunting and fishing we had been thinking about. We improved pastures and surface water, raised cattle and hay and learned something new every day. Not all we learned was in text books. One of the first things we learned was you can not get away from a farm for very long. One year for Christmas, we went to my brother Steward's house near Avery, Texas. Christmas Eve night, we slept on a mat in the back of a suburban. Tom and I had seldom been closer, partly due to the space between the wheel wells and partly due to the night temperature. We were SO COLD! We came home after Christmas Dinner.

The other time we got away was to visit friends in Mesa, Arizona. We had just arrived when the reports of torrential rains in northeast Texas got us on the road for home. Brother Bob had come from Dallas to the farm every night while we were away.

Other things we learned: Over twenty cats in two barns are too many. A twelve pound channel catfish is about as big as my hands can hold while cleaning it. POD stands for post hole digger. You cut and bale hay in the sunshine and haul it in the

evening. You help your neighbor when you can. You'll need their help before long. Take care of your live stock. If you can not feed them all, sell one cow and buy feed for the others. If you are angry with your mate, keep your own counsel. If you get too much rain, celebrate. It beats being too dry.

In 1982 when I retired from the telephone company, we started thinking about selling the farm. Tom wanted to retire too. By 1984 we had sold all our land, livestock and equipment. Next stop was Hide-A-Way Lake near Lindale, Texas. Our home backed up to the 15th fairway of the golf course and we were across the street from a small lake. The same things we liked about it, made it easy to sell in 1993.

Since 1987 we have been spending summers in Pt. Ludlow, Washington, on the Olympic Peninsula. Our home overlooks the mouth of the Hood Canal and the Pudget Sound. On good days, the Cascade Mountains from Baker (at the Canadian border) to Rainier (south of Seattle) are a magnificent sight. We've lived here permanently since February of 1992.

Among other things, Tom and I share this philosophy: If there is anything you want do in this life, get on with it.

LISTEN TO THE MOCKINGBIRD
(or ignore it if you can)

The mockingbird is aptly named for a habit of imitating other birds. Occasionally, I have even heard one imitate a cat. There are catbirds, but that's not what I'm talking about; they are not good imitators.

The mockingbird is the state bird of Arkansas, Florida, Mississippi, Tennessee and Texas. It's a protected little big-mouth and easily recognizable with its slender bill which is about nine inches long, a white underside, white wing patches and white along the outside of the tail. The rest is various shades of gray. Its wing beats are slow enough in flight to be counted.

The mockingbird is not found in wooded areas. It skirts them. On clear summer nights it perches on high places, telephone poles, television antennas, etc. There it sings its best, loudest and most repeated songs. It will leap straight up in the sky—but if you are hoping it will fly away—don't count on it. It just goes straight up and straight down, imitating other song birds and repeating its song several times without changing its program.

When we farmed in Texas, most of our grass work, cutting and hay baling, was done in hot dry weather. If we worked hard all day, we needed our rest at night. That seemed to be the time the protected little bugger sang the loudest. Before we built a modern house, we had two different trailers at the farm. Neither of these was air conditioned, so they were open for ventilation. The mockingbird loved these nights.

One summer afternoon after lunch break, Tom went back to cutting grass for hay. I stayed in the pasture with him, parked the pickup under a shade tree, stretched out on the truck bed with the tool box and thought I'd catch a few winks. But Mr. Mockingbird thought he'd sing. He was singing his next to best. (Nights are best.) When he finally took a breath, I whistled to him the only bird song I knew, "bob white, bob white." Mr. Mockingbird didn't like my whistling. He flew away and I fell asleep listening to the steady hum of the tractor and mower. I had slept no more than fifteen minutes when Mr. Mockingbird returned to the tree and corrected my song, "bob bob white, bob bob white," and I'd swear an oath, he laughed!

Living in Washington State for several years now, I miss the mockingbird and his endless song. But I remember that's not all bad.

Ruth Ford, '44

OUR CLASS SONG

It's been hard these long years,
But we've finished them in style,
And today we know it's been worthwhile.

We've had chemistry, biology, arithmetic and
    speech.
Now it's here, that goal we've tried to reach!

We're leaving you with hearts so full
And words we cannot say.
We hate to leave you, dear old Buckner,
But we must confess: this is a grand old day!

Sarah (Heckethorn) Haley, '44

Once when I had table duty and my table was the last one on the row, farthest from Miss Mamie, I was getting ready to do my dishes and facing nothing except the back window. I decided to face the other table and talk to the girl in front of me. Suddenly Miss Mamie called "Sarah, Sarah Haley" in her high pitched voice, and she pointed the one finger at me saying, "Come here." She asked me why I was talking and I told her I just wanted to talk. She then said for me to start coming after school to clean the tables and benches in Manna Hall. I did that for about three days. When she finally let me go she said, "Sarah, why can't you be nice like your sister Marie?" So much for being nice.

Another time at Buckner when I was working in the kitchen, I had gathered all the dish (cup) towels from the top of Manna Hall where they were drying on the flat roof. I had just finished folding the towels when the guys from the bakery brought the dessert for the evening meal. It happened to be cream puffs. They looked so good I decided to snitch one. Just as I was putting it into my mouth, guess who walked in the door? None other than Miss Mamie!

She caught me red handed. Obviously there wasn't anything I could do but go ahead and finish eating it. She then said, "Sarah, was the cream puff good?" I said, "Yes." Needless to say, I had to come after school again to clean. This time I only had to come back for one day. When she told me I didn't have to come back anymore, she even had a smile on her face and just told me not to snitch anymore desserts.

I remember the time Barbara Waller, Doris Ridge, Fay and I had to dig up the grass and make a flower bed down by the hospital in order to get permission to go to a football game between Buckner and Garland. If we did that, Mrs. Brady said, she would let us go to the game. We sure did get it done, but gosh that was work.

MY LIFE AFTER BUCKNER

I left Buckner, the only home I knew, on graduation night, May 26, 1944. When I went with my sister Mildred, to Houston, Texas, I was a scared girl not knowing what to do. She took me under her wing as always and taught me about

life outside the gates of Buckner. I didn't think I would miss Buckner, but I was completely lost without the security of the place I had called home for eighteen years. I think I cried more at that time than any other time in my life. I finally got hold of myself and found a job at Straus-Frank, a big wholesale company, keeping inventory and learning how to keep books.

I met my husband Howard when I visited Marie in Las Vegas, Nevada, in the summer of 1953. He was the brother of Marie's husband. I made several trips to Vegas and finally we decided to marry on July 14, 1956.

I loved Las Vegas, but missed Texas and all my family and friends in Dallas and Houston. In Vegas at that time, I knew only my sister Marie and her family. I wasn't used to living in the desert and had to learn to do things differently. For example, in planting a yard, I always thought you used grass sods, but there was much more to it than that in Vegas' climate. I missed the greenery of Texas, but I finally adjusted to a different kind of life and a town that never closes.

Six months after we married, I went to work for E G &G, a contractor for the Atomic Energy commission. While there I saw them test an atom bomb at the Nevada Test Site, sixty-five miles away. It was an awesome sight, also a bit scary.

I worked until I had my first child, a girl, Carol. I stayed home with Carol, Susan, and then Gary until they were in middle school. After they entered junior high, I worked at a car dealership just a few blocks from home until I retired.

We have five grandchildren, who have kept us busy the last few years. About three years ago the whole family decided to buy a condo in Brian Head, Utah. There the young ones can ski and the old folks can just enjoy the beautiful mountains and scenery. Also it is a great place to go in the summer when the temperature reaches 110 degrees here in Las Vegas.

Looking back through the years and thinking about my life at Buckner Home, I'm glad my father decided to put me there. I wondered why then, but as I grew older, I understood. I developed close ties there with my classmates and friends which I will always cherish.

Leston Lee McNeil '44

COMING INTO BUCKNER

The year was 1931, and the Great American Depression was in full swing. Throughout the nation people were losing their jobs, their homes, and even their farms; and my family was caught up right in the middle of it all. I was only six years old at the time and understood little of what was happening in the world, but I knew things were not going well on our small farm as I always went to bed hungry. My family consisted of my father, Jake McNeil; my two brothers, Travis and Estel; and two sisters, Addie and Gladys. My mother, Lila Levine McNeil, had died two years before of a disease known as pellagra, and that's when the fortunes of our family began to change. The girls, Addie at fifteen, and Gladys at thirteen, were old enough to accomplish the household chores, but it wasn't the same somehow, and we all knew that it would never be again.

Our father was trying to farm 160 acres of sandy-loam soil in Leon County, Texas, but no matter how hard he tried, the end of each year's harvest season found him further in debt. Father never realized that the soil was wrong for growing cotton, so he planted cotton year after year with one poor crop following another. There were no farm agents in our part of the state, but in 1931 Dad got some advice, from someone he apparently trusted, to try planting peanuts. He planted them that year, going deep into debt to purchase enough seed, and we had a fantastic crop at harvest time. Our barn was completely full of peanuts, and there were additional huge canvas covered piles scattered around outside the barn.

The problem then came to light. Because of the Depression throughout the country, no one was purchasing peanuts that year. The previous year's peanut crop had made some of the local farmers wealthy, but they all, including my father, lost their shirts in 1931. We ended up with plenty of peanuts to eat but precious little else.

In October 1931, Father received word from his brother, Lewis, who lived in Burkburnett, Texas, that the oil field there was booming and the oil companies were looking for men to hire. Uncle Lewis promised Father that he would make sure there was a job for him in the oil field if he wanted to leave the farm and come up there to work. It seems the offer came just in time as Jake realized that he was broke, deep in debt, and based on his lack of success in previous years, in all probability would be unable to get another loan. He had nothing to lose as he knew he was not going to be able to feed himself and five kids through the winter.

He loaded us all into the back of a truck with a canvas cover over the back, and we were soon on our way to Burkburnett and a job in the oil fields. Father had talked one of his more prosperous friends into driving us to Burkburnett in his almost new, two-ton truck; a product of his last year's peanut crop. We traveled for three days and two nights, stopping only for gasoline for the truck and a sandwich with a drink of water for us kids. There was little to do during the trip and nothing to see as we were holding the canvas cover down as tightly as possible to keep the rain from soaking us and the few items of household goods we were able to take with us. It was with a great sigh of relief that we finally arrived at Uncle Lewis' place. As if to help us celebrate, the sunlight burst through the clouds and a warm wind began to blow from the south, making for a wonderful day for October. Uncle Lewis seemed genuinely glad to see us, and told Dad that the oil company had a pumper's job waiting for him, and that a small three room house came with the job as part payment of his salary. We would stay with Uncle Lewis for the night, and in the morning he would escort us to the house.

What I remember most about the night we spent at Uncle Lewis' house is that his daughter, about my own age, bit me on the hand, and when I began to cry, my sister Gladys returned the favor by biting her hand. For awhile it looked as though we would be escorted to our new house that night. But it was not until morning that we piled into the back of the truck again for Uncle Lewis to deliver us to what we called our "new house." It was only about a mile from where we had spent the night, and I was pleased that we were so close to Uncle Lewis.

We were located in a place known as Stringtown, as the small houses were strung out about one quarter mile apart along the oil company's main road. Each pumper had his own house located near the center of the area for which he was responsible. Our new home had three rooms, a kitchen/dining room on one end, a living room on the other end, and a bedroom in the middle.

The toilet was an outhouse which was all right with me as I had yet to see my first indoor plumbing. The shack did have running water in the kitchen. We thought it was a real nice house.

Dad's job was to check the oil wells to make sure they were greased and running right, to turn them on and off on schedule, and to monitor the level of oil in the giant collection tank which loomed above our house. The smell of crude oil was everywhere, seeping into everything.

Even with Dad's new job and some money coming in, things did not improve much. By purchasing only what we could not do without and with weekly donations of food and milk from Uncle Lewis, we were able to scrape by. Dad's other brother, whom I never met, nor whose name do I remember, got a divorce from his wife who then came to live with us. This, of course, put an additional strain on our resources, and things began to get slowly worse. We called the lady "Aunt Deal," and soon I learned to love her as a member of the family. Aunt Deal taught me several nursery poems that I still remember to this day.

We had lived in our little house in Stringtown for about six months when Dad became sick and could not go to work. Weeks passed and he could not get out of bed; his sickness got worse instead of better. We were able to keep his job with the oil company by the older kids doing his work. Uncle Lewis, although he could ill afford it, finally paid a doctor from Wichita Falls to come to see Dad. As expected the diagnosis was pellagra and consumption. The doctor said there was nothing he could do to make him better. I can still remember how it hurt to see my father in his weakened condition, for he had always been so strong and full of life. Now he was little more than skin and bones with huge sores all over his body.

Father died of pellagra in May of 1932. I found out years later that pellagra, which killed thousands during the depression, was nothing more than the lack of fruits and vegetables in the diet. Now the plight of our family could hardly get worse. The loss of Dad's small income meant that we were now unable to purchase even the basic essentials of food, and we soon received word that we would have to vacate the house so the new pumper, hired to replace Dad, would have a place to live. At the time I was too young to really understand the problems, but I knew that I missed my Dad something awful.

What happened next seemed a mystery to us

all. A few days after Father's funeral, a shiny new car pulled off the road and stopped in front of our house. A well dressed man and woman got out of the car and came up to the porch where we were sitting. They asked for the adult of the house. We had already received word that we must move out of the house, but since we had nowhere else to go, Aunt Deal had decided to stay in the house until we received an eviction notice. We expected these two people were delivering our eviction notice, so we were not surprised when they departed and left Aunt Deal crying.

After the shiny new car had turned around and left, Aunt Deal came over to where we were on the porch, and no matter how hard we tried, she would not tell us what the man or woman had said to make her cry. We suspected they had used the "Poor White Trash" phrase with which we were all familiar.

The next morning while it was still dark, the car again pulled up and stopped in front of our house. Without our notice Aunt Deal had packed a few of our personal items, and now she awakened us three boys, got us dressed in our best clothes and ushered us out the door into the waiting car, without waking the girls. She told us that we were just going for a little ride, but we all suspected it was more than that because her voice sounded funny and she kept wiping her eyes and nose with her handkerchief. The car turned around and pulled away, and we three boys, even though we did not know it, were on our way to Buckner Orphans Home and to a life a thousand times better than anything we could have had otherwise.

Someone had reported our plight to Buckner, I am not sure who it was. I suspect it was my Uncle Lewis, but whoever it was, I will always owe them a debt of gratitude as it proved to be one of the best things that could have happened to my brothers and me.

In recalling the events of that day so long ago, my only real regret is that we did not get to say goodbye to our sisters. In fact, it was the last chance we would have had to say goodbye to Gladys as she died some six years later from the flu. I did not see Addie again until 1944 after I had graduated from Buckner. It had been twelve years since I had last seen her, and she no longer felt like my sister; just another woman who happened to have the same parents as I did. I do not understand why Buckner declined to accept my

two sisters. My brother, Travis, was older than Gladys, so the decision could not have been based on age alone. One would think that girls would have needed help and protection more than boys in a case like ours.

I do not know what happened to Aunt Deal, but I pray she had a full and happy life. She was a wonderful lady who helped ease the pain in my life when I needed someone the most.

We traveled in the car for the better part of the day, and I enjoyed most of it. At first I was a little car sick as it was the first time I had ever ridden inside a motor vehicle. The man drove the car without talk, but after it got daylight the woman turned around and began to talk to us. She had pretty, well kept brown hair, and her face had a roundish look, but I think most people would think of her as pretty. She asked us our names, our ages, and all kinds of questions.

At first we were reluctant to answer her questions, but as time passed and she continued to talk to us, we began to feel more at ease and began to answer her questions and to ask some of our own.

Soon we realized that she meant us no harm with all of her questions, and I actually began to enjoy her being with us. We stopped three times during the trip. Our first stop was in a big city where we were taken into a large store. There the lady purchased each of us a pair of shoes, a pair of socks, a pair of pants, and a shirt. These were the first shoes I had ever worn, and walking in them really felt funny. Boy did we feel rich in our new clothes. Since these were my first pair of shoes ever, it took me some time to get the feel of walking in them with their stiff, slippery, soles. I felt like someone had tied two boards to my feet. However, these gifts went a long way toward breaking the ice between us and the man and woman and also made the remainder of the trip quite pleasant.

We then were taken just outside of the city to a café where we were served the best breakfast I had ever had. Travis, who could read, was really tickled by the name of the eating place. He kept wondering out loud where the "COW" was.

We left that city, which I now realize was Wichita Falls, and drove on down the highway through several small towns and a lot of countryside. Later in the afternoon, we drove through a city even larger and more spectacular than the one before. This city had street lights, stop lights, and signs made from colored lights on some of the buildings. I kept Travis busy telling me what the signs said. They even had their streets named.

We left the big city and after driving for some thirty minutes, came upon a place at the junction of two highways that had many red brick buildings with red tile roofs. The buildings were surrounded with green grass and trees, and they almost all looked very much alike. The car went through a gate, drove up a straight street with trees on both sides, and entered a curving road running in front of all the buildings. The road actually formed a large oval, and we drove about half way around the oval before we stopped in front of a large white building with great white pillars holding up the roof of the front porch. I noticed that there was an entrance into the building under the porch and steps running up to the porch on both sides in front of the building.

The man parked in front of the building and went under the porch. He was gone for some fifteen minutes, so the lady told us to get out of the car and stretch our legs. I was awed by the beauty of the place. Everything was so green and clean. Sidewalks ran everywhere. There were also kids everywhere. Some playing ball; others just sitting and talking to each other. The thing I noticed most was that they all seemed to be happy. The man returned to the car, and after we were all reseated, he turned to the lady and said that we were in the wrong place, that we would have to go back to a place called the Receiving Home.

The car made its way around the remainder of the half circle, back down another straight drive, and out the gate to the right of the one we had entered earlier. A few minutes later we pulled up in front of another building which was a dead ringer for those we had seen facing the oval, except this one was in a large open field with a few trees around it.

We had arrived at Buckner Orphans Home, and soon I was in love with the place and with the little girl who lived with Mr. and Mrs. Saddler at the Receiving Home.

It was 1932 and almost the whole nation was hungry except for my two brothers and me, and the hundreds of other orphaned kids who were lucky enough to be taken into Buckner during those hungry years.

Yes, we had come into Buckner and found it to our liking.

BUCKNER RECEIVING HOME

Upon arrival at Buckner Receiving Home, we were led from the automobile into a beautiful red brick building with a red tile roof, exactly like the ones we had seen during our first stop a few minutes before. The grass in Stringtown had just began to show green, but here it was growing solidly around the building and as green as green gets. The building, the grass, and the trees combined to make a beautiful picture in the late afternoon sun.

I found myself awed by the fact that the trail was paved from where the car was parked all the way into the building. Sidewalks were new to me. Once we had reached the large white door and entered the building, I was amazed by the beauty of it all. We came into a large living room with overstuffed chairs, sofas, a piano and various other kinds of equipment I assumed was used for games of some kind. The most profound thing was that they had stained the wooden floor a dark brown and had polished it until it shined. In fact, the floor was so slick and my new shoes so untested, that after a few cautious steps I managed to land flat on my back. Embarrassed beyond belief, I scrambled to my feet the best way I could and with my back pressed tightly against the wall for support, blurted out my apologies.

I remember very little about the wonderful things I saw and experienced in my first few days at Buckner, but I do remember shiny floors, overstuffed chairs, flush toilets, and bathroom sinks with hot and cold water spigots. One of the biggest surprises was the bathtub, made of some kind of hard smooth stuff that looked and felt like white stone. It also had hot and cold water, a plug, and if you pulled a small lever, water would squirt on you from above. This was a strange and wonderful place, and I could not believe that my brothers and I were to live here.

The food was great. We were all served at a large table in an enormous dinning room by girls about my sisters' ages, who thought it very funny watching my brothers and me as we sampled unknown foods and tried to follow instructions as to what to eat what with. We each even had our own bedroom and our own bed. Life couldn't be any better than that. Could it?

There was a little girl, named Betty Sue O'Malley, living at the Receiving Home at the same time as I was there, and it was years later before I found out that she was not the Saddlers' daughter. Betty Sue was a very pretty girl, as friendly as she was pretty, who would let us play with any and all of her many toys. She had a large tricycle which we spent hours taking turns riding around the building on a concrete path they called a sidewalk. There were also swings and see-saws in a grove of trees in back of the building where we spent many happy hours.

We had been at Buckner for only three days and had begun to think we had landed in heaven, when we were herded into a car and driven to the Buckner hospital for physical examinations. We were pricked, prodded, pushed, and pulled! We received immunization shots and gave blood samples. We received the best physical examination that could be given, which dragged on for three days before it was over. After the weekend we were again driven to the hospital, but this time it was to see the dentist. He learned right away that I had a gag reflex when something touched my tongue near the back of my mouth, and never again during my stay at Buckner was I really welcome at the Dental Clinic.

After we had been at the Receiving Home for two weeks and thought we had really settled in, gotten used to all the nice things, and to all the new clothing, the second shoe dropped. We were called into the beautiful parlor which we had been forbidden to use, and Ms. Saddler explained to us why this place was called the "Receiving Home." She explained that we had passed the health examinations, had our hair cut, learned how to take a shower and to get along somewhat with other people, so it was time for us to move in with the other kids on the Buckner campus. She even told us that we would be separated from each other as we would live with kids of our own age. This last part didn't sink in at the time, but I was soon to understand. The following morning, with all our possessions packed into card board boxes, we were loaded into Mr. Saddler's car and driven onto the Buckner campus.

After entering the gate to the campus, our car took the road which led up a drive between rows of trees, to a round or oval shaped drive, curving around so that all the pretty brick buildings we had seen on our first day were facing it. The car drove slowly around the oval and we could see only girls playing around the first three buildings we passed. We then passed the large white building with the large columns holding up

the porch roof that we had seen before. We later found out that this magnificent building was the church and main office. The next building we came to on our left was unique in that it was made of large grey stone blocks and was the only building located on the inside of the large oval formed by the road. The car stopped at this ugly gray building, and I was taken by the hand, led up the steps and turned over to a woman I had never seen before. I was then told that this was the Buckner Nursery and that it would be my new home. To my surprise and dismay, Mrs. Saddler, without unloading my brothers, got back into the car and drove off, taking them away from me.

I had felt lonely, sad and lost when my father had died earlier that month, and when I realized I would probably never see my Aunt Deal or my two sisters again, but I was really hurting now much worse than before. Now, standing on that ugly porch with this strange woman, I was engulfed in a total loneliness such as I had never felt before. My whole world had been taken from me, and I was not prepared to cope with the loss. I was six years old and had lost my entire family in the past few weeks. First my father, then Aunt Deal, my two sisters and now my two brothers. When my father died, I had made a vow to myself that I would never cry again, but I was now alone, totally alone among strangers in a strange and ugly place.

I found that I could not live up to my vow, so I began to cry, and I continued to cry for a long, long, long time!

THE OLD NURSERY

I'm not sure if losing one's entire family in a few weeks is the kind of trauma that can affect a person for life, but I do know that I went into a deep depression after arriving at the Buckner Nursery. All I could do for days after arriving there was to stand by a window and cry, hoping to see Estel or Travis among the boys passing back and forth in front of the window.

I do not remember anything about my first month at the nursery except that a beautiful young woman was assigned to take care of me and my stuff. She was Ernestine White, an older Buckner girl assigned to the nursery to help. I was one of five kids entrusted to Ernestine, who took care of us and our clothing; washing and pressing it as needed. I remember that I had a favorite shirt of white cotton with a blue collar, blue trimmed short sleeves and a pocket. Ernestine was always good to me, and for a long time she was my only contact with reality.

Slowly, as the memory of my lost family faded, my interest in life, and in things going on around me returned. By the end of summer I was playing with the other kids and somewhat enjoying my new home. I remember when Luther Hamlin broke his leg while playing on the merry-go-round. I remember playing in the sand under the concrete porch with Jacky Dobbs, Alma Jay Sherrell, and Peggie Farris. I was Flash Gordon, Alma Jay was Dale Arden, Jacky was Doctor Zarkov, and Peggie was his wife. I'm not at all sure how it was that we knew of these cartoon characters as there was no radio at the nursery and we couldn't read. Funny what one remembers of life as a six-year-old.

In the fall I was taken across the oval road to the school building and enrolled in the first grade. I had never been to school before; in fact, I had never even heard of school before. This was a new experience and I liked it. I guess I could say that to me school was fun and I was ready to learn. I became seven shortly after school started, and I now suspect that was the main reason that I was moved up to the second grade so soon after school started. The kids in second grade did seem to be more my age than those in first grade.

The most vivid recollection I now have of life at the nursery has to do with a cat. The way I remember it there were only two bedrooms at the nursery, one for the boys and one for the girls across the hall. All the beds in each room were lined up side by side with an aisle between. There were about twenty beds in each room. My bed was near the center.

One night I awakened because I couldn't breathe, and there sitting on my chest with its face in my face was a large cat, making some kind of noise similar to purring. I panicked and sprang to my feet, right there on my bed. The cat went flying, and I ran for the room door, jumping from one bed to the next and howling for all I was worth. I wasn't about to get down on the floor if I could keep from doing so. The matrons came, searched the room, and pronounced that I had just had a bad dream and sent me back to bed. To this day I'm convinced this actually happened,

and I doubt if anyone could convince me otherwise.

I don't know how long I lived at the nursery, maybe more than a year. At any rate I was moved into Rupard Hall before the old nursery was torn down. Rupard Hall was known by us kids as "The Little Boys' Building." Some also knew it as "The Dehay Building," which referred to the head matron of the building. I was then about eight-years-old and ready for all the things to happen that can happen to an eight-year-old, living in a building with some fifty boys, ranging in age from eight through eleven. I do not remember George Sherrell, James Zackery, Thomas and Frederick Van Pelt, Bobby Daniels, Leon Curl, Joe Bryce, and many many more, having lived at the Nursery. I'm sure some of them did, but I definitely do remember them from "The Little Boys' Building," where they came to be a part of my life that I hope I never forget. A lot of old friendships date back to those days in Rupard Hall.

DECLAMATION

Do you remember when kids used to get up on the stage to say a poem or give a speech? We called it declaiming. Do you remember George Ebbie? George was a kid of about twelve when he gave his declamation poem—well, sort of gave his poem. George was kinda' funny looking. He was skinny, had black hair and eyes, but his most distinguishing feature was his ears. George's ears were large for his size, or maybe it was just that they looked large because they stood straight out from the sides of his head. Everyone teased George about his ears; in fact, his nickname was "Big Ears" Ebbie.

Anyway, on the day George gave his speech, he was all cleaned up and really looked pretty sharp. When it was time, he walked straight out to the center of the stage, did a right face, and after a brief pause, began in a loud clear voice. "You appreciate me and I'll appreciate you." At this point a look of panic came over his face, and it was obvious he had drawn a complete blank as to what came next. He looked all around; then someone in the wings of the stage could be heard telling him the next line. George listened, turned back to the audience and said, "And we'll appreciate each other."

Again the look of panic and again he turned to the stage wing for a clue. I guess he couldn't hear what was being said so he cupped his hands behind his ears and leaned toward the wings. He was still unable to hear his prompter so he turned back to the audience. His face filled with panic. George then threw his arm up in front of his face and was heard to say, "Gah, I forgot my part," as he bolted off the stage. According to my recollection, the audience appreciated George's little skit better than anything else presented that day.

CHANGING THE PECKING ORDER

Do you remember when Chicken Zackery, a wimp of a kid that liked girls and played the piano, whipped everyone in Rupard Hall. We all called James Zackery "Chicken Zackery," not because he was a coward, but because when he ran, he would hold his arms funny—kinda' like a girl does—when she runs. Anyway, we decided to test Chicken. We took him to the attic, where we all had to stay on rainy days, and when we found someone higher in the pecking order than he was, we would tell him that Chicken had said he could whip him. Being macho and pecking-order conscious, everyone of them would start a fight with Chicken, and Chicken would whip everyone of them, one by one. It's safe to say after that day of testing, no one tried to bully Chicken Zackery. I was one of the top "peckers," and I can remember that I didn't get too bossy with Chicken thereafter.

WHEN SOMEONE SHOT
DOROTHY HEITMAN

Do you remember when someone, using a rubber band, shot Dorothy Heitman in the rump with a paper clip (actually half a paper clip) which pinned her skirt to her body? She screamed bloody murder and had to go to the medic for a tetanus shot, so I'm told. Anyway, it wasn't me, and I'm not going to tell on Thomas Van Pelt. I wonder if Dorothy remembers?

THE GREAT MELON CAPER

Each year during the months of July and August, the melon growers of East Texas sent hundreds of semi-tractor trailer loads of watermelons to Dallas to feed the melon-hungry masses. The only road from East Texas to Dallas was Highway 80, which came right by Buckner Home campus. Now Buckner had a farm, but we never raised anything as good to eat as melons. Our crops were cotton, corn, oats, cane and hay; almost anything that had tons of work associated with it, instead of something good to eat like watermelons. It was, therefore, natural that when we saw all those thousands of watermelons going by on the trucks, our mouths began to water, and we began to ponder about how we were going to liberate some of those melons. Lord knows we couldn't afford to buy even one as there was seldom a nickel among the bunch of us. So there had to be another way.

It so happened that Highway 80 ran along the north side of the Buckner campus and crossed Buckner Boulevard at the northwest corner of the campus. There was a traffic light at that intersection and as luck would have it, the campus fence row of hedges was well developed near this intersection.

We devised a plan which we found to be effective—most of the time. We found, by experimenting, that if we took a rock in hand and rapped the traffic light control box a good whack, it would freeze the light in its present position for ten to fifteen minutes. Two or three of us would go down to the intersection around 2:00 A.M. and wait in the bushes for a melon truck to come over the hill some thousand feet from the light. We would wait until the light turned red, then give the control box a good whack. As the truck slowed to a stop at the light, we would sneak out of the bushes and approach the truck from the rear. One of us would climb up on the truck to hand the melons down, and the others would catch them to place them on the road behind the truck. We worked until the driver either got tired of waiting for the light to change, or the light turned green, and the driver would drive on down the highway toward Dallas.

This little scam worked well, especially at night, unless another vehicle came over the hill and illuminated the whole scene with light. In that case, we abandoned the melons to the oncoming vehicle and made a mad dash for the safety of the bushes. There was very little traffic on Highway 80 during the wee hours of the morning, so we were seldom interrupted in this manner.

Sure, we knew it was stealing, but we were not sure exactly from whom or what the value of our theft was to the owner as compared to how much the melons meant to us. The truth of the matter was we did feel bad about what we were doing, but not bad enough to stop doing it.

One Sunday afternoon, Bobby Daniels and I decided we could make a daylight acquisition of melons. When the truck stopped, we rushed out and Bobby climbed up on the truck. He had passed down only one melon when he gave a whoop and landed on the road beside me, running for the cotton field across the road. Knowing we had been spotted, I tore out after him at full speed. Looking back, I could see the fat trucker and his slim helper hot on our heels. I always suspected that we lean and hungry kids could out distance grown men, and it proved to be the truth, but only barely so. The men gained a few yards on us, but I guess their endurance was not strong enough, because we were a good thirty yards ahead of them when we left the cotton field and plowed into a tall cornfield. The men soon gave up, and it was just in time because running in the soft dirt was taking its toll on Bobby and me.

We continued through the cornfield to a hilltop on the far side before we stopped. As we looked back, we could see the two men return across the cotton field to their truck. They loaded the melon on the truck and moved on down the highway. We had by now caught our breath and breathed a sigh of relief when Bobby said, "Gah, they must have seen us." I didn't get a melon that day, but I did get a good laugh. They must have seen us, indeed; they almost caught us.

BUCK, SON OF BROWNIE

The troop train with its load of soldiers bound for Korea, gave several huge lurches and ground to a squeaking halt to let the east bound express scream past. I recognized the railroad siding we were on as the one where many years earlier, as a fifteen-year-old, I had faced a Mexican kid with a hunting knife in his hand.

From my seat on the train, I could see the lights on the Buckner Home Campus where I had been raised. This siding was one mile from the Buckner Campus and just a few hundred yards from Evans Store, where as kids we had spent our pennies. Then we had thought it great sport to come to the siding and push the freight cars up and down the track, causing them to crash into and lock up with each other. At times, we would find a car open and would prowl the insides as well as over and under them. It doesn't sound like

much now, but to a group of fifteen-year-old orphan kids with time on their hands, it seemed like great fun.

Our gang, which we never thought of as a gang, spent a lot of time walking the railroad tracks. Now that I am older, and I hope a little wiser, I can look back on our activities as similar to those of the wolf packs in Alaska. We prowled a rough circle, one to five miles around the Buckner Campus, and little transpired within that circle that we did not know about. We would gulp down our breakfast, and as if time were important, hastily leave the Buckner Campus on foot via a trail beginning at the hole in the fence behind the commissary. The trail took us through cotton and corn fields to a small lake about one mile southeast of the Campus—Bull Pond.

Here we would strip naked and swim in the warm water until we were satisfied, then dress and search the shoreline of the lake for water moccasins to kill. We often killed several snakes before departing the pond. Now that I look back, I can't help wondering why we had no fear of swimming in a pond which we knew to be loaded with poisonous water snakes. Yet the truth is, we never gave it a thought. From Bull Pond we would cross the nearby Farm to Market Road and go up onto the railroad tracks. We would walk west along the tracks, throwing rocks at everything imaginable and challenging each other for the title of champion rail walker. It was only a mile from Bull Pond to the siding, and it never took long to cover the distance. From the top of the parked freight cars, we had a perfect view of the Dallas skyline some seven miles to the west.

The events leading up to the knifing, had started to unravel some six months earlier. At Buckner we were not allowed to have pets, but several of the older boys owned dogs in sort of a loose manner not common to the conventional relationship found between pet and owner in normal societies. The dogs were on campus and were free to roam anywhere they chose to go. Everyone knew the dogs and who they belonged to, yet everyone took every opportunity to feed and pet them as though they were theirs. It was as if the dogs belonged to everyone and to no one.

During the years when I was thirteen to fifteen, there was one large male dog on campus named Brownie, which I'm told belonged to Johnny Wright. Brownie was a legend in his own time as "the best darn rabbit hunting dog there ever was." Brownie's heritage was questionable, but he was a dead ringer for a dog in a movie called "Old Yeller." As things happened, there was also a female dog on campus—just passing through, I guess, for no one ever kept a female dog. This dog we called Lady and that she was. She was so full of happiness, so frisky and friendly, that one couldn't help liking her. In the course of time, Lady came into heat, as female dogs are wont to do, and she and Brownie disappeared into the cotton fields for a few days.

Time passed and soon it became evident that Lady was going to have puppies as her sides were bulging, and she was no longer her bouncing, frisky self. Unfortunately, it was February and the weather took a turn to ice and snow. As I remember it, James Zackery became concerned that Lady would not be able to find a dry, warm place to have her pups, so he took her up the back stairwell of the three-story building where we lived and put her in a box against the locked attic door at the top of the stairs. James acted just in time, for on the very next morning, Lady brought seven cute puppies into the world.

A few days passed and we received word that our matron of the building knew about the dogs and had asked Shorty Collins, the Buckner farm operator, to come and haul them away. We knew this meant that Lady and all her pups would be killed, so we gathered them up and moved them with their box into a hay field just south of the hospital. The hay fields in this part of Texas have what we locals called "buffalo wallows," which are round depressions about two feet deep in an otherwise flat plain. So we placed Lady's box in a buffalo wallow and left her there for the night.

We woke to sleet and snow the next morning, so we rushed to the hay field to make sure Lady and the pups were OK. We found two of the pups frozen; knowing the others might freeze too, we moved them near the front gate into the Thornhill Bushes. James Zackery, Joe Bryce and I were just about frozen when we completed the move, and when we got back to the warmth of our room, I noticed that James was crying. I knew orphan kids don't cry, but looking closely at him, I finally realized that he had lost his shoes somewhere in the hay field and his feet were purple and bleeding from the cold and ice.

Fortunately James recovered, but I can imagine the pain he must have endured. Time passed

and our daily trips to the Thornhill Bushes to feed Lady, and check on the puppies, became routine. The puppies soon had their eyes open and it was great fun playing with them. Someone must have picked up on our daily visits to the bushes, or maybe they just noticed the trail we had inadvertently created, for one day we arrived at the box to find Lady and her puppies were gone.

We searched everywhere, thinking Lady might have moved them, but to no avail. When we got back to our building, we were told that Shorty Collins, and a group of larger "farm gang" boys, had picked up Lady and the pups in a pickup truck and driven away. Several weeks passed before the hurt of losing Lady and the puppies, knowing they had been killed, diminished somewhat.

The season turned to spring and several of us decided to go "bumming" as we called our forays away from the campus. We took the trail through the barren fields to Bull Pond. The water was still too cold for swimming, so we continued toward the railroad tracks and headed west towards Evans Store. When we reached the railroad siding, there were no freight cars to explore, so we proceeded on towards the store.

It was then that Joe noticed a bunch of puppies at one of the small shacks, located by the tracks and occupied by a Mexican family. Even though Lady was nowhere to be seen, we just knew that those were our puppies. We approached the house and asked a woman out front if we could have our puppies back. The Mexican family apparently spoke no more English than we did Spanish, but they sensed that we wanted the puppies. Before we could get a good look, a teenage girl and her brother scooped up the pups and rushed into the shack with them. Two teenage boys and a man came out of the house and began to yell and push us away from the front porch. A fight started, and it was then that the boy, about my age, came at me with his hunting knife. The boy was quick as a cat, and it wasn't long before the hunting knife had sliced a six-inch gash on the inside of my left arm from the wrist up, and blood was spurting everywhere. Sure I was scared. I had never fought anyone with a knife before and it was an unhappy experience. So I like to think of it as a "tactical retreat," and remember that "discretion is the best part of valor," and stuff like that.

The truth is, we left the area as quickly as we

could, and I, for one, had no intention of going back. We did, however, stone the house from the railroad tracks. The man and the two boys came after us. I tied a string around my arm, but it's safe to say I could have been tracked home by the bloody trail I left.

On reflection, I suspect the puppies were not ours at all, and the Mexican family just wasn't going to let a group of gringo teenagers take their pets from them.

I learned later that Johnny Wright was one of the farm gang that had helped Shorty Collins haul Lady and the pups away, and he had decided to keep the one that looked the most like Brownie.

Johnny named the puppy "Buck" and Buck grew up to take the place of Brownie for a new generation of kids. Buck also became a legend in his own time as "the best darned rabbit dog there ever was."

Finally, the troop train lurched and moved ahead with me, full of memories, still in it. On to the West Coast and on toward Korea.

GOING BUMMING

Our gang, the one which we never thought of as a gang, used to go bumming. We left campus through the hole in the fence behind the commissary and took the trail through the cotton and corn fields to Bull Pond. (We never used the article before Bull Pond!) A family named Smith had a small farm near Bull Pond, and in late summer we would visit the Smith watermelon field to select a nice melon. We would put it into the lake to cool off before we ate it. I can't honestly say it was any cooler when we ate it than when we stole it.

We also found great sport in hunting water moccasins along the shore of the lake and trying to kill them. On occasion Clyde Smith, who owned a .22 caliber rifle, would join us in our snake hunts. I can remember the day he killed six snakes. In spite of knowing this, we swam in the lake without fear!

Our route from Bull Pond was up the railroad track towards Dallas some seven miles away to the west. As we passed near Evans Store, we would stop for a cold drink if anyone had any money. We would follow the railroad west, through the area where Urbandale is now located, and into an area known to us as Blue Haven. Blue Haven was a lovers' lane for the locals, and

we enjoyed hiding and spying on the lovers in their cars. Blue Haven also contained a Hobo Jungle, or Hobo Camp, where we at times talked to the hoboes.

We left the railroad at Blue Haven and entered the woods we knew as Rockbottom. There was another swimming hole in Rockbottom, and we never passed up the chance for another swim. There were trees overhanging the pond at Rockbottom, and we delighted in swinging from a rope out over the swimming hole and dropping into the water. The pond was created by a dam on which a road was built. It had a culvert which came under the road and turned up. The level of water in the pond was maintained by the height of the culvert. Following a hard rain, the water running into the top of the culvert created a dangerous condition in the pond. Several Buckner boys, including my brother Estel, were washed down and through the culvert. This phenomena drowned one boy, Everett Ingram, who got hung up on the supports under the road.

From Rockbottom our trail turned back east, towards home, through fields and an area known as "Willows," because of the dense growth of willows found there. The total trip was about ten miles, but we never thought of it as a tiring trip as it never ceased to be a fun trip. We always kept an eye out for a rabbit or squirrel to take back to roast on an open fire under the shed. Things didn't get better than to have a rabbit roasting over the fire and a bucket of coffee boiling in the coals—especially if there was sugar to go with the coffee.

BLUEBEARD'S CHAMBER

Don't ask me how it got its name. Perhaps it reminded someone of a cave once used by Bluebeard the Pirate on some isolated island. In truth the thing we called "Bluebeard's Chamber" was a room located on the lower floor of the two story commissary building in which all the most exotic things handled by the Commissary were kept. Things like coffee, sugar and spices. I'm not really sure what all was found in Bluebeard's Chamber, but I do know that it was always locked and Mr. Porter, who was in charge of the Commissary, had the only key. He had the only key, that is until Herbert Ray White came to work at the Commissary. Herbert was good with his hands and he was smart. On one occasion when Mr.

Porter gave Herbert the keys to get something from Bluebeard's Chamber, Herbert made an impression of both sides of the key in a piece of clay. He then went to work with a small file and a blank key and soon had his own usable key. He did the same thing for the front door of the Commissary.

Now I can't say what Herbert may have done with these two keys, but I did notice that he always had coffee boiling in a bucket over a fire out near the shed when no one else had coffee.

Coffee was looked upon as a luxury, to be prized even above ice cream, especially when it had sugar in it. Anyway, when Herbert left Buckner, he passed these treasures on to me. Now I never worked at the commissary, but the barber shop was on the second floor over the commissary. On my trips to the barber shop, I looked the place over and found there to be very sophisticated alarms set up in the commissary. On the stairwell there was a light beam sensor that when broken activated an alarm. There were also several other alarms on the lower floor; one near the entrance and another in front of Bluebeard's Chamber. I also noticed that workers on the second floor would throw their trash down an open hole to the lower floor to be put into the incinerator.

I took my best friend, Thomas Van Pelt, into my confidence; and we, with visions of hot steaming coffee in our heads, planned our attack on Bluebeard's Chamber. We knew full well that if we were caught, we would be expelled from Buckner, and we accepted the challenge.

We accumulated our gear, a twenty foot section of rope and a canvas pack to carry our loot. We entered the commissary at two in the morning and climbed to the second floor, up the rail of the stairwell to keep from setting off the alarms. There was a steel gate closing off the lower floor from the entrance door, so we knew we had no chance of getting to the Chamber that way.

In the dark we found the hole used for throwing down the trash, found a sturdy steel beam to tie our rope to, and soon we were standing on the lower floor in front of Bluebeard's Chamber. We had never had a chance to test our key, but it fit perfectly. We were soon loaded down with coffee and sugar and on our way back to our rope. Thomas went up the rope like a squirrel, but I found it to be quite a challenge. We had failed to tie knots in our rope, and it proved to be

almost beyond my capability to climb with the extra forty pounds of goodies in tow.

We did get out of the commissary and back to bed, without being caught, and the next day we hid our booty in the rafters of Rupard Hall, the building we lived in. To hide it, we had to crawl under a section of the wall and through a small opening into a section of the attic where only the rafters were located.

Two days after we hid our loot, Mr. Taylor called me into his office and there on his desk were our ill gotten gains. That day I told Mr. Taylor the only lie I ever told him. I denied any knowledge of the coffee and sugar. To this day I'd give a lot to find out how he ended up with our booty. I know he did not crawl through that tiny hole in the attic himself because as a hundred and twenty pound weakling, I had had trouble getting through the hole myself.

TRASHMAN

Do you remember Kate? I do. I remember her well! Looking back from this viewpoint, I can say that my 1942 summer involvement with Kate made it one of my best summers ever. I was sixteen that summer and, as is the truth about most sixteen-year-olds, my perspective of the real world was shaded by how I felt about a matter.

Kate had brown hair and big brown eyes that always had a twinkle of mischief in them. She was typical in most other respects. She had strong clean-cut legs and a strong supple body which actually was quite small. She had a firm well-shaped mouth, and her nose was attractive enough. Kate's ears were a little large, but they did not detract from her overall appearance, as they were covered by her brown hair. Kate made my summer of '42, and we spent many hours together.

My job at Buckner during that summer was to be the trash man. I used a one-mule wagon to pick up the trash from designated trash deposit points on campus and haul it all to the dump. The job really wasn't hard, but it did keep me busy five days a week. On occasion my days were much longer than they needed to be.

Immediately following breakfast, I would walk the half mile to the Buckner farm, located northeast of the campus, capture, harness and hitch the mule to the wagon. The one-mule wagon contained six fifty-gallon trash cans in which to transport the trash to the dump. At first I was worried that I might not remember where all the trash deposit points were located, but I soon found that I had no cause to be concerned. The mule was used to pulling the trash wagon; in fact, had been on the job for years and knew exactly where each deposit point was, having memorized the whole routine.

She would pull the wagon up close alongside the deposit point and stop. Then she would remain stopped at that point until I climbed down from the wagon and climbed back up again. When I was back in the driver's seat, and only then, would she proceed on to the next point.

This routine was completed at every deposit point on the route, and it made no difference whether there was trash to be picked up or not. After the six trash barrels were full, I still had to dismount and climb back on the wagon at all the remaining stops in order to complete the route. Not because I wanted to do this, but because that mule insisted!

After all stops were made, the mule would pull the wagon out the north campus gate, turn west onto Highway 80, and proceed to the dump, located in Walkers' Woods, two miles west on Highway 80 and one mile into the woods. After the wagon was unloaded, the mule would pull it back to the highway and head back to the barn two and a half miles east. The whole trip from the barn, around the campus, to the dump and back was eight miles and took close to eight hours to complete.

It seemed great to have a mule to do my thinking for me until the day came when there just wasn't enough trash in the deposit points to warrant picking it up and taking it to the dump. Nevertheless, the mule insisted that I get off the wagon, climb back up, and make each deposit point. I could live with that so long as she proceeded on the route as soon as I was back on the wagon, but the real problem surfaced when the mule pulled the wagon out the north campus gate onto Highway 80.

With the reins, I signaled for the mule to turn right and head for the barn. She ignored me completely and turned left, heading for the dump three miles away. In my effort to turn right, I pulled the reins until the mule's head was touching her shoulder. To no avail. The mule continued to pull the wagon right on down the highway toward the dump. I got down from the wagon, took the mule's bridle into my hands and led her around to head her toward the barn.

After walking and leading her by her bridle for about one hundred yards, I climbed back onto the wagon. As if this had been a signal, the mule turned around in the highway (almost getting us both killed by an oncoming truck), and headed back west toward the dump. I learned that day that I must always not only stop and remount at each deposit site, but also take the trip to the dump each day, like it or not.

Actually, the mule ensured that I did a good job that summer. It was just as easy to haul a load of trash to the dump as it was to make the trip empty. So you can see the mule would have nothing to do with a short, easy work day. I went to the dump each day, like it or not.

My workday ended back at the barn. I would unhitch, remove her harness, and turn the mule into her own corral. The last thing I would do each day was dump a bucket of oats into Kate's feed box and stroke her long brown ears as she ate her fill. Those big brown eyes would look at me and sparkle with mischief. Yes, I would say that Kate really was "My Summer of '42."

GRADUATION DAY

I will always remember my graduation day. Not for the elaborate ceremony or for anything unusual that occurred during the ceremony. I couldn't even tell you who the speaker was or even if there was one. It was what happened to me during and following the ritual that sticks in my memory to this day, some fifty years later.

I do remember that my older brother, Travis, who had graduated five years earlier, did not show up. It may not have been so, but I felt like I was the only one in the class who was completely alone after the ceremony was over. There was no one to pat me on the back and to say "Well done, Kid. Let's head for town for something to eat."

I well remember it was raining as I left the auditorium. Not coming down in sheets but as a cold, steady drizzle. After picking up my gear back at the dormitory, I bummed a ride with someone who was driving in to Dallas. It was someone with a car already packed full, but who was still kind enough to squeeze in one more. The sad part is I don't even remember who that kind person was.

Billy Ray, Jake, and I had already rented a room in Dallas, on Columbia Street. I had been there once, but all I could remember about the location of the place was that the "H" streetcar ran past the front door. As things worked out, it was already dark and still raining when we got into Dallas. To keep from being perceived as an idiot who didn't know where he lived, I asked to be let out when we came to the first set of streetcar tracks, stating that I would catch the trolley home from there.

I stood in the cold rain at the streetcar stop for hours. Streetcars came and went, but none was the "H" car. I finally decided that these tracks might be running parallel with the right set of tracks further into town, so I set off walking. It was perhaps forty blocks later that I came to the second set of tracks, and sure enough I had no sooner arrived than the "H" car came to a screeching halt in front of me. I had never ridden on a streetcar before and didn't have a clue as to what to expect.

My joy knew no bounds as I climbed the steps and entered the warm, well lit car. My joy was short-lived, however, for the trolley operator pointed to the money collecting box and said, "Fifteen cents, please." A feeling of panic and overwhelming embarrassment, swept over me as I realized that I had no money with me, not one red cent. I put on a show of searching my pockets for the change I knew I did not have as the driver feigned patience while glaring at me. I finally blurted out that I must have left my money in my other pants and bounded off the car and back out into the cold dark rain. I realized that the only way to the warmth of that rented room was to walk, so I set off down the street. It must have been about three in the early morning when I finally found the house and entered to find Jake and Billy Ray fast asleep. Graduation Day, Friday, May 26, 1944, will not be forgotten for a least a few more years.

FIFTY YEARS LATER

Following graduation, several other Buckner kids and I moved into a boarding house in Dallas and went to work making ammunition for the Government at the Murray Gin Company. However, I soon learned that General Electric Company was offering better wages, and what ap-

peared to be a better prospect for the future, so I left Murray Gin and went to work for them.

After about a year, I decided to move to California to be with my brother, Travis. One of the most interesting jobs I had while in California was with the Pan Pacific Theater on Wilshire Boulevard in Hollywood. While there I saw and actually had conversations with many of the prominent movie stars of that time. As a part time job I jerked sodas at the Snow White Waffle Shop located a few doors down from Grummans Chinese Theater on Hollywood Boulevard. Even then it was a real show just to watch what came strolling down that Boulevard. Travis and I enjoyed going to some of the famous watering holes such as Earl Carrol, The Brown Derby, The Palladium, and the Hollywood Stage Door Canteen. We didn't have a lot of money to spend but it was something we liked to do.

We left Los Angeles to work the wheat harvest from Wyoming on up into Canada, but we moved too late as the harvest was already into Canada before we could catch up with it. So, we moved on to Seattle in hopes of getting onto one of the tuna boats working out of there. Again, it was not to be, so Travis entered the University of Washington and I got a job with the Post Office. I also took a part time job jerking sodas at the Chimes Cafe just off the University campus—for reasons clear to any 19-year-old young man. Life in Seattle was different, but fun. However, we soon burned out on "Seattle in the Rain" and returned to Dallas.

General Electric rehired me, and I moved into a boarding house where several other Buckner exes lived. We had a lot of fun—especially on weekends—and I was content for about two years. Going nowhere, not saving a penny, but having a lot of fun. In 1948 during a conversation with my boss at work, I asked him how much the boss of GE's maintenance shop made each payday. To my great surprise the figure he gave me was only about fifty cents more per hour than I was drawing. Mr. Shans was a brilliant man and had been with the company for over twenty years. I took a long look down the road, and I could see myself in his shoes in twenty years or so—so I hung it up and joined the Army.

I spent the next twenty-five years in Uncle's Army and loved most of it. It was, in a way, like being back at Buckner, only on a much larger scale. The Army provided me with travel and adventures that I would never have been able to afford any other way. I saw things, went places, experienced all kinds of unusual things like being shot at in Korea and being buried for two years thirty feet under the ice on Greenland's ice cap.

I was fortunate enough to attend many schools on all kinds of subjects. I learned Auto Mechanics at the Electrical and Mechanical Maintenance School in Aberdeen, Maryland, attended the Adjutant Generals' School, the Military Police School, the Army Missile School, Officers Candidate School, the U.S. Army Nuclear Power School, and the Nuclear Power Superintendents' Course. Since the schools were all related to the duty assignments I had at the time, after each school I was able to put what I had learned into practice.

During my Army experiences I served in the Infantry, Armored, Artillery, Missiles, Military Police, Adjutant General Corps and in the U.S. Army Nuclear Power Program.

I spent the years 1952 through 1955 working between Korea and Japan. I married my wife, Nobuko, while in Japan in 1953, and our first child was born at Kanoka Army Hospital in September of 1954. I was in Korea when the Chinese came boiling across the Yalu River, and we began to pull back.

Returning to the States in November of 1955, I was stationed at Fort Carson with the 10th Mountain Division. While at Carson I became a local celebrity—known Division-wide as "that damn paper shuffler from Division Headquarters who made the highest score in the Division on the Division Annual Physical Fitness Test." I was assigned to a desk job under the Post Adjutant at the time, and the men I caused so much grief had no way of knowing that I spent almost every off duty hour out in the mountains around Pikes Peak, hunting the wily mountain lions, and thus was in top shape.

After my tour at Fort Carson, I attended the Corporal Missile School in Fort Bliss, Texas, and was then assigned as an Instructor at the Missile School in Fort Sill, Oklahoma. The hunting and fishing in the Wichita Mountains in Oklahoma were just about as good as it gets.

I applied and was accepted for the U.S. Army Nuclear Power Program with its school located at Fort Belvoir, Virginia, just outside of Washington, D.C. This was a two year education.

I finished in 1961 and was posted to the PM-2A Nuclear Plant under the ice in Greenland where I spent the next two years—buried thirty feet beneath the Greenland ice cap, a hundred and thirty miles from the nearest person—no radio, no TV, mail only about once a month. We did have a pretty good library and an NCO Club. Life wasn't a bed of roses, but it could have been a lot worse.

When I returned from the Ice, I was assigned as an instructor at the Nuclear School for about one year. Then I received orders to report to the SM-1A Nuclear Plant at Fort Greely, Alaska. Hooray! My greatest wish had become a reality.

I and my family—now in addition to a wife, I had two girls and one boy—enjoyed our assignment in Alaska as we had never enjoyed any other place. We hunted moose, bear, caribou, dall sheep, wolf, and mountain goat, and were successful in all our endeavors. We caught fish until we were tired of catching fish, then caught some more—one King Salmon at 78 pounds and many Halibut over 100 pounds.

Alaska was the place we had been searching for, and we managed to remain there for nine years. I retired from the Army on 30 June, 1972. At retirement I was the Supervisor of the SM-1A Nuclear Power Plant at Fort Greely. I guess this was the most important position I have ever held, as the equipment, which I was responsible for, cost millions of dollars.

In 1973 I went to work as a Federal Civil Service Employee and an Electric Power Controller at the Fort Greely Power Plant. The Plant is a fuel-fired boiler and diesel generator power plant and child's play to operate as compared to the Nuclear Plant.

As our family had spent the last nine years in Alaska, we decided to make it our permanent home. So we bought a house in Delta Junction, Alaska. My son, Travis, and I started building a hunting/fishing resort on property we had purchased at Quartz Lake, about twelve miles from our home in Delta. We finished the Lodge and opened for business in 1979. The Black Spruce Lodge soon caught on, and in the summer we had all we could handle in people, boats, cabin rentals, entertainment and fishing. Life was good and we lived it to the hilt.

I retired from Federal Civil Service in 1993 with a total of forty-four years of Federal Service

—and believe it or don't, they didn't even give me a watch.

Both Nancy and I are fully retired, and it's nice to go, and stay, and come back when we want to. It is a good life here in Alaska, and our prayer is that all of the Buckner kids are as happy as we are. It has been a long road, but fun. I'm ready to start all over again when this tour is up.

Janie Lou (Ellis) Nash, '44

After graduating from Buckner, I worked for the summer as mail clerk at Eighth Army Headquarters in Dallas, Texas. In September of 1944, I entered nursing school at Parkland Hospital through the Cadet Nurse Corps. After three grueling years, only 21 out of 101 students graduated in 1947.

Shortly after passing the State Board Exams and becoming an R.N., I moved to San Antonio, Texas, and went to work for Civil Service at Brooke Army Hospital, Fort Sam Houston. I met Air Force Sgt. John DiBella and married him in 1949. We had four children, two boys and two girls born at various air force bases. We spent time at Air Force Bases in the Philippine Islands, San Marcos, Texas; Weisbaden, Germany; Yuma, Arizona; Fairbanks, Alaska; and finally Nebraska. In 1962 my husband retired from the Air Force.

During the years of being a military wife, between all the moves and four babies, my nursing career consisted of many short term and part time jobs. It was not until we bought a home and settled in Las Vegas, Nevada, that I could work full time. I worked at Southern Nevada Memorial Hospital, was staff R.N. on Med-Surg, and finally progressed to nursing supervisor. It was not until I became Emergency Department Nursing Supervisor, that I became really interested in emergency nursing.

I was instrumental in getting the Paramedic Bill Passed in the State Legislature and then put together the 500-hour course as Nurse Coordinator for the Paramedic Pilot Program for Nevada. Later I was the Nurse Coordinator for the first Nevada Critical Care Nurse Program for R.N.'s, sponsored by the American College of Orthopedic Surgeons. After several years in emergency medicine, and becoming Admitting Department Supervisor, I retired from nursing in 1988.

I divorced John DiBella in 1978 and married Robert Ellis in 1985. Robert retired after twenty-seven years as a captain with the Clark County Fire Department. We still reside in Las Vegas but spend four months, May through September, on the coast of Northern California where it's cool. We keep a boat in Trinidad Bay, just north of Eureka, Ca., and do a lot of ocean fishing.

Now we enjoy traveling and have been to Europe, New Zealand, Australia, Canada and Mexico. We have a motor home and have traveled most of the Western United States. Our goal in life is to have as much fun as we can for as long as we can.

Edna Mae "Foxie" Reynolds, '44

One funny incident happened one day in the Manna Hall while I was carrying a pan of dishwater. I took a flyer. Well, several girls helped me clean up the spilled water, but I went back, refilled the pan and fell again. Even Miss Mamie broke down and laughed! I must have held the record for working in the dining hall and kitchen; Miss Mamie always asked for me. I think it was because I wasn't afraid to talk back to her. She didn't like it, but she did seem to respect you more when you stood up to her.

Also, do you remember the time we got food poisoning at the home on Christmas Eve? We must have been sophomores. There was a radio show that gave us silver dollars. Right after the show everyone started getting sick. It turned out to be from the ham sandwiches we'd eaten for supper.

Buckner had to bring some doctors out to tend to the sick. I was one of the few who had not eaten the ham sandwich, so I had to go around with the doctors to assist. I remember the next year one of the cooks asked Miss Mamie if we were going to have ham sandwiches, and I thought Miss Mamie would kill her. She said, "Don't ever mention ham sandwiches to me again."

Doris (Rusciano) Ridge, '44

In March of 1935, George W. Ridge, my father, who was only thirty-seven years old, died from a stroke. As a tenant farmer, he had made a meager living for his wife and six children. Neither he nor mother had much education;

both, therefore, had limited skills. The U.S. was still going through the Depression. Mother worked at anything she could find—mostly cleaning and ironing for other people. After two years she placed me, my younger sister; Norma Loy, and two younger brothers; Charles and Glyn in Buckner Home. My two older sisters remained with her. Norma, Charles and Glyn were excited about going to Buckner, but I was very shy and withdrawn and felt only resentment. After a stay at the Receiving Home—to make sure we didn't have nits or any communicable disease, we were moved to the main campus. The Home was overcrowded then and there was not room for us in the dormitories with our own age groups, so we were placed in the old nursery, a building slated to be torn down—until they found room for us in the regular dorms. There I learned that sleeping on a pillow is not good for you.

From the courtyard I could see the kids in the regular dorms at play. I often heard them singing, "There is an orphans home not far away, where the kids get beans and bread three times a day. Oh how those kids could yell when that paddle hit their tail. Oh how those kids could yell three times a day." Needless to say this didn't help my already low feelings and discomfort.

I had not met any of the kids my age when school started. I was in Miss Mary McCorkle's homeroom sixth grade class. She realized that I was timid and shy, so she talked to the class about making new students feel good by being friendly. I soon felt a tap on my shoulder by the boy sitting behind me, "Happy" Corbett. I looked around and he asked, "Will you marry me?" in a voice loud enough for the whole class to hear. Of course everyone laughed, even me. This broke the ice.

As I began to make friends, I felt better and better about myself and began to realize that I could be happy at Buckner. My special friend was Fay Dewberry, who had a very outgoing personality, and before long she brought me out of my shyness. After lunch in Manna Hall each day, we went to a place we called "the corner" and met with our brothers and sisters for a quick visit with them. At the corner we made friends with other families. I especially remember the Richardsons —Bobbi Nell, Billy Dean and Angie. Through the years, I have kept in touch with Bobbi Nell and have been thrilled by her many accomplishments. Billie Ruth Gary, four years older than I, became

my "big sister." In fact, she was big sister to a group of us. Billie and I have remained good friends and still visit in each other's homes.

CHRISTMAS AT BUCKNER

The school auditorium was the place we all gathered on Christmas Eve. There was a big Christmas Tree on the stage along with a Santa. Under the tree were "strings" for all the kids. The presents we got were all tied together in a bundle with string, so we called the bundle our "string." We went back to the dorm to cut the strings and see what our gifts were. Each year in our string we got an apple, orange, sometimes nuts and peppermint candy. These were the ingredients for a dish we called "pig wash." In a jar we placed cut up apple, orange, and peppermint candy; and then set the jar outside the window to chill. On Christmas morning we ate "pig wash."

One year, a week before Christmas, a radio station from Dallas conducted their weekly quiz show from Buckner. I was one of the students selected to answer a question. The question was, "Name the two bodies of water separating Texas and Mexico." I answered, "The Gulf of Mexico and the Rio Grand River." For that answer, I was paid twelve silver dollars. They took up all the money that we kids won that night and divided it between the contestants equally.

THE RADIO

The boys were always telling us of the programs they listened to on their crystal radio sets. In the dorm the girls had only one radio in the parlor, and we could only listen to it at certain times. We never got to hear the programs the guys told us about. With the crystal set, you had to have earphones, and there had to be an aerial wire to go out the window to tie to a tree or light post. Fay and I gave James Knight money to get the parts to make us a crystal set. When he made it and presented it, we put it under my pillow, ran the wire out through the screen, then tied it around a post.

After lights out, we put on the ear phones, but all we could get was static. We told James, but he couldn't figure out what we had done wrong. Leston McNeil had the job of changing out burnt-out light bulbs in all the dorms. We arranged with him to come check our crystal set

(We made sure the light in our room was burned out.) to see what we had done wrong.

The day before Leston was to come, Miss Hardy spied the wire going out the window and traced it to the set under my pillow. She took it to Mrs. Brady. I was called to her office after school that day along with Fay. We could not convince her that we had not been staying up half the night listening to the radio.

Campused again! We had to bargain with her to allow us to dig up "our flower bed" in exchange for the punishment of being campused, so that we could go to the football game. We always rode in the back of a cattle truck to go to the game to cheer for the Buckner boys. It was very cold riding in the back but we didn't mind. We sang all the way there and back. I referred to the flower bed as "our bed," because of the many times we had worked off our demerits working in that flower bed. It was a disappointment to go back to Homecoming years later and find that "our flower bed" was no longer there. Are the children better behaved now than we were in our days there?

THE ARITHMETIC TEAM

In elementary school, Buckner students competed with each other to get a team of two with two alternates for UIL Math. Jake Corbett and James Knight made the team, and Billy Ray Clark and I were the alternates. Jake and James competed in the area contest against other schools and won first place. Bill and I got to go along.

We all became good friends—the three boys have always treated me like a sister. Later we all attended Howard Payne College. When I graduated, Bill and Jake told me that before I married anyone they wanted to approve the fellow. I think the reason I went out for the math team and not spelling was that I wanted to show that I could compete with boys on their own turf—so to speak. The spelling team was an all girl turf.

THREE LITTLE KITTENS

Since Fay, Janie Lou and I were on the first floor of the dorm, we had to go up stairs during quiet hour. Visitors to Buckner might come to see our rooms on Saturday and Sunday, so our beds had to remain neatly made. Fay had an aunt and uncle who lived not far from Buckner on a farm. According to Fay, their farm was only one mile

away. We were not supposed to leave the campus without permission, and permission was seldom granted.

The three of us decided to sneak off campus during quiet hour one afternoon and pay Fay's aunt and uncle a visit. We managed to get off campus without trouble. We walked and walked and walked. It was getting to be a very long mile and very hot. The Buckner night watchman drove by but did not spot us. Our next mishap was worse. We were passing a corn field when three starving kittens ran out—one for each of us. We petted them, but when we tried to move on, they insisted on following us. We were really a sight, three girls running down the highway as fast as we could, each with a starving kitten on her heels. We did out run them and finally got to the farm. After we had sat a while and rested, Fay's uncle kindly drove us back to the campus.

As we were sneaking back to the dorm, Dorah Newton met us with bad news. Janie's sister had called her by telephone from Dallas, and Mrs. Brady was looking all over for her. Dorah helped us get in the back door and told Janice to go to Mrs. Brady and explain she had been sleeping on the floor under Dorah's bed on the second floor. Dorah walked behind Janie and verified the story to Mrs. Brady. Safe at last! We had already made up our own cover story that we had been on the shady cool steps of the grade school the entire afternoon, but we didn't need it.

CHARLIE

One day when Fay and I were acting silly, I sat on her lap. Barbara Waller said we looked like Charlie McCarthy and Edgar Bergan. Fay said, "Doris is a dummy like Charlie, too." From then on, I was known as "Charlie." We called Fay "Edgar" for a while, but it didn't stick. When I went to Howard Payne College, I thought I would get away from my nick name. Not so—there were too many Buckner kids at Howard Payne, and soon I was "Charlie" to everyone there. Even my husband calls me "Charlie Girl" half the time.

THE DENTAL OFFICE

Work assignments were made for six months at a time; then there would be a change—except for dental office, the plum of all assignments—which lasted for four years in high school. Billie

Ruth had it until she graduated, and she recommended me to Dr. Robb. Dr. Robb thought I was too small, so she asked for two girls. Patsy Corbett was the other girl assigned with me. We were trained to be dental assistants.

Dr. Robb didn't work on Saturdays so Patsy and I cleaned the office then. Mrs. Mayo was the hospital cook. When we went through the kitchen to empty the trash, she would always have goodies ready for us. We hid these goodies in the trash can and took them upstairs to eat. Sometimes, when they made hospital deliveries, the boys from the commissary would signal us, and we would go to the kitchen where they would give us fruit or other goodies. We had to hide them in the trash can, because the big fat nurse hated us just because we worked with Dr. Robb, whom she also didn't like. She got wise one day and looked in the trash can. She almost had Mrs. Mayo fired when she saw what we had hidden there.

WW II was in progress and as was the custom, interns came out each Saturday to remove tonsils and appendixes. Before the war they had brought plenty of nurses with them, but since so many nurses were in the service, they had Patsy and me scrub instruments for them after the operations.

My brother, Charles, was repeatedly in the hospital with fever. He was even turning yellow. Fat Nurse would send him back to his dorm, saying there was nothing wrong with him. I guess he would have died if Dr. Robb hadn't intervened. She told Fat Nurse to take him to a doctor in Dallas to have tests made or she would go to Brother Hal and tell him what was going on. She took Charles to the doctor and found he had to have his appendix removed right away.

I was at the hospital, scrubbing instruments, when the interns operated on Charles. The next summer I also had my appendix removed. The interns all teased me as I was going under the ether. I was very angry because I couldn't talk back.

Dr. Robb was more than just my boss. She was like a mother to Patsy and me. She took us to her home. She brought us things, gave us money, and even mailed letters for us so that Mrs. Brady wouldn't censor them. We were very sad when she told us she had cancer. She died when I was a freshman at Howard Payne.

THE BUNSEN BURNER

As we grew and developed, we became more concerned about our looks. Hair was growing on our legs and we got tired of shaving it off.

I had a bright idea. Fay and I would go to the dental office on a Saturday and we would singe the hair off our legs with the Bunsen Burner and never have to shave them again. We lit the burner and gave it a try. Can you imagine how much pain fire causes? We didn't have to imagine. After a couple of tries, we decided shaving was the better way—just as soon as we healed! Fay made the mistake of telling her boy friend, Herbert Ray White, about our experiment. He managed to spread the news all over the campus. We still have not lived down that escapade.

KITCHEN

Kitchen duty was considered one of the worst job assignments, next to laundry duty. Patsy and I felt bad because we never had to have these assignments—just dental office. We talked it over with Dr. Robb, and she agreed that we could take kitchen duty for three months each. When it came my turn, I was the person selected to wake up the other "kitchen girls." We had to wake up at five A.M. and be in the kitchen in fifteen minutes. The night watchman would come to my window and wake me; then I would run to the beds of the others and awaken them.

All went well for awhile. Then the night watchman awakened me late, just as the six o'clock whistle blew. When we got to the kitchen, Miss Mamie blew up and bawled me out. I told her what had happened, but she wouldn't believe me.

The next day the same thing happened, and Miss Mamie told me if it happened again she was going to slap me across the Manna Hall—and she could do it! The next morning the night watchman awakened me again as the six o'clock whistle blew. I yelled at him and told him to wait on the sidewalk for us. He did and we made him tell Miss Mamie he had awakened me late. She let me off the hook and gave him a lecture.

The thing I'm proudest of learning from working in the kitchen? I can crack an egg with one hand!

Helen Roller, '44

After Buckner, I attended Parkland Hospital under the Cadet Nurse Program, and to repay the U.S. Government for the training, I went into the Navy. My motive was not just to see the world; seeing the world was incidental. However, during my twenty-three years in the Navy, I saw a lot of the world. I was stationed in Japan, Vietnam and many many states in the U.S. until I progressed in rank from Ensign to CDR and eventually retired in Amarillo, Texas.

I had already learned to follow rules at Buckner, but I encountered even more rules in the Navy. For example, the first car I purchased was a 1955 Olds 88—green with a white top. I learned about conflicting rules with it. I had it delivered to my carport on base in China Lake, California; whereupon, I called the gate to get a sticker and was not only told that I could not learn to drive on the base, I also could not get a sticker without a valid driver's license. Impasse. Eventually we resolved the problem. They sent a base security guard each afternoon to take me off base and teach me to drive.

I received several decorations: National Defense Service Medal with Star, United Nations Service Medal, Korean Service Medal, Navy Occupation of Japan, Vietnam Service Medal; U.S., Vietnam and Navy Unit Citations.

When I retired, I worked for the Foreign Mission Board of the Southern Baptist Convention in Rhodesia, Korea, Columbia, Australia, Ghana, Italy and Sicily, Thailand, Brazil, Indonesia, the Philippines, Ethiopia, Minsk, Belarus, Russia and Burundi.

Though there was political unrest in several of these places while I was there, I can honestly say I was not afraid—even of being in foreign lands and not speaking the language. Someone was always looking after me. I did nursing, training, feeding etc., at these locations. I have also worked for the Home Mission Board in Texas, Arizona, New Mexico and Wisconsin.

Not having seen enough of the world while working, I visited many other countries all over the world for pleasure. I even have pictures of people on camel back. However, I've not been called on to travel that way yet. Someone told me in Burundi recently it would take an hour by foot to get over the mountain border into Rwandi. I am sure if necessary, I could make it much faster.

Now I work with my church, Buckner in Amarillo, Hospice and a nursing home. Since it is all volunteer work. I am free to travel more anytime I want to.

Martha (Durant) Stanley, '44

FIFTY YEAR HIGHLIGHTS

There are a couple of real highlights in my life since I left Buckner over fifty years ago. Not much happened in my earlier years because I was busy raising a family and working.

I'll never forget leaving Buckner; they helped me get my first job with Floyd West Insurance Company. I was very grateful to Buckner and to Floyd West.

Since then I have married, divorced and moved from job to job. I married a second time and my husband died in 1963. I raised two boys alone, which was not easy, but we managed. My mother, who was still living, gave me much help and support.

My time is filled with hope and doing some things I really enjoy. My travels are very limited, but genealogy has filled much of my time the past few years. This takes me to different places—searching out records and kin. I never had a chance to know many relatives, so this search has turned into work.

One of the most interesting things in my past fifty years happened after my children were grown. In 1980 I took a job with E-Systems, which sent me overseas to work for about three years. No other place would I rather have been than the places they sent me: Israel and Egypt. I went to many places where our Lord had lived during His ministry. We were in the middle of the desert (the Sinai Peninsula) not far from the Suez Canal, at a base compound made up of peace-keeping civilians called the "Sinai Field Mission." I visited many places of interest while there: Bethlehem, the Sea of Galilee, the River Jordan, Jerusalem and the pyramids.

Then I was transferred to the southern tip of the Sinai Peninsula, where there was a multinational force, made up from the United Nations. I felt as if I were in the service. We were under military rule. Here we walked many times by the Red Sea, waded along the edge of the water and could even see the mountains of Saudi Arabia.

I was fascinated by the St. Katherina Monastery, at the foot of Mt. Sinai. In fact, some of our group walked up to the top of Mt. Sinai, where it is believed that Moses wrote the Ten Commandments. In 1983, I came home by way of Holland, a pretty sight with all the tulips in bloom. After such a fabulous trip to the Holy Lands, I was quite restless, so I traveled with my grandchildren and then visited my sister, Rosemary, and brother, John.

When I came back home to Sulphur Springs, Texas, I worked until 1992 when I retired. Now I am just trying to live one day at a time with my good memories, friends and family.

Ella Mae (Liebrum) Taylor, '44

After graduating from Buckner High School in June of 1944, my work experience began with the Floyd West Insurance Company. At the end of that year, James and I married on the first of December. In February I changed jobs and went to work for Dallas Bank. Both of these jobs gave me a lot of good experience for my very next important job.

In June of 1945, I left the banking business and began a full time business of raising a family for the next thirty-five years. The Lord blessed James and me with two girls and two boys. My life was very full during those years. I was involved with all their church, school, social and sports' activities. I was a chauffeur, tutor and an avid fan for all their many endeavors. Although I have been very involved with our church and the Baptist Women's organization in our church, I found that after my youngest son graduated from school in 1980, I wanted to be more involved with helping those who could not help themselves.

I first started doing volunteer work at Doctor's Hospital. Later, I found myself going to Mary Trew Home and visiting with the elderly people there. Soon I was helping teach ceramics to them. Through the next several years, I gained a lot of fulfillment from adopting several widow ladies who lived in our area of town. James and I would take them to church, shopping or even out to dinner. I have also enjoyed being a part of the Baylor Auxiliary at Baylor Hospital and going to my Book Club each month.

In 1989, James retired and my life made some more changes. James had been interested in wood crafts for several years. Between our children and friends with all of their ideas and projects, James keeps the saws buzzing. I keep the paint brushes stroking our crafts. We now have two craft stalls that keep us very busy.

Our youngest grandchild was born this past March. Our two oldest married in April and July. James and I have celebrated our fiftieth wedding anniversary. My life has been full and I look forward to seeing what the Lord has in store for the rest.

Joyce (Galaway) Work, '44

Can it be possible that we have celebrated our Fiftieth High School Reunion? It seems only yesterday that we all expressed a sigh of relief when the closing words were uttered at our graduation ceremony, and with much excitement and a little fear we entered into civilian life.

After a brief visit with relatives in Denver, Colorado, I moved to Shreveport, Louisiana, where I began my career in banking. Mother and I moved to Dallas a short time later where I met my first husband and was blessed with the birth of a beautiful boy. About eight months later, I moved with my beautiful boy and my mother to Houston, which has been my home ever since.

During the last forty-five years, I met and married my second husband, Bill. We had two wonderful daughters and have made a home for our three children. We now have eight grandchildren and a great-grandchild who is the apple of our eye. It has been my great fortune to have had a helping hand not only in raising our children, but also the grandchildren.

I am now retired and hoping this year to move to the country and travel around this beautiful country that God has permitted me to be born in. I also hope to lose twenty pounds.

LaVoe (Potter) Brown, '45

AN UNFORGETTABLE MOMENT

The Manna Hall kitchen is the setting for this story. The year is 1944; the "kitchen crew" is Jean Tilley, LaWanda Kight, Eva Lois Thomas, and yours truly, LaVoe Brown.

The "crew," dressed in their "granny dresses" (old dresses that came to our ankles—pants were not allowed in those days), were busy about their chores, transferring food from the big steamers in the back of the kitchen to the steam table in the front of the kitchen—under the watchful eyes of the cooks—for serving hundreds of very hungry orphan boys and girls. When all the food was transferred, it was our duty to clean the steamers. We took turns cleaning the big steamers because the "lucky one" had to climb up on a stool, stand with feet together while another member of the crew gathered her skirt around her ankles and held tight, as she, bent from the hips and with feet in the air, reached down into the steamer to clean and dry the interior.

On this particular day, the crew had finished cleaning, the cooks and other members of the crew had left the kitchen, and Jean and I had agreed to wait until Miss Mamie inspected the steamers. However, we had time on our hands since Miss Mamie had been detained in the dining room.

Jean sat down on the edge of the short, pot-bellied rice steamer, swinging her legs as we joked back and forth. On impulse, I pushed her into the steamer and closed the lid, which I immediately opened. But not fast enough! She was screaming—LOUD! We didn't have to wait for Miss Mamie any longer. She was there! "LaVoe, why did you do that? I thought I could trust you; you've never been in trouble."

I stood there with my head down, embarrassed and ashamed. Knowing she could pack a wallop when she administered punishments, I dodged as she motioned for me to sit down at the nearby table.

That table was my "after school work station" every day for the next three weeks. Looking back over my punishment today, I recollect that those fifty pound bags of beans just seemed to get bigger with each passing day, as I went through them cleaning out the rocks, etc. To this day, I reminisce about this experience when preparing pinto beans. Thank goodness, pinto beans come in one pound bags!

Louise "Redtop" (Kirby) Cumbie, '46

In the early 1940s, Miss Lester, our choir director and music teacher, chose four girls to be a quartet. She had a unique way of determining who they would be. Each auditioned individually, then by two's, then all four together for singing accapello harmony. I was fortunate to be chosen to sing soprano, Joyce Duckworth; second soprano, Yvonne Ward; alto, and Wanda Swindall; bass. Miss Lester said she knew she had chosen the right girls when our harmony was so close it hurt her ears.

So we became "The Melody Four." Our uniforms were navy skirts and gold blouses, decorated with a treble cleft. Later Miss Lester's mother made us dresses alike. What good times and opportunities we had. For example, when she was hostess, Miss Bertha would have us sing for her WMU meetings. In turn, other WMU hostesses would invite us to sing at their meetings. We almost became regulars at Gaston Avenue Baptist Church revivals and WMU meetings. We also sang for the R. C. Buckner Masonic Lodge that met upstairs over the shop on old Highway 80 across from the Receiving Home. We were even invited to sing on KSKY radio station, "atop the beautiful Hotel Stoneleigh overlooking downtown Dallas."

Miss Lester had gone to Baylor University and knew several young ministers who had been in school while she was a student there. One comes to mind, named Chester Cadwalder. When he was holding a revival at Rowlett, Texas, we were asked to sing at the services. Rowlett seemed miles away at that time, but we loved going every mile that we traveled for our performances. We were just teens and for the first time were noticed by boys outside the home. What a thrill!

I suppose our biggest thrill was when we went to a recording studio in downtown Dallas to cut a record. I remember standing in a sound-proof room with a mike, looking at Miss Lester through the plate glass window as she directed us. We cut two records (old 78's). I listen to mine from time to time to reflect on all the good times the four of us had singing. I feel young when I hear our voices blending in harmony again.

I have tried to preserve those recordings on cassette, scratching sounds and all. In spite of the scratchings, we still sound good to me. I will be forever grateful to Miss Lester for recognizing the talent in us and giving us opportunities to enjoy experiences we might never have otherwise had, so in memory of her—and the other "Melody Fours," I submit this story as a record of our good times.

Mary Evelyn (Guinn) Bearden, '47

At Buckner we would always have a devotional time on Wednesday night. One day some of the girls were planning to run away. During another girl's prayer that night she said, "And, God, bless the girls who are planning to run away tonight."

Of course the Matron's eyes flew open, and she wasted no time—just had everyone involved come to her room right away for a full investigation and assigned punishments.

Cleo (Mosely) Wharton, '47

MY FIRST LESSON AT BUCKNER

In 1936 in the old Girls' Dormitory, I was six-years-old and had been assigned a bed at the end of a long row of single white iron beds with white covers on them. My bed was next to the door that opened to the hallway on the second floor.

Standing by the bed next to mine was a friendly blue-eyed blonde with delicate features named Lela Faye Melton. She smiled at me and asked if I knew what I was supposed to do. If I answered her, I don't remember or maybe it was just the blank expression on my face. (I was tongue-tied and rarely talked to anyone.) She came over and explained, pointing to the bell above the door, that the bell would ring in the morning and "your feet will hit the floor."

I nodded and she proceeded to tell me how to get dressed. When she said, "Tie your shoes," another blank look was on my face. "You do know how to tie your shoes, don't you?" I was learning fast, not a blank look on my face anymore, but a blank shake of the head. We then sat down on the floor by my bed and she taught me how to tie my shoes.

Once that task was over, Lela Faye asked me if I could count by "tens." I didn't even know what she meant so I shook my head again. She taught me, although I had no concept of what I was saying when I rattled the numbers off in order. She asked then if I could count by "fives." Another shake of the head and she started teaching me. When we got so far, she looked at me and said that there were more, but that was all she knew right now, and when she learned more she would teach me. I was soon to learn that some of the older girls loved to play school and would teach the younger girls what they themselves had learned at school.

Our friendship was made that day. My first friend—reaching out, caring, teaching. The first of many of my Buckner sisters to come—always helping and looking out for one another.

The next morning the bell did RING! What a sound! It could wake the roosters. By the way, my "feet did hit the floor" and continued to do so for the next twelve years.

AN AWARENESS OF GOD

On a rainy stormy night, the lightning and thunder woke the six-year-olds in Miss Orr's charge. All the children began scrambling out of bed and running to her room. Miss Orr got out of her bed and took us to the little sitting room where we sat at night when she would read to us or where we sat waiting for her to comb our hair after we were dressed. However, she did not turn on the lights, but moved toward the window and explained to us that although we would actually never see God, this was one way we might look at Him. Miss Orr compared the thunder to a clap of His hands and the lightning to His hands writing in the sky.

We sat in silence, listening to the rain and waiting for the clap of His hands and anxious to see what He would write in the sky. In the darkness of the night during a fierce rainstorm, the six-year-olds huddled and watched in awe of the power of God. Somehow the sound of the thunder no longer frightened us, and we watched the lightning as children today watch fireworks. As we soon settled down and became sleepy again, she had us to calmly go back to bed with an awareness that God was over all and we were safe in His hands.

THE JOY OF A COLD CRISP MORNING

I was talking to Joy McCleod Cowen. She remembers the cold, crisp mornings when we would leave the Manna Hall for breakfast and what fun it was to exhale our breaths with the smoke-like effect we could make.

I remember Mary Merle Bryce actually mastered "smoke rings." It stirred so much excitement because we all wanted her to teach us how to do this neat trick. The matrons frowned on this because of the connection to smoking. Poor Mary Merle—her moment of glory was short lived.

Miss Wilva Evans, '48

TO THE SENIORS OF 1948
(With apologies to Henry W. Longfellow)

Listen, my children, and you shall hear
Of the Senior Class that knows no peer:
There were twenty-four who lined up at the start,
But before the year was out some had to part.
Judy found out she was one year ahead;
So she went back to the Juniors with a heart full
    of lead.
Thus the race continued till the middle of the
    ride
When Jimmy Bishop fell by the wayside.
Then Juanita Thompson, by some known as
    "Pitter,"
Made plans for the future and left in a twitter.
Corene too grew tired of the race
And left the track before she could place.
Twenty to finish—a goodly number,
But even then there was little time to slumber.
Let's take the rest of them alphabetically,
And speak of them truthfully or deal propheti-
    cally.
Evelyn Callaway won't stray far away;
She's going to Forney to answer phones by the
    day.
Myra Clarkson, keep well, and the best of wishes
That you'll not end up by washing dishes (unless
    they're your own!)
Luck to you, Willie, and many more successes
At making headlines (or making the right guess-
    es).
Jack or "Beaneye" much luck fellow teacher (?),

'Tis really great fun unless you decide to become
    a "speech-er."
Mary Lou Hall, you've a cute turned-up nose;
Keep it out of others' business and keep on your
    toes.
Play the game, Wallace, and follow the rules
That you've learned these years at the Buckner
    Home Schools.
Beatrice, I hear you're going college ways;
Cross your T's, dot your I's but don't count the
    days!
Christine, the follower of Florence Nightingale,
When you get your RN, I'll let you know if I ail!
Wanda Louise, I wish you well
In the business world or if it's dresses you sell!
Ruby Lee, step up; here's some advice:
Do your work well at first; so you won't need to
    do it twice.
Mary Ann, I know you'll win his heart.
If sketching won't do it, cooking's the art.
Betty, please come back when you're able;
And all I ask is—Don't marry Clark Gable!
Bennie Mae, cast your eyes to the top of the hill,
And you'll reach it, I know, if you only will.
Nora Sue, you know that with your personality
Your every dream can be a reality.
Tommy, you leave with my very best wishes
For a good catch in life—and I don't mean fishes!
Franklin, please keep your sense of fair play and
    good disposition;
You'll need both, I'm sure, whatever the condi-
    tion.
Lurlene, my right hand partner in crime,
Keep up the good work and come to see me
    sometime.
Jimmie Sherrell, you're a versatile lass,
And I'm sure you'll always be at the head of your
    class.
Billie Joe, may your vision, like your jumps, al-
    ways be broad;
Then at your successes we'll all applaud.
President Prentice, though you're last in name,
I know you won't be when they pass out fame.
Now I couldn't forget the leader of your house;
So now I'll give three cheers for dear Miss Rouse.
Now these are only my sentiments in rhyme;
So good night, Seniors, it's past my bedtime!

Billie Joe Stanley, '48

THE GROWING YEARS

I was born in Texarkana, Texas, but very soon, my family and I moved south of Commerce to the small community of Riley Grove. We lived on a farm in a small shack that was well-ventilated, which was fine for the warm months, but obviously very drafty and damp during the extremely cold winter months. As a result of these harsh conditions, my father died of pneumonia. I have been told that he was a hard, strict, but strongly devout Christian man. Mother said that we would all have been farmers without an opportunity for an education if my father had lived.

When my father died, I, along with my brothers and sisters, Rosemary, Martha Lou, John, and Edward, was placed in Buckner Orphans Home. Only my oldest brother, Allen, stayed and lived with my mother. According to a copy of my birth certificate, which was prepared by the officials at Buckner, I was placed in the Home as an inmate in June of 1936. I was housed in a large frame building, the Nursery, located in the middle of the campus just north of where the statue of Father Buckner now stands. This building was soon demolished and replaced by a modern brick structure, the Sunbeam Home, located on the southeast corner of the campus. Prior to placement in the Nursery Building, all of us were housed at the Receiving Home, just north of the main campus. The Receiving Home processed all the incoming inmates before placement in appropriate housing on the main campus. Every one remembers Sally Pope, the person in charge of the children there.

I remember several things about life in the old Nursery Building. One was the fear of what may have been in the basement below the building. Many of the children talked about scary things that were supposed to be down in the dark and mysterious basement. Another memory was having to eat oyster soup, which I disliked and still do. Also, I recall using a potty that was placed on the floor between the rows of beds during the night. While in the Nursery, one of the ways we were disciplined was to have us sit on the floor with our legs spread apart; after which we were required to place our head on the floor between our legs.

From the Nursery Building, I followed the usual progression through the dormitories according to age and sex; boys in dorms on one side of the campus and girls on the other side of the campus. Pires Home was the first dorm I was placed in after leaving the Nursery. At the time I graduated from high school, I was living in Rupard Home.

While in Pires, I can recall the times when we lined up at the clothes closet and the house mother fitted us with a clean pair of overalls, the times we had our throats mopped out with a swab containing mercurochrom, the delicious anticipation of getting to go barefooted for the summer, the "plat-rubber" toys we made and played "war" with and the times we had our mouths washed out with soap when we were caught saying vulgar words. I also remember having to stand with our noses against the wall for punishment when we misbehaved on the playground, the "bully," who made us do whatever he wanted us to do, the tetanus shots that made our arms swell with a big knot which ached for several days, the leather aviator caps with goggles that I loved to wear, my effort to read through the Bible during the nap time we were required to take in the summer months (but I quit when I reached either First or Second Kings), my bout with the mumps (and since I didn't stay in bed and rest like I should have, I had a relapse with swelling down to my groin area), and the new pair of shoe strings we got occasionally for our "brogans" which made them seem like a new pair of shoes.

In August of 1941, I accepted Christ as my Savior and was baptized. My decision was made during a well-attended revival. The church sanctuary wasn't large enough to hold all the persons attending the revival, so some of us were placed in the school auditorium just below the chapel, and the sermon was relayed to us via the public address system.

During the invitation at the close of the service, I went forward to profess my acceptance of Jesus as my Christ. Over the years I have sometimes doubted my conversion, because I thought that perhaps I had gone forward only because some of my friends did. I also thought that perhaps my decision was only an emotional response. However, as I grew and matured as a Christian over the years, I truly came to believe that I did let Jesus come into my heart that day.

Some of the things I recall while in Freeland were the times we would gather in the parlor on the first floor and have family devotions, led by the house-mother before we went to bed in the evening, the many summer nights I spent lying awake in a pool of perspiration, the times I would wet a towel and lie on it to try to keep cooler, and best of all looking out my northwest window and seeing the Flying Red Horse on top of the Magnolia Building in downtown Dallas.

As I grew older, my next move was to McElroy Hall. The things I can remember the most at this age were the games we played. Since we didn't have the luxury of having many toys as the children of today do, we had to make do with inexpensive toys and improvise many of our games. For example, we played with tops, washers, marbles, hockey (with sticks and a tin can) and various other simple games.

I also remember being assigned to yard work while living in McElroy. We had many beautiful flower beds around the dorm; cannas, zinnias, periwinkles, and moss rose. Once each week, usually on Saturday, we hosed down and swept clean all the sidewalks around the dorm for Ms. Clark and Ms. Dehay, two of our dorm mothers.

The next and final step up the line was the dorm that housed the older boys, Rupard Hall. I was living there at the time I graduated from high school and left the Home. My room was on the first floor in the southwest corner. This room, occupied by three others, was connected to another by a bath room. Mrs. Bearden was the housemother, and I can rate her as one of the strictest and toughest housemothers I had while in the Home.

While in Rupard, I developed an ear for country/western music. We made crystal radio sets and would lie awake at night listening to the top ten country/western songs broadcast over KRLD on a show called the "Hillbilly Hit Parade." It really boosted our self-esteem whenever we were able to stay awake long enough to hear the number one tune so we could talk about it the next morning. Another program we enjoyed listening to at night was the wrestling matches, live from the Sportatorium.

We entertained ourselves in many unique ways. For example, we went rabbit hunting with a large group of boys armed only with "rabbit clubs," fashioned from broken softball bats, large limbs or sticks; we dressed and cooked the rabbits over an open fire, using margarine brought from the Manna Hall. We loaded up once each winter in a cattle truck and went to Rockwall or Terrell to the big rabbit hunt of the season and would return with over a hundred rabbits. We played touch football in the large vacant area east of Rupard Hall or sat at the "top of the hill" waiting and watching for our girlfriends to leave the Manna Hall after their chores. Sometimes we'd even sneak across the campus at night to rendezvous with them.

The highlight of our social life, one which was approved by the Home, was our visit to Buhrman Hall on Sunday night. After BYPU each Sunday night, the older boys and girls were allowed to sit together in the parlor of Buhrman for an hour or so under the supervision of a house parent. Except for school hours, school activities and the times we slipped around after dark, this was the only time we were able to see our girl friends.

Talking about girl friends, my "first love" was Jo Nell Brown. While in the first grade, we had a rhythm band, where I played the sticks and Jo Nell was the student leader. My next "love" was Elizabeth Atkinson when I was a freshman in high school. Elizabeth was several years younger, but I believed she was the cutest thing I had ever seen. One day while returning to the dorm from the cotton fields, I waited for and "jumped on" another younger boy because I had heard that he was flirting with Elizabeth. I believe that was when I experienced my first taste of jealousy.

The next and final "love" while I was at Buckner was Dorothy Simmons. She was also several years younger than I. I "went with" her during the last two or three years of high school and continued to return to see her after I went off to college. She was the girl friend I sneaked over to the girls' side of the campus to rendezvous with after dark.

Each inmate, whenever we became old enough, was assigned a "chore" each year. The assignments varied from year to year, depending on our age. The boys were assigned to duties at the dairy, the barn (farm), custodial work in the dorms, custodial work in the schools, the commissary, the campus bakery, and the campus power plant. The girls worked in the Manna Hall (dinning room and kitchen), the campus laundry, and the girls' dormitories. The last three years of high school, I worked in the bakery with Pap Grube, along with Hoyt Lang and Billy Ed Taylor. Some special events I enjoyed while working in the bakery were the times we got up early in the morning to put the turkeys in the oven for Thanksgiving and Christmas. The other times were in the late summer when the older boys stayed out late in the fields baling hay and missed the supper in Manna Hall. We prepared a meal for them in the bakery, a meal far superior to the ones normally served in the Manna Hall.

Although we had duties assigned to us that

we performed routinely each day, the older boys and girls helped out during harvest time with the various crops that were farmed on the land owned by the Home. We were let out of school in the fall to pick cotton. We were paid two to three cents per pound for the cotton, and we saved our money to spend at the State Fair in Dallas. Other crops that the older boys helped with in the fields were: chopping cotton, hoeing corn, picking corn, shocking oats, and gathering in silage to be stored in the two silos on the dairy farm.

While we were in the Home, our connection with the outside world was very limited. An older brother or sister could get a pass to go into town and take us with them. When this happened, we would get up early in the morning and wait at the bus stop, just off the campus on Samuell Boulevard, to catch a bus into downtown Dallas. These trips into town were rare because we didn't have the money to make them often.

As I got older, I did the same as many other boys; we would hitchhike into town or walk to several places close to the Home to attend a movie or go to the store. There was a grocery store at the corner of Buckner Boulevard and Forney Road, a variety store in Pleasant Grove and a movie theater in Urbandale that we visited whenever we had the money.

When we didn't have money to attend the Saturday afternoon movie in Urbandale, we would "borrow" a bicycle from the bike rack in town and ride it around there while the local boys were in the movie. We didn't have bicycles at the Home and it was a special treat for us to ride these "borrowed" bikes. In fact, for the annual Junior-Senior Picnic, we would go to White Rock Lake, have a picnic, and rent bikes to ride around all day. I did not own a bike until I started to college. My brother, John, who had just mustered out of the Coast Guard, bought my first bike for me.

Occasionally, we would slip off to go into downtown Dallas to see a movie. We would either walk to Urbandale and catch a suburban bus into town, or hitchhike into East Grand and then catch a streetcar. At that time, in the early 40s, the cost of riding the street car was seven cents, the movie was eleven cents, and the return on the street car was another seven cents. So you see, a quarter was all we needed for going into town to see a movie. Sometimes, if we were lucky, we had extra money to buy popcorn or a soda pop.

There was another incident that happened when I was ten to ywelve-years-old. One Sunday morning while we were going to Sunday School, a black Model T Ford pulled up and stopped at the curb some fifty yards away, and a large lady in a black dress backed out of the car. I made fun of her size to the boys there with me. We proceeded on into church, and later I was summoned and told my mother had come to visit us. Yes, she was the person I had called the "big fat" woman when I had seen her getting out of the car. On many occasions, since I have been an administrator in the public schools, I have used this example of how cruel kids of this age can be to anyone who is unusual or extremely different from the norm.

I remember many events that took place in school, for in many ways school was a real "testing place" for us. I remember well my first grade teacher, Miss Sweatman, and later Mrs. Gregory of Waco, Texas. I believe the reason I remember her so well is that I was one of her pets. Franklin Nash and I were allowed to stay after school and help her with dusting erasers and other small chores. When we did, she always gave us candy. Billy Ed Taylor was very timid and would hang his head most of the time. Miss Sweatman, who worried about his shyness, cut a piece of cardboard and tied it under his chin to hold his head up.

I don't remember much about second or third grade except for one incident involving Pasty Jo Motes. She won't like my telling this, but once she was misbehaving and was punished, as we frequently were, by having to stand and bend over to catch our ankles and stay that way. While in this torturous position, she wet her pants and made a big puddle on the floor.

I also remember what may have been my first paddling while I was in the fourth grade. Several of us boys had some parched corn in our pocket and were eating it in class. Our teacher, Mrs. Powers, took us out into the hall and gave us a good spanking. During the next few school years, the main thing I remember was recess. Most of the boys would go to the dirt basketball court toward the north end of the campus and play basketball. I seemed to be pretty good at this game and later proved to be a successful basketball player in high school.

An account that is indirectly related to school during the junior years of my life is my recollection of all the memory work I learned in Sunday School. When I was twelve, my Sunday School teacher was Ms. Zapp, a dorm mother in one of the girls' dorms. She required us to learn many verses and chapters of scripture in the Bible. The things I learned at this age were the things I could recall and easily recite with very little assistance many years later. Some of these were the Twenty-third Psalm, I Corinthians 13, the Preamble to the Constitution, and the Gettysburg Address.

I remember when the Second World War began. The Japanese bombed Pearl Harbor and the next day, we listened to the radio in school and heard President Roosevelt declare war on Japan and her allied nations, Germany and Italy. I still have as one of my possessions, a spiral notebook that I had in the eighth grade. On the back cover of the notebook are listed the names of all my classmates, and on the blank pages inside I have drawings and pictures of airplanes, newspaper clippings, and other items related to the war.

The ninth grade was my big jump into high school. Mr. G. G. Dickey was the high school principal and Superintendent of Schools. Two of my favorite teachers were Effie Watkins and Ms. McCullough. They were my favorites, not then, but now, because they were more strict and taught me more than any others. The subjects they taught, math and general business were my better subjects. I wasn't what you would call an outstanding student, but was usually able to make B's with some A's and some C's. I don't recall ever failing a subject.

My greatest accomplishments in high school were through the athletic program. We participated in only three interscholastic sports; football, basketball and track. I was involved in all three. During my junior and senior years I was one of the better athletes in each of the three sports. In football I was a halfback while on offense and the safety on defense. We didn't do too well in football because we were small and few in number and competed against much larger schools; Pleasant Grove, Mesquite, Irving, Grand Prairie, Carrollton, Garland, and Vickery Hillcrest. Mart Hit, who had returned from the war as a Navy Commander, was the head coach for football and track. He was assisted by Morris Greenwood, who was the head basketball coach. In 1947 our basketball team won the co-championship of our district and the right to go to the regional playoffs by defeating Pleasant Grove in the best two-out-of-three playoff games. We were defeated in the regional playoff by Plano High School.

On the track team I was a broad jumper, ran the 100-yard dash, the 220-yard dash, ran on the 440-yard relay team, and was a member of the mile relay team. During my senior year I placed second in broad jump in the regional meet held at Owenby Stadium, on the campus of SMU. This earned me a trip to Austin for the State Track Meet. I didn't do so well in the two events I entered; broadjump and the 100-yard dash. Although I didn't place at the State Meet, it proved to be quite an experience for me, and I felt honored and proud that I was able to represent Buckner.

As a result of being on all the teams, I lettered in all three, football, basketball and track, for two years. At the May graduation exercises, I was awarded the Paul Danna Trophy, which was presented to the Outstanding Athlete of the Year. This trophy is a perpetual trophy displayed in the high school trophy case, and my name was added to it. Paul Dana, a deacon in the First Baptist Church of Dallas, made the trophy possible. My experience and training in high school athletics enabled me to make the track team at East Texas State University in Commerce, Texas, as a walk-on. Later after making the team, I was awarded an athletic scholarship.

THE LEARNING YEARS

When I graduated from Buckner High School, I had already made up my mind where I would attend college. It was natural that I would go to Commerce, where Mother was living, and attend East Texas State University. For the summer and fall semester, I lived with Mother on Pine Street, but when I received a scholarship for making the track team, I moved to the Athletic Dorm on the college campus.

My intention when I enrolled in college was to major in mathematics since that was my strongest subject in high school. As the result of poor counseling by the professor assigned to me, I was placed in a college algebra class that was far too advanced for me. This discouraged me from becoming a math major and I changed to accounting. In the meantime I was also taking education courses and physical education theory classes, and ended up with a major in them. In the spring of 1952, my senior year, I interviewed with Dr. E. D. Walker from the personnel department of the Dallas Independent School District and was hired as a physical education teacher to begin in the fall semester.

As a member of the college track team, I had a successful year on the freshman team. During my sophomore year our first official track meet was the Border Olympics in Laredo, Texas. While participating in the broad jump event, I pulled a hamstring muscle and wasn't able to perform much the rest of the year. A similar experience occurred during my junior year, which made me inactive the rest of the track season. Soon I developed back problems and learned that I had a ruptured disc in my lower back. Therefore, I had to begin treatment and was unable to participate on the track team my senior year.

While at East Texas, I met, dated, broke-up with, but later married my wife, Patsy Ruth Hayes of Deport, Texas. Patsy graduated from college one year later than I and also came to Dallas to teach. After a year had passed, we met again and the rest is happy history.

I have my mother to thank for making it possible for me to stay in college and earn my degree. She worked as a nurse in Dallas and sent money for me to pay my way through college. Without her, college would have been impossible for me.

I graduated in May of 1952 with a Bachelor of Science Degree, and started my Masters Program the summer after graduation, taking classes on Saturdays and some evenings until I completed the work in 1954.

Eventually, some twenty years later, I earned a Doctor of Education Degree from North Texas State in Denton. I had decided earlier to work toward becoming an administrator, quit teaching PE and turn to math and earth science to gain some experience in classroom teaching. After five long years of attending classes and surviving the tough testing and admissions requirements, I realized that all anyone needs is determination and "stick-toativeness." There were many times while taking the qualifying exams and working on my dissertation that I became discouraged and almost gave up. I told myself, "I am not a quitter," and by staying with it, I was able to succeed.

I spent eleven years as a teacher of PE, math, and earth science, learning new things all the while. In September of 1967, Dr. W. T. White assigned me to be assistant principal at Marsh Junior High. One day I was a teacher and the next day an administrator in a school with an enrollment of 2,200 students.

I was assigned as administrator to five different Dallas schools, but finally decided it was time I retire from the public schools, a difficult decision, but one that has proven to be right for me.

My last school position was as Headmaster of Royal Haven Baptist School, housed in the church I have attended for the past twenty-five years. I was very happy with the job though our enrollment was low and we were in a financial strain the entire time.

The Golden Years are finally here for me. I have fully retired. I am spending my time doing some traveling, playing golf, and indulging in my penchant for collecting stamps, coins, barb wire, old school books, and antiques. Perhaps I'll set up somewhere at a Flea Market with all my collectibles and just watch the people go by. Sounds exciting, doesn't it!

Bobby Lee Bray, '49

[Submitted by Dessie Hamrick, who wrote a note saying that Bobby had so few fingers, only stubs, and that he typed with his toes. Ed.]

THE TYPEWRITER

A typewriter is a swell machine, but it is not for me.
When I sit down to type a note, I can't find a single key.
"Use the tabulator," you will say, or "Back space to twenty-three."
And I get so dad-gummed mixed up I can hardly ever see.
When I finally get the paper fixed and start to bang away,
I don't know whether to shift gears or throw in a bale of hay.
So I will stick to pencil stubs and a tablet paper letter
Till I can figure this thing out or till they make it better!

Jo Nell (Fulton) Brown, '49

Remember the Girls' Woods? One year when my group went there, we all slept on the usual pallets out on the ground. We had slept like that for years without any mishaps at all. Then one morning I woke and looked up to see a cow standing at my head with her face about two or three inches above mine. Talk about letting out a scream! I jumped up, started running, fell over Jane Tilley, who had been scared out of her wits by my scream, and cut my knee on a stick on the ground. The stick jabbed my knee deeply enough that I had to be taken back to the campus and to the hospital for a couple of stitches. I could have hit the rest of the kids because they were all laughing hysterically. Later it dawned on me that I must have, indeed, been a funny sight trying to get away from that cow—my scream probably scared the cow half to death!

Going to Evans Grocery Store—what a thrill it was when we got old enough for one of the older girls to take us to shop there. One day Mary Sue Culbertson invited me to go with her, so we squeezed through the hole in the fence behind the hospital and walked about a mile across a plowed field up to the store.

Mr. Evans had some really nice looking watermelons outside the store. While I went in to shop with my quarter, Mary Sue picked one of the melons she liked and carried it aside. When I came out of the store, we started carrying that thing until we reached the field, then rolled it across that plowed field to the hole in the fence.

We looked up just in time to see Dean Dora Brady step up to the fence with orders for us to pick up the watermelon, carry it to the front gate of the campus, then up the highway back to the store with her following us in her car. That was the longest mile I ever walked, the heaviest watermelon I have ever seen or carried anywhere, and the last time I ever helped anyone "take" what they wanted.

Betty (Doughtie) Clark, '49

At cotton picking time during my sophomore year, I thought I'd have an easier time of it if I picked along with the right group.

Mr. Dickey was the overseer in charge, perched on a big horse and handling a long-reaching whip to ensure that we didn't goof off.

I thought I was so smart and decided to pick alongside Mr. Dickey's beautiful daughter, Jo Nita. (Understand now that Jo Nita didn't have to pick cotton, but she chose to do so to be one of us, as she often did.)

Let me tell you that I wasn't so smart. Mr. Dickey didn't leave our row. If we stood to stretch our backs too long, we would hear the sound of that whip and bend back over to get back to work. He rode Jo Nita more than anyone one else that day. Naturally when we returned to the fields after lunch, I stayed as far away from Jo Nita as possible.

I also remember in the summer after supper, that sometimes the commissary trucks would come around with ice cold watermelon—as much or more than we could eat. We'd stuff ourselves silly and then have watermelon fights until dark. Our matrons would hose us down before we went back inside. Then we'd be up all night crowding the use of the johns.

I never have had another melon that tasted quite as good as those.

Mary (Kelsoe) Curda, '49

When I was about six or seven years old, I belonged to the Rhythm Band. There must have been fifteen or twenty kids in it, and most of the members were girls. When I was a member, Jo Nell Brown directed the band. I always wanted that job of directing, for it appeared to be such a delightful thing to stand up before everyone and wave that little stick. No one ever gave me a chance to wave the little stick. I played the bird whistles, and I liked them well enough. I also played the sticks. I really didn't care much for the sticks, for I truly had a greater desire to play the drums. No one ever let me play the drums either. We used to play little songs, such as "Glow Worm," and "Twinkle, Twinkle Little Star." We were generally dressed up pretty cute, and we went to various churches, playing to raise money for the home. I guess our performance was mainly to remind people that there were children in the Home needing help. It was fun for us to get out and away from the home; everyone treated us quite well.

Another thing that I wanted to do was to be a cheerleader, and I never got to do that either. I always believed that the cutest girls were chosen, more of a popularity contest. In the pep squad, I always yelled so loud and so hard that before the game was over, I always had a sore throat. Yelling never got me what I really wanted either.

We always had sack lunches on Christmas Eve Night. Usually, the sandwiches were passed out for us at noon to take home to eat that evening. On one particular evening, something dreadful happened with terrible consequences. A cup towel was usually placed in the bottom of the aluminum pans before the sandwiches were placed in them, but this year, someone forgot to use the towels. There were almost six hundred sick kids early Christmas morning, as almost all the kids came down with ptomaine poisoning. Every available doctor in Dallas was called out to attend to all the sick children. To this day, I have been unable to eat peanut butter and banana sandwiches.

What most people called Christmas stockings and what we called them was not the same. Ours were made from big chunks of cloth sewed together. One side had rippley candy, hard candy, and stick candy. On the other side were the fruit and nuts. The toys and clothes were wrapped up inside the bundles, "strings" as we called them. We always went to the school auditorium where there was generally some sort of Christmas play or program. The lights were dimmed, and the curtains were opened to reveal beautifully decorated Christmas trees, which sometimes rotated. Since they were in the auditorium, we only got to see the trees that one time. I always wished that they could have been placed where we could have seen them often. As soon as the curtains were opened, the "strings" were passed out. The high school seniors were the ones to pass out the Christmas bundles. I went back the year Mildred Ann was a senior and took several pictures of her passing out "strings."

Profanity was never permitted at Buckner; no one ever used such language. We had an art teacher who used profanity, and how she got away with it, I never knew, but she did. When things went wrong for her, she always used a favorite curse word, and we kids always thought it extremely funny.

We had summer camp, and everyone loved it. We were permitted to wear our jeans and shorts. Generally, shorts were a "no no" on the Buckner campus, but camp was a whole different story. Each girl was assigned little jobs at the camp, and if she cooperated and did what was expected of her, if she didn't fuss and complain, she was considered a "good camper" and was often permitted to return to camp again that same summer. I always made the good camper list, as I always went over and above what was expected of a camper. I recall my last time at summer camp. I believe that it was V-J Day, and we all had to return to Buckner to go to church to pray because the war was over. Most of us kids would have preferred to stay at camp.

We senior girls had to make our graduation dresses and suits, and we thought we looked pretty fine in them. If one did a sloppy job on the outfit, she still had to wear it. We failed the course if we did not wear the outfit. I also remember that we seniors always had a banquet in which we girls wore evening dresses. I think that those dresses were delivered to the dormitory with particular girls in mind for each dress. Somebody else must have pressed them up, for we knew nothing about such clothes. I imagine that those evening dresses were surplus, sent to Buckner from some of the local Dallas stores. At any rate, we did feel quite high in the in-step. We also received our first high heels about graduation time. I believe that we got to go to town to pick out our shoe selection, and I mean to tell you, it took an act of bravery for some of us to walk in those heels for the first time.

One thing really annoyed us girls. Every time the swimming pool had to be closed for cleaning, it was on the day that the girls were supposed to swim. I don't remember just how we went about obtaining swim suits, but I rather suspect that the matron already knew what size we were and brought over appropriate suits. If they did not fit so well—tough cookies! The boys always peeked out of the windows to watch the girls swim, and I think that the girls always managed to do the same in devious ways known only to those girls. You know that old saying about "sauce for the goose" being "sauce for the gander."

Catherine (Thomas) Goodwill, '49

The past fifty years have gone by so fast. They nave been very normal and uneventful, but happy and fulfilling. I have balanced my life with church and charity work, and I have many fond memories of Buckner.

After graduation from high school, I received my nurse's degree from Baylor University School of Nursing in Dallas. Back when I was in the first grade at Duncan, OK, Felix Thomas was in the third and best friends with my cousin, Alvin Arterbury. After I went to Buckner, I never heard from Felix until I went to Duncan following graduation from Nurse's training. He was home on furlough from the Navy. After Felix was discharged, we married in 1952. He is such a blessing to me and treats me like a queen!

We started our married life in Odessa, TX, where I worked as a nurse in surgery and the emergency room. Felix graduated from Abilene Christian College in 1958 and I got my PHT degree (pushing hubby through) working for Joseph C. Snow, MD, as office nurse and surgical assistant. Then we moved to Fort Worth where he was an accountant for Stratoflex and he and Royce Stephens, from Buckner, worked together. We moved back to Abilene where I went back to work for Dr. Snow. (It was while I worked for Dr. Snow that I met up with James Cutshall when he became one of our patients. He didn't take well to my giving him injections in the hip . . . ask him about it!) I retired from nursing in 1996 after 36 years in the office of Dr. Snow and later Dr. Stackhouse.

Several years ago we had a Buckner get-together at our home. Those attending were James and Sarah Cutshall, Dessie & Wayne Hamrick, Bill and Geneva (Scurlock) Starrett, R. D. and Thelma (Goodwill) Stewart. W. L. and Marie (Wilson) Smith would have attended but were out of town.

Felix is a pilot, avid reader, has preached for many small congregations, and now is teaching our Sunday morning class. His favorite toy is an award winning 172 Cessna Skyhawk. My toy is a 1965 Thunderbird in mint condition with 61,000 miles. I volunteer as a special duty nurse when my time allows. We do a lot of church visitation, practice hospitality (1 Peter 4:9), and love to travel.

It has been a tremendous 50 years, and I feel that there is still more I can accomplish if God is willing.

BUCKNER HOMECOMING, 1999

Come stroll with me down memory lane
And spin a yarn or two.
Let's flip the pages back in time
And live old days anew.

Let's play the games we used to play
And find the friends we knew.

Let's walk the paths we used to walk
Where sometimes flowers grew.
For just a time, let's catch a glimpse
Of what our world was like:
I see a shining Christmas tree,
And presents to delight!

I see such happy faces glow.
I see us running through the snow.
I hear the sounds of childish play
And wish for a while we could stop and stay.

But years have passed, and time has flown
And all who were young have long been grown.
We've gone our own way like wind-blown leaves;
Some to new lands, across the wide seas.

But once each year from far and wide,
We lay all work and cares aside,
For we have an appointment that just can't wait.
We'll all meet at Buckner so throw wide the gate!

For there I found family who first were just friends,
But now they're my relatives, my special "close kin!"
So we'll see you next year from wherever we roam.
We'll always return to the place we call home—Buckner.

Wayne Hamrick, '49

(1939-1949)

One time Kenneth Thompson and Harvey Ellis asked me to run away with them. I didn't have anywhere to go if we were caught, so I stayed behind. About midnight Kenneth and Harvey came back, soaking wet and looking like two drowned rats. I was glad I had stayed home.

We boys in Rupard were full of mischief and would wait until our matron, Mrs. Bearden, would run water and get in the bathtub and then roll the metal garbage cans down the stairs. Can you imagine what went through her mind as she heard the noise?

In the 1947 football game against Highland Park, on their field with about ten minutes to go, I plunged for a player—which someone else beat me to. There was nothing for me to hit but the ground. With nothing to cushion me, I landed on my left shoulder, breaking it. No one even looked at it. I had to hold it up with my right hand. I rode the bus back to Buckner in a lot of pain, took a shower, and changed clothes. Finally, Coach Greenwood noticed and suggested I go to the Hospital. I walked down there by myself. Still nothing was done to help the pain. I spent the night there. The next morning they took me to Baylor where I was put into a body cast from the waist up. I spent the next six weeks in the Hospital on the campus.

In another of the games I took a hard lick, which knocked my senses right out of my head. I played anyway for a whole quarter, not knowing what was going on. I must have passed out, for I finally came around to find the coach bending over me and hollering at me, "Hamrick! Where are you? What time is it? Are you OK?" and lots of other silly questions. I didn't have to go to the hospital that time.

Once in a game with Corsicana we were playing pretty rough. The referee threw his flag down hollering, "Fifteen yards for squeezing." The guilty player was none other than Bobby Baker. We still get a good laugh at that one.

While showering one day and "boys being boys," as they say, someone took my towel, putting it into the door where I could not get to it, and leaving me standing naked. I tried to kick in the wood part of the door to get to the towel, but instead, hit the glass with my right leg. I cut that leg really bad. Blood was running everywhere. Kenneth Thompson carried me to the Hospital on his back. I still have a nasty scar as I could not get it sewed up until the next day.

Many times some of the boys would catch the train out of Urbandale, see how far they could ride and jump off before it picked up much speed. They would jump onto the train as it would slow down going up a hill toward Urbandale. One day Obert Long, Bobby Lee Bray, Kenneth Thompson and I all jumped on the train for a free ride. Kenneth and I got off in time before it picked up too much speed, but Bobby Lee Bray and Obert Long did not make the jump in time. The train carried them all the way to Terrell before they could get off. Bobby and Obert had a much longer train ride that day than they wanted. They got off when it reached Terrell and had to walk all the way back to Buckner.

Grinding feed one day at the Farm, the mixer would not go fast enough. I put my right hand in a little too far, trying to make the mixer feed faster. My hand was caught, cutting two fingers. The middle finger was cut at the second

joint and the leaders were cut in the index finger, leaving it stiff. By the time I got to the Hospital, word was all over the campus, "Wayne got his hand cut off." Even though I was hurt, I still had to shift the gears for Mrs. Martin to drive me to get help. No one else but me knew how to drive that truck.

Many a young child has been broken of sucking his thumb by my showing him my finger and telling him what might happen to him if he didn't stop!

Dessie (Hamrick) Hardin, '49

(1936-1949)

There were five of us Hardins there, Paul, Marion, Jesse, Frankie and me, all together in the Receiving Home. You know how they always gave the "beloved" shots, DPT, small pox, etc. Paul and Marion always were teasing us younger ones. They built up such a fear of the shots that Jesse and I hid in the closets! They finally found us and we still had to get the shots.

One day we decided we were not going to stay there any longer. I think it was after Frankie, who was just a baby, left the dining room with some bread in the roof of his mouth to suck on. They got on to him about it and made him spit it out. I did not like that one bit. I got angry with them and, in turn, I was also punished. The next morning we took off, taking nothing with us and not knowing where we were going. They caught up with us at the red light on Highway 80 and Buckner Blvd. I don't remember being punished for that. I think even those adults were frightened that we got away so quickly.

In the first grade, Miss Howard and Miss Howell wanted to take Paul, Marion, Jesse and me to the Dallas Zoo one day. Everything was arranged. I was all dressed up in a pretty blue velvet dress with white socks and black patent leather shoes. All the boys were cleaned up nice also. They picked us up and we started out, but I don't remember getting to the Zoo. Marion, who was sitting in the back seat, got sick and threw up. I think we had to go back to Buckner before we got very far.

We, the entire family, were all put in the first grade together for about a week. We had never been to school before. We were given crayons to learn to use, but Marion got into trouble for coloring freckles all over a boy's face in the picture we were assigned to color.

Wayne tells the story that when he was in the second grade, for some reason the teacher made him sit out in the hall in the little cubby-hole locker. School was turned out and still nobody had told him he could go home. The cleaning man came and found him still sitting where he had been instructed to sit, and told him school had been out a long time ago, and to scuttle on back to his dorm!

In the early forties at Hardin dorm, we girls discovered a dog that had had some pups outside our window in the northwest corner room. Their mother kept them hidden in the brush in a hole near the foundation. We would hold one of the girls by the feet and hand her out the window. She would pick up one of the puppies and we would pull her back up, play with the puppy for awhile, then let someone else put the pup back the same way. Of course we would sneak food from the Manna Hall to feed them. One day while we were getting one of the puppies, it was Johnnie Shurlock's time to get a turn picking up the puppy. While we were holding her feet, something went wrong. We dropped her out the window! Needless to say, we could not get her back inside, and she had to walk around to sneak in through the door. After she was safely in, she kept saying her arm hurt, so we had to go tell Mrs. Zapp what had happened and go to the hospital to get the stretcher to carry Johnnie to the hospital. The puppies were removed, and we had to face our punishment, missing stunt night again for several weeks.

Friday night in Hardin was "Stunt Night." We could put on plays, sing, say poems, anything to entertain. It was something everyone looked forward to and planned for all week. We would compete by rooms to see who could put on the best show. One winter Myra Locklear got it into her head to sit on the hot radiator. Of course, she received a pretty bad burn. She told the matron we had dared her to do it. We had to miss a whole month of stunt nights for punishment, and we weren't even guilty this time!

One Halloween when we were in Hardin Home, the older girls had fixed up the attic for a Spook House. Our matron took us younger girls for a walk while they put the finishing touches on

things. It was about dusky dark and our walk took us by the Manna Hall. We saw this woman with long gray hair blowing in the wind. We just knew we had seen the Halloween witch or a ghost of some kind. It turned out to be Miss Mamie out for a stroll.

I will never forget that day, December 7, 1941. I was in Hardin Home, and we all just knew that we would be bombed. We had gone to church that morning. Brother Hal made the announcement of the bombing of Pearl Harbor from the pulpit, had a prayer and sent us back to our dorms. We were no longer allowed to have lights after a certain time at night for fear that enemy planes seeing them might be led to bomb our building. We would see search lights, probably advertising something, but we thought they were looking for missing planes. We would save foil from chewing gum wrappers. I don't know where it was supposed to go, but we felt very patriotic helping the war effort in this way. We saved what little money we could for War Bonds and gave the foil we saved to the Red Cross. I remember one year having a real patriotic program with all the Armed Forces songs and Kate Smith singing "God Bless America!" We all dressed up in red, white and blue, and felt we had really done something worthwhile. Later my brother Paul went into the Navy and sent me a picture of himself in his uniform. It reminded me of a little bull dog. Oh, but I was so proud of him. Then in 1945, after the war was over, he came to the high school and walked me to my rooms carrying my books. I thought I was the Queen of Something!

One summer morning when we were in Hardin, the cattle truck took us to the Girls' Woods. We played, rode the horses with Daddy Buck, and had a good time. When it came time to go home, the truck did not show up. We waited for what seemed like a real long time. Finally, we started walking home. You know Miss Mamie did not like us to be late for our meals! We were almost half way home when the truck met us. Don't you know that was a sight—all those little girls with identical short hair cuts walking down the highway. Anyway, we were late to dinner, but we were fed! This was the only time we were ever late to a meal!

When we were in Hardin, we had to take rest periods. We would lie on quilts in the living/play room and the matron would read us stories. She read a lot of things to us: Raggedy Ann and Andy, the Nancy Drew books and the Hardy Boys. We did not have to go to sleep, but we had a "Quiet Hour." I guess that's why I still enjoy a nap after lunch.

You know, when I think about it, we really did have it good. In thinking back there are some really good times, but it is hard to put some of the good things into stories because they were such everyday living.

I remember on the spring and summer days when we lived at Crouch Home, we would go out to play and someone would bring out a ball and bat? Of course we did not have baseball mitts, but it was time to play scrub ball. We would have a catcher, pitcher, and a batter, three bases and the rest of us would be in the field. We would try our best to catch three flies or to get six balls so we would get the chance to bat. Sometimes it would take us a long time to get a turn at bat and some days no time at all. Some of the girls could hit the ball real far and some would take forever to hit the ball. Those were some fun days.

On one spring afternoon while we were playing scrub, for some reason or another I threw my bat and Wilma Jean Hildreth was the catcher at the time. The bat hit her in the nose and broke it. Well, it made matters worse because her older sister was graduating that night, and she did not get to see her graduate. People were not very happy with me for awhile. It really was an accident or I think it was.

Does anyone remember Mary Alice Higginbottom? You recall she did have a problem, being always a littler older than most. Because she would do anything asked of her, we sometimes took advantage of her. One day when we were in Crouch Home, on the third floor, we girls saw a bird nest in the top of a tree. The tree was as tall as the windows on our third floor. We could not reach it and since we were not allowed to go outside at will, we knew we needed help. We said to Alice, who was taller than we were, "Would you get us the bird nest?" She opened the window and reached for it, but as she did, she took a fall all the way down to the ground. We just knew she was dead and didn't know what to do.

While we were frantically trying to decide what to do, she just got up and walked upstairs with only a few scratches on her.

Beside that tall tree was a Chinaberry, which we could reach. In fact, we used to reach out the window to the limbs and climb out onto it. It also

reached up to the third floor but was closer to our window. We collected the Chinaberries and had some pretty good fights throwing them at each other. The berries really did hurt when they hit, especially if they were thrown hard.

One day when we were living on that same floor, everyone on one side of the hall got mad at the girls on the other side. We didn't allow anyone from the other side of the hall to enter our territory. Once, we were even so angry that we threw ink at each other, but most of the time our fights were just noise; hollering and screaming.

Our matron, Mrs. Marrow, once had us line up in the hall facing each other. Then she said, "OK, you want to fight so get with it!" She stood there and watched us, making us hit each other. Of course, we could not fight. We ended up laughing and pretending to fight. After a while, she said, "Now, hug each other and make up." We obeyed and went back to our rooms, peaceful until the next argument.

I don't remember all the things we got demerits for, but it seems I always had too many. We had one matron on the third floor of Hunt Home who delighted in making us drink a big glass of warm water to work off our demerits. One glass, one demerit. Some of us threw up after drinking. We did not have to put up with that lady too long. We reported her and she found another home. She was a meanie.

Mrs. Ratcliff was head matron of Hunt and once while she was on her week-end off, we had an adventure. The third floor girls would always have to go in the back door after we had been to a movie, ball game, etc. The parlor was waxed and cared for carefully. We were not allowed to walk on it so that when visitors came it would be shining and clean.

I had just had my ears pierced. You know how someone would rub alcohol on the earlobe, pinching it to deaden them and then poke a needle through it. Then we would put a broom straw into the holes until they got well. Our ears had not yet healed when we came home that day to find our door locked and could not get in. It was very cold that night, probably raining. Our matron sat there on the stairs with her keys in hand and made us all go around the building up to the second floor and come down stairs into our room. Everyone was fussing about it. I guess I was the loudest one. She flailed out at me and just happened to come down on one of my sore ears.

This really hurt me, so I came back at her, grabbing her hand so she could not do it again. Of course I twisted her arm just a little bit.

She told her story the next day and I told mine. Mrs. Ratcliff was very understanding, but said she would have to punish me.

I was campused until I apologized to the matron. Of course I had to miss movies and ball games, everything, but I could not make myself tell her I was sorry. I don't remember ever doing it. I could be pretty stubborn.

Anyway I had to let my ears grow back together again after all. That should have been punishment enough.

Does anyone else remember Brother Oscar, who used to come out to Buckner just about every Sunday afternoon? He would ask riddles or jokes, and if we could answer them, give us a piece of candy or a small trinket of some kind. He would always ask us to sing a song for him. The most important thing he gave was his time and what little he had to make us orphans happy.

In thinking back, I believe he must not have had very much himself. I recall the old beat-up van he drove that we always looked for on Sundays because we liked having a regular visitor to look forward to. One day he did not show up, and we learned later that he had died.

He was a lonely old man when he first started coming to Buckner. I like to think we brought a little happiness to him as he did to us. He did mean a lot to our lonely Sunday afternoons. Wayne said he came over to the boys' side of the campus doing the same thing for them.

I can remember a lot of the details about Manna Hall duty. On Saturdays we always had to wash all the salt and pepper shakers and put fresh salt and pepper in them. We had to scrape all the gum off the benches and we had a special ritual for washing dishes. We would go to the kitchen service window to get our pan of hot soapy water and then go back for rinse water. It was difficult not to spill it while we were carrying it back to the table. I remember tucking it between my waistline and right arm to carry it. We were in a hurry because we were always trying to see who could be the first for inspection and were unhappy about the slow pokes.

We would stack the dishes for our table in the order we were going to wash them; glasses first, plates and then silverware. We washed everything, dried the whole bunch, and then would set the table for the next meal.

I remember once when I was the youngest girl at the table with Mrs. Orr, we had kidney beans for lunch. I could not stand kidney beans, so I did not eat them.

They were in my bowl the next meal! I did not eat them. They were there at the next meal. I still did not eat them. The third time Mrs. Orr said I would eat them.

I finally choked them down, but they came back up! After that Miss Mamie did not make us eat our leftovers the next meal anymore. And in all honesty, I just love kidney beans today.

One time Richard Holder had to wear a dress to Manna Hall for not polishing his shoes to play in the rhythm band. This seemed to be some matrons' favorite way to punish their boys. Needless to say, the boys in dresses were really made fun of and laughed at.

Miss Mamie finally put a stop to that. She told those matrons to punish their boys at home, not in her dining room!

Nearly every winter the older girls took turns picking chickens. One year in 1948, I was in the lucky group. It was cold outside, but very hot in the small room with 30-50 girls. First, the boys broke the necks of the chickens and brought them inside to us. We then dipped them into the Big Black Pot of boiling water. Oh, the stench of scalded feathers that I can remember to this day. Then we steamed them and crowded around the table ready to pick the feathers quickly and pass the chickens on down the line for the next step. Miss Mamie called out, "Be sure to get the lights out," to the ones who were gutting them.

Well, suddenly I came to my senses and realized someone was holding my feet and my head was whirling. I did not know what was going on. Eventually, I found out I had fainted and hit my head on the Big Black Pot.

Lucky me. After that I never had to pick chickens anymore. I was only allowed to inspect to make sure there were no pen feathers and that the lights had been pulled out of the cavities!

It was many years before I could bring myself to cut up a chicken. But as a housewife, the time came for me to cut up a chicken to serve my family. Wayne would usually do it for me, but he was not always there when I needed one cut up, so I finally had to make myself do it. This was one of the hardest things I had to learn because it continued to make me sick to my stomach.

Sometimes we were just full of mischief. One

day Dora Brady had campused us for some reason we felt was unjust. That night we went out and let all the air out of her tires. She was so proud of her car, but she never did find out who had done it. Lucky for us! If we had been caught, we would have deserved to be punished.

We were allowed parlor dates after we got older. One time in the winter we did not have church on a Sunday night because of the weather. At that time Fred Powell, who was older, was trying to get me for his girl friend. He was nice enough but not for me. I think Edna Heitman and Ernestine Webster were encouraging him.

That night I was studying in my room, not expecting a date, but Mrs. Hardy came to tell me someone wanted to see me in the parlor. When I went downstairs, there sat Fred. Mrs. Hardy would not let me go back to my room. She said that he had come to see me and I had to sit there with him for our full hour.

I did not know Fred or anything about him to talk about, so we sat quietly, and all the time, Fred was nervously pulling and tugging on the drapes behind us. I finally got bored and told him that I really did need to go do homework. I just got up and walked out. He went home, but later Mrs. Hardy told me she was so glad I had left because she had been afraid Fred was going to pull the drapes down.

Wayne and I were in the parlor for a date one Sunday night when the lights went out. Mrs. Hardy nearly broke her neck trying to get to her flashlight. We did have a good laugh about it. The lights came back on before she got back with the flashlight, even before anyone was able to steal a kiss.

It was always a real treat to go off campus—fun just to be in the woods out in the beauty of nature. When we were older, senior girls in Burhman Home, one year we stole peaches from the people across the road from The Girls' Woods. The peaches were not ready to be picked, just little green things, but that didn't stop us from eating them and getting a real good stomach ache. We did get caught and were punished. Ironically, several years after we left Buckner, Lisa Harvey married Bill Scott, whose relatives, as it turned out, owned the orchard from which we had stolen those peaches!

I will never forget my first encounter with Wayne Hamrick. We were in the fifth or sixth grade. We had just come in from recess and Jo

Nell Brown, a cute blond-haired, brown-eyed girl, said that she "liked" Wayne. Well, me with my big mouth—since Wayne sat behind me in class, I thought it would be so smart to ask him, "If I give you a piece of paper, would you write Jo Nell a love note?"

Before I knew what had happened, wham! Wayne slapped me in the back and knocked the breath out of me. I could not breathe for a moment. The teacher was out of the room, but for some reason I never did tell on him. He said he did it because my brother Paul had whipped him. By the time he left the Home after graduation, Paul had grown to like Wayne and told me he would make a good husband. Of course, I never dreamed at the time that we would be together for forty-eight plus happy years.

David Dan Reynolds, '49

Remember along with me—as a barefoot boy of six or seven in 1939—playing on the playground of Pires Dorm with my knickers (knickerbockers) up to my knees and little vest on, watching in awe as the piper cub airplanes flew over low above Samuell Boulevard—being punished (for some silly, minor infraction—like fighting with another boy) by having to stand with my nose pressed against the red brick wall of Pires for one hour (an eternity). Remember as I walk (run) only fifty feet to the swimming pool on Tuesdays, Thursdays and Saturdays, pausing for a mini-second to disinfect my dirty bare feet in the chlorine cleaning pit just inside the pool gate. Watch me as I take like a fish to water (after all, I'm a Pisces) and learn to swim and dive on my own at age six. Those prickly wool swim trunks were really uncomfortable!

Then, remember with me as a lad of ten, eleven and twelve, living in Freeland Dorm. We would go swimming in Bull Pond, or better yet in Rockbottom (once, getting a spanking from Mrs. Day for sneaking off to Rockbottom without permission). Remember the big boys—like Herbert Dewberry—swinging and diving off a tree limb fifteen feet above the water, and my bravely emulating them. My brother Jack—three years older than I—always had me under his wing during those early years even though we always lived in separate dorms.

Then recall the beginning adolescent years of thirteen and fourteen in McElroy Dorm. It was those years when I remember the "lawn mower brigade," where several of us boys would tackle the vast (or so it seemed at the time) acres of campus lawn with our push mowers lined up in a row. There was the hoeing of corn, chopping cotton and picking cotton into those long "toesacks" under the watchful eye of Mr. Dickey on horseback, the stacking of insulage in the silo, packing it down with our bare feet inside the tall, dark silo. These were the years of World War II, and I remember the sugar and gasoline rationing cards (the teachers and matrons had them), and anxiously awaiting WWII fighter pilot/war story books mailed to me monthly by my Aunt Hollye, as well as the Hardy Boys and Nancy Drew series of books which I read from cover to cover. Those were the early years of piano lessons from Helen Hutchins (Henderson), and then later Helen Buster Roberts. Such hard work—that relentless practice on the pianos in those tiny rooms above study hall.

Ah, the final years as a big boy of fifteen, sixteen, seventeen, in Rupard Hall. Jack had graduated and left Buckner when I entered high school, so I was then really on my own. There was eagerly awaited camp at the lake every summer, and I would always hope my name would be on the list posted of boys to go first. At around age fifteen, I worked for Mrs. McKinney in the laundry, delivering clean clothes and linens in those big rolling carts all over the campus. My favorite and last job was as janitor in the high school building, where I would spend hours after school sweeping the wooden floors with those wide push brooms, scattering the red-powdered cleaning compound all over the floors before beginning to sweep. I took great pride in being assigned to blow the campus siren at given intervals. (The siren button was located in the high school study hall.) I couldn't be a minute too soon nor a minute too late in pushing that button!

I also remember Miss Mary McCorkle asking me to wash her black 1939 Plymouth on a sunny Saturday morning and Coach Greenwood and his wife taking me one evening to my first Starlite Operetta in Dallas. I remember bicycling all the way around White Rock Lake—all of us eleventh graders humming together in Miss Effie Watkins' class just to aggravate her—wanting so badly and studying so hard to be '49 senior class valedictorian, and just having to settle for salutatorian when David Ezra Ward nosed me out by a couple of grade points—my crush on Jo Nell Brown in third grade, my crush on Elisa Harvey in fifth grade, and high school girlfriends Betty Joan Clark and Billie Juanita Graves, and friends like Veoma McClung, Alice Ann Ward and others.

I loved Saturday night cliffhanger serial movies and Sunday church in the Chapel where I occasionally played the piano. Additionally, I loved playing as everyone marched into Manna Hall and later while the girls sang a hymn before our prayer. The truth is I also loved RC Colas, Moon Pies, and ice cream from the new Campus Mart.

Then it all ended in September of 1949 when, with the help of Buckner, I headed for Howard Payne College in Brownwood to continue my education.

I'm so happy I finally returned to the Buckner Homecoming fold in 1998! I was absent for too long from all my brothers and sisters!

Class of 1940, 1st Row: Raymond Gafford, Gene Morris, Mahala Hildreth, Doris Titus, Helen Patterson, Nellie Frank Carver, Thelma Howard, Arnold Jones, R. D. Sampier, Jeff Dobbs; 2nd Row: Carroll Davis, Louise Caskill, Ruby Vaughn, Louise Malone, Vivian Ford, Leroy Gafford, Tommie Taylor, Robert Taylor, Billy O' Connor; 3rd Row: Milton Haley, Pearl Taylor, Dollie Gee, Mary Etta Barnes, Bertie Myers, Christine Pace, James Reid; 4th Row: Billy Harting, Joy Moore, Mary Moore, Laurine Davis, Byron Duckworth, Harold Reid.

Girls' Gathering, 1944-45; 1st Row: Dollie Gee, Willie Mae Davis, Beatrice Brown, Jeanette Collins; 2nd Row: Alma Ricks, Hazel Humphrey, Ruby Davis, Lorene Chick; 3rd Row: Georgia Taylor, Eunice Arrant, Elizabeth Pollard, Dorothy Motes, Mamie Curl, Louise Rushing, Helen Duffer..

The Spanish Song Group, 1940.

Robertine Woodall and Steward Dewberry, 1941.

Class of 1941, Seated: Mamie Curl, Alma Ricks, Mary Pollard, Ruby Davis, Standing:Louise Rushing, Hazel Humphrey, Rubye Arrant.

Class of 1941, Seated: Carl Farris, Dorothy Motes, Willie Mae Davis, Earl Dobbs,
Standing: Beatrice Brown, Lorene Chick, Helen Duffer, Jeanette Collins.

Billy Joe and James Smoot, 1942.

The Corcoran Family Arrives:
Billy, Leonard, Charlie, Louise, and Margaret, 1942.

Open House for Sewing Classes: Willie Mae Davis, Ruby Davis.

Fay Dewberry by the flower bed, 1944.

Girls' Chorus with Miss Lester, 1941-42, 1st Row: Joyce work, Sue Farris, Sue Day, Fay Dewberry, Wanda Swindall, LaVoe Brown, Helen Hildreth, Wilma Alvey, Billie J. Dickey, Winifred Brown, Margaret Pierce; 2nd Row: Dorothy Heitman, Ruby Bolton, Ella Mae Taylor, Lorena Brasfield, Alma Jay Sherrell, Joyce Ford, Viola Rougea, Sarah Haley; 3rd Row: Lanell Green, Virginia Woods, Zelna Hildredth, Helen Harrison, Miss Lester, Avie Calhoune, Lucille Pollard, Thelma Davis, Yvonne Sherrell, 4th Row; Twila Brice, Lucille Brasfield, Maydell Morris, Hazel Duckworth, Willa Jean Reed, Ruby Atwood.

80

Third Floor of Hunt, 1944.

Big Sis for the younger girls:
Roberta Howard.

Below:
Class of 1944; 1st Row: Doris Ridge, Dale Worthington, Joyce Work, Janie Lou Nash, Jake Corbett, Patsy Corbett, Laura Mae Graves, Sarah Haley, Sybil Ellis, Ruth Ashley; 2nd Row: G. G. Dickey, Principal, Mildred Mast, Fay Dewberry, Barbara Waller, Billy Ray Clark, Dorothy Heitman, Ella Mae Taylor, Katherine Kirby, Ruth Ford; 3rd Row: Martha Stanley, Leston Lee McNeil, T. W. Harper, Helen Roller, Lizabeth Stanton, Joan Haggard, Edna Mae Reynolds.

Buckner Boys at War: Bobby Manor, James Smart and Johnny Wright, 1944.

Robert Dewberry, c '44.

Mrs. Hutcheon's Boys Choir.

Girls of the Class of '44 find treasures in the trash.

Joyce Work and Owen Thomas, 1944

Helen Roller, Fay Dewberry and Doris Ridge commune with Father Buckner, 1944.

Girls Camp "Out" House.

Evans Store; within walking distance.

Letter Jacket Winners, 1943, First Row: "Red" Mason, James "Hollywood" Carter, Jack Reynolds, Leston McNeil, Jacky Dobbs, Benny Jo Locklear; Back Row: Leo Curda, Truman Bearden, Frank Curda, Jake Corbett, T. W. Harper, Billy Ray Clark.

Johnny Wright with the horses.

Jack and David Reynolds, 1946.

The Girls' Pep Squad, 1947-48.

84

Barbara Waller and Patsy Corbett working hard, 1944.

Billy Ed and Cotton Taylor in front of Freeland, 1945.

The Melodeers in Song:
Joyce Duckworth,
Louise Cumbie, Yvonne Ward,
Wanda L. Swindall.

Edith, Mary, and Eva Nell Turner.

The Melodeers in Uniform: Wanda Lee Swindall,
Yvonne Ward, Louise Cumbie,
and Joyce Duckworth.

GIRLS OF THE CLASS OF 1946; Seated: *Louise Cumbie, Norma Henslee, Mary Tom Harrell, Jenna Day;* Standing:
Velma Patterson, Sue Mast, Bobbie Sinclair,Dorothy Mason, Geneva Scurlock, Fern Horsley, Dorothy Lookado, Anna Lee McLeod,
Margaret Fritchie, Hazel Graham, Jo Dickey, and Jeanne Tilley.

86

Miss Roberts' Music Class of 1948.

The Girls' Basketball Team, c 1940s 1st Row: Mary Curda, Betty Lookadoo, Mary Ann Leamer, Dessie Hardin, Jimmie Sherrell, Dorothy Barnet; 2nd Row: Norma Lookadoo, Helen Curda, Gladys Hall, Juanita Minitra, Elizabeth Atkinson, Daisy Morgan.

The Boys' Track Team, 1947-48; 1st Row: Edward Stanley, Billy Houston, Kenneth Murray, Obert Long, (In Front): Pete Campbell; 2nd Row: Bobby Baker, Prentice Ward, Vance Horsley, David Ward; 3rd Row: Coach Greenwood, Vernon Horsley, Robert Bleakley, Red Stephens, Harold Campbell, Cigar Smith, and Billie Joe Stanley.

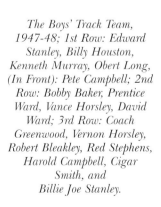

Fall Cleaning for Homecoming: Mattye Lou Sowell, Mary Evelyn Bearden, Betty Clark, Dessie Hardin, 1947.

Crouch Home Girls, c 1940s.

Girls Basketball Team, 1947-48; 1st Row: Betty Lookadoo, Wanda Tucker, Tressie Perkins, Dessie Hardin, Beatrice Hendricks; 2nd Row: Gale Keeter (Coach), Mary Curda, Marie Hall, Jimmie Sherrell, Juanita Minatra, Mary Ann Leamer, Betty Boatright, Helen Curda, and Nora Sue McLeod.

*Letter Jacket Winners, 1948: Wallace Hall, Jack Hall, Royce Stephens, Prentice Ward, Billie Joe
Stanley, Tommy McWhorter, Franklin Nash, and Marion Hardin.*

Bobby Lee Bray, 1949.

*Clara Joyce and Royce Stephens,
1949.*

*The Football Team, 1948;
Kneeling: Vernon Horsley,
Prentice Ward, Billy
Houston, Vance Horsley,
Charles May, Ira Lee
Henslee, Billie Jo Stanley,
M. C. Greenwood (Coach);
Standing: Jessie Hardin,
Edward Stanley, Red
Stephens, Bobby Baker,
Harold Campbell, Obert
Lone, Wayne Hamrick,
Tommy McWhorter, and
Kenneth Thompson.*

89

*Ms. Brady's Car: Jo Nell Brown,
Betty Clark, Jane Tilley,
Dessie Hardin, Mildred Mallette,
and Wanda Tucker.*

Miss Jo's Girls' Choir, 1948-50.

*Weldon Smith working at
the farm, 1949*

*The Opening of the Campus Mart: Colonel R. C. Buckner serving
a group of girls from Crouch Home, 1949.*

Mr. Callahan's field gang, c 40s.

Wayne Hamrick, Mutt Holcomb, Harold Ingram.

Ironing at the laundry, c 40s.

Dessie Hardin, Mary Lou Hall, Ernestine Webster spent a lot of time on roller skates, 1947-49.

A Favorite Pastime: Jimmie Sherrell, Betty Lookadoo, Christine Henslee, Nora Sue McLeod, and Mary Ann Leamer.

The Fifties

"For in you alone, O Lord, the fatherless find mercy."
Hosea 14:3b, RSI

Robert Bleakley, '50

GOOD TIMES AT THE BAKERY

One of our favorite places to spend some of our leisure time was at the Bakery, run by Mr. Ed (Pap) Grube. It was a joy just to be around him because he was so nice to us. He was a real gentleman, and sometimes a big cut-up. Of course we helped him with all the work he had to do while providing us with all the wonderful desserts that we enjoyed. In addition, he made bread every day, several hundred loaves. We got to eat some of those desserts and wonderful slices of fresh bread. After work, he allowed us to hang around and entertain ourselves. Sometimes, we would clean off the long bread table and play table tennis on it.

He would make a different dessert every day. One day it would be cookies; the next day pies, cinnamon rolls, cakes or some other tasty treats. Billy Ed Taylor was one of his regular workers assigned to the bakery as his regular job. In the kitchen there was a huge sink, used to wash up all the big mixing bowls and other utensils used in the bakery.

One day this sink got stopped up, so Mr. Grube took the drain pipe off of the bottom of the sink and was catching the water out of the sink in a five gallon bucket. Billy Ed was watching the bucket fill up, and worried, he finally yelled at Mr. Grube that the bucket was getting full and asked, "What do you want me to do with it?" Mr. Grube told him to pour it back into the sink, so

Billy Ed picked up the bucket and poured the water back into the sink as he had been instructed. Everyone in the bakery just broke up laughing, and only then did Billy Ed realize what he had done and that Pap had only been teasing.

While we laughed, he just turned away with that familiar big sheepish grin on his face. We couldn't resist telling him, "Billy Ed, it sure would take a long time to empty that sink at that rate!" We had lots of good times and many fond memories from our time spent in the bakery.

TOP OF THE HILL

Located at the corner of Rupard was what we called "Top of the Hill." Underneath a large tree there were several benches, where we boys would gather to fellowship and have a good time. Of course, as boys are prone to do, a lot of our conversation was about the girls.

Some of them would have to pass by this popular gathering place on their way across the boys' side of the campus to their work place at the Teacherage. They were terrified to walk by this area because they knew we were watching them closely and commenting about them as they walked by. They were sure our comments were derogatory. I admit that we teased them, but sometimes our remarks were actually very complimentary.

We always enjoyed our time spent at this gathering place. We usually had a lot of friends with us and a few of our favorite dogs on hand.

Surely it was the barking of the dogs that scared the girls. We were really harmless.

GOOD TIMES

As I think back over the years I remember other good times that we had at Buckner. There were the rabbit hunts, the watermelon feasts that we had on the lawn, the yearly camps we went to at Lake Dallas, our annual trip to the Texas State Fair, our trips on the big boat on White Rock Lake, all our swimming at Bull Pond and Rock-bottom. Of course we had lots of brothers and sisters to enjoy these things with us. That made up for a lot of things lacking in our lives.

Harold Campbell, '50

THE FAMILY

There is something unique about the Buckner Family in that wherever you meet a Buckner Ex, you meet a brother or sister. Being from Buckner and meeting someone else who is also from there makes me understand the meaning of the words in the book of Proverbs, "A good friend sticketh closer than a brother."

In 1960 I had been working for seven years for Reynolds Metals Company of Gregory, Texas, just north of Corpus Christi. One night a tall guard who worked at the plant showed up at the warehouse window and said, "I'm looking for Harold Campbell."

I said, "That's me."

He stuck out his hand and said, "I'm Carol Ford. I understand you were raised at Buckner."

I said, "Yes."

He said he was too, and then we began to discuss times of the past. He had left the Home in 1937, and I didn't go there until 1943. After he retired, he moved near Bastrop, and though I had been all over the country, I had finally landed in Bangs. At Reynolds they called him "Model T" after the Model T Ford.

After leaving Reynolds Metals Company, I taught school and attended many conferences in South Texas, and never went to any of them but what I made arrangements to go by and see Model T. His wife Ruby Longacre (Ford) would not allow him to smoke in the house, so he'd lead me to his shed out back where he would reach up

over the door, get down his pipe and light it. There we would sit and share times gone by as well as the present. He was like a brother because we were both from Buckner.

Again in 1997, I experienced some serious health difficulties which made me feel I needed counseling just to get through them. I contacted a man in Brownwood, Texas, and through our contact I invited him and his wife to our place on Lake Brownwood for hamburgers, fellowship and fishing. While he and I were outside solving the world's problems, our wives were in the trailer preparing food for the evening. Something brought up the subject of Buckner and my wife said, "That's where my husband was raised."

Ruth Robbins said, "That is where my husband was raised too." Lo, and behold, it was Bill Robbins who had left in 1931 before I was ever born, and yet at our meeting, we immediately felt that unique bond that comes when two Buckner Exes meet, regardless of when they went there or when they left.

At Homecoming I find that same feeling of oneness and closeness each time I meet another Buckner Ex. It is a unique experience, and I'm not sure there are many others which can compare with it.

MOVING TO BUCKNER

My family moved to Buckner in January 1943. I remember the welcome that I got when we moved to the main campus.

James Cutshall and Tommy McWhorter had more marbles than I had ever seen in my life. They were good at playing marbles and usually won every marble anyone would play them for. I don't know why, but on the day we arrived on campus, they gave me about a hundred marbles each. And I'm sure that it wasn't two days before they had every one of them back. They both would have done well in Las Vegas because they could let it out and then win it back.

When you had a birthday, if you were in Freeland Dorm, it was widely announced that your birthday was a certain day, and all the kids would wait outside Manna Hall, grab you and give you a good whipping. One year I remember Billy Ed Taylor had him a little short lead pipe, and on his birthday he would just look at us and hit that pipe in the palm of his left hand. When he came out of the dining hall that day not a soul touched him. There were no whippings for him that day.

Mrs. Day was commander-in-chief of second floor of Freeland in 1943. She was a good matron; we just thought she was too strict, but then what kid didn't think the matrons were too strict? At night she would have us all sit in the room across the hall from her room, and she would read us stories from Peter Pan. She could do a good job of reading. Then she would read a scripture, after which each boy had the opportunity to pray. She would close with her prayer and send us off to bed. That is where I learned to pray.

She would always send us off to bed with the admonition of no talking. And many a time she would step out in the hall and say, "All right you boys hush that talking." There were about twenty-five of us, and I was in a room on the other end of the hall from her. I don't know if anyone was really talking or not because I never did hear anything, and yet the message would keep coming to "stop that talking!" Then after about four warnings, she would step out in the hall and say, "Whoever is doing that talking, step out here in the hall." After about four of those commands and a no show, she would say, "All right everyone of you get up out your bed and come out here in the hall."

Sleepy-eyed, everyone would come out into the hall and again she would say, "Whoever was doing that talking, confess." Then it was, "You're all going to sit here until someone confesses." After a long time she would say, "Get you a partner and you are going to have to whip each other. If you don't do a good job, I will take over and whip you."

Sure it hurt, but before we were finished, everyone was laughing at the antics and gyrations that each recipient of the lashes would do as the rubber hose approached the point of emphasis on the posterior of his partner. It became hilarious. Then we were finally off to bed for a good night's sleep. She was usually laughing too in the end.

SMOKING AND GOING TO THE MOVIE

I have many memories of days at Buckner. On the northeast corner of the second floor of Rupard was a room that was ideal for smoking. We had windows on the north and windows on the east. If the wind was out of the north, we could raise a north window and an east window, and the draft out the east window would suck the smoke right out the window. At noon all who smoked would head to that room to smoke before dinner, thinking that the meal would take the smoke odor off our breath. The teachers passed by those windows on their way to the Teacherage to eat, and I'm sure they knew what was going on, or else they would have called the fire department because of the amount of smoke that was going out that window. However, never once did they tell on us. At night we did the same thing, and sometimes there were times that room was so filled with smoke that Mrs. Mabry would knock on the door and all cigarettes would go under the bed. She would say, "Now you boys go to your room. It is late."

Seeing all the smoke she would say, "I did not actually catch you smoking so I can't report it." As she left the room, we would listen to see if she went to her room and then we would all get our cigarettes out, finish smoking them and move off to bed.

Wallace Hall did not teach me how to smoke; however, in that smoky atmosphere by candlelight, he taught me how to play chess, a game I still enjoy to this day. He had a table about 18 inches square, and he would put a candle on one corner so that we could see. Obert Long, who was also there, always had money, so they always had cigarettes. I lived on the other end of Rupard (south end) and Uncle Thompson would make me make coffee for him and anyone else who wanted it. We'd take a gallon jug, put it in one sink and run hot water on it, then take an undershirt and put it down in the mouth of the jug. Afterwards I would put a cup of coffee grounds in and then slowly pour hot water over them. When the water ran through the grounds, we had a gallon of coffee. That is when I learned to drink coffee. I didn't really care for it, but I said that if I had to make it, I was gonna learn to like it. Too bad they didn't know what decaf was then; I think it would have been easier to learn on. Those who smoked and drank coffee managed to have their coffee and cigarettes at night even though both were strictly prohibited.

Every Saturday we could get a pass and go to the movie. We were allowed to go to downtown Dallas once a month, but we could go to Urbandale every week-end. If we wanted to go to town more than once in a month, we would just get a pass to Urbandale and catch a bus to town. The cost of the movie was 11 cents when we were under nine years of age and 35 cents for those ten years and older. Someone was always short a few coins having enough to get in to the movies. Once Red Stephens told some boy, "Just go around to everybody and tell them, 'I sure would like to go to the movie but I just lack a nickel having enough.' They will each give you one and in a little while you will have enough to go."

That kid did as told and eventually came back to Red. When Red asked him how he was doing, he said, "Great, but I just 'like' a nickel having enough." Red just reached in his pocket and gave him another nickel.

A SERMON BROTHER HAL PREACHED IN MY YOUNGER DAYS

I was working on the Home Farm, and one Saturday out of the month we had to haul off the glass that was in 55 gallon barrels at the commissary. My two helpers and I had the wagon loaded and were headed to the woods north of the dairy where we always dumped the glass. As we were riding along the highway, a nice car pulled alongside and Brother Hal leaned over and asked, "Is Harold Campbell there?"

I said, "Yes, I'm Harold Campbell."

"Get in the car."

I got in and as we drove along, he asked, "Harold can you tell me what a bully is?"

"I guess it is some big guy who beats up on a little one."

He then asked, "How much do you weigh?"

"About 185 pounds."

"Would you say that a 185 pound boy beating up on a 65 pound boy would be a bully?"

How could I say anything but, "Yes sir," after the definition I had given him?

At this point he took me to the waiting area where Frankie D. Parks' switchboard was and told me to sit there. I sat there for about an hour, and when the whistle blew for lunch, he told me to go on to dinner.

I thought that was the end of it until Sunday morning when the topic for the morning church service was "A Bully."

It was about two years later when he helped me prepare the first sermon I ever preached and the longest one—ten minutes. We never had any more words, but I certainly learned a lesson from that encounter and his sermon. I wish I could remember the text that Brother Hal used that day. I'd like now to check him out scripturally.

DISCOVERING MY ROOTS

When I finished Seminary in 1971, I was called to a church in Sacramento, California, a small church which had to have Home Mission Board approval and financial support. In order to get the financial support, I had to write a brief life sketch and in so doing I found out some things I had never given thought to; some of which are as follows:

My father died in 1938 leaving my mother with seven children. Early on she decided that she was going to raise us, and she saw to it we went to church every Sunday morning when there was a ride to the nearest community church, four miles away.

Every Sunday morning she would have us dressed and ready to go, believing that someone would be there to pick us up and there always was. Sometimes she would stay home because of a sick one. The two younger ones were one and three years of age when Dad died. My mother wrote to Buckner, and asked if she could put us there while she worked in the defense plants, jobs the women did then because the men had gone to war. Buckner responded with a no, but said, "If you will come and work here, you can come and bring your children." She did this on January 30, 1943.

We did not have much, materially speaking, as a family, but we had much—much more as a family than I had ever realized before. When we arrived and were placed in the Receiving Home in the middle of that field just north of the campus, that was the loneliest time of my life because Mom was not there. I recall it must have been like being a prisoner in a jail cell, looking out the window and realizing he could not get out. As I looked across the highways at the campus each day, I longed for the time I could go over there. The Horsleys were at the Receiving Home when we arrived. They were about ready to move to the main campus, and it was really rough when they left.

As all Buckner kids know, we were drilled in Christian Education, but we made that choice for Our Lord and Savior on our own, under the influence of the Holy Spirit. It was there in the Buckner Chapel that I was saved on October 30, 1943. That began a long walk of faith that has helped me survive some difficult situations; one was a daughter's death when she was only four and a half years old. That same year, 1966-67, I was diagnosed with terminal cancer and was given two years to live. After radiation treatment, the cancer (bone cancer) was arrested.

You do not know pain until you know bone cancer, and it hurts twice as bad when you're lying down as it does standing up. I must tell you that I had faith in the Lord, but when the doctor said, "Mr. Campbell it looks 100 percent fatal," it was like being hit in the pit of the stomach. It knocked the breath out of me. When he told me I had two years to live, I spent about two weeks trying to figure out what to do. After several radiation treatments, I was digging up a tree stump in our front yard and I prayed, "Lord I'm not dead yet; help me to live till I die."

I have never looked back. But I want you to know that what kept me going was that walk of faith in my Lord which began in 1943. Now I would be quick to say that there are some things worse than cancer, but it was from here that I went on to Seminary to prepare for the ministry of the gospel. I have never had a reoccurrence of the cancer, but there have been times I thought I did and rushed in to have it checked out. When they did the radiation, I prayed that it would kill every cancer cell. So far, after thirty-two years, God has faithfully kept me well.

Anyway these are the things I learned from writing my life sketch: Six of us seven children went to Buckner. Five finished high school. Of the five finishing high school there, three hold masters' degrees and the two others have at least two years of college. That would not have even been a remote possibility had we remained in the environment we were in before we come to Buckner. Two are ministers of the gospel; one is an active layman today. All are Christians because of Buckner.

I'm sure there is much more that can be said about this. I did not know of one person at Buckner who did not know Christ as Savior. None of us became criminals. There were no out of wedlock children. I attribute this to the Christian education we received and to the influence of the Christian employees who worked with us.

Helen (Swift) Curda, '50

ADVENTURES

Each child received just so many pairs of shoes per year; if the shoes wore out before the allotted time to receive new ones, we just had to make the best of it, and we often did in our own unique Buckner fashion. Holes always appeared in the soles of those well-made shoes; we must have shuffled a great deal for such sturdy shoes to wear out so quickly. We always managed to find stiff cardboard to poke down into the bottom of the shoe, but sometimes, the entire sole came loose from the rest of the shoe.

We just flopped down the sidewalk—flop, flop, flop. Most of us were skilled in flipping the shoe forward and then bringing it down quickly so that the sole landed flat on the sidewalk. Masking tape probably hadn't been invented then, for I don't recall we had access to tape or to string with which to secure the offending part. Perhaps we were denied access to such means of repair in order to teach us a valuable lesson in conservation. Oh, we were forever learning lessons! Flopping down the sidewalk wasn't too bad if we walked; it was when we found ourselves in danger of being late to school that we forgot and ran. It was then that we incurred the spite of the little shoe demons. Instead of going flop, flop, flop as in walking; running consisted of skippity, skippity, flop. It was generally on the third skippity flop that our luck ran out, and we found ourselves tripped up. Somehow the sole failed to flop back into place; probably, in our haste, we lost our rhythm, and rhythm was so very crucial in negotiating the "loose sole shuffle." I always favored my knees and elbows, but they often got skinned in the shuffle. Buckner kids sported perpetually skinned elbows and knees, a real badge of courage. Make no mistake—it took real courage to be a Buckner kid, especially when the shoe demons had it in for you!

Skating was probably pretty rough on our shoes. Everyone skated. If one didn't own a pair of skates, he borrowed a pair when possible. I suppose that skates became the most desirable objective of every girl on the campus. One Christmas, Mother gave all three of us girls a pair of skates! How terribly excited we were! I can't ever recall if we thanked her properly before flying out the door, racing back to the dorm to show off our presents and then back outside to find out if they were as fast as the next girl's skates. We skated the entire day with only a lunch break and minimum pit stops. By the time we went inside that evening, we possessed enormous blisters on our feet, but they were happy blisters. What were a few blisters compared to the delight and euphoria we experienced as we whizzed over the sidewalks?

As we grew older, we went camping in the local woods during the summer months, and one of the fondest memories was of climbing trees to pick wild mustang grapes. They were so sour that we were unable to eat them without puckering up; however, we Curda girls always came home with a pillowcase full of grapes to give to mother. She turned them into jelly, and when there was nothing else to snack on, she brought out the jelly and bread. There was nothing more delicious to ever-hungry kids. Throughout the years I conjured up that smell of grape jelly cooking.

When the State Fair of Texas rolled around, all we kids were turned out of school to help pick cotton in various neighboring fields. It made no difference whether we wanted to do so or not. In this manner, each individual earned his spending money for the fair, according to the amount of cotton he picked or didn't pick. I was never much of a cotton picker, for I never forgot the pain in the back from bending over a row of cotton, row after row after row. It was always more painful the second day. Anyone pulling cotton and leaving a messy row had to go back over the row and clean it up. The superintendent was sitting upon a horse, supervising the clean-up job. It may have been such experiences that taught us to do things right the first time. I suppose that good habits were just as easy to form as bad ones.

Sometimes, for punishment, we worked in the yard, pulling weeds, spading and raking. I never recalled that we had a particular yard job assignment as such, but we surely must have been expected to complete a specific project. (Boys usually did yardwork and most other outside assigned jobs.) Once I worked on the other end of a spade, and surprisingly enough, I rather enjoyed it. Working in the yard was a matter of my enthusiasm holding up until my back got used to it. One night I went to bed with large blisters on the palms of my hands, and in the course of time, they became infected. I required hospital

treatment, but I never regretted those blisters. No sir! I always imagined that the matron requiring me to do the yard work had a guilty conscience for keeping me at the chore so long. I rather suspected that Mother, who really never defended us too much, probably spoke her mind about working a young girl the entire day. Creating confrontations between adults gave such a stimulating sense of power, and we delighted in sniggering over such accomplishments. We had absolutely no shame at all!

GLORY BE! I'M SIXTY-THREE

How strange and unsettling to awaken one morning with an uncanny insight I never dreamed to possess, the realization that I am truly growing older. Oh, I always knew my age in years, for at each birthday there was chatty person, more than willing and even determined to remind me, in exact years, just in case I conveniently forgot. I do not think we Buckner kids really paid much attention to age unless it was associated with another unfortunate individual, and I seriously doubt that we held a healthy and proper respect for such vulnerable citizens. I suppose we always expected to remain the same in appearance and in abilities. I assure you that the shock was acute when I finally realized that the inevitable had come to me in person and all but introduced itself.

There were the tell-tale signs with my advancing years, but as long as I could still motivate, under my own power, to continue doing the many and varied things I wanted and loved doing, to think and to determine situations in my own particular style, I was satisfied and confident that life was ever so much more desirable with the advancement of years. True, in the case of a woman, her hairdresser worked over-time, reminding her that unless she got a color job soon, she may as well join the ranks of other sweet little old ladies who had already given up on their appearances as being too much bother. Each morning my mirror reflected the wrinkles and the sagging features, but as though they were some honored badge of merit, I assured myself that I had earned every wrinkle, that they were dignified and respectable wrinkles.

Oh, the girth of my mid-section expanded to such a degree that I sadly reflected the necessity of giving up my beloved soft drinks, particularly

Cherry Pepsi. A recent trip to Colorado with the kids delivered another surprise, a personal delivery, if you please. Being forced to move slowly and deliberately at the 14,000 feet elevation while panning for gold was an exercise in regret and frustration, for standing up quickly could be a "heady" experience. Getting myself into condition beforehand would have been a wise decision.

At my advanced age, I believe I can already see into the future, dim though it be. I know that I shall meet the day with regret when I can no longer function on my own, when I shall need someone younger to do for me and to make decisions in my behalf.

Being a Buckner kid, I hope I can still contrive to make the best of a bad situation, to continue enjoying life to its fullest, for life at this time is such a tantalizing gift. There is so much catch-up to make up, so much still to investigate, so much more to experience, and ultimately, so much more to enjoy in order to store up memories. An old saying goes: "The spirit is willing, but the flesh is weak." Wouldn't it be amusing to prove that saying a "hoot?"

Juanita "Jerre" (Simmons) Graves, '50

FORTIETH REUNION, 1990

I want to ride with you again, Class of '50, for
    miles and miles
In a full bus or cattle truck,
And sing every song from our past
Until I am hoarse from the strain
Of pleasure and melody of adult voices
Blended with the memories of younger echoes.

I want to eat peanut butter and "zip"
Slathered on pieces of bread made by the boys in
    the bakery,
And apples furtively cooked on steaming radia-
    tors overnight,
And little pies from Mr. Grube's special recipe,
And Miss Mamie's potato salad that I can never
    duplicate.
I also want to recall singing the "The Soup Song"
    once a week,
And commiserate with you because I smell that
    same soup
Whenever I hear the strains of "On Jordan's
    Stormy Banks I Stand."
Do your eyes tear up the same as mine; do you
    remember me

As I do you as those notes dance across years of
    faces and events?

I want to remember short haircuts, even for the
    girls.

I want to remember, with you, Christmas Strings
With oranges and apples and nuts
And some toys,
And the unfamiliar odor of sizing in new dresses
    and shirts
Brought by Santa, especially wrapped and
    labeled for us.

I want to remember the Manna Hall and mop-
    ping and sweeping,
Setting tables and washing dishes,
Killing flies and collecting them on dustpans for
    inspection
To prove that we had served our punishment
    time.

I want to save candles to read in the shower after
    lights.
And meet my boyfriend in the parlor on Sunday
    nights
Hoping that the electricity will fail
So that he can steal a kiss before
The power failure is over.
I will, of course, be wearing the dress that Eva
    Nell
Wore the first time Bobby kissed her,
And Peggy also wore it and it worked for her and
    Bobbi Nell too;
In fact, it went the length of our entire hall
And almost everyone who has worn it has been
    kissed in it,
So I am expecting magic for me.

I want a chance to listen to Mrs. Ratcliff's radio
While the Hit Parade is on,
And climb that tree in back of Hunt Hall
With all my friends dangling from a branch be-
    side me.

I want to see Mrs. Bearden
And Mrs. Knot.

I want to swim, for once, on Tuesdays and
    Thursdays
With a pool full of boys!

I want to hold hands with someone adventurous
And weave my way over fences and bushes
To go to that grocery store down the road,
Or to a movie in Urbandale
And find Miss Willie with her aged limbs
Hanging, trying to get over the fence
To catch us "running off" again!

I want to remember the "boys' side" and the
    "girls' side"
Of a campus that is split by gender

And a church sanctuary with the same division,
And the boys on the benches at the "top of the hill"
Passing judgment on everything that moved.

Was it I who loved to play Knocking on Doors at parties,
And attending the State Fair,
And catching the city bus to go into Dallas for a day?

I want to go to a blue and gold football game
Where my heart is in my throat every time anyone is tackled
Because the field is full of boys I love and am bonded to
In some love feast of communal identification
Whose power I can feel but not understand completely, even now.

I want to go to school and find Mr. Dickey,
Miss McCorkle,
Miss Coleman,
And Miss Sikes
And Miss Isbel
I want to hear Miss Effie Watkins say "prolly,"
Miss McCullough talk math, Miss Rohm make speeches
And Jean Hack talk about LITERATURE.

I want to show my poetry to Miss Ruth Rouse
And do shorthand and typing for Mabel Wells.
I want to get another chance to listen (this time!)
To a sermon from Brother Hal
Or Robert Cooke Buckner,
And clean that statue of Father Buckner
From the marks of birds and weather and time.

I even want to recall spankings, sitting on the wall,
And pulling weeds on the front lawns,
And drinking Sal Hepatica in large glasses
As a special punishment for talking after lights!
How could we not talk after lights in a room full of girls?

I want to remember Mrs. McKinney and the laundry
And ironing, ironing, ironing,
Then stumbling down those iron steps, curling in tiny circles,
With threateningly empty spaces between each tread
Which might trip some unwary girl, loaded down
With shirts and dresses and sheets folded for delivery.

I want to remember snow storms that woke us early
Enough to play before the whistle blew for breakfast,

And ice storms that brought, not just icicles, delicious on the tongue,
But also a truck loaded with a treat of free cokes
Because all the water pipes were frozen and we had nothing to drink.

I want to sing at the wedding of dear Mr. and Mrs. Hyden.
(Nobody else ever invited me to sing at a wedding!)

I want to see one of those lovely hats perched atop
The head of Mrs. Taylor.
And hear Dean Taylor talk about "his boys."

I want to go again to The Woods and camping
And frolicking with friends across fences
Guarded by Daddy Buck.
I want to take my turn riding Freckles
And sit around the camp fire telling tall tales
And sleep on quilts on the bare ground.

I want to wait until night
And climb out a window in Buhrman Hall and down a tree
To meet my own true love of the moment
In a stolen adventure that could lead to disaster.

I want to sing again in Miss Jo's girls' choir,
And play the piano for Mrs. Roberts.

I want to giggle for hours
And say "pigeye,"
And "I claim first,"
And "Yum, Yum, Fiddle Diddle Dum"
With people who will understand my eccentricity.

I want to walk every inch of the old campus,
Even the boys' side,
Right through to the days and months
And years of our youth!

MEMORIES

It was a dramatic moment for me when I realized that Father Buckner's birth year was 1833, for I had been born in 1933. The recognition that one hundred years before I was born, God had been preparing a man with the energy, ability and sense of mission, to provide a place of safety and security for my family even before we needed one, gave me assurance that I could and should tell my story to all who would listen.

In 1943 after seeing an article about the deaths of my parents and a picture of my brothers, sisters and me on the front page of the *Dallas Times Herald,* Brother Hal came that very same day to my grandmother's small apartment and offered to take all five of us children to Buckner to live. He promised her that she would not regret such a decision and that Buckner would give all of us the opportunity for a stable, Christian life.

His act changed our lives forever. I moved from a two-room apartment, where we five children had slept on pallets of quilts on the floor, to the third story of a red brick dorm, Crouch Hall, with about twenty-five other girls my age and grade. I didn't know it then, but I would be with these same girls for the next seven years until our graduation. They would become my family.

At Buckner we had our own church and school on a large campus, split down the middle by gender. The Manna Hall, the church, the school and a statue of Father Buckner were in the hub of the wheel. On one side were the boys' dorms and on the other, the girls' dorms. Ideally for the administration, the girls would stay on their side and the boys on theirs, meeting only for church and school activities. Tall fences and thick shrubs surrounded the entire campus. The gates to the entrance were protected by a guard, and we did not leave, except for three days in the summer and then only if a family member came for us. All that we needed was there within those walls.

Whistles blew to signal the scheduled activities for each day. We lined up for a trip to Manna Hall to eat, tallest first; smallest last, and marched into the dining room three times every day. We each had a job assigned us to clean our dormitories, and when we grew older, to iron for the campus, serve food, wash dishes, mop floors and help in the kitchen.

This last duty was not an attractive one; for the kitchen girls had to rise at 4:30 A.M., peel three large washtubs of potatoes, two dishpans of carrots and one of onions for each day. Also we had to help clean up the kitchen, an enormous and very hot task. My least favorite chore in the kitchen was cleaning the oatmeal pot. It was much taller and rounder than I, and deep enough to fall into. My only possible approach to the job was to climb up a stepladder of about four steps, then place my hands into the water to scrape the sides of the aluminum pot. I then had to flush the water and detritus out by an opening in the bottom and rinse it with fresh water which I carried from a sink.

Surely oatmeal has been improved since then, for I remember the slimy soup that the soaking water produced. I finally learned to like oatmeal, but in those early days it took a strong stomach to be a kitchen girl.

Our menus did not differ from week to week. We knew what we would eat for breakfast, lunch and dinner every Monday of our lives and every Tuesday, Wednesday, Thursday, Friday, Saturday, and Sunday. We did not complain about that. In fact, it was only later that I, personally, recognized the structure of the daily food choice.

We loved the Saturday night meal that promised an apple and peanut butter. We ate the peanut butter mixed with syrup on bread and saved those apples. Then when we got back to our buildings, we furtively set the apples on the radiators to roast. We thought we kept it a secret from our matron, but now that I've roasted apples in my own kitchen, I'm sure those matrons turned a blind eye, for they surely detected the permeating odor of apples baking everywhere. Our favorite day was Sunday lunch, chopped roast beef and a square of vanilla sheet cake with white frosting, served along with a small bowl of canned peaches! Thursday night was pie night; Mr. Grube and his bakery boys made wonderful pies. Friday was soup night—always before every meal an older girl or boy played the piano as we marched to our places on the benches at the tables, a matron said a prayer and we sang a hymn, selected by the students. Every Friday we sang "On Jordan's Stormy Banks I Stand," and to this day when the strains of that song's melody come to my ears or even waft across my mind, I can still smell the aroma of that weekly soup.

By today's standard our punishments sound very cruel. We were paddled, yes, sometimes because we were never quiet at night—all lights went out at 9:00 P.M. every night. After we got into high school, we no longer had to have our hair bobbed and trimmed every two weeks. So, we set our hair after lights—rolled it with bobby pins stuck onto curls, formed by wrapping strands of our hair around a pencil. Even when we were seventeen, those bouncing Shirley Temple curls were our models. Older girls could go to Mrs. Bird's Beauty Shop in Dallas for a free perm if we wanted to. How gracious of that lady to allow us such a benevolence!

One matron was named Mrs. Knot. I am embarrassed to admit we secretly called her "Miz Snot!" She was responsible for getting us quietly to sleep each night at nine. We were from three to six girls in every room and life seemed to be one slumber party after another. Now I can imagine the frustration of trying to get twenty-five girls quiet every night, but I remember also the impulse then to talk. One night Mrs. Knot spanked us, made us sit on the wall, assigned us to pull weeds from the lawn the next day and finally made us drink Sal Hepatica. (It tasted horrible and upset the innards!) We still could not stop talking and giggling, so she finally bedded us down to sleep in bath tubs far away from each other, no pillows, no quilts. That must have worked because I don't remember any other punishments that night.

It is true that we all feared the wrath of Miss Mamie. Her punishments were swift, sharp and imaginative. One of her famous punishments was killing flies. Yes. We had to report to her after school and kill flies. We were given a dustpan and a flyswatter to clear the Manna Hall from the blight of flies. Naturally our campus was not air conditioned in our years there, so the windows were almost always open on hot days and the doors were always held ajar for the multitude of boys and girls going in and out three times a day. I was very near sighted and it was a long time before anyone recognized my disability. We all just thought I was simply inept in lots of physical areas. For example, I could not see well enough to find a fly to swat. So my dear friends would swat multitudes of flies, and when we could hide behind one of the columns without Miss Mamie's seeing us, they would transfer a goodly number of flies from their hoard to my dustpan. Sometimes even tediously cutting them into to share a paltry harvest. Naturally I'll love until I die, those girls who so generously shared the "fruits" of their labors with me so that I wouldn't feel Miss Mamie's hand on my cheeks. "Greater love hath no man . . . nor orphan girl!"

In Miss Mamie's favor, I have to admit that she taught me to clean. That is one thing I can do to the max! I must give her credit for setting those high standards even if my memories of her are of a very stern and unyielding tartar. However, she was in charge of feeding seven or eight hundred kids and at least two hundred adult helpers three times a day, every day. What a job!

Since we were a campus physically divided by gender, even in church there was a boys' side and a girls' side. We did have Training Union together Sunday evenings and could sit together in school. However, in most of the classrooms we

girls still sat in clumps on our own side of the room.

When we were sophomores, we could have dates after evening church, which we called "Vespers." Girls and boys could walk home from church at night together to go sit for one hour in the parlor of the senior girls' dorm. We sat on folding chairs arranged in a circle around the room, and Mrs. Hardy, our matron, side by side with Mrs. Brady, Dean of Girls, sat with us, reading their newspapers upside down! Eventually the boys devised a plan to have a moment of darkness together in that parlor. Since we had a power plant on the campus with switches that turned off all the lights, the boys agreed to take turns staying home, climbing over the fence into the power plant and turning off the lights. It worked for awhile, but finally the chaperones caught on and began bringing flashlights for any power failures that threatened the decorum of the evening.

My first kiss, a very chaste peck on the check, was a disaster. After a basketball game in the gym, Herman Mangum pulled me behind a thick cedar bush just long enough to mark a memorable moment. My matron saw it or someone reported it—we orphans never told on each other so she must have seen it. When we got home, she called me into her room and told me about boys—in such embarrassed and allegorical terms that I was reasonably sure I was pregnant because, according to her, it was even dangerous to sit in a chair where a boy had just sat. Very puzzling to me.

She told me that she had always loved to look at me in the choir in church and thought I was pretty and a good girl, but that now I was a rose whose leaves had been crushed and that the damage could never be completely restored. I am sure she meant well, but I misunderstood her completely. After time passed and no baby appeared, I finally forgot to worry about it. However, it was some time before I was willing to get involved in such hanky-panky again.

According to stories we hear, the boys—though not allowed to—had pets. There were "campus dogs." But the boys wandered farther afield than we girls were ever allowed to do. Hence, I had no significant relationship with the lower species, unless you count that close relationship that Miss Mamie encouraged with flies. However, the love gift that our boyfriends honored us with (sort of like a friendship ring might be given today!) was a captured flying squirrel.

Herman brought me many. Because he "liked me." We kept the squirrels in our shoe drawers, a closet shelf with small holes to allow for the shoes to air out. We used those holes to get air in for our pets. Poor animals. I see now it was cruelty. We brought them food and water, even played with them as if they were dolls or dogs, but I imagine they got away as quickly as possible. There were always doors open and confusion in progress, so escape must have been easy; consequently, we needed new pets often.

As we grew older, punishments were sometimes changed—spankings still, but demerits, pulling weeds in the yard, or no Saturday night movie were added. We usually saw movies on Saturday night in the school auditorium. However they were always censored. Someone blocked any embraces, kissing, smoking, etc. We developed terrific imaginations, so the damage was done anyway. Eventually I realized that if it were true, as we seemed to have been taught, that God allowed no one to go to heaven who smoked, danced, drank, cursed, kissed, stole, lied, gossiped etc., then the only safe way to get to heaven was to die before we left Buckner where our behavior was rigorously monitored. I had already read enough books and heard from enough graduated Buckner friends to know that outside the Buckner walls few people managed on a daily basis to avoid every one of these

Some jobs were fun. I can still hear us laughing as we polished floors. Every dorm had a formal parlor with lovely wooden floors. Periodically, on our knees, we waxed those floors with old rags, and after the wax was all dried, we pulled each other on old quilts to polish the floors to a mirror shine! Two of us would lie down on one end of a quilt while two others would grab the other end and run, pulling us from one wall of a room to another, thus putting a great shine on the waxed floors. We took turns "riding the waves" as we called it and "handling the boat" on our sea of wax. We knew nothing of surfing or skiing, but I see now that we had invented a new sport of Olympic proportions to us. Some ski on snow, some on water, but we skied on wax!

Another fun job was cleaning Father Buckner's statue. We loved to be selected to do that. Unfortunately the birds—irreverent creatures—also loved landing on that statue and deposited their gifts liberally as they flew over, so frequently we cleaned the statue for Sunday visi-

tors. Bon Ami was our all-purpose cleaner, and it worked well on that statue (as it did on windows, mirrors, tiles, tubs, floors, muddy shoes and brass door decorations). We were much in awe of Father Buckner, "the founder of our feasts." I have always thought that God must look a whole lot like him, but we controlled our awe enough to love cleaning the statue. Recognizing our irreverence, I admit it was mostly because that statue was smack in the middle of that campus and we, cleaning it, were very close to that forbidden boys' side of the campus. In fact, as we polished, we posed for anyone looking on. With intricate athletic moves, we practiced clinging and clambering as if we were high wire artists. Though ostensibly we were cleaning, we were actually showing off for any boys who might be in sight!

Buckner had a pool out by the gym and we loved swimming. Naturally we had separate boys' days and girls' days with absolutely no mixed bathing. Even today, I am very uncomfortable swimming on Tuesday, Thursdays and Saturdays. Those days were the boys' days in the water.

However, on Mondays, Wednesdays and Fridays, those same boys used to sneak under the stadium seats beside the pool to peek at our swim-suited bodies! For this infringement we broke our unwritten rule and tattled on the boys to any adult who was around. Such shrieking and shouting! We thought peeking was quite sinful. In looking back we seem almost fully clothed in our suits when they are contrasted to the shorts and halter sets and swim suits so popular today.

We were horrified at this intrusion on our swimming days, because we were inordinately modest. We had no real privacy, so we had devised methods to maintain our dignity. We could completely undress or dress under our gowns without "showing a thing," but our main ploy for maintaining modesty was simply to announce we were going to undress by warning, "See no evil!" We always turned our backs or simply closed our eyes until the undresser announced that looking was permitted again. I doubt any of us have grown up to be exhibitionists.

Reading was always my salvation. I read everything I could get my hands on. I have always loved the printed page. If I'm too tired to read, I simply relish caressing the page with my eyes or meandering through the paths that the white spaces leave between the words. My friends at Buckner did not like me to spend time reading.

They wanted me to play, so when the lights went out, I was always wanting to finish a book. If I had money to buy candles, I would sneak into the bathroom, hide in the shower, sit on the floor with a lighted candle beside me and read as long as there was candlelight. If I had no candle, I had to be more resourceful. I read by the light from the outside night light. I simply opened the window, even when it was cold, and leaned out to see to read by the lights on the side of the building. I had to be on the lookout for the night watchman so that I could finish in peace the latest Nancy Drew or Grace Livingston Hill or even eventually a play by Shakespeare.

Once I ran away with Wanda Faye Godsey when we were about thirteen. She was angry about something and asked me to go with her. I agreed and we planned carefully. First, we collected pepper in envelopes from the Manna Hall, so that we would have protection if anyone bothered us. We planned just to open our envelopes and throw pepper in any attacker's face. (I thought later when the Dallas Police began using pepper spray that Wanda and I were really ahead of our time.) We left just after lunch and walked all the way to downtown Dallas, to the streets where the huge watering trough for horses used to be, at the intersection of Jackson and Commerce. Sadly, that landmark of Dallas's early days is no longer in existence, but we were glad to see it and rinse our blistering faces in its cooling water.

We were pretty tired and decided to take a street car ride across the Trinity River to my grandmother's apartment in Oak Cliff. We asked one of the men standing at the horse trough where we could catch a street car. He must have thought we looked lost, for he asked if we had any money for street car fare. We had not planned for that. I'm not sure we even knew riding a street car would cost money. Fortunately, he gave us each a dime and showed us where to catch the right streetcar. We rode on those fearfully and deliciously open rail tracks across the Trinity River by the old Houston Street Bridge. (Alas, the entire tracks and all the cars are gone now.) It was as exciting to us as any roller coaster ride has been since then. Miraculously we found my grandmother's apartment. She was red-eyed with weeping for she thought I was lost forever. Brother Hal was there already, waiting to take us back.

We had had quite an adventure and thought it all well worth the subsequent punishment.

I also clandestinely left the campus again when I was older. Somehow we had heard about "The Outlaw," a famously touted wicked movie. I have no idea how we knew it was playing. We had no access to newspapers and listened to the radio only when one of our matrons allowed us to. Nevertheless, we wanted to see that movie, so we decided to go to the theater at Urbandale. We started out after lights out.

We had been told that Urbandale was just across the field from Buckner Boulevard. Unfortunately it was the rainy season and there had been a deluge earlier. Therefore we had to a cross a wet ploughed field. We were wearing jeans (strictly forbidden outside the dorms) and after a while we were so bogged down in the mud we could barely lift our feet. Eventually we had to bend down and with our hands pick up the bottoms of our jeans to help us raise our feet to make every step. This was hard work.

By the time we arrived at the theater, it was midnight and the movie crowd was heading for home. We were too late. We simply hadn't realized that the movie would not be showing continuously. We thought we had all night! Nor had we realized how long it would take us to get there. What a mess we must have looked. Greatly discouraged, we trudged back in the mud and falling rain. Part of the trip was down Forney Road. Then down Urban Avenue to Urbandale. Every car that passed seemed threatening to us. Perhaps it was a policeman or someone from Buckner searching for us. So when we saw headlights coming, we lay down beside the road until they had passed. Our trip was one mud bath after another. Somehow we managed to get in, clean up the mud and were not caught though we would have been severely punished if we had been. It was years later before I saw that movie—by then it seemed not so wicked, or even as interesting as we had thought it would be.

Later, as a mother of teenagers, I had a difficult time confessing to them about climbing out the window and down a tree limb to the ground and then walking around outside after lights with my boy friends. I certainly did not want my girls crawling out our upstairs window to meet anyone. But in all honesty, I did climb out that window of Buhrman to meet first, Herman Mangum; and later, David Reynolds. We held hands (very exciting to us) and probably kissed. There was no single torrid embrace—we were much too shy, but if we had been caught outside, we would have had to leave the home. Where would we have gone? Obviously, we had no other place to be than Buckner. How did we get the nerve to disobey the rules? We were like all teenagers. We could not yet think in terms of anticipating or accepting the consequences of our actions.

With so many girls around, we were best friends with everyone at one time or another, but I had two very close friends and roommates; Eva Nell Turner, the prettiest girl; and Peggy Grusendorf, the craziest. We were roommates during all my years there. All three of us at some time went out the window. One person always stayed in the room to open the window to let the others back in. No one had a clock or watch, but if we made Eva Nell drink lots of water just before bedtime, we trusted her bladder to wake her and us after the matron had gone to sleep. Sometimes we went out the upstairs window, catching a branch of a tree and climbing down to meet someone, just to walk freely around the campus in the dark. We had gone to bed every night since our arrival at the home at 9:00 P.M. The lights were always turned off all over the campus at that hour, so it seemed a real adventure to be out after lights.

No one who is a teenager today in a much more sophisticated world would believe how very innocent those few little jaunts were. There may have been a kiss or two exchanged, but not of the intensity that I see taking place daily in the corners of the halls of the high school where I have taught for years. In fact, in all the years I was at the Home, I never heard of any single orphan on that campus getting pregnant. Most of the time I was there, the intricacies of producing children remained a mystery.

At Buckner we were never alone, always in groups, such crowds! But, it was an individual teacher who encouraged me, persuaded me that I could go to college and teach someday. Surely her influence and that of so many other teachers whom I admired were responsible for my choice of profession.

Pinky Sikes, who eventually married Bill Gray and spent twenty-five years with him as Baptist missionaries to Mexico, literally arranged Howard Payne for Eva Nell and me. I was Pinky's laundry girl. She paid me for taking care of her laundry chores, and I was able to spend some time with her since I had a weekly delivery of finished laundry for her every week. (The Teacher-

age where she lived was on the boys' side of the campus!) I didn't realize at the time that her friends referred to me as "Pinky's orphan!" It was after we were both older, and I had been a bridesmaid in her wedding that I was introduced to some of her friends who said, "Oh, you're Pinky's orphan." I am glad I was. For many insecure teenagers, it takes some personal attention to give them a boost into their future. I was one of those. Until Pinky came along it never occurred to me that I could attend college.

She got the applications from Howard Payne for us, helped us fill them out, told us how to apply for jobs, and forced us to see Colonel Buckner to ask him if he would recommend us for college. What a terrifying thing! We didn't know then that if Buckner students were deemed good scholars, Baptist colleges would give them scholarships. Thanks to Pinky we both went to Howard Payne. I worked in the dining hall the entire four years, and with my scholarship and some help from my grandmother who was living meagerly on a pension from her oldest son, killed in WWII, I graduated with a teaching degree in Speech and English.

Eva Nell graduated also, then attended Southwestern Seminary, married Gene Kimler and went with him to Venezuela as Baptist missionaries.

I met my Bill in college—we were in a play together. We fell in love and were married on the day we graduated from college. After a stint in Korea with the army, he took a job as DJ at Radio Station KSKY in Dallas, and when he retired had been general manager for years.

I taught thirty-eight years, two of them at Buckner High School and thirty-six at Duncanville. My two years teaching at the Home gave me a unique perspective of our lives there. One thing I noticed right away. The people who had been my teachers had gotten younger while I had been away at college. They were very gracious to me as a new teacher and became my dear friends.

I loved my students at Buckner. They taught me how to be a teacher. I realize now that I tried in a single year to teach them everything I had learned in college. I had been reading about street theater in New York, and was excited at how actors simply went into the streets and did dramatic things, pretending they were real. Critics said this was the true test of acting abilities; if an actor could convince people in real life situations, then he was really gifted.

Fearlessly, I flung myself into testing this theory with my speech students. We set up several situations to test our abilities. Joann Cannon, the student council president (She later got her doctorate at Baylor and, according to what I hear, eventually helped train Peace Corps Volunteers!), staged a very noisy altercation with the principal, J. W. Perry, who had given us permission to conduct all our stunts. He and Joann had agreed to speak very loudly and confrontationally with each other. My intent was to have my students write about it all when it was over and compare recollections. However, Earl Ray Miles overheard their very spirited argument and stepped right in to defend Joann, frightening us all with his righteous indignation. He almost came to blows with the principal. I had to take him aside very quickly and let him in on our secret.

We had had Jody Summers plant stories about her despair over a fake boy friend who had written her a "dear John" letter earlier. On the day of our performances, she climbed out on the upstairs balcony of the high school and shouted that she was going to jump. What a sensation it all was. Everyone ran out of their classrooms, down the stairs and out the door to plead with her not to jump and to be on hand to watch in case she did. It was very realistic, and I blush to admit my lack of discretion in precipitating all of this.

Miss McCullough, that wonderful lady, sprained her ankle as she hurried outside to help Jody. I have never forgiven myself for that. The students were so distraught. One girl in the watching crowd fainted. We finally decided that to prevent a riot on the spot we had to do something. The principal, Mr. Perry, called everyone into the school auditorium where my speech class and I explained that we had only been performing. I think I probably deserved to be fired, but it was an exciting interruption to days that tended to be very uneventful on our campus. The students kept telling the stories of our adventures over and over, but I wanted to forget the whole thing as soon as possible.

Earlier I had bought my first rock music record, "Rock Around the Clock" with Bill Haley and the Comets. I took it to school to play for the students. I intended to have them write about it, explain their responses to it, but I realize now that its beat must have been very disturbing resounding through those very sedate halls. I doubt that anyone other than the students and I

agreed that that assignment fit the prevailing pedagogical theory.

In addition to these youthful improprieties, my class almost started a fire when we were studying *Macbeth*. I had them doing scenes from the play; they made wonderful wooden mock-ups of The Globe and loved doing scenes from Shakespeare. Some of them brought in a large black wash pot for the witches' scene and proceeded right there in the room to burn old rags soaked in oil to simulate fog. That simulation was successful, but produced a cloud of smoke that sneaked its way down the halls and into the doors of other classrooms. Near riot again. In retrospect, I am amazed that my fellow teachers allowed me to stay on.

My classmates and I used to make fun of Miss Effie Watkins, our General Business teacher, for mispronouncing words. We didn't realize then that she was hard of hearing and tended to drop some syllables. Nor did we realize that we would also very likely have that same problem some day. For example, she said "prolly" instead of "probably." Little mischiefs that we were, we imitated her pronunciations and entertained ourselves greatly, giggling behind her back. Poetic justice has won out though because I eventually found that I had said it so often, teasingly, that I had gotten into the habit of saying it her way. I deserve to be embarrassed by my mispronunciation, for she was a very sweet lady who truly loved the Buckner kids she taught, as I discovered when we became fellow teachers.

Every Buckner girl learned to sew in Home Economics Class. We had those pedal sewing machines in our classroom. We all made an apron, a housecoat, a baccalaureate suit, and a graduation dress. Eva Nell and I made twin blue suits with white cuffs and a pleated peplum at the waist, but we made individual statements with our graduation dresses, our *piece de resistance*. I don't remember Eva Nell's, but mine was a pale blue waffledy piqué, sleeveless dress with scallops at the waist and neck. I had no idea how difficult the insetting of those scallops would be, but Miss Ophelia Isbel, my teacher, helped me persevere until the dress looked at least wearable.

Not everyone was good at sewing. I do remember that on graduation day Miss Isbel was desperately whipping seams by hand, pinning hems and stitching zippers, trying to help slower students. She even penned in the sleeves just before the marching music began so one slow-sewing girl could walk down the aisle with her proud accomplishment straight-pinned on. How we held our breaths, fearing she would stick herself with one of those pins and ruin our graduation with her screams of pain.

I loved Miss Mabel Wells, my shorthand teacher. She was a member of the exclusive and famous "redhead club" of our day. She, Pinky and the Hydens were all red-haired and in spite of the stereotypical belief to the contrary, very even tempered. To this day I remember many of the loops and curlicues Miss Wells taught. When I am nervous or bored, I still practice making the shapes of shorthand words in the air with my rheumatic old fingers. Perhaps that movement will keep my fingers working and my mind clear into old age!

It was Miss Ruth Rouse, my typing teacher, who discovered I could write poetry and helped me find my way though rilling rhymes, galloping similes and tumultuous metaphors to many a finished product. She sent one of my poems to the *Baptist Standard*, which published it and made me feel quite equal to Shakespeare and Milton for a little while at least.

One reason I think we Buckner kids managed to deal with the tragedies in our lives was that we talked (incessantly) to each other and comforted each other. We told our stories over and over, not to a counselor, but to friends who understood us and had no urge to blame us or make us feel guilty. We were all wounded; therefore, we all seemed normal to us.

We were not kissed or hugged. We were very undemonstrative. This was probably a mandate, though I don't remember any one moment when it was decreed. I was encouraged not to hold hands with my brother if I met him walking across the campus. Some good Baptist, we were told, might see us and not knowing we were relatives, disapprove of our display of affection.

Together, we invented paper doll life stories from pictures in the Sears Catalog, moved our iron bedsteads into rows and played circus tightrope walking on their connected tubular roundnesses, stood in line to get endless inoculations; sometimes fainting and falling down as if a wind had passed by and flattened us. We sang the songs we loved—knowing every verse and every word— until our throats and our ears were mightily distressed; ate, slept, cried, laughed together for years, but I had no idea that I loved those people. Not even Peggy and Eva Nell or the two Wandas or Bobbi. Nor did I imagine there was anyone around who loved me. But as time has passed, I see that I did love, even Vernon who teased me mercilessly and called me "Henita" instead of Juanita for some unknown reason. I just knew then that nickname was derisive because of his expectantly teasing tone. But in spite of not recognizing it at the time, I loved every one of those I spent my youthful seasons with, even the boys on their forbidden side of the world.

Buckner did many things for me and I remain eternally grateful. I learned there that God is real and provides for His children. I can still hear Brother Hal and Colonel Buckner, even now, quoting that scripture in Psalms 68:5 and 6, that records, that *"A father to the fatherless . . . is God in His holy habitation. God setteth the solitary in families. . . ."* We were comforted by this scripture, for we believed that God was our father in a special way because we were orphans.

We also learned from the Buckner family and our teachers that we must serve Him. We didn't know what was happening then, but as time passed, we became a family of people who helped, comforted and protected each other in the world opening up to each of us. Learning to love and serve those around me was just one of the priceless gifts that Buckner gave me.

My brother, James; left the Home early and became a Marine. His joining was influenced by our older half brother, Frank, who was already in the service when we went to Buckner and a career Marine—one who at seventeen was present at Pearl Harbor when it was bombed. Later James worked for the National Geophysical Year for a while, but ultimately settled into a sort of wanderlust, seeing the world. He is now retired and living in Oklahoma City. My brother, John, joined the Navy and during the early Korean War years, served aboard an oil tanker. Eventually, he became a Hospital Corpsman aboard some of the first nuclear submarines. In fact, he and his crew took out the new subs for six month trial runs underwater. He married a girl from Boston, Barbara, and had two children, a girl and a boy. His son, Johnny, was just six (the age John was when we were orphaned) when John suffered a massive coronary and died. My sister, Barbara Ann, married and became the mother of four children. She died a few years ago of cancer. My youngest sister, Peggy, was adopted by a friend of one of my aunts when she was small. I consider us to be a success story for Buckner.

I still find it difficult to tell how we managed to arrive at Buckner where such kindness awaited us, but I allowed Steve Blow to write that story when I retired. He convinced me that my story would be inspiring to young people and since I have devoted my life to teenagers, I could not say no.

"TEACHER HASN'T BEEN A PRISONER OF CIRCUMSTANCES"

[Reprinted from an article by Steve Blow in the Dallas Morning News, *Sunday, May 19, 1996. Ed.]*

Her father was a raging alcoholic. The desperately poor family moved from one dump to another. And when she was 10, her father finally carried out his threats.

He shot her mother to death in front of all five children. And as they ran for their lives, he turned the gun on himself.

With no family to care for her, she was shipped off to a children's home. And you can probably guess the rest . . . .

Right, she became a wonderful, happy, well-adjusted wife, mother and teacher.

Hmmm. Not what you expected?

We tend to believe these days that childhood cements our destiny. Jerre Simmons stands as a one-woman refutation of that theory.

This week, the beloved teacher at Duncanville High School will retire.

"She is gracious, loving, supportive—all those things," colleague Frances Phillips said. "She doesn't know how wonderful she is."

"I call this my palindromatic moment," Mrs. Simmons joked. "I'm 63 years old, and I've been teaching here 36 years. It's the perfect time to retire."

Palindromatic? Can you tell she's an English teacher? As Mrs. Simmons tells her life story, it's hard to believe she's not reciting from some tragic Southern novel. "I was born in Honey Grove, Texas," she said. "My family had lost everything in the Depression. And I don't guess they had ever had much. My father was a tenant farmer, and we moved a lot. My father was also an alcoholic. The very worst kind—the kind who took his pay, got drunk and then came home and abused his wife and children. He tried many, many times to kill my mother."

Mrs. Simmons was the oldest of the five children. She remembers one drunken, murderous rage in particular. "My mother and I carried the

babies and ran into the cotton fields and hid. The cotton was high or he would have found us."

When the rage passed and they slunk back into the house, her father had smashed every dish and shredded every piece of clothing in the house.

Later, the family moved to a two room house in Dallas. She remembers that the children were washing their hair that day. "He came in with a gun. My mother's last words were, 'Oh, John. No, no . . . .'"

The children fled from the house. "As I ran, I heard another shot and remember thinking, 'She wasn't dead. He shot her again.'" It was the suicide shot.

I looked up the local newspapers for Aug. 5, 1943. Front-page photos show solemn-faced waifs. "Home Sought for Children After Slaying," said the *Dallas Times Herald* headline.

"I keep saying I'm going to write it in a book one day," Mrs. Simmons said. I already have the first line. I want to say: 'I grew up in a foreign country, just outside Dallas.'"

That was the Buckner Orphan's Home. "It was like its own country, with a fence around it," she said. Mrs. Simmons has come to love the place only in retrospect. "We felt like we were just in a holding pattern, that life would really begin only when we graduated and became like everyone else."

We expect children to be permanently scarred by such trauma. How could Ms. Simmons have emerged so whole?

"Well, I never have seen a counselor," she said with a laugh. "My people don't go to psychologists."

She certainly credits Buckner with providing safe haven. And she brags on husband Bill, "my rock," for 42 years, support.

But, fittingly, this celebrated English teacher says her primary salvation came through words. Just words.

She talks about the books that sent her imagination soaring from a lonely orphanage. She talks about the poetry of John Donne and Emily Dickinson that helped her fathom the human condition.

Most of all, she recalls the words of encouragement that people in her life provided at exactly the right moment. "It seems that at times when I faltered, there was always someone there," she said. "To me, it has always been words that have healed and comforted."

In her classroom, in her life, Mrs. Simmons has been a testament to the transcendent power of words. And now she's earned two of the sweetest: *Happy retirement.*

Ira Lee Henslee, '50

Jerre, I'm sorry for such a delay.
Just couldn't help it—I had to go play!
I gave lots of thought as I sat by the pond.
I knew in my heart that I should respond.

But what do you say about childhood adventures
When your mind is not clear and you've had to
add dentures?
It's always easy to reminisce over the times that
we had—
Most of them are good, but a few of them; sad.
But I'm looking forward to checking anew,
How classmates are doing and what they've been
through.
So just save me a place in old Manna Hall.
I'm looking forward to one thing—just having a ball!

FRANKIE D. PARKS

*[Written by Ira Lee Henslee for a tribute when he was just a
young teenager. Also read at the ceremony when she received
the Outstanding Employee Award. Ed.]*

I admire this person because she has a physical defect, and she is still cheerful. She goes
about her work in such a way that it seems she is
a part of it. She greets everyone with a smile. [She
was the receptionist and answered the phone in
the Home Office. Ed.] Not only is she a good
business woman, but she has a great sense of
humor. She can take hardships with a smile.

I also admire this person because she is a devout Christian. Although she is hindered by her
physical defect, she takes part in the work of her
church. She attends church each Sunday unless
something makes it impossible.

When I am inclined to worry about my troubles, I think of all the ways she is hindered and
what a cheerful person she is. After I think matters over, I am ashamed of my thoughts and
actions. I thank God for my health and resolve
not to worry about my small troubles. I try to do
my work in a way that will help others as she has
helped me with her pleasing personality.

Vernon Horsley, '50

THE DAIRY

During the late forties, I worked at the Dairy.
One summer day when we had finished our
chores of putting out feed and washing down the
sides of the buildings, we were ready to go home

for lunch, but we couldn't find Bobby Lee Bray.
All that work always made us hungry, and we just
assumed he had thumbed it home, so we left.

I guess we forgot about him. We went back
after lunch, and Dennis Tucker and Donald Johnson, who were chasing chickens, found Bobby Lee
on the ground, paralyzed from the waist down.
He had fallen off the silo that morning and been
unable to get anyone's attention. After a long
time of hospitalization, he died.

He had always been famous for being a dare-
devil and walking the top of the rim of the tall
silo. He was also noted for having a mischievous
grin on his face and hair cut in a flat top that
seemed to be forever growing taller. It grew, as he
had trained it, to stand straight up on his head, a
mighty crown of long locks, standing firmly upright without the help of mousse. The girls
thought him handsome and adventurous.

He was the first to die in our age group, and
his loss was very frightening to us. If Bobby Lee,
who loved to scale the heights wherever he found
them, could die, then so could we. (Perhaps it is
irreverent, but I can't help wondering now why
Dennis and Donald were chasing chickens. To
steal them?)

A HEROIC RESCUE

Some of us were swimming in Bull Pond one
summer, as we did as often as we could get a
chance. I swam out to the rock as all the others
were doing, but when I attempted to get back to
shore, I got scared and was going under!

Pat Green pulled me out. I will never forget
that day, my fear, and Pat Green's heroic rescue. I
attempted to find him or his brother, Martin,
after I had grown up and realized what a fearful
moment he saved me from, but I have had no
luck. They also had a sister named Gloria Faye.
I'd like to find someone in his family so that I
could say a proper, "Thank you!"

"RECALLING MEMORIES OF BUCKNER"

[Reprinted from an article by Steve Blow in the Dallas
Morning News, *October 14, 1990. Ed.]*

As we toured the sprawling grounds of the
Buckner Children's Home, Vernon Horsley was
recalling memories of "lights out."

In those days in the 1940s, bedtime was 9

P.M. But that didn't mean all the little rascals went right to sleep.

"Some of the boys had these little crystal radios," he said. "We would stay awake until 10:30 waiting to hear the *Hillbilly Hit Parade* or the wrestling matches with Wild Bill Longston."

Larry Crisman interrupted Mr. Horsley's recollections to point out another building, bringing us back to the present with a jolt. "Here is where we have our after-care substance abuse treatment program," he said. "This is for boys and girls who have already gone through drug detoxification."

The appearance of the Buckner Children's Home has changed little in sixty or seventy years. The imposing red brick buildings sit far back off Buckner Boulevard on the eastern edge of Dallas. The manicured lawns, the red tile roofs, the austere architecture—they all give it the look of a bygone era.

But behind that dated exterior, great changes have taken place at the 111-year-old institution.

And those changes are especially clear when hundreds of former residents return to campus every year. This is the weekend for homecoming.

Last week, I took a little then-and-now tour of the campus. The "then" was provided by Mr. Horsley and Connie Miller, the outgoing and incoming presidents, respectively, of the alumni association. The "now" came from Mr. Crisman, public relations director for the home.

Though it's still known to most people as the "Buckner Orphans Home," very few orphans ever lived there.

"I recall only one family that was true orphans when I was here," Mr. Horsley said. "That was the Smith brothers. Their parents were killed in a wreck."

Back when Mrs. Miller and Mr. Horsley lived there, most of the children were economic orphans.

"My mother died when I was six years old, and my father just couldn't take care of us," Mrs. Miller said. So she and a younger brother were sent to the home in 1936, and they remained there until graduating from high school.

"Daddy ran off and left us," Mr. Horsley said. "He had mental problems. Mama had six kids. She was working in a sewing room making $30 a month. When she got laid off, we had to come to Buckner." He arrived there in 1943.

Today's residents of Buckner are what administrator Weldon McElreath calls "social orphans." "They are socially abandoned kids," he said. "They come through that front gate suffering from drug abuse, physical abuse, sexual abuse, mental abuse, a multitude of problems."

Needless to say, it's a far cry from the day when rebellious behavior meant listening to the *Hillbilly Hit Parade* after curfew.

In Mr. Horsley and Mrs. Miller's time, more than 640 children lived at the home. Stern faced "matrons" presided over each dormitory. And the residents typically spent their whole childhood at Buckner.

Today, the home takes in about 250 youths. They live in small group settings, shepherded by "child care specialists." Most stay about a year before returning home or going to a foster home.

In the old days, Buckner Orphans Home was almost puritanical in philosophy. "They showed movies on Saturday night," Mr. Horsley said, "but the projectionist would always block out the screen when the actors were about to kiss."

Today, the atmosphere is spiritual but far more relaxed and contemporary. "We've got the Dallas Cowboy Cheerleaders coming in about a month. They come every year to perform for the kids," Mr. Chrisman said.

I asked Mr. Horsley what kind of entertainment the community provided when he was at Buckner. "Baptist people would come and bring fried chicken once or twice a year," he said. "And in the summer time, farmers would bring watermelons."

It would be easy to think of the Buckner Home as a sad sort of place, then and now. But Mr. Horsley and Mrs. Miller certainly don't see it that way.

"It looks good," Mr. Horsley said. "It looks like home."

Let's hope today's residents agree someday.

Miss Alma Rohm, '50

[Who came more than 9000 miles in 1996 to receive "The Distinguished Former Employee Award," Ed.]

In 1949 a star, an intellectual upheaval, an angel, a new thing in our world—perhaps we could even say a meteor blasted to earth and landed right here at Buckner, leaving in its path sparks whose flashes of light still shine on those fortunate enough to have been orphans at that time. I'm not completely sure whether we students saw ourselves as her victims or something worse at the time. She kept us too busy to judge then, but we soon knew we loved her because she made our lives so exciting. She had arrived with her unstinting enthusiasm, love for God and dedication to our improvement whether we wanted it or not. Miss Alma Rohm allowed for no shirkers in her high school classes.

A lover of music, she quickly did what seemed impossible in that age when guys with musical talent were considered "sissies," and rock groups and idolizing them were still social trends waiting in the future. She allowed the girls to sing, but she convinced the boys to sing, even started a boys' choir and to their surprise, persuaded some talented few, terribly macho guys to sing in a quartet in church!

She produced plays with us as the unbelievably wonderful actors and actresses. "What could she not do?" we asked ourselves and knew that she had persuaded us by her example that there was nothing we could not do.

She shared the adventures of her application for placement with the Foreign Mission Board. We thought they ought to be able to tell by looking that she could do anything in the world. We could. We had introduced her to "real live orphans" and she had introduced us to a "real live missionary." What an exchange!

In 1996 when asked to list her three most important accomplishments—a difficult task for a woman whose entire energetic years are full of spiritual mountaintops and accomplished goals— she modestly thought seriously for a long time as though it were difficult to think of three (that magic number of points that we had learned for the first time from her, that makes up a good speech or composition). Eventually, we learned that she is a woman of many accomplishments over the years, our oldest missionary in active service and that she considers Nigeria home until Heaven. We also discovered a Baptist School and a Baptist Church in Nigeria that bear her name, and a full length sculpture of her, shaped by loving hands, inspired by loving hearts, deeply influenced by her Christian life and teachings. In the view of Buckner High School's class of '50, fifty years of service as a missionary in Africa have made her the "Lottie Moon of Africa."

She has sung the songs of the faith in a strange land that has become home for her and has taught those songs to thousands in the music school that has become only one of her major projects. Most of the organists playing in Nigerian churches today have been taught by her or by someone who was once her student.

We wanted to do something for her and asked what we could do. She simply said, "I need more music; sheet music, hymns." Since she needed more, we, her ex-students have raised some money for her to use to purchase what she needs or wants for her work.

For almost fifty years we have remembered her contributions to our lives. Until now few of us had seen her after our graduation. But in letters she wrote again and again of Buckner kids who were communicating with her.

And now, "Momma," and "Chief," as she is lovingly called, with you here this Homecoming, we see that even though some of us have grown old and tired, even retired, you have not lost your sparkle or your energy. You can still think and work twice as fast as anybody else; you still have wonderful plans for the future that we know you can carry out, and you have not lost that sense of fun that so enchanted us as teenagers.

Ellis Smith, '50

It must have been late summer or early fall of '46. The war was over and people's attention was turning to domestic issues and problems. One major problem of that time was polio. No one seemed to know what was causing it or how it was spread. Officials once suspected that it was spread in swimming pools. The city of Dallas promptly closed all public pools. Another time those same officials thought it was spread by rats, and the city had a massive rat eradication program. Once it was even rumored that polio was spread by bananas!

Now bananas were not a part of our normal diet at Buckner. We did get an apple every Saturday night to go with a wedge of cheese and a couple of crackers, and half an orange occasionally for breakfast. That was primarily the extent of our fruit diet. But suddenly we started getting bananas, many bananas. At first there was a banana at each plate set in the Manna Hall, then two and then three. This lasted for perhaps a week and just as suddenly as they had appeared, they stopped. I guess something else came along that was suspected of causing polio, and therefore, we had bananas added to our menu. Or maybe, with our sudden experiment of eating them, we just shot the banana theory down, for never was there a case of polio at Buckner!

Billy Ed Taylor, '50

I was born on October 10, 1930, in Big Springs, Texas, and only weighed two pounds at birth. My mother died in the same month and year. I was the youngest of nine children. In 1934, on a cold November day, my two sisters, Ella Mae, Wanda, and I were brought to the Receiving Home, probably kicking and screaming all the way there. That started my life at dear old Buckner Orphans Home. These are some of the good things I remember while I was at the Home.

GORDON S. TAYLOR

About a year after arriving in 1935, I was walking out of Manna Hall between the High School and the Church with Mr. Taylor. I was feeling lonely and sad, and when we got about to the curb on the driveway that circles the campus, I reached up and grabbed his hand and asked him if he would be my daddy. Some years later, after I had left the home to join the Marines, and while I was on leave attending one of the Homecomings, he reminded me of that time so long ago.

When I was about nine years old and in Pires Home, some kids talked me into going over the fence to swim in the pool even though it was closed. Some time later Mr. Taylor came by, saw us and took us into his office. He closed the door, took down the razor strap and whipped each of us on our bottoms. For some reason he didn't whip me as hard or as much as the other kids. I think I know why!

THE BAKERY

Mr. Taylor was the one who got me the job to work with Mr. Grube in the Bakery. On Saturdays after work, Mr. Grube would always give each one of us twenty-five cents to go to the movie at Pleasant Grove. The movie price at that time was thirty-five cents. We had to come up with the other ten cents.

One time while I was working in the Bakery, Mr. Grube had to be at the Lake Dallas Boys' Camp, and Donald Johnson, Robert McKinney and I were left to bake the pies for supper that night. We were making up the dough for Boston Upside Down Pies. Part of the recipe is to add ice to the dough. On the first batch we didn't get the right consistency in the dough and had to pour it out there next to the commissary and start over. The next one we got right. The kids loved it, said it was even better than Mr. Grube's pies.

We would always make about 100 pies at a time, cut each one into six slices and take them over to Manna Hall from the Bakery. Before telling Miss Mamie how many there were, I was asked by some of the girls to lie and say there were one or two short of 100 so they could have some before supper.

LAKE DALLAS CAMP

Sometimes we would go with Mr. Grube to the Lake Dallas Camp and cook for the kids there. One of the best things we would make was French toast and giant cinnamon rolls which all kids loved. I haven't tasted any toast or cinnamon rolls that good to this day.

MAKING OUR OWN RADIOS

When we were about thirteen-years-old, we didn't have radios of our own, so we had to make them out of old wooden chalk boxes.

We would get chalk boxes from school and take them over to McElroy. Using all the copper wire we could find from the trash dump, we would stretch a long piece of wire from the top of old Rupard Hall over to McElroy, run it down the side of the building and attach it to our home-made radios. We made those radios out of 6 to 8 screws, a spool of wire, crystal sets and pieces of tin cut from Prince Albert tobacco cans. By touching a needle and wire to the crystal, moving the piece of tin back across the spool of wire and by touching the needle on top of the crystal with our old telephone receiver (or those who had money, could buy headsets for about a dollar at that time), we were able to pick up KRLD, WFAA and WRR on our radio sets late at night. However, we had to keep the receivers under our pillows and not make noise or the matrons would take them from us.

HUNTING FOR RABBITS

Billy Dean and I, about every afternoon after school, would take off to Bull Pond and the cotton fields to hunt rabbits. I only caught a half-grown jack rabbit once. Our hunting and killing was more of a chance to get away from the matrons and just have fun than it was about really catching anything.

MOVIES

Every once in a while the matrons would give us a pass to get off campus and go downtown Dallas to see a movie. Around 1943, I remember going to the movie with my sister Ella Mae. Before each movie, they would show a short news feature. One time when the news came on, the picture showed a close up of a white cross worn by one Marine among the hundreds of corpses on an island in the Pacific Theater of Operation. The News Caravan focused in on that one cross. I did not have any idea at first that the Marine shown was a boy from Buckner Orphans Home— not until I was able to read the name on his dog tag: Pfc. James O'Connor. I had known him.

Little did I know then that some several years later I would join the Marine Corps and spend some twenty years there seeing combat in Korea and Vietnam. I was proud to serve my country.

Buckner will always be a part of my life. I thank Buckner for taking my sisters and me on that November day in 1934, for teaching us right from wrong and taking care of us all those years.

Eva Nell (Kimler) Turner, '50

MEMORIES

How frightened and lonely I felt when my mother left Mary, Edith, Ray and me at the Receiving Home at Buckner Children's Home a few days before my 12th birthday in October 1943, to go to her job in the dining hall. Those were two of the loneliest weeks I have ever spent, but soon it was time to move to the dorms—each of us four children in a different building. We three girls got our hair cut off and it was so sad to see Mary Louise's long pig-tails gone. We had to cry about that. Though eventually we all adjusted to our new dorms, dorm parents and to school, the new

adjustment showed in my school work, so much so that I was detained for another year in the 6th grade. Perhaps I couldn't understand the good in that at the time, but it didn't keep me from going on after high school to get my Bachelors and Masters Degrees.

Soon after I arrived at Buckner, it was time to get tonsils out. We were all lined up in the beds at the infirmary and had our tonsils removed, one by one. My appendix was removed shortly afterward, and I was detained in the infirmary for two weeks during which time I was not allowed to walk, so when I finally was allowed to walk, I held myself all bent over for awhile.

Then there was that first boyfriend. How thrilling to pass notes back and forth and sneak a smile or wave at each other when the opportunity presented itself. We called that "going steady," but we really didn't go anywhere.

High school days were fun. One of my favorite experiences was singing in the Girls' Choir and though I have a soprano voice, I sang base in the all-girls' choir. The choir trips off the campus of the home were enjoyable and a chance to get away to see other things and people. Our Sunday morning attire was robes, but our traveling attire was pink blouses and brown skirts. How special for the choir to sing on the balcony of the chapel "Bless This House" at Dr. A. A. Hyden and Marjorie Barnett's wedding. We also sang "Under His Wings" later at a funeral. Miss Jo, our choir director, was not only a beautiful person on the outside, but lovely on the inside too and kind and patient with us.

Music lessons were interesting with Mrs. Helen Buster Roberts. After practicing all week on my lesson, I would be so nervous with Mrs. Roberts that I couldn't play anything right, but thanks to her perseverance, some of her hard work with me stuck, and the music that I had learned served me well for my forty-year missionary career. I not only played hymns for the worship services, but was also able to train many Venezuelan young people to do the same. Recital time at the Home was especially a difficult time as I became so nervous, as did most of the students, and made many mistakes in the well-memorized piano pieces. However, the audience was kind, and it was always a relief when recitals were over.

High school football, basketball games and track meets were exciting. Being in the pep-squad, then being a cheerleader was even more exciting, as was singing "Fight On Buckner Hornets," and being able to walk a few steps from the field or gym to our dorms with our boyfriends after the home games.

When the snow came during the winter, it was sheer delight to play around Father Buckner's statue and throw snowballs at each other.

There was a lot of anticipation when work assignments were made; what would we be doing next? Would we have laundry duty where we had to iron those shirts just right? Would it be dining hall duty, where Miss Mamie made sure we had everything spotless, or kitchen duty where we had to wash those large pots and pans or even commissary duty in the building where all the clothes were stored until given out. One duty that no one really anticipated eagerly was cleaning chickens on Saturday mornings, but we did like to eat the fried chicken the next day.

Camping out in the woods, cooking our own food over an open fire, sleeping out on the ground under the stars and riding horses in the summer were welcomed times for all of us.

Then that senior year came—our outing at White Rock Lake, presenting the Senior Play, "Mama's Baby Boy," and finally graduation. It was certainly an honor to receive the award "Most Representative Girl" for that year's senior class; then in 1982 to receive the "Alumnus of the Year Award."

Thank you, Pinkie Sikes (Nadine—Mrs. Bill Gray) for helping us to enroll in Howard Payne College and assisting us with getting jobs to help pay our way.

I would say that I was blessed and learned a lot of things that enriched my life because of those Buckner years and the people who touched my life during that time.

Viola (Hooker) Wright, '50

The memories of my years in Buckner Orphans Home are good memories and grow sweeter as years go by. While I was there I wished I could be elsewhere; but after leaving in the fall of 1948 to live in far off Michigan, I'd have given anything to be back in the Home. Buckner was truly home.

Remember lining up when the first whistle blew and at the second whistle going over to Manna Hall? I remember the meals I liked best: Monday morning (always) hot chocolate and scrambled eggs, Tuesday noon (always) a big bun and a slice of bologna with mashed potato salad, and always our tin pitcher of syrup and butter.

Remember Friday nights; soup and the piano players always played "On Jordon's Stormy Banks" and how we'd keep chanting "soup-soup-soup"?

Remember how on Sundays we always got a piece of cake, and many times, being a waitress, we would get behind one of the big poles and scarf down an extra piece of cake without Miss Mamie seeing us?

Remember looking at our "changing jobs list"? I dreaded getting the laundry job and ironing all that bundle of shirts. I just never could iron to please Mrs. McKinney.

Remember having the job of going to Manna Hall early in the morning to mop? Oh, how I hated to open the door to where the mops were kept—it smelled of sour wet mops.

Remember roller skating from our building to the Manna Hall? Unfortunately, we never could get away with skating on the boys' side of the campus.

Remember on Saturday Night we could go to the movie—if we didn't have too many demerits? I don't remember the number of demerits that really got us in trouble. I'm sure grades had a bearing on it, and I know I missed quite a few movies because of that.

Remember that we couldn't turn on our room lights after coming home from the movie?

Remember going to the commissary to get our new order of clothes? I remember at one time seeing a pair of shoes that had thick rubber soles. I wanted them so badly, but my matron said my shoes were still good. So, when I went back to my building, I scraped those shoes on the sidewalk until they were worn out, and somehow I got the shoes I wanted so badly.

Remember after the noon meal we could visit with brothers and sisters in front of church, but only a short while?

Remember picking cotton? The best part was when the girls and boys got to pick the last field together and we threw green boles at the boys when Mr. Dickey couldn't see us as he rode through the fields on his horse.

Remember the "slop-hack" that was horse drawn and made the rounds behind the buildings picking up refuse? I remember because I "liked" one of the boys who drove the slop-hack.

Remember the pride we felt at the football games? I still recall one of the yells. I guess I've repeated it once too many times to my grandchildren as they say "Grandma, did you really say that?"

Yum-yum-fiddle diddle dum
Hump stump, flop-diddle, air bubble
Rig-dom, gig-dom-bobo-kiro
Deck-o diro fuzzy wuzzy cat-gut rat-gut bat-gut
Billy, Billy Hoo-rah hoorah hoorah.
Buckner High School, Rah, Rah, Rah.

So many good memories. I firmly believe we had the best. The discipline was firm, but we were taught well.

Our Christmas Strings and the beautiful Christmas trees are also stories I've shared with my children and grandchildren.

I remember too the "Family Hour Devotions." We would always end our nightly devotional by singing a good farewell song, "God Be With You Till We Meet Again."

Doris (Woods) Bleakley, '51

My favorite thing is telling Buckner stories even to people who are not particularly interested. I think every day of my life I come to appreciate more the life that my brothers and I had at Buckner.

I have had a full and happy life since I left Buckner. I am married and have one son. While my son was growing up, I worked mostly in temporary positions. Now I am partially retired as an Executive Secretary to a Vice President at Brown and Root in Houston, where I have worked for eighteen years. One of my accomplishments at Brown & Root that I am proud of was to organize and write the bylaws for the Brown & Root Women's Clubs on project sites where my husband worked.

I also worked for thirteen years in public service type positions such as churches and schools and have done lots of volunteer community service through clubs, Boy Scouts of America and schools. I was church secretary for Central

Baptist Church, Port Arthur, Texas, for almost thirteen years.

Margaret (Borden) Corcoran, '51

KEEP ON KEEPING ON

In high school we had a Young Women's Christian Organization on campus. One day Mrs. Bertha (Brother Hal's Wife) was speaking to our group. She was telling us about their experiences as missionaries in China. I don't remember everything she said or her exact words, but her story was fascinating to me.

Her narrative began after they had already been in China for many years, and God had been using them in a wonderful way. Brother Hal had a burden on his heart but didn't know what God was trying to tell him. Every day for weeks he prayed about it, but God was silent. The burden remained.

Then one morning he said, "Bertha, I'm going to the church to pray, and I'm not coming back until God gives me an answer."

When he returned, his face was glowing and lit up with a smile. Excitement was in his voice. "Bertha, Bertha," he said, "we're going home."

"Oh, Hal. Did you hear from the Mission Board?"

"No, but I heard from God. Start packing. Get the children's things together. Decide what you want to take with us and dispose of everything else. I'm going to the shipping office and booking passage on the first ship headed that way."

Everything was packed or disposed of and they were ready to get on board the ship when they got a telegram from the Foreign Mission Board.

It read, "Come home. Your father has died and we need you and your brother Joe to run the Children's Home."

When Mrs. Bertha finished her story, I knew I wanted to be just like her and Brother Hal in my dedication to God. I hadn't known Brother Joe, but I did know Brother Hal. Even when he was getting older and a little feeble, he still preached every Sunday morning. As the girls' choir left the choir loft after each service, he waited until I started to go down the steps from the platform and put his hand on my shoulder. We walked down the steps together. When we reached the bottom of the steps, he always said, "Smiles, I couldn't do it without you."

Then one day he wasn't able to preach any more, and we heard that he was very ill. Occasionally Miss Jo, as we called her, took me to their house to do some cleaning. After the work was done, I spent a few minutes with him. He always said, "Keep on keeping on."

Before he died, he said to Jo, his daughter, "Go and get Smiles; I want to see her."

She didn't know who Smiles was and asked him who he meant. He replied, "You know, that girl who always helps me walk down from the podium."

She finally figured out who he was talking about and came to the campus to find me. He took my hand and in a weak little voice said, "Smiles, just keep on keeping on."

Even on his death bed, he had his papers spread out around him and was busy making plans for the future of Buckner.

When I'm a little down or discouraged, I still remember his voice saying,"Smiles, keep on keeping on."

Katherine (Vance) Henslee, '51

I was six-years-old when my sister, baby brother and I were brought to the Home. (My three other brothers followed later in 1939.) At first, we were placed in a building called the Receiving Home, where we had to spend more time than usual because the kids on the main campus had whooping cough.

When everybody got well, we moved to the main campus. My sister and I moved to the "girls' side" and my brothers moved to the "boys' side" of the campus, forever to be separated by gender. I was also separated from my sister. We were in the same building, Hardin Hall, but in different units since she was older than I and in a higher grade. That was the rule; you stayed with kids your own age and in your own grade in school.

Miss Dolly Orr was my first matron. I remember her as a nice lady. When it was storming outside and the lightening and the thunder were scary, she came around in the rooms to see if every thing was all right, even in the middle of the night. She taught me to say, "What time I am

afraid I will put my trust in Thee." Sometimes I had to say it a lot before I wasn't afraid anymore. I still do.

I gradually got used to the other girls and started learning how to live in a group. There were some unspoken rules among the kids that we just came to know. Some were: Don't tell on anybody, leave other people's things alone (some things were sacred), and don't criticize. Especially don't criticize names. I was used to being called "Jane." My father called me that after a heroine in a Zane Gray novel. The administration told my Grandmother that nick-names were not used out there, so I would be called by my first given name, "Melissa." I didn't like that name so I chose to be called "Katherine," which was my middle name.

For a long time I thought my father and mother would get well, come get us as soon as they could and I would be Jane again. That never happened; Jane was gone forever.

Katherine learned that you could make it easy on yourself or you could make it hard on yourself. There were many different personalities among the children and matrons. Most of the time I tried to make it easy on myself. Sometimes I just wanted to be left alone. I wasn't a "goody-goody" kid, but I wasn't bad either. I got into trouble with matrons and teachers and the powers-that-be. I got whippings and other unique punishments along the way. For instance, sitting on the wall, standing in the hall, drinking hot water, working extra in the Manna Hall or having to iron extra shirts in the laundry. One I will never forget is sitting in the attic in the dark. This was for talking after the lights were turned off.

Miss Mamie had a good one, killing flies. This was a punishment for breaking a dish, being late for work, or talking too much. I had to kill flies nearly every day in the summer. The problem was that I couldn't hit a fly. Miss Mamie would have you save all the flies you killed in a dust pan. She would count them and if you didn't have enough to suit her, she wouldn't dismiss you. So, you see the problem. I never had enough flies. I tried to remedy this by saving my flies from one day to the next. I wrapped them carefully in wax paper and hid them in the mop closet. One day Miss Mamie inspected the mop closet and found my little cache of flies. I wish I could have seen her face when she unwrapped that wax paper and only found dead flies. That was just one of the unsolved mysteries she took to her grave.

Miss Mamie was famous for her disciplinary acts, but she never struck me. I have come to the conclusion after leaving the Home, that she actually liked me. One reason is she never "boxed my ears," although I did a lot of things that would have gotten the other kids in a lot of trouble.

One time I broke a broom handle trying to kill a giant roach. That was a slappable offense, but she just told me to put it in the trash. Another reason is she requested me to work for her as a monitor when she knew I didn't know how to tell time. Who do you think, confused the whole campus once by blowing the last whistle in the morning five minutes after the first whistle? I confess! Remember there was supposed to be thirty minutes between them. Maybe she just wanted to teach me how to tell time.

There were four buildings on the girls' side of the campus that we progressed to, depending on our age and what grade we were in. There was Hardin Home (primary girls), Crouch Home (junior girls), Hunt Home (intermediate girls), and Buhrman Home (senior girls). I lived in all four of them. Some of the matrons I remember not at all, some fondly, but some not so fondly.

My first Christmas at the Home was different, to say the least. I already knew there was no Santa Claus, courtesy of my older brother. When I had lived at the Home for almost a year, the other kids were all excited about Christmas and what Santa was going to bring them. We made red and green construction paper chains, sang Christmas songs, and dreamed about what we all wanted more than anything—to go home. I already knew parents were really the ones who brought the Christmas presents. I also knew that we, my sister and brothers, had not heard from any of our relatives since coming to the Home. I thought there would be no presents for us this year. The other kids kept telling me that everybody got something for Christmas. I didn't believe them; there were too many kids.

Christmas Eve finally arrived, and we went to the school auditorium for the Christmas program. The decorated trees on the stage were so beautiful. Then someone started handing out something to the youngest kids first. It wasn't a Christmas stocking or even a box wrapped in Christmas paper. It was a bundle of things tied together with flannel string. This was the first of many "strings" I received at the Home. That year I got a big doll and a doll bed that had wheels. I

was so surprised and delighted. I don't remember everything on that first string, but I know it had a bag of candy, nuts and fruit. It always did. The doll and the doll bed were the most wonderful toys I had ever had.

They were second hand, but I didn't care; they were new to me. I couldn't imagine where these things came from. They could have come from the fairy god-mother of Christmas strings for all I knew. Now I know they came from the good Baptists of Texas. And I want to say, "Thank you very much."

For some reason the girls in my room saved the flannel string for weeks after Christmas. I suppose it was like people save the pretty ribbons on birthday and Christmas packages today.

One Christmas when I was in Miz Zapp's unit, we all got food poisoning. The chicken sandwiches we were served for supper had not been kept cold enough. There were some pretty sick children, but nobody died. I was very sick for several days myself. Doctors and nurses from Dallas Hospitals came out to the Home to help care for the sick kids.

At some point between living in Crouch Home and Hunt Home, when I was about eleven or twelve-years-old, all the kids were required to take a TB test. The results showed that two of my brothers and I had active TB. I was sent to the Campus Hospital to live until they decided what to do with me. I understand now that people with TB had to be quarantined because it was contagious and there was no cure for it then; nevertheless, this is the most unhappy memory I have of the Home. I didn't understand why I was not allowed to just talk to my sister or any of my friends. I didn't feel sick. Why did I have to stay in the Hospital? I had been able to see and talk to my sister every day even though we didn't live in the same room or unit. She was my security. Nobody explained what was happening or what I could expect to happen in the future.

One day a suitcase full of clothes, which they said were mine, showed up at the Home Hospital. I was told that I would be going to the Sanatorium the next day. Nothing in that suitcase was mine. Where were my things? I learned later that they had been destroyed.

The next day, late in the afternoon, Mrs. Brady, Dean of Girls, came to the Hospital, picked me up and took me to the train station in Dallas. The workers at the hospital had given me

$3.00 for spending money. A little six-year-old boy named Danny Joe Wynn was being taken to the Sanatorium too. Danny started asking for candy as soon as we got to the train station. Mrs. Brady told me to take him and get him some candy; he had his own money. I didn't buy anything for myself because I wasn't hungry and I didn't think I could get anything past the big lump in my throat. Mrs. Brady insisted I go back and buy something, so I got a 5 cent package of Tom's Peanuts. I had just put them in my purse when Mrs. Brady suggested that Danny Joe might like some of my peanuts. I just sort of ignored her. She must have taken this to be belligerence on my part. She continued trying to get me to share, and by the time I got on the train and settled in my berth, I was crying uncontrollably. Everyone on the train noticed, and Mrs. Brady was very embarrassed.

I cried until I finally went to sleep. They were taking me somewhere I didn't want to go. I didn't have any control over anything. I wondered if they had told my sister where they were taking me. Would I ever see her again?

The next morning when I got up and went to the bathroom to dress, Mrs. Brady was already there. I was so sick to my stomach. I guess it was motion sickness or anxiety or both. I started vomiting all over the place. Mrs. Brady was afraid to get too close to me because she was afraid of my disease or because she didn't want to smell bad, I guess.

I had brought the suitcase to the bathroom with me, and while I was cleaning myself up, I just laid the peanuts on the top of the suitcase. Mrs. Brady sent me to her berth to get something for her. When I got back, I noticed the peanuts were gone. When I asked her if she had seen them, she became angry. She started telling me how selfish I had been for not offering her and Danny Joe any peanuts last night and how she wanted me to straighten up and act like a lady, etc. Though nothing more was said about the peanuts, I knew where they were.

I guess I had cried out all my tears because I was dry-eyed from then on, but I was still so sick at my stomach. When we got off the train at San Angelo, I picked up the wrong suitcase, and a man had to chase me down to get it back. Mrs. Brady was not enjoying this trip. I had never seen that suitcase that had been given me as if it were mine, until the day before yesterday, so it should have been easy to see why I hadn't recognized it.

We still had a long bus ride out to the Sanatorium, and I don't remember anything about it except getting on and getting off. I must have slept all the way out to the Hospital.

After I checked in, I was taken to the children's building and put to bed. The nurse unpacked the suitcase. She put the pajamas in a drawer of the bedside table and hung the dresses in a closet in the hall. When I was packing to leave, nine months later, I found three or four dresses I had never worn because I didn't know they were mine, but they had my name on them.

I was very happy to leave the Sanatorium of Texas. Mrs. Brady showed up again to take me home. This time I was just as nice and polite and quiet as I knew how to be. I didn't want any trouble.

I was so glad to see the old red top buildings and my sister and friends. Now I realized that I considered the Home to be my home. I knew no relatives were going to come get us. I was there for the long haul. Until graduation I never tried to run away, as some of my friends did. I knew I had no place to go. Some of the kids would sneak off the campus and go to a show in Urbandale. I never went with them, but I would open the window and let them back in when they came back. I wish I could say that I settled down and became a model student, but I didn't.

I mentioned earlier about having to sit in the attic in the dark; it was supposed to be a punishment, but my best friend and I were marched off every night until we came to look forward to it. We called ourselves "attic pals." We would jump on the stack of quilts up there and tell ghost stories, and look out the windows. We could see the lights of Dallas and even see the Flying Red Horse on the Magnolia Building. We watched for falling stars, and the moon and just talked.

The matron never stayed with us, so we just trooped back to our beds whenever we felt like it. I guess the matron thought we could do no real harm in the attic so she went on to bed. I realized later that being the matron of twenty-eight to thirty-eight girls must have been a hard job. I never let that thought bother me then. This took place on the third floor of Hunt Home where Mrs. Jeter was our matron.

When we moved into Hunt Home, we got to start going camping in the summer. This was just a day camp but I loved it. They would take us to the woods and we could just go wild. We could roam all over the woods; of course there were fences that we couldn't cross. There was a stream to wade in and many trees to climb. We could go off all by ourselves or with a bunch of other kids. It was a taste of freedom.

We could also ride horses. This was a supervised activity and two had to ride at the same time. I didn't care much for horses. They were so BIG. One time a friend asked me to ride with her because nobody else was interested. I knew she was one of the few good riders, so I climbed on behind the saddle. The minute the horse, Freckles, got out on the road he decided to go to the barn, and he was in a big hurry. I was scared to death. I tried to hold on, but I saw a limb up ahead that I thought was too low for me to go under so I bailed off the horse. As I fell to the ground, I reached out to the fence, not thinking that it was a barbed wire fence. Well, I split two of my fingers open, the ground hit me in the face, and maybe the horse kicked me because my face sure did hurt. I thought my nose was bleeding so I kept wiping it with my hand. I had blood all over me by the time the teacher got to me. After the blood was washed away, we found only my fingers needed attention. As soon as we got back to the Home, I was sent to the Hospital. The nurse told me she was not allowed to put stitches in a wound, but she bandaged it real well and it healed nicely.

At the end of the summer season, the teachers and matrons would choose the girls they thought were the best campers, and they got to spend the night in the woods. I really wanted to be a "best camper." I did get chosen the last two years I was there. We were assigned jobs at camp, and I had to peel a lot of potatoes and clean the "john," but I loved it. I had a wonderful time.

When I moved into Buhrman Home, I was old enough and had enough sense to work in the kitchen. The "kitchen girls" had to get up early. (The matron would wake one girl and she would wake all the others.) There were always six of us. We would get dressed in the dark and meet in the stairwell to go to the Manna Hall together. We wore old dresses, the uglier the better and our hair rolled up with a scarf on it. We looked more like refugees than workers in the kitchen. This was when we peeled tubs of potatoes. There was a potato peeler in the kitchen which we used, but we still had to pick out the eyes. We also had to clean the oatmeal pot. It was so huge that we had

to practically stand on our head to get to the bottom to clean. Then there was the scrambled egg pot which needed attention, too. After that the floors had to be scrubbed everyday. We did a day's work before school every day.

The kitchen and Manna Hall were Miss Mamie's domain. For her everything must be done a certain way. It was so certain it was like it was carved in stone. Everything had to be reported to her, and she had to inspect it before you could even think of going home. If you dropped something (pan, plate, spoon, etc.) it had to be reported. You had to say. "Miss Mamie, I dropped this." or "Miss Mamie, I broke this." You always had to say "Miss Mamie" first or she acted like she couldn't hear you. Miss Mamie was in charge of the kitchen girls, the pantry girls, the table waitresses and the Manna Hall girls. I dare say any girl that worked under Miss Mamie never forgot her.

Buckner had a very fine school system, a fully accredited grade school and high school on campus. In 1950 Buckner decided to restructure the high school into a five year school to create an Academy. My senior class was given a choice to graduate from high school with a diploma or stay another year and be the first Academy Senior Class. I chose to stay, along with eight other girls and one boy. Actually I didn't have much of a choice because I had goofed around in my sophomore year and failed some classes. I could not have gotten a high school diploma if I had not stayed. The extra year helped me make up those classes and get my diploma. Besides at this point I had no idea what I would do after graduation, or where I would go for that matter. College was out. No money.

Actually school was not my favorite thing. I was not a good student. I was in no way a leader; I was a follower. I was a quasi "B" student. I had some "C's" and once in a while I would make an "A." (Glory!) I was a slow thinker. I still can't do 100 multiplication problems in three minutes. So all those spankings for not getting problems correct were wasted on me.

I liked to do things with my hands like crocheting or knitting. Those skills weren't in the curriculum. We did have classes in sewing and cooking though. I liked the sewing class; we made our own graduation dress, a simple dress and a made-over garment. I got the medal for sewing when I graduated. The teacher said it was because I was the most improved. I should think so since I had known nothing about sewing when I started class. I was also dumb enough to try to make bound button holes. They were so hard for me to get right. I have never made another bound button hole, but sewing was a skill Buckner taught me that has helped me all my adult life. I was able to learn to crochet after I left the Home.

Now cooking is a horse of another color. I can get by in the kitchen but I wash dishes better. (Miss Mamie taught me that.) However, it was necessary to cook such huge portions of food in the Manna Hall that I was used to seeing great big pots of potatoes and beans, etc. It was hard to scale down the portions for just two people. I lived with a friend from the Home for a while after graduation, and we just cooked until all the pots in the house were full; then we figured we had enough.

While we were at the Home, we went to church twice on Sundays. In the morning we had Sunday School and then the Church services. In the evening we had BYPU. (Baptist Young People's Union.) Our own definition for those letters was "Button Your Pants Up."

I was baptized when I was in Miz Zapp's unit in Hardin Home. It didn't take though, because I was just telling her what I thought she wanted to hear. I had already had some experience telling her what she didn't want to hear! The girls she called in before me, told me what she was doing and what to say. When I left her conference room, she pronounced me ready to be baptized, and so I was.

Later when I was on the second floor of Crouch Home, I did make a true profession of faith but was not baptized again. After I left the Home though, I took care of that matter.

I am so grateful that Buckner showed me the way to Christ. I keep realizing every year what a valuable treasure Christ is. If it took spending my growing up years in an Orphans Home to lead me to salvation, then it was worth it all.

When the time came for me to leave the Home, I still wasn't sure what I was going to do, but I had to leave. I don't know how it came about, but my aunt and uncle came the day before I graduated and let me go home with them. They came and got my sister when she graduated too. I don't know if the Home called them or if they just wanted to come. It made me feel like maybe I could go back to my family. I hadn't

called them or written to them. I just couldn't ask to live with someone who didn't know me very well. I didn't know them either. I guess God called them. They were wonderful Christian people. They were not rich and could ill afford to take on another mouth to feed. They had two small children, and my grandmother lived with them also. I came to them just like I went to the home without a penny in my pocket. They never asked me for anything ever. I lived with them about a year, which was long enough to help me make the transition from institutional life to normal life (whatever that is).

Rena (Carkeet) Key, '51

THE FLY BANK

Thanks to Miss Mamie, to this very day I am a Champion Fly Swatter.

> On a table, in a chair,
> On the wall or in the air;
> Where's that fly? I don't care—
> I can swat it anywhere!

Under the watchful eye of Miss Mamie, some of us had table duty (serve and clean); some, Manna Hall duty (sweep and mop); some, kitchen duty (potatoes and pots). Whatever the job, tardiness and talking were not tolerated. The offenders were required to return early after school was out to catch flies.

Knowing that we were doomed if we failed to report back without a reasonable number of dead flies, we began with dust pan and swatter in hand. Woe be unto us on the day that no flies were flying. For just such days, some ingenious Buckner minds set up a Fly Bank.

Far from "The Eye" in the rocking chair—with columns blocking the view—a window or corner was selected to store any extra flies killed on the lucky days. To keep the bank fresh, we exchanged the new kill for passable substitutes and cleared out all the old ones.

On any given day, how could we know how many dead flies would be considered enough for absolution? That could only be learned by experience.

It has been said that "practice makes perfect," and the talkers got plenty of practice. While perfecting our swatting skills, it never occurred to most of us to perfect our behavior instead.

Thanks to Miss Mamie, I did learn some useful life lessons: how to serve, wash dishes, sweep, mop, eye potatoes, wash pots and swat flies—"but the tongue can no man tame."

Bobbi (Batchelder) Richardson, '51

Every person from Buckner has a story and my strong desire is to read each one. These stories will be enjoyed by friends and families. I want to write my own but when I try, I literally get sick. Your memories are my memories, so I thought if you could be cajoled, begged or bribed to write, it would be okay if I didn't. But, Jerre Simmons (Juanita Graves) has shamed me. So, in spite of disliking every minute of it I will try.

After the death of my mother, who was shot by my father, with all five of his children looking on, my world, as seen through the eyes of a five-year-old, was turned upside down. It wasn't much of a right side up life before my mom's death; however, the episode certainly changed life as I knew it.

It was easy to identify with the other children in the Home, as we called the orphanage, because others' stories were as bad or worse than the Richardsons'. These are some of the stories from my eleven and one-half years' stay.

RECEIVING HOME

There was another family waiting to be placed on the main campus (The Wallers). Betty Fern Waller was about my age. She was almost at the end of her stay, so a strong friendship did not develop then. However, for the years we were at Buckner, it was a joy to be in her company. We were successful cooking partners in High School, making up concoctions that included bugs etc., and trying to get the boys to eat them. We also tried cooking up the real food (frying chicken) and telling them it was fried cat to see if they would be brave enough to taste it. When they refused, we showed them how brave we were by boldly eating it. They looked on in horror, until we were down to our last bites, then we told them the difference. It was too late for them to beg us

for a piece. We counted it a "special" time anytime we could put one over on the boys.

The Ward family came later. Alice Ann Ward and I developed a friendship, sharing an interest in books and poetry that has lasted to this day. I still admire her gift to memorize and to write poetry. She went on to become a serious writer. While there we used verse to talk to the other kids. Some of the same type of sing song verses heard in any play group today are like the ones we created in 1939.

My brother and sister were housed with me in the Receiving Home, but we were later segregated by sex and by age. My brother, Billy Dean, was eight and Angie, my sister, was three. I was six. We realized we were a part of a much larger family. Our friends became family. It was difficult to keep in touch with our real family since we all three had different schedules.

The Receiving Home was a modern brick building like the other buildings on the campus, with terrazzo floors, hot and cold running water, tubs and showers, (one's own choice for use), steam heating, many windows for good ventilation and a bed for just me! No more getting blamed for bed wetting when my sister would roll over me and leave me in the wet spot. There was indoor plumbing, a first; with rolls of toilet tissue, also a first. Just how many sheets should one use for that type of paper work? We took a poll to determine. Also, do you fold or crunch it? We soon learned a lot of useless information about everyone in the building.

Even though we had to have naps everyday, the good raisin and oatmeal cookies, toys, books and the other children made this a good place to begin a new life. An average stay at the Receiving Home was two weeks.

Two girls from the main campus helped in the Receiving Home. They became like "big sisters," showing concern and interest. Barbara Markham was one of these girls. We've had a strong relationship since first we met. Years later she married Mark Williams, and the couple treated me as a blood relative. Barbara and Mark often got me passes from the Dean of Girls to go off campus with them. It was Barbara and Mark who introduced me to the Starlight Operetta and South Pacific. They took me to the drive-in theater and cooked me special meals, including plenty of desserts and also introduced me to foods I'd never tasted. They made it possible for me to have my first real date, an unchaperoned one with their nephew. I wonder if they ever knew just what we did or didn't do?

HARDIN HOME

The move to the main campus was to Hardin Home, a two-story brick building with an attic which housed girls six to nine-years-old. One of the six beds in a corner room facing the inside of the campus was mine. In hot weather during the after lunch nap time, we rested on the cool floors underneath our beds. If we were quiet enough we could play games that we invented. Sometimes we could get away with a game of rolling under the beds until we piled up under the last one and rolled back again to the other end. It was fun then. But how could any six six-year-olds, keep from giggling while rolling? Other fun times were pillow fights and a game of hide and seek which meant hiding each other's stuffed animals. We only did this when Miss Orr had a day off, and the matron at the other end of the hall had to supervise the whole floor. Miss Orr understood us. We in turn behaved for her. But, when the other matron was on duty, we tried everything we could think of to break the rules. Other mischief was running away from the matron in the hall and hiding in other rooms, so she couldn't identify which kids belonged to which room. We would also knock on her door at all hours of the night and then run back to bed before she could get the lights on to catch us. This matron knew if she left the punishing to Miss Orr, it wouldn't get done, so we were often all spanked because it was too difficult to find out which kid had done what. Miss Orr's return was always celebrated.

Each room had three closets with storage for two kids' belongings in each. The quality and quantity of clothing were always second hand, but were almost equal to that of any middle class Dallas child of the day. This included dresses for school with tam, sweater, coat, shoes and socks. A separate complete wardrobe for Sundays was issued with our names stamped in the back of each garment. As older kids we would sometimes see the dresses we had once owned being worn by younger kids. We would even sometimes remember which roommate had which dress and bet our dessert or piece of fruit on whose name was stamped in the back of which younger kid's hand-me-down dress.

It was a real show of growing up when we no longer had to wear the long stockings that were held up by rubber bands. In spite of the elastic, they still slipped down our legs, which was most irritating. That and having the elastic break in our panties (without a safety pin handy) were the most irritating things about clothing. Oh, yes, I forgot to explain that I was always losing my tam, but never my gloves. If any one asked why I was always being punished by having to sit on the wall, hold my ankles in the hall or sit beside the matron during playtime so no one would talk to me, it was because of losing my tam. Sometimes my roommates would help me devise ways to not get caught until we could locate my tam. I'd wear my Sunday one, and the girls would group around me pushing me behind them when the matron was around.

The playroom was shared by all the girls on the floor. The room was lined with windows, and the walls under these windows had scores of built-in, wooden window seats. Each, when opened, made a toy box that could be shared by two children. Sometimes willingly, we would crawl in and get our toy box mate to close the lid, pretending we had run away from the orphanage. Other times we would capture a kid and stuff her into the toy box—our way of punishing someone for doing what we thought was unfair to the rest of us. Other playroom fun was making peep boxes and playing jacks.

THE MEDICINE CLOSET

The medicine closet was visited each night and after breakfast. We soon learned what would get us a band-aide, bandage or a hug and pat or even a dose of milk of magnesia. Best of all was a trip to the hospital. Since I didn't like school, it was a good excuse for missing a few days.

HOSPITAL

This building was a place on the edge of the west side of the campus that had a ward on each end of the first floor and some private single bedrooms, a kitchen, operating room, and a day clinic on the first floor. The large basement held supplies, laundry and an incinerator that burned the hospital waste. I enjoyed the stays there because it was a place where I was given special attention. I frequented it often because of having changeable fever. Once I became accustomed to being in the HOME, the fevers never returned. However, getting my tonsils removed, having chicken pox and measles gave me a good shameless way of skipping school. Even my gum ailment warranted late passes to class.

DENTAL OFFICE

This office was part of the Hospital. Going upstairs and sitting in the dental chair made me feel important. The dental hygienist, Doris Ridge (nicknamed, "Charlie"), became a good friend and tried to influence me to care for my teeth. She did a great deal to assist me in keeping my gums healthy. Needing attention and getting it for having bleeding gums, I had done everything I could to keep them bleeding. However, Doris's friendship changed the focus from hurting myself to pleasing her. She met my brother, my sister and I after lunch each day in front of the Chapel and we visited. Her friendship lasted even after she graduated. We have kept in touch all these years.

Even though Billy, Angie and I were not close as a family, we did try to stay in touch. We could visit Angie when she was in the self contained building, the Sunbeam Home. We could visit her on a Saturday or a Sunday from 2 to 4 P.M. Some of the time Billy Dean would visit her at the same time. We really didn't know how to visit or what to say. We just stood around and looked at each other. When Angie became older, she and I visited each other in our dorms on a Saturday or Sunday. I became aware of what an interesting person she was. She had a delightful sense of humor. I soon forgave her for all the times before going to the Home, when she had chased me with rocks, sometimes hitting me with her wild throws. If I restrained her or hit her back, I was punished because she was the youngest. Billy Dean had some good stories about our time at home with our parents that kept the memories alive for me. So being with my brother and sister was enriching. We liked each other then and still do.

VISITORS

Many people visited the Home every week. It was fun to see people come and stand on the balcony in Manna Hall to watch us eat and later come through some of our rooms to see how we lived. Every day at least one room in each dorm

was kept extra nice to show visitors who happened to be on campus that day. The same neatness was required of every room. Every orphan had a beautiful handmade quilt and stuffed animal on her bed. The older girls on the campus acted as guides to show groups of visitors around the campus. In answering their questions and anticipating questions that would be asked by other groups, I learned a lot of background about Buckner. My appreciation and respect for everyone from the founder to the night watchman increased tremendously. Showing the Home off was of special interest to me.

CHAPEL

Chapel was a place where we practiced choir, went to church services and had Vacation Bible School. What we learned at church was stressed throughout the day in many ways. When we lined up for breakfast in the mornings, we had prayer. After breakfast several of the matrons talked to us about putting Bible teachings into everyday actions. Bible verses were used to remind us how to behave. I learned to use the same technique with my children. *"Honor thy father and thy mother. . . . Man looks on the outward appearances but God looks on the heart. . . . A soft answer turns away wrath but grievous words stir up anger. . . . Do unto others as you would have them do unto you. . . . Love thy neighbor as oneself. . . . A merry heart makes a cheerful countenance."* These were only a small example of the verses that are still with me today: Whole passages of the "Song of Solomon," "Psalms," The Ten Commandments, The Beatitudes and Luke's account of the birth of Jesus are just some of those pointed out to me in Sunday School and Training Union that I committed to memory.

Once a week in small groups, we studied our Bible. Everyday we were taught to read the Bible and pray. In school we prayed after we said the pledge to the flag, and often we would say the pledge to the Christian flag and the Bible. This training touched my heart, and at the age of eight, I was so overwhelmed that God sent Jesus to earth as a living example and that He loved me so much (at a time when I thought I was the most unlovable) that I accepted Jesus and have since tried to follow Christian principles. In spite of the rude things I did afterwards, such as slam the seats in the Chapel to create a lot of noise or make fun of others or become jealous of the other girls, I think that my conversion was truly a spiritual experience. It taught me that we cannot start too early to influence a person to live by Christian principles. As a teenager I dedicated my life to Christian service.

SPECIAL DAYS

Any break in our routine was always welcome. Founder's Day in January, Fourth of July, Homecoming in October, Thanksgiving and Christmas were the special holidays. These days we had special lunches with an abundance of food and a sack provided so we could pack it with enough from that meal to take to the dorm to have for supper. At Easter everyone received a new pair of shoes, a new dress and the boys a new shirt. Everyone received a new bright colored sweater. Mother's Day and Father's Day were Sundays where every child wore a white flower, if that parent were dead, and a red flower if the parent were alive. There were only about ten percent who were true orphans with both parents dead, but no one placed in the Home could be adopted.

We looked forward to football, basketball and track competitions. These became special days. In the summertime on Mondays, Wednesdays and Fridays we could go swimming. Every third week we went to the girls' woods to ride horses and have a special snack known as syrup deckers. Some days in the fall we could go to the boys' woods and pick up pecans. Most of us looked forward to Thursday's supper when we had a piece of pie. We had soup once a week, so many of us looked forward to that day, because we always sang "On Jordan's Stormy Banks I Stand." I always thought Saturday was a special day. There was no school, and we got an apple for supper that we could take out of Manna Hall and eat at the Saturday night movie. Even picking chickens was a special day, because we got out of school. However, picking cotton was even a greater time when we could earn money, for we knew we would have a very special opportunity to spend it at the State Fair of Texas.

Going to events off the campus was special, not because of the event as much as it was for the riding in the cattle truck or on the school bus where we sang every song we knew and felt a bonding between classmates that we remember to this day. Graduation was a sad day for those of us not graduating, but a very special day for those

who were. This was the day the graduates left the campus. Most graduates' stay at Buckner had made up the largest portion of their lives and they were like kin to the rest of us. However, Baccalaureate Day helped prepare us to break the ties. It was a Sunday when a special church service was held for the graduates and after lunch the graduates, in their suits (the girls made theirs), hats and new shoes, walked about the campus with their brothers and sisters and special friends. It was like a farewell visit among just "us," the orphan family. The graduates were honoring the matrons and helpers, classmates, friends, brothers and sisters. We, in turn, had great respect and were proud of those who were leaving. Each year I thought, "This is the best group that ever graduated from Buckner."

Sometimes a relative or acquaintance from the past would visit us Richardson kids. We could go off the campus on a day pass or once a year get a pass for seventy-two hours. My older sister, who was a teenager when we went to Buckner, could not be enrolled because no teenagers (thirteen-year-olds and older) were accepted in 1939. This sister, nine years older than I, and her husband would visit us during the year and get us a pass each summer. She provided us a link with our past and upgraded our wardrobes so that we could have shoes, bows, belts, etc., selected according to our taste. This act of kindness, at great cost to her and her husband, made a lasting impression.

Special programs made up special days for me. The Quiz Kids radio program came to the campus when I was about seven years old. Special scientific programs were demonstrated. Sound controlled by a beam of light made up a program as well as the demonstration of a microwave years before they were available. A consultant for movie stars came to give us tips on proper hair styling, posture and public graces. Music programs brought by bands, symphonies and choirs were also special. We always looked forward to the music programs from our own students and even more so from graduates such as Major Thomas, whose style of piano playing entertained us while he was on campus and also when he would return for a visit. We were sorry to have to give up the popular minstrel program performed by the men and boys. Banquets, when we were able to wear long dresses and sit by our boyfriends, made us feel very grown up. Having a wedding on campus was an event we never forgot.

ELEMENTARY AND HIGH SCHOOL

All schooling was on the campus. Grades one through eight were in one building and nine through twelve were in another. There was a gymnasium, swimming pool, track and football field, a stadium and school auditorium, all on the campus. The first two grades of school were interesting, but for some reason very difficult. While I was in the second grade, the administration increased the grades from eleven to twelve and students moved up a grade. I was already one of the youngest in the class. I had had a chance to go to a one room school before I came to Buckner (the school was just across the road from our house). Many children had never been to school or their early education had been interrupted because of the tragedy that was part of their lives. Many classes had students two or more years older than was considered normal for that grade level. It was just the opposite with me. I was two years younger than I was supposed to be for my grade.

Music was the best thing about school. The Rhythm Band was my favorite subject. We went all over Texas playing in the Rhythm Band. Jo Nell Brown, an older girl, was our leader and my greatest inspiration. Hazel Brown, Mildred Campbell and I were three bird whistlers and wood block players. We wore uniforms and paraded and played before many Baptist Churches in the area. Once we went all the way to Houston, Texas, to perform for the Texas Baptist Convention. When the choir performed, I was enthralled and looked forward to the time I could sing or listen to music.

There was a time in the early forties that the music program at Buckner was one of the best in the State, and the students received honors in interscholastic league competition. It was equal to our sports program, where Buckner excelled in football, basketball and track. For several years students participated in Interscholastic League, winning honors in interpretive reading, creative writing, slide rule, debate and typing.

The part of school I disliked most of all was the unorganized part. Anything that had to do with free play was boring and dreaded. This included art, free reading, science and recess. It was true we had balls, jump ropes, bats and softballs, but without organization it was just a free for all, and I disliked it immensely. Therefore, I tried to stay in from recess as much as possible, once having it written on my record that I was disobedient. I was just staying in to finish a poem I was trying to write.

When there was a diversion in school, it was exciting. Several times I was chosen to be a part of the plays in high school and was allowed to take time out from my elementary school to practice. I watched everything the older girls did and looked forward to the day when I would be "a big girl."

Each year as we progressed through the grades, we were moved to another part of the building we were in or to the next one. This was the progression for the girls. The boys had similar ones on their side of the sixty acre campus. With each move special privileges were given. Hardin Home generally housed girls in first through fourth grades. We were given special opportunities in Hardin. We had excellent playground equipment, jump ropes, skates, balls of all sizes, bats and even one bicycle. When the weather was too cold or wet, we could play in the attic. Halloween was celebrated there as well. The fourth graders could have Stunt Night and opportunities to walk about the campus with a matron in small groups at least once a week. We could buy candy at the Gatehouse. Two or three times each summer we went to the girls' woods to hike, ride horses and have special treats. I remember: Mildred Campbell, Alice Ward, Barbara Ann Dean, Betty Jo Harwood. Mary and Helen Curda, Elisa Harvey and Joyce Stephens, Betty Scurlock, Jean Tilley, Hazel and Jo Nell Brown.

Crouch housed girls fifth through seventh grades. We could visit each others' rooms without permission, and the seventh graders could listen to the radio everyday at 5:00 P.M. We were given opportunities to develop skills in sewing, memorization, developing skits and readings to perform in dorm assemblies. Mary Beth Cutshall was especially talented in crocheting, knitting, tatting and various types of embroidery stitchings. To no one's surprise she won the Home Economics Award for sewing in High School. We were given tutoring after school if needed. We could visit other dorms on Saturdays and Sundays. We didn't have much play equipment but were given opportunities to dig in the dirt, go swimming three times a week, ride horses as a single rider and play softball. There were more girls per matron here, so there was a sense of greater freedom. I remember Mary Turner, Noni Duckworth, Veoma Clung, and Imogene Woods.

HUNT

Hunt housed girls eighth through tenth grades. We could go to overnight camp, play outside anytime we wanted to (as long as we stayed in designated areas), grow our hair long, go off campus (into Dallas) with an older girl as chaperone. We could walk in small groups one mile off campus to Evans Store. We could have a declared boyfriend and sit with him in the gymnasium and at church on Sunday evenings. We had work schedules that changed every three or four months. We were assigned jobs. Some of these were in the Manna Hall (dining hall) or Laundry. One of my favorite jobs was working in the Hospital. I enjoyed cleaning the floors, washing the dishes and changing the beds. In the Sunbeam Home it was fun seeing the little kids. After they ate, we cleaned their floors and washed their dishes. I also enjoyed being the door girl in Manna Hall, which meant I stood and held the door as everyone came in. That meant I could see and greet everyone.

It was my job to call the Manna Hall girls early to get them to do their work before each meal. I liked waiting on tables and didn't mind washing the dishes. I disliked laundry when I had to iron clothes, but I didn't mind using the mangle. I remember Alberta Disch, Nelba Jo Jennings, Sara Crouch, Rita Mae Tarlton, Viola Wright, Rosa Lee Woods, Doris Bleakley, Gladys Hall, Jane McWhorter, Willie Mae Stringer, Betty Jean Nelson, Josephine Newton and Mary Nell Oliver, Frances Moore, and Imogene Stringer.

BUHRMAN HALL

At last we could be counted as "big girls" with all their privileges. These included being a part of Student Council, being a pep squad leader, wearing hose and high heels, playing on a basketball or volleyball team, having a parlor date after church every Sunday night, being with a boy at the Fourth of July Picnic at White Rock Lake, The State Fair of Texas and "hanging out" with a boy after school each day by walking with them down the school sidewalk. Also we could make money by doing a teacher's laundry and continue with all the privileges awarded before. But we still had to line up to go to Manna Hall and wear socks, even with sandals. We could use the telephone about once a month. I remember Dorothy Thedford, Eva Nell Turner, Dessie Hardin, Catherine Goodwill, Peggy Grusendorf, Roberta Clarkson, Juanita Graves, Dorothy Simmons. Juanita Minatra, Judy Miller, Betty Lookadoo, Betty Clark, Joy Smith, Pearl Griffin, Elizabeth Atkinson, and Dorothy Kimbell.

ACADEMY SENIORS

This new program started the graduating year of my senior class. Before the school year started for the class of 1950, we were given a choice to stay another year or graduate with the class. If we chose to stay another year, then we were told we would be taking Bible classes for most of the school year 1950 and 1951. The administration even hinted that they would try to get some of the classes we were going to take accepted in the Baptist college we would attend. It wasn't a very popular idea with the boys, but several girls thought it was a good idea, so nine girls and one boy chose to stay. This new program was to be separated from the High School classes and was to be called the Buckner Baptist Academy.

Because I was so young (sixteen), I was one of the ten students who elected to stay. I didn't think I was mature enough to go to college. There were some positive and negative aspects of staying. In fact, we had two senior years. Yet, the first year wasn't great because we weren't graduating. The second year wasn't a special year because most of our classmates were gone and we were somewhat segregated. We didn't fit in anymore. We did not have classes with any of the other kids. However, even going to the Texas State Fair, the Junior and Senior picnic and taking special trips off campus to sing or to give some information about the Home were all lacking without those that had been in our class for so many years. We were used to having boys our age or older in our classes and in our plays. Now the boys all seemed younger and all matched up with their younger female classmates. I was lonesome for my classmates that had graduated. But we did get to know those who stayed much better. They were Marie Bailey, Margaret Corcoran, Frances Fulton, Wanda Godsey, Katherine Henslee, Rena Key, Jeanette Phillips, Wanda Mae Polk and I. The only boy our age left was Willie Hall.

The good part was we had another year to work out where we would go to college. There were new teachers on the campus, and many of them were couples. The adults on campus, for the most part, had always been single women. The rules seemed relaxed for us, but when I try to think of what exactly was different with the rules, I can not think of a change. Teachers seemed more friendly and engaged us in serious conversations. They seemed to be in a counseling rather than disciplinarian role.

We seemed to have different ideas that did not fit in with what we had been doing, such as not going to the dining hall on Saturday with our hair up in rollers. We wanted to dress nicer even when we were not going to school or to church. The last year at Buckner we no longer wanted to have our hair in rollers or pin curlers outside our rooms. We took better care of our personal hygiene. We wanted a different type of clothes that we were not issued. We did not want to wear socks with our sandals. We did not want our mail read by the matrons. We wanted to visit friends off campus.

As graduation from our Academy Year was nearing, we were given still another choice. We could stay during the summer at Buckner, and we could be the first occupants in a brand new dormitory (Pender Hall), where a married couple would supervise us. We would have many of the old rules abolished for us. We did not have to go to Manna Hall with the others. We ate where the teachers ate and had special food. We worked in the Maris Center, with children in the Sunbeam Home or with the Campus Mart. Our work earned us money. We taught Vacation Bible School and Sunday School classes. We could go anywhere on the campus that we wished when we wished, except in the boys' rooms. We could use the telephone, our mail was not read and we could date boys off campus, unchaperoned. I remember Joan Bye, Ruth Nevil, Norma Lookadoo, Daisy Morgan and Doris Bleakley from those days.

A few of us stayed that summer and really enjoyed a different aspect of life at Buckner. At one of the off campus programs that we gave to Baptist groups, I met Mrs. T. C. Bateson who introduced me into her family that eventually became my foster family. I left the Home, staying with the Batesons for a few weeks before going to Howard Payne College for my undergraduate work. This family truly became my family, sponsoring me through school, and being Godparents to my children. From 1950 to 1989 when Mrs. Bateson died, we remained family. Even now

their adopted son is like my brother, and he calls me his sister. That summer of 1951, I remember that Rena Key, Margaret Corcoran, Marie Bailey and I were the last Academy Seniors to leave Buckner Orphans Home.

Hazel (Kinnard) Brown, '52

I was placed in Buckner at a very young age and went first to the Sunbeam Home. I remember back in those days that our caretakers were worried about our not getting enough vitamin D, so weather permitting, we were marched single file out to the yard, boys and girls separately. There we would spread our little blankets on the ground, take off our sunsuits, and lie down on the blankets, "toasting" first on one side for a short time and then on the other. No wonder I was as brown as a coffee bean! My nickname was "Brownie" for a long time.

Also, at a young age (probably six or seven) we were taken, twenty or twenty-five at a time and our tonsils and adenoids were removed, whether they needed to be or not; this was to prevent illnesses of various kinds. I remember being brought orange juice for breakfast the next morning and finding that drinking it set my throat on fire!

Being the youngest of three girls, I had to follow suit in every way. First LaVoe was a rhythm band leader, then Jo Nell, then me. I remember the maroon velvet dress with the white lace collar, and climbing up on the offering table in front of the pulpit in church. There I would turn and curtsy to the audience, then turn and lead the band. Also, since both LaVoe and Jo Nell had taken piano lessons, so did I, in spite of having no talent for it. The first two years we studied composers' lives which I found uninteresting. Another girl and I got caught two in a room playing chopsticks together—this was not allowed—and had to work off a number of demerits.

One of my duties was getting the girls who worked in Manna Hall up in the mornings. I remember getting up very early and going to each floor and yelling down the halls "Manna Hall Girls!" While working kitchen duty, I got caught by Mrs. Mamie "sampling" the mashed potatoes one day. She told me had I tried to hide it, I would have been punished, but since I hadn't, a reprimand was all I got. I also ate so much whipped cream I got sick, and for years afterward, I wouldn't even look at the stuff.

I remember working in the laundry and folding hot sheets as they came off the mangle, ironing starched shirts "dry" and "without wrinkles." Mrs. McKinney was a stickler for properly ironed shirts!

I remember picking cotton, riding in cattle trucks, football games, going to the State Fair, Saturday night movies, Sunday School and church, parlor "dates" on Sunday evenings, Christmas in the school auditorium, picking and cleaning chickens, making "bean boats" out of fresh, hot bread from the bakery, and Mrs. Ratcliff's pecan divinity.

I remember being baptized by Brother Hal, the Fourth of July picnics where we always had RC Cola to drink, sing-songs in the parlor, waxing and polishing those beautiful wooden floors in the parlor by having girls lie down on a quilt and several others pulling them up and down the room to shine the floors, and shine they did!

I remember "cooking" bologna on the radiator and making sandwiches, and talking after "lights out."

Some of the girls sneaked out of the dorm at night to meet with their boyfriends out at Father Buckner's statue. We used the phrase "going with" about our relationship with our boyfriends. Where did we go?

I am grateful to have grown up at Buckner—I received a good education, never lacked for food or clothing, was taught values, and was a member of a very large "family" of brothers and sisters.

The Day Brothers' Day at Buckner

by Vernon Horsley

In 1936 the Day family came to Buckner from Winnsboro, Texas. After losing her husband to cancer, Gussie Day came to work at Buckner and brought with her four children. They were Fon, three years of age; Carroll, four; Virginia Ann, eight; and Sue, ten. Mrs. Day became the housemother on the second floor of Freeland, where she remained until she left the home in

1950. When she died in 1987, she was eighty-two years old.

Sue graduated from Buckner High School in 1943. Virginia Ann followed in 1946. Virginia Ann started the Day tradition in basketball; however, Fon and Carroll received all the notice with their athletic abilities.

Fon won the shot put as a freshman. He also won the 200-yard low hurdles and placed second in the high jump. From this record, you may have guessed he was the high point man of his freshman class. No record survives of Carroll's achievements as a freshman, but as a sophomore he won the high jump, tied for 1st in pole vault, placed 3rd in shot put and ran on the first place mile-relay team. He also placed 4th in discus.

The next year both brothers not only starred in football and basketball, but were also outstanding in track. Both Caroll and Fon were named all-district in football in 1950.

The year of their greatest achievements was 1951. Buckner won the District Track Meet by 67 points. The meet was really a "field day" for Carroll and Fon. Carroll won two individual events. Fon won three individual events. Each of them won two second places. They were also on the first place mile-relay team. Carroll was named as the Dallas County Athlete of the Year for 1951. [The Horsley twins, Vance and Vernon, had won this award in 1950, Ed.]

Buckner won its second consecutive regional meet in 1951. Carroll set a new regional record in the high jump (6' 3"). Fon set new records in the shot put and the 440-yard dash.

At the state meet they did not fare well. Carroll tied for 2nd in high jump and Fon took 2nd in shot put. Carroll also tied for 4th in the pole vault.

The following year, Buckner dropped out of state sponsored athletics, and the records during those years are not available at the present time.

The Day brothers left the home in 1952 at the height of their athletic careers, and eventually both joined the Coast Guard. Though I have no access to the records of their Coast Guard years, I'm sure they continued their athletic careers in the service.

Carroll died of lung cancer in 1979. Fon lives with his sweet wife in Levelland, Texas. His sister, Sue, lives in Lubbock. Virginia Ann, now retired, lives in Dallas. She took care of her mother from 1950 until her death in 1987.

The passing of the years and the scarcity of records from so long ago erase their legend somewhat. Our memories and some paltry records can't truly show the outstanding athletic abilities of Carroll and Fon.

Their kind of ability comes only from God. They were truly blessed. The proof of their exceptional gifts is in the fact that they began their careers as outstanding athletes while the rest of us had to strive to compete for greatness and never reached it.

Daisy (Breland) Morgan, '51

GRADUATION DAY!

May 1944. Excitement could be felt all over the campus. For those graduating it must have been sheer delight and high expectations; the end of one era of their lives and the beginning of one with high hopes and dreams of success for the future. To the "little girls" it was an extra event for the week since the only events that we were privileged to attend were the movies on Saturday night and church on Sunday morning.

At the age of twelve, I had a different reason; I had never heard of, much less attended, a graduation ceremony. In Panama before I came to Buckner, I had attended school on a limited basis only, and for just nine months in American schools. From hearing the other girls talk and observing the actions of the "big girls" about this event, I simply could not imagine what a graduation was all about.

I determined that I would attend this ceremony. There was only one hitch to this intention; I was in the hospital with the chicken pox. Nevertheless, I simply had to attend this event. I made my plans for sneaking out of the hospital, pajamas and all. I wish that I could remember exactly how I did it, but I only know I did manage just that, pajamas and all.

I sneaked into the Crouch dormitory, went to my room to change my clothes and prepare to get into the line to attend this high school graduation. Well, what was I thinking? Did I think that I would not be noticed by the matron? Did I think that my presence would go unnoticed by the other girls? I really didn't care; I had to take my chances to see this thing called high school graduation.

Needless to say, one of the girls (I wish I knew who) reported to Miss Mays my escape from the hospital and my intention of attending the graduation. That was the end of my escape; I had to return to the hospital with my chicken pox, totally devastated and disappointed. I would have to wait a whole year before I would find out what these graduation exercises were all about. And eight long years before I experienced my own graduation.

EAR PIERCING

I believe it was in 1945 when we had a new girl to appear on the scene in the Hunt dormitory. Her name was Tressie Perkins and of all things, she had pierced ears! Certainly none of the younger girls had had that experience although some of the older girls might have. I don't remember, but I don't believe that they did. Tressie told us that there was nothing to ear piercing and she would be glad to accommodate us.

At the time none of us even had earrings to wear after the ear piercing and of course, no possibilities of getting earrings to wear. What in the world were we thinking and what were we going to do to keep these holes open once they were placed in our ears? The only thing that we could think to do was to wear broom straws in our pierced ears, hoping that at some time we would be fortunate enough to be the owners of a pair of earrings.

I took my turn piercing the ears of various girls. It really didn't hurt that much, and all you had to do was to get a needle, alcohol, cotton and something to put behind the ear lobe to make it rigid. I chose the back of a lipstick tube!

One night after the lights were out, several of us got together for an ear piercing episode. We sneaked out on the landing of the second floor since the lights were left on all night on both stairs of the dorm. We had our necessary materials together and I went to work.

I had already pierced several pairs of ears with success when I started to pierce the ears of Betty Jean Nelson. The first one went very well. However, something was amiss about the second one, so I had to insert the needle a second time. When I did, blood spurted out of her earlobe and she turned pale. We were scared to death! We had no idea what would happen. Someone ran to get a wet washcloth to wipe her brow in hopes that she would not faint right there in front of all of us. Luckily, she did not faint, but that was the end of our ear piercing episode for the night. In fact, I did not attempt to do any more ear piercing after that, ever. We proudly sported the broom straws that we had simply plucked from the brooms that we used to sweep the floors in the dormitories and the Manna Hall. Though we were taking an awful chance by ignoring the laws of good hygiene, fortunately no one got an infection from our ear-ring derring-do.

Mary (Jackson) Turner, '52

As I have been thinking about Buckner, many things come to mind. I still remember the consuming, lonesome feeling when my family entered the Receiving Home, but later there were happy times.

Some fun times included going to the Girls' Woods for summer camp and experiencing my first snipe hunt; finally realizing those girls were just pulling my leg. It took a very long time to realize that. Also, I remember cooking out and how delicious everything tasted; however, that first taste of celery made me know that it was not a favorite of mine. We loved sleeping outside with about four of us pooling our quilts, piling three on the bottom and saving one to cover with when the dew came. We awoke to a damp bed, but what fun. Picking up wood for the campfire where we sang and told stories, going trail riding, and learning to play 42 were some additional memorable times. The teachers who went with us were no longer just our teachers, but our friends as well.

Going swimming every other day at our scheduled hour was a time I looked forward to as much as anything. Because I wanted to be brave and show how I could dive, I dived off the side and just hit bottom hard on my knees, skinning both. But to show just how brave I was, I got out of the water smiling instead of crying (at least on the outside).

Some other summer special times were: sitting around outside singing songs such as "Don't Fence Me In" while looking at the fence surrounding the Home, waiting for the truck that would bring us watermelons. Then the matrons sliced them and we dug in with our mouths and hands—juice everywhere, but how delicious. However, the favored special moment was watch-

ing for the church groups that would bring us that fried chicken lunch. We would say, as the visitors watched us from the balcony, that they were up there talking about those "poor little orphans."

I especially loved those long summer hours of reading to my heart's content.

Going to the State Fair each fall in the large cattle trucks was something we eagerly looked forward to, and when we were a certain age, we could even ride on the rides at the Midway with our boyfriends. We were given some free rides, after seeing the exhibits first, of course. Usually our boyfriends had more cotton picking money saved than we girls did, so with their financial assistance, we ate and rode the rides to the last penny. When the returning cattle truck turned a corner, we all fell to one side, screaming as we did, but it was an exciting time.

I wanted to take piano lessons, and when Mrs. Roberts came to teach piano there, she let anyone who was interested try out. As a result my two sisters and I all got to take piano.

Singing in the Girls' Choir was a treat, not only because I loved music, but also because we often got to go to churches and sing. Naturally, we always laughed about "singing for our supper" because, of course, there was an appeal for financial assistance for the Home before we finished the program.

The outstanding teachers, Mrs. Dickey, and others who encouraged us, made us feel capable and also made us want to excel. Principals such as Mr. Browning gave us support and encouragement that we still remember.

Having friends was very important though some were merciless pranksters and got us into trouble. When I had a boil in a strategic spot, I went to bed early one night and jumped right up when I discovered a horned toad in my bed. (Jumping up and down hurts if you have a boil in a strategic spot!) Of course, when Daisy Morgan laughed the loudest, I immediately knew it was she who had hidden the toad among my sheets.

Some jobs were more enjoyable than others, and laundry was one that was dreaded. We sweated (not perspired) and lost our hair-do as well— hair spray had not been invented then. We often had to change clothes when we finished work for the morning, noon or afternoon.

Working in the Commissary was an envied job, and especially with Mrs. Pharr in charge of us. If we worked there, of course, every so often we would get to pick out something new for ourselves that had come in and been put in the clothing bin. (Usually our matrons selected our clothes.) One other advantage was that sometimes the boys downstairs in the bakery would throw us up a loaf of bread through the chute, usually with Pap Grube's approval.

I can still remember the anticipation we had as Christmas drew closer. We went to the auditorium with our matron and usually had a short program. Then the older girls and boys would pass out the strings—all our presents, which consisted of toys for the younger ones, along with a new dress (We did look forward to the new dress we got only at Christmas.), socks, and underwear. Then we ran back to the dorm and couldn't wait to untie the string.

I can still taste the bread and butter melted on the old radiators after we would sneak it out of the Manna Hall. It tasted better than what we had eaten at supper after marching in to the sounds of the piano playing and raising our voices in singing a hymn. We all especially looked forward to hearing Major Thomas when he would be on leave from the service and come for a visit. He could tinkle those piano keys and entertain us royally. I also enjoyed taking my turn singing and playing as I got older and more proficient at the piano.

As we moved into the oldest girls' and boys' dorms, we could walk from the Chapel on Sunday night with our boyfriends and sit in the parlor for an hour with them—while the matron sat there reading her magazine upside down. Sometimes we sneaked in a little hand-holding on the way to the parlor.

I also remember Mrs. Ratcliff, whom we all learned to love after we discovered her soft, tender side. She went down the hall when the rooms were not clean, telling us she was separating the sheep from the goats. Some were definitely with the goats, but it was so encouraging to hear her say to me that I would be with the sheep.

While the loneliness at Buckner sometimes overwhelmed me, I felt very fortunate that my mother, Mrs. Gussie Turner, worked there and we were allowed to visit her. With the encouragement and support of her, my teachers and matrons, I received a scholarship to Howard Payne College. Thus, I was able to fulfill a lifelong desire to be a teacher and eventually to receive a masters in counseling.

I am thankful for a Christian mother who, when left with seven children, had faith that she could keep the family together. She was blessed with children, grandchildren and great grandchildren, forty-three in all. Today, some are homemakers, some in the business world, some in church work, and some on the mission field. I can honestly say to my students and to the world, "Yes, there are adversities, hardships and obstacles in life, but you can make it in spite of them."

Edward Stanley, '52

Rabbit hunting was a legendary pastime for boys at Buckner. As was the custom, we would line up across a cotton field, armed with cut-off baseball bats. As we moved along the rows, rabbits would scurry away to be chased by dogs until they circled back to be pounced upon by the boys.

My older brother, Billie Joe, a very fast runner, chose an alternative to throwing a club. He would chase the rabbit (outrunning the dogs). As he pulled even with the rabbit, he would feel the rabbit's ribs to see if it were prime for eating. If satisfied, he would scoop it up. If not, he proceeded to catch up with the next rabbit.

I cannot attest to the accuracy of this story, only what I have been told. I believed it, however, and enjoyed hearing stories of his running prowess as we sat around the cookout fire (after he had graduated and left the Home). I also enjoyed eating fried rabbit and roasted ears of corn.

Mildred Ann (Reed) Curda, '53

We had to wax the parlor floors at Hardin, Hunt, and Crouch Home. We first waxed them, and then we all got on a quilt. Two or three other kids, possibly four, squatted down on their knees while two other kids pulled the quilt. There was always an argument as to who got to sit down on the quilt and who had to do the pulling. The two pulling grabbed the end of the quilt and pulled the people sitting, and thus, the floors were polished. There were no electric floor polishers, but we made excellent floor polishers, always making a game of it.

We had those beautiful hardwood floors. They were creaky, and our idea of getting into mischief in those days was silly by today's thinking. Some girls did get into trouble by sneaking out the window to go across the campus to visit the boys. I never did anything like that because if I had been caught, it would have meant, not only a spanking from the matron, but also one from Mother. "Miss Goodie Two-Shoes" kept her nose fairly clean in that respect. One evening, someone dared me to sneak across the parlor floor into Mrs. Ratcliff's rooming area in Hunt Home. I took the "double-dog-dare" and proceeded with my mischief. I hit that stupid creaking parlor floor, and Mrs. Ratcliff came out and asked me what I needed. I thought myself so very clever; I told her that I had a stomach ache. She invited me in and gave me something for it; three tablespoons of Milk of Magnesia. When I finished taking that medicine, I went back into my room and told all those girls that I was going to kill them! I had a terrible temper, and I yelled: "I'm going to kill everyone of you!" Of course, the other girls cracked up laughing at me on the spot.

Once again I had been naughty, and the matron told me that I was going to stay at home from the movie that Saturday night. We had movies every Saturday night in the school auditorium. At that particular time, we not only had the movie, but we also had a serial before the main feature. *"Zorro!"* We were going to see *"Zorro,"* and I was in love with Zorro. Guy Madison! There was no way that I was going to miss that serial! Mother was sitting in the chair on the aisle, and I sat right next to her. The wooden seats were like the church seats, rolled arms with a high back and a lot of scroll work on the edge of it. I huddled behind the edge of the seat. When I saw my matron come in, I huddled down even closer to Mother. Mother kept asking me what was wrong. I couldn't tell her that I was hiding. Either I was seen at the movie, or else I was missed at the dormitory when they made a head count of those having to stay at home. I was missing from the list. Yep! I got into it again. Boy! Did I ever catch it!

When I was older, I drew kitchen detail, which was actually one of the better jobs to my way of thinking. We rotated jobs about every three or four months. The kids who worked in the dining hall washed the tables, dishes and mopped floors. Those were the gross jobs. As we became older, we graduated to what we considered the better jobs. At first, I thought the kitchen job was great, but now that I have thought back, it wasn't such a hot deal. We had to be up at four in the morning to go over to the kitchen to peel onions. We had a potato peeler, but we girls also had to dig out the eyes from the potatoes. Whoever had the alarm clock went around, whether it was assigned or not, to wake up everyone. I always shut off the alarm clock and went back to sleep. Being a sleepy head kept me in hot water. My biggest promotion was that of being moved to the pantry. Now that was the job! Everyone aspired to a pantry job. That was where all the food was kept. We never went without food when we had that job. We simply picked up anything we wanted. We called it stealing because we certainly hadn't asked for it. When we took it without permission, we often as not had to eat it on the spot. Miss Mamie knew every pea, every bean and every quart jar that came into that kitchen from the good Baptists of Texas.

Saturday morning was the day that the bakery sent over the week-end bread. The dairy sent over fresh butter, and the bakery also turned out sweet rolls, cakes, pies—all mighty good eating. Our sweet rolls looked like a cow chip, and so we called them "cow piles." We literally unrolled the "cow chip" as we ate it, never even being bothered by the ugly name we had given it. When the fresh bread came over on Saturday, we learned to rip out the end of a hot loaf, fill it with beans and then gorge ourselves. Saturday noon was pinto beans, corn bread, and fresh onion day.

We had different desserts each night; one night there was cake; on Tuesday nights we had Boston Creme Pie. Everyone loved Thursday nights, and I loved it especially when there was chocolate pie, even though there was no meringue on the pies. Mary, my sister, no longer cared for chocolate pie as much as before, and we often swapped out desserts. Actually, I thought Mary liked it as well as I, but was just pampering her little sister.

It turned out that Mary had been caught with a whole pie in her possession. She and several others snitched it, but before they could divide it, an adult came on the scene. Mary had to eat the entire chocolate pie within minutes. No wonder she didn't care for chocolate pie so much after that affair! Mary always traded me her chocolate pie for my lemon pie when it was served. On that day, my slice of the lemon pie traveled across the entire length of the dinning room to Mary. When chocolate pie was served, she then sent her trade-off pie across the same route to reach me. That was a weekly ritual. I had previously thought it generous and sacrificing of Mary to trade me her pie. However, after being a party to pie stealing myself, I figured that she always had her fill before dinner. I didn't find out the truth behind that story until the summer of '89.

There were times that various country churches affiliated with the Southern Baptists sent out cakes and fried chicken to the home. We tried to pick out the most beautiful, the most delicious cake, and the one with the best chocolate icing on it for our own personal attention. We only got what we deserved, if it turned out to be a funky cake with only a beautiful icing on it—dried up already. Actually, we did receive some mighty good cakes in those days.

There was always a ritual in the dining room; we sang a hymn and had a prayer before we ate. Various matrons led in the prayer, and everyone always dreaded when Miss Zapp returned thanks, for she prayed for ten minutes, or what we thought was ten minutes. She absolutely blessed everyone and everything in this world. She was one of our favorite matrons, along with Miss Orr. Miss Zapp might have made number one on our list had she not been so long-winded.

James Graves, '53

THE TRIBE

On the journey to manhood, the rites of passage that young men face usually happen late in their teens. However, lesser rites occur earlier and as surely shape the man through the boy. In the early forties at Buckner Home, we were as far removed from Dallas as Jamestown is from England. We still used "pigeye," a shortened "in a pig's eye" from the speech of the English Middle Ages. Our meaning was "I take back what I said" or "I was only teasing," usually uttered under heavy duress.

Isolated by miles of farmland, shielded from outside influence by a secular curtain, we tended to a tribal social order. What we knew of the outside was from homemade crystal radio sets, old books or rare visits with kin.

By age twelve we boys were set in our pecking order. Entering the tribe early, we were all pushed, from the largest to the smallest, till we claimed our lot. Securely ranked by our now friends, each did not cross the big boys, nor bring wrath from above in harming the little boys.

Lords of all, the big boys stayed near their "hill." We below were male cubs in harmless play with undercurrents of menace toward weaklings or outsiders. Rare status moves were foreshadowed by growth spurts or a perceived weakness and heralded by shouts of "fight! fight!" Watched by all, 'ole so and so turned on 'ole such and such. With more posturing than pain, the weak link was reforged, the chain strengthened.

Dodging an occasional spinning top amid cries of "slips" from the endless marble games, we talked, read, or whiled the days in seemingly timeless childhood.

THE INTRUDER

The murmur of play slowed, then stopped. Heads turned in alert to a dimly felt call of danger. A breeze stirred the neck and lips curled in an ancient reflex. The newcomer saw smiles. Our dogs glimpsed teeth and rose with us.

Cane in one hand, arm slung in a cast, he emerged from the car and limped into our world. His goal was the office of Ms. Clark, first floor matron.

Secure in ourselves, we watched as little ones, younger and in a different branch of our tribe, danced a gauntlet of excitement just out of reach. He struggled on, ignoring their cries. As he neared our marble pits, excitement spread to some who sensed advantage in weakness. A few moved nearer, uncertain in purpose. No one in memory had broken the chain for years. Entry had been early or not at all, since outside older ones might corrupt us.

Pushed forward by the more timid, a red-head blocked the way. The newcomer half raised the cane in alarm. Silence fell and time slowed as they faced each other, the untried and the unsure.

The hill stirred; then a message moved our way. Keepers of the unwritten had spoken. Fairness postponed any reckoning. Security for all lay in safety as one.

Eying our toes, we scuffed sand into circles

while a big boy talked, then pointed him to the dorm. Moving away, other voices rose behind him with the words "accident . . . car wreck . . . lost both . . ." threaded through. Slightly shamed and with a lesson learned, we returned to our play.

Alone, unranked, but one of us already, the boy labored up the steps toward his new home.

THURSDAY

Friday means weekends. Saturday's for chores. Sunday to church. Monday runs uphill. Wednesdays are halfway. This much is true for everyone.

For Buckner Exes though, one day has a different connotation than it does for others. Thursday is blessed and peculiar. With their memory dimmed by age, perhaps the lightness still in their step is unrecognized in origin, but I say it's because they remember Thursdays at Buckner.

Manna Hall to a child was a cavern abuzz with conversation. Endless tables stretched from the boys' side to the girls' side. A piano rested on a small stage where girls sang hymns before the blessing.

In the kitchen Miss Mamie ruled and stood by the line as the older girls moved food to their assigned tables. Mistakes brought sharp words to stinging ears.

The girls moved as dancers, arms raised with trays full, in an innocent ballet of sureness. Unfamiliar feelings stirred the older boys to follow their movements as they filled plates and returned for more.

Finally seating herself at the table's head, the waitress brought to the little boys a softness needed in their lives. As close to being a family as we could be, the plain nourishing food was eaten.

On rare nights the voices stopped abruptly, followed by hopeful whispers of "ice cream." The silence was almost painful as the girls rose at a signal, moving to the line. Returning with the prize, they rejoined their table families amid voices raised higher by anticipation.

Afterward, always wanting more, we wondered when the next treat would come. In our uncertain lives we had learned that little could be reckoned on. Then remembering, we quietly hugged ourselves inside. There was always Thursday. Thursday was special. Thursday was Pie Night!

Anonymous, '54

I don't know why the following happened to me. I had forgotten all about it until recently, when I needed something to cheer me up.

The event happened in the 1950s in East Texas, and at that time there was a great deal of racial prejudice. White people did not treat Black people very well. The Blacks were not allowed to eat or drink in the same places that whites used.

I was sixteen-years-old and in Buckner Orphans Home where all the boys had to help do the oat harvest. The oats were cut and tied into bundles that we called shocks. The shocks were left in the fields in sacks. We went from stack to stack and used pitchforks to throw the shocks into a large semi-truck with high sideboards.

After we loaded the shocks into the trailer, we then rode on top of the oats to the location where a large thresher was operating. The thresher was north of the main campus and just outside the area of the farm buildings. Since the weather was really hot and humid, most of us were working without our shirts. We used the pitchforks to throw the oat shocks off the truck and into the thresher.

We finished the unloading and then we all had a drink of water from the water cooler hanging on the side of the thresher. We were using a pint mason jar for our community glass. I was the first one to get a drink. Just after I had put the mason jar down beside the water cooler, one of the boys touched me on the shoulder and said. "He wants a drink of water." I turned to my right to look and there was a middle-aged Black man in a suit and tie, standing right with us. I had not seen him walk up. His black suit was clean and well pressed and his tie was red. His shirt was brilliant white with no signs of wrinkles, ring around the collar or sweat. His shoes were shinny black and not dusty.

The Black man looked right into my eyes and said that he had come a long way and still had a long way to go before he was home. He asked if he could have a drink of our water. I said sure and started to reach for the jar to fill it for him. One of the older boys jumped up on the platform beside the thresher and said that we only had the one jar to drink out of and that he could not use it. Someone said that the Black man could kneel down below the water cooler, and that he would hold the spout open for the man to drink by catching the water in his hand. I realized that the man would be kneeling in the mud below the water cooler.

While they were discussing various ways that he could get a drink, I just took the jar and filled it for him. I handed it to the Black man. He drank about half of it and handed the jar back to me. I felt so bad for him and the humiliation that he was feeling. I wanted him to know that not all of us were like that. I started to drink the water. I had a hard time with the first couple of swallows, but after I started, the water tasted very good and I drank it all down easily. I put the jar back on the thresher by the water cooler. The same boy that initially objected, grabbed the jar and threw it against the thresher, breaking the jar. He then drew back his fist and called me a "nigger lover" as he started to hit me. Then he stopped and had a very puzzled look on his face.

He just turned and walked away. I turned to speak to the man, but he was nowhere to be seen. The two or three boys that were standing with me could not agree as to which way he had gone. He would have had to go a quarter mile to the nearest place that we could think of for us not to have been able to see him. He had simply vanished.

This was not the last time that I saw that old man. I had one more encounter with him.

The year after the incident at the thresher, Chico, Wendle and I were exploring a piece of Home land that we had never been on before. It was to the south of the Home. The land was not cultivated and had a few scrub mesquite trees on it. We were attracted to one spot by a few buzzards flying low. When we got to the spot, we found a dead cow. Of course, Wendle had to poke her bloated belly with a stick. The smell and the heat made me feel a little sick and very thirsty. Wendle pointed out that just a short way to the south there was a road and a row of shacks. They were the type that Black people occupied all over east Texas. I was afraid to go there but could not say that. We decided to walk to the small houses and ask for a drink of water. Most white people feared the Black people as much as they feared us.

The houses were built up higher than usual off the ground with front porches just about belly button high. We had to climb a barbed wire fence and then cross a blacktop road to get to the houses. We started across the road toward one house where a large Black woman was sitting on the

porch. The yards were all green and neatly mowed. About forty feet behind the houses, the mowed grass ended and there the weeds, about a foot high, began. I was almost across the road when that same Black man that I had encountered the year before, just appeared out of nowhere right where the backyard ended.

I realized that something strange had just happened. I did not see him come from behind anything. He was just suddenly coming toward me as though he had walked through a tear in the sky. He was wearing the exact same clothes that he had had on the first time I saw him. He was spotless. The shirt was starched, white and without a hint of sweat or dirt. He had a friendly smile, and to my surprise I felt a tremendous sense of relief that he was there.

"Where did you just come from?" I asked in amazement.

"I was just around back doing some work."

"Oh, no, I saw where you were when you appeared. Where did you come from?" Because he ignored my question this time, I just stopped asking about where he had come from and asked him if we could have a drink of water. He replied, "Oh, no, for you boys we have some iced tea." He turned to the lady on the porch and told her to get us a glass of iced tea and she got up out of her rocker.

Then he said, "Let's feed them too. Give them a plate of fried chicken and mashed potatoes and gravy and some green beans. Let's give them a big piece of pie too. Let's make it apple pie."

"We don't have anything like that." Her amazement was obvious from her tone.

"Oh, yes, we do; go and look on the kitchen table."

She suddenly had the same puzzled look on her face that the boy had who wanted to fight me after I had given the man the water. Then she turned and went into the house.

When I asked him if he remembered me, he chuckled and said, "Remember you . . . I know you very well and have been watching over you for years. I pray for you every day."

I still didn't get it. I was trying to figure out how he could watch me at Buckner without anyone seeing him. He would not have been able to come onto the campus.

About that time the lady came out on the porch with three plates heaped with food. She had a strange look on her face. The food and drink were delicious. We started to eat quickly, but I wasn't really hungry. The excitement got to me.

I wasn't ready to leave when Chico said, "We have to go." We thanked them and walked toward the road. After a few steps I turned to wave good-bye, but only the lady was there in her rocker. The man was gone. I wish that I had been able to ask the man more about himself.

I never saw him again. But now after many years and a lot more experience, I know who and what he is. I just wonder why he allowed me to see him.

Verda Bea (Grantham) Giles, '54

MEMORIES FROM BUCKNER

I remember so many good things from Buckner. They were rather routine at the time but are dear memories to me now.

I recall:

Sitting in the choir during church and looking out at the people in the audience. How routine it was to see everybody clean and well-dressed, awake, alert, attentive, looking at Brother Hal preaching.

Chemistry class and the labs with Mr. Lundy. He gave teams of two an element to identify. We then did experiments to determine its properties to help us identify the element. One time we made salt crystals in the lab.

Piano lessons with Mrs. Roberts. I would not have had those lessons if I had not been at Buckner.

Going to camp during the summers. I still have pictures from the woods near the Buckner campus, and some from a summer at Lake Texhoma. I wonder if the teachers from school were there because they volunteered to go on the trip, or if they were assigned to go? Anyhow, it was great fun.

Going to the Mart every Saturday, being a life guard at the swimming pool during the summers, and the training required for that job with Miss Music, who was in charge of the pool. I did flips off the diving board and learned how to jump into the pool without getting my hair wet. All of us girls had identical one piece swim suit designs.

Getting my ears pierced one evening while sitting on the bench waiting to do clean up duties after the tables in the Manna Hall were cleaned. The holes are still open.

Living in Hunt on the second floor with Ms. Sue Morrow as matron when I first went to Buckner. Getting up early in the morning to go to Manna Hall when I lived in Buhrman with Betty Hamrick in a two-girl room at Buhrman. (We had the same birthday, July 8.)

Waving at a boyfriend as I walked all the way from the dormitory until we could no longer see each other because of the church building.

Being a cheer leader with Patsy Butler and Mildred Curda, watching football in the fall (going to games, riding in the cattle truck), track in the spring, and baseball in the summer and then playing basketball myself during the winter.

Algebra with Miss McCullough, English with Mrs. Hack, History with Miss Musick, Bookkeeping with Mr. Browning, Shorthand with Mrs. Bolden, Religion with Dr. Colson, Life of Christ with Mr. McBride, and the Bible trip to New Mexico; a reward for passing the test.

Going to "the corner" after lunch to see my family members, the Strings at Christmas, and the programs that preceded the handing out of the Strings.

Working in Manna Hall—helping to receive all the fried chicken for a special Sunday for sack suppers—and then separating the chicken and putting pieces in pots for the tables. I well remember picking chickens in the back room of Manna Hall, singing songs of all kinds to take our minds off what we were doing. I especially remember "Buttermilk Skies."

Getting pies in from the bakery for Manna Hall, and decorating them before we cut and passed out individual slices on all the tables.

Saying "pig eye" to mean, "It is not so," or "I was teasing," visitors at Maris Center and on the balcony during lunch. And finally, going to Abilene with Josephine Campbell and Mr. Browning to apply for a scholarship to Hardin Simmons.

Buckner really molded my life in a positive way; not only by the strong work ethic, along with religious and moral teaching, but also with extracurricular activities associated with school, such as the paper; "The Hornet," and the annual. I wonder how it happened that we had an annual at all. Perhaps it was the special talent of the faculty at that time. I feel as if I should give something back to society for the wonderful opportunities afforded me because of the good academic education, as well as the Christian upbringing at Buckner. Both areas of learning have served me well in my personal day to day choices, and my professional experiences. What have I given to society? Well, not a lot, I suppose. I have stayed out of trouble with the law, and have worked as a nurse for thirty-three years. Nursing is a caring profession. Since I work as a school nurse, I care for children in their formative years. I demonstrate Christian values in my every day life and work. I recognize Christian values in children and adults, and am drawn to help them when they need it. I still go to church and take my fourteen-year-old grandson. I guess I am really using the church to reinforce my own values to him, and to keep him busy, and out of trouble. I still give money to Buckner, but the program is so different now. I hope the help will be as useful to today's recipients of Buckner's efforts as it has been to me and that Buckner will continue to be a respected name in the field of social services. I know I am proud to be identified with Buckner.

Gordon John Ratcliff, '55

by Vernon Horsley

Another great athlete from Buckner has been outstanding in every endeavor from his first days at Buckner.

Gordon John Ratcliff arrived at Buckner with his mother in 1940. After she lost her husband, Gordon's father; Dr. George W. Truett, Pastor of First Baptist Church in Dallas, helped her and Gordon to get situated at Buckner.

Mrs. Elsie Ratcliff spent twenty years at Buckner as a head matron at Hunt Girls' Dormitory. Indomitable to the end, even after leaving Buckner, she continued working, selling Avon right up to her death at age eighty-eight.

Gordon John was always an excellent student in school, and was recognized as the Class Valedictorian at his graduation. Track was his favorite sport, and he excelled in it by winning the mile run at the Texas State Track Meet in 1954.

Texas University was Gordon John's choice of a place to further his education and also another opportunity to continue his running. While there, he lettered twice in track and cross-country. Additionally, he won the two-mile race at the Southwest Conference Track Meet in 1957.

He graduated with a degree in physics and

went to work at Texas Instruments in 1959. I believe he retired once, but continues to work at TI on a contract basis as an Engineering Market Analyst.

One indication of Gordon's talent is that while on location in France several years ago, he wrote a professional article in French!

Gordon found a wife in 1957. He and Kaye have been married over forty-one years. They had three sons. Their oldest son, David, is in medical school and Brian is a financial advisor. Their youngest son, Scott, was lost in an auto accident several years ago. He was a twenty-one-year-old premed student at Baylor University at the time.

Gordon and Kay are both active in their church. He is the chairman of the school committee, and also consults in financial areas. Gordon John likes gardening and has continued his running. He gets up early to run, sometimes six miles. In a recent high profile track meet in Dallas, he won second place in his age bracket in the Turkey Trot.

He and Kay now have a grandson, who gives them great joy.

Gordon has always had a great deal of respect for Buckner and has contributed in many ways. He has always been willing to share, and he and Kay give financially when they can.

In my opinion, Gordon John is a true reflection of the success of Buckner Children's Home. Buckner truly makes a difference!

Sammy Sims, '55

WE WEREN'T ALL ORPHANS

As a small child living at Buckner Orphans Home, I often thought that I didn't belong there. I remember lying awake at night in Pires dorm; I would tell myself that we still had a mom and dad. We were not like the rest of the orphans. Besides, I would tell myself, my Dad loved us. I wasn't sure about Mom, because she had left us, and we never heard from her again. Dad, I would muse, would come and get us soon, but right now he had to get some problems worked out and then we would go to live with him again.

One day he came to see us. I remember it was on a Saturday in November just a week after my birthday. There were five of us and I was the middle child with a brother and a sister older than me and a brother and sister younger. I've heard it said both ways that being the middle child is a curse—destined to being ignored. On the other hand, I've heard it was a blessing not having the concerns or pressures the others do. I can't testify to either result in my life. But on the occasion, when Dad came to visit us, we were all assembled to see him. It was a joyous occasion. We hadn't seen him for about eighteen months. I remember how he would tell us stories, most of which we knew were made up, and tease us a little. We knew he loved us, or maybe we just wanted to believe he did; but he made light of the fact that we had to live apart. He never really told us about the life he was living. About his and Mom's divorce, his living with another woman, about his illness, his drinking, his unemployment and much more I'm sure.

I asked him why we could not leave the orphanage now to go live with him. He chuckled a little and said that we wouldn't understand. When I pressed him, he said that some day he would come for us. I believed him and the thought was comforting. "But why not now?" I said. He answered that he needed to work and get more money, and then buy a place to live first. He told us to be good to the matrons and teachers, to do well in school, and not to get into trouble until he visited again.

That seemed to help me understand. He had given me a reason and now I knew he really loved us, but there was this little problem that stood in the way. He just needed money.

All of a sudden, the solution came to me. I remembered last Saturday when all the boys in our dorm had gone to the woods, a place full of pecan trees. I had picked pecans for about two hours and had filled a small gunny bag. I was so proud of myself. Those pecans could be sold. I knew so because there were pickup trucks with their big signs "Pecans For Sale" at the corner of Highway 80 and Buckner Boulevard. I had seen cars stopping often to buy the pecans.

I told Dad about the pecans, that he could have them to sell, and I would go back and pick pecans all day to get more money so that he could solve this problem. Well he just laughed and ruffled my hair. "You keep them, son." That hurt, but I didn't tell him, because he hugged me. I no longer wanted even the pecans I had already picked after that.

I felt his pain, but I couldn't understand why he wouldn't let me help.

He never came to see us again.

Today, I recalled those feelings as I was reading in Romans 8:14-17, *"Those who are led by the Spirit of God are sons of God. For you did not receive a spirit that makes you a slave again to fear, but you received the Spirit of sonship. And by Him we cry, "Abba, Father." The Spirit himself testifies with our spirit that we are God's children . . . Now then if we are children, then we are heirs, heirs of God and co-heirs with Christ if indeed we share in his sufferings in order that we may also share in his glory."*

According to my childhood view, my Dad, my brothers, and sisters and I were a family, just separated, but soon to be rejoined. It is the same today with my relationship with God. He is my Father, and I am his son. He doesn't need my pecans.

When something bad happens to our family, we all suffer. I am an heir both to the riches and sufferings of the family. If God is praised and glorified, our family is glorified. If evil men trash God, I feel it. What do I do about it? Well I try to fix things my own way. I lash out at evil men, and then turn to God and say, "Look what I'm doing for you." Then I wonder why my deeds don't fix the problem. But God is loving, and He does not laugh at us. Instead He teaches us to love our enemies and do good to those who hate us. He teaches me to be obedient to His calling. God will show us what we can do to bring praise and glory to Him and His family. God is faithful. He will not leave us alone. His Spirit is with us to comfort us in lonely times, in troubled times, in sickness, and in heartaches. He will come again to take us home. He keeps His promises.

He said in John 14:3, *"And if I go and prepare a place for you, I will come again and receive you to Myself: that where I am, there you may be also."* We are not orphans; we do have a home.

John Vaughn, '55

My recollections about Buckner in themselves would be sufficient to fill up a book, but I'll try to be brief. With so many brothers and sisters, I enjoyed the camaraderie immensely. Many of the boys had nicknames, which were unique and colorful, such as "Hangeyes," "Hooknose," "Sawbones," "Piggy," "Deathgrip," "Uncle," "Corky," "Flickie," "Mutt," and "Beller." My own nickname, "Bookworm," was acquired when I was in the sixth grade. "Pinky" (another nickname) Sikes had given me a research paper to write, so I had checked out a lot of books and carried the stack back to my dorm room. One of the "big boys" saw me and said, "Hey boy, what you doing with all them books? Are you some kind of book worm?" From then on I was Bookworm; in high school it was mercifully shortened to "Bookie," but unfortunately that had certain connotations associated with gambling!

On one occasion I had to do some yard work for Mr. Callahan on the Field Gang. It was a very hot day so I sat down in some shade to rest and cool off. Mr. Callahan saw me and thought I was loafing. "What's your name, boy?" he asked. I was so scared that I couldn't reply.

One of the other boys said, "His name is Bookworm."

"BOOKWORM! WELL, YOUR NAME IS GOING TO BE SCREWWORM IF YOU DON'T GET BUSY," he shouted.

Among my cherished achievements in high school, I would cite the following:

* Lettering in football, basketball, and track
* Making all A's except for two B's throughout high school
* Winning medals in English, history, and Bible for the highest average
* Serving as editor of the *"Buckner Hornet"* and as class president four years
* Winning the Citizenship Award in my senior year
* Serving as MC for the athletic banquet in my senior year
* Having a poem published in the *Baptist Standard* during my junior year
* Graduating third in my class and writing the class motto
* Getting to go on a trip to Carlsbad Caverns and Old Mexico as a reward for memorizing, in order, 186 sentence statements pertaining to the life of Christ.

Those were great days, were they not? I have my doctorate now and have been happily teaching English at ETBU for the past thirty-two years. Prior to that, I taught one year at Tarleton University and three years in the Dallas public schools. I have served five years as president of the Poetry Society of Texas and currently am

Librarian for the National Federation of State Poetry Societies.

Clark Watts, '55

AUSTIN'S RENAISSANCE MAN

[Reprinted by permission from an article by Leigh Hopper in the Austin American-Statesman, *September 16, 1996. Ed.]*

Brain surgeon. Researcher. Lawyer. Professor. Army Reserve brigadier general. Writer. Editor. Any of these would be career enough for one person, but Austinite Clark Watts has done them all—usually several at once.

And that's not counting his stint at the Pentagon, the master's degrees he holds in public health and pharmacology, the terms he's served on professional boards. His resume is forty-three pages long. (Lest anyone think he's perfect, please note he doesn't cook or clean house.)

At fifty-eight, Watts may sound like the busiest man in Austin, but he has blended multiple pursuits seamlessly, making it look easy.

"This guy has more irons in the fire than you or I could count. I sometimes think Clark is running from something, but I can't figure out what," says close friend Gerald Livingston, an attorney in Dallas.

Watts has been married to Patricia Watts for twenty years and raised eight children.

Watts is a product of Buckner Orphans Home in Dallas, where he lived from age nine until he graduated from high school and went to the University of Texas. His siblings and colleagues all agree that Watts' extraordinary success has been because of his roots, not in spite of them.

Watts, tall and distinguished-looking with white hair, is not given to telling colorful anecdotes about himself.

"I've never had a lampshade on my head," he says.

But inside the man whom friends describe as "extremely serious-minded," "a superachiever," "a perfectionist," is a boy who knew what hunger felt like, who kept a pet squirrel named Admiral Peabody in his room at the orphanage, and who once took a pitchfork through the hand when he stepped between two boys fighting in the orphanage dairy barn.

"He's just been a special person. There's just something inside Clark that once he decides he wants this goal he's going to work to get it," says his sister, Eva Watts, a Dallas school teacher who is a few years younger and also grew up in the orphanage. "I think a lot of it is, we were self-starters. We were very motivated. And Clark has reached the heights of that motivation."

Last week, while serving as on-call neurosurgeon for the Brackenridge emergency room, Watts finished up a paper on nervous system injuries he is going to present at a legal conference in Chicago. (He composes them in his head while jogging or swimming.)

He also assisted his colleague, Dr. Byron Neely, in a neurosurgical procedure. Later in the week, wearing his lawyer hat, he flew to Houston for a medical malpractice case.

Watts, who got his medical degree in 1962, began teaching medical ethics courses at the University of Missouri and was editor of the National Medical Journal *Neurosurgery* from 1982 to 1987. The journal was a 25-hour-a-week job, and when it ended, he decided to use the time to study law, earning his degree in 1990. He says he did it because he knew he wouldn't be able to continue performing surgery throughout his lifetime, since those skills decline with age.

"If I try to be both (doctor and lawyer), maybe I'm neither," Watts says. "But I've learned how to take the best of both and combine them."

He joined the U.S. Army Reserve in 1963, holding posts at military schools. He was a flight surgeon in 1985 and has trained special forces medics for troops heading to developing world hotspots who have to rely on themselves for trauma care.

In 1993, he and Patricia returned to Texas, moving to the Cat Mountain area off RM 2222 to be closer to their eleven grandchildren. Watts accepted a job as clinical professor of surgery at the University of Texas Health Science Center in San Antonio and joined the Austin law firm of Ford & Ferraro as special counsel.

"I think that sometimes his involvement in things that are so removed from ordinary conversation makes him seem . . . aloof," says his friend Livingston. "But that's not the case if you touch upon a subject in which he's interested; he'll engage to a great extent. He's out there where most of us are not walking around. What would you talk to Einstein about? He's not elitist; he's just focused on his interests."

It all seems to have started when Watts and four of his seven siblings were placed in Buckner Orphans Home. His father had left home, and his mother, who had a ninth-grade education, couldn't care for them alone. Children thrived on the 3,000-acre farm, with boys learning to milk cows, drive tractors and keep the grounds tidy. Watts' mother stayed nearby, even working at the orphanage for two years.

"I don't think there has been a period of my life I have more satisfactory memories of than that time," Watts says. "I have to think there was something about that experience that contributed to those accomplishments. We were constantly exposed to new skills, new learning experiences. . . . They created an environment in which the kids could work and excel."

Watts maintains that he has simply followed his interests throughout his life, but the man remains something of a mystery. He sleeps six to eight hours a night and says he tries to be organized. Apparently, there's no "dark side" other than a recognition that at times he paid more attention to his profession than to his family. Other people who know him fill in a few of the blanks:

He once published a book of poetry under an assumed name. He took piano lessons. In his twenties, he was a fencer. He keeps a photo of his bulldog, Murphy, in his wallet. He's a Republican. He likes listening to the blues. He visited his mother regularly until she died March 1.

In Eva Watts' photos from their childhood, Clark is never pictured. That's because he was always the one holding the camera.

"I think it was through his guidance we all stayed together," she says. "Two years ago I was diagnosed with advanced-stage breast cancer, and it was Clark who talked me into fighting it. I thought it was all over and he said no, we have to try." (The cancer is in remission.)

"I hope it doesn't sound like I think he's God. But he's always been there, and I really appreciate it. I will always love him for that."

[Eva is now deceased. Ed.]

Nettie Jo (McLeod) Woods, '55

MEMORIES

Does anyone else remember . . . Brother Oscar, who came out to the home frequently with candy and trinkets for everyone . . . when one of the matrons in Crouch took us all out late at night to watch the stars . . . quiet hour at Crouch when you weren't allowed to go to the bathroom, and if you went anyhow and got caught, you had to stand in the hall with your nose in a ring on the wall for punishment . . . getting to ride horses at the Girls' Woods . . . the smells of cooking breakfast out at camp . . . picking cotton?

The first time I picked was a few months after I came to Buckner as an eight-year-old. I believe I picked about eleven pounds. I had to write my daddy and ask for some money for the State Fair.

Do you remember the same meals on the same day every week . . . getting up at the first whistle and going to Manna Hall to crack eggs for breakfast and peel potatoes and carrots for lunch . . . picking pinto beans for punishment . . . killing flies in Manna Hall for punishment and if you knew you had to do it the next day also, cutting them in two after reporting the number to Miss Mamie and then hiding them in a hole in the brick wall of the mop closet in the kitchen to use the next day . . . conversion (I accepted Christ as my Savior and was baptized at twelve.) . . . going to the State Fair in the cattle truck and being scared to death if I was on the outside, afraid the sides of the truck would fall off when the truck turned a corner . . . Campus Mart and getting a nickel allowance a week to buy a big ice cream cone, or bottle of soda or a bar of candy? There are so many other memories, too numerous to put down on paper. Maybe these few will spark a recollection that has been forgotten.

Leonard Corcoran, '56

PIE IN THE SKY

Some people say they can remember things that happened to them when they were real young, but not me. I was sickly as a youngster, and I guess I tried to wipe out the memories of privation and pain. Do people remember back that far, or do we tend to forget things which are unpleasant to us? So with that in mind I have to rely on what was told to me by my two older sisters.

We were poor like so many others during the 30s and sometimes food and the proper nourishment were hard to come by. When mother bought

toothpaste it didn't last very long because we would eat it.

One day while my sisters were making some mud pies. I must have been awful hungry because after the pies were "finished." I ate some of one.

I guess I was carrying the Story of Creation a little too far, maybe recreating myself. So if at times you wonder why I do not see things clearly, now you know.

THE TEST

After my return from the Army in March of 1959, I tried several jobs. I even got a job at $1.25 per hour for my uncle in his appliance store. At the end of about three years, I got a raise to $1.35 an hour, which meant that instead of buying an empty milk carton, I could get one with milk in it.

I thought it was about time for a career change. But what should I change to? I could be a Brain Surgeon; nah, I'm too talented for that. I tried college for five weeks and found out that I couldn't teach them anything. The question was, "What do I want to do for the rest of my life?"

Then it came to me in the form of the *Dallas Times Herald,* Headline: FIRE FIGHTER, CITY OF DALLAS.

I put in my application for the position and reported for the written test. I passed, but during my physical I was weighed, which was OK; measured for height, for which I had to stretch my neck about three inches to be tall enough. (I now wear a neck brace to keep my head from falling over.)

I then went to the eye chart. The test consisted of ten sheets full of dots of different colors. All that I could see was a bunch of little old bitty dots. So ended my career with the Dallas Fire Department before it ever began.

Finally, I filled out an application for employment with the Garland Fire Department. When I found the Nicholson Library where their test was to be held, there were about 250 people to take the test. I almost went back home, but I remembered what I had been taught at Buckner and said to myself, "Hold it. Don't leave. You are as smart as anyone here."

The results of the test were posted, and I not only passed but was tied for the first place score.

You guessed it, the eye test was still to come —my old enemy. It turned out that I was not color blind. I had just had trouble with some of the colors that day in Dallas; I saw things in a different light, to say the least. I guess you might say I saw red.

After two weeks of Fire Training School, Class Number One, we were assigned to our station duties. I was assigned to Station Number Two, on South Garland Avenue. When my probation period ended, I asked Chief Sharp about the eye test and he said forget it. I was sure glad for I had found what I wanted to do for the rest of my working career. Starting November 1, 1962, until I retired because of Parkinson Disease, on May 14, 1995, I was in a job that I looked forward to for thirty-two years.

JUST PEDALING

Coming home from the Rocky Mountain National Park with my wife, and on the way to Dallas for the Buckner Homecoming, we meet them again! The wife is driving our four-cylinder, Nissan Station Wagon, not known for its mountain climbing abilities. Anyway we are creeping up the road when we run into this traffic jam. We inch our way up until we come to the road block.

Then we see the cause of the trouble.

You are apt to run into them anywhere. Who? The bicyclist. It seems like everywhere you go, they show up in their tight outfits with the colorful shorts and tops, which show everything God gave us clothes to keep hidden. They look like refugees from a comic opera. On top of their head rests a biker's helmet, louvered and reminiscent of the customized hood of a 1932 Ford coupe hot rod.

They are usually riding the latest fashion in the biking world, the cross country or mountain bike. We are talking 101 gears forward and 25 gears for back peddling in case of an emergency! They are equipped with the latest onboard computer, which tells them how fast they can go on each revolution of the pedal, time of departure, time of arrival, number of calories burnt, the best place to camp overnight, and which bush to use when nature calls.

Also, their bike is usually equipped with a water bottle containing enough water for a couple of swigs, and on their back is the invaluable pack stuffed with granola bars, dried fruit and a change of underwear in case of an accident.

Included in their array is a small bicycle pump.

They are even sometimes seen on the highway, pumping up a flat tire for a stranded semi truck driver, so they are not all bad, just aggravating to me when traffic is stranded behind them.

As we wait for the traffic jam to unjam so we can get on with our vacation trip, I begin to amuse myself by imagining escape scenarios:

I am climbing Mount Everest, and as my hand reaches up and curls over the top to pull myself up to the peak, someone on a bicycle runs over my fingers causing me to lose my grip and fall all the way to the bottom of the mountain.

I am in an airplane flying at 45,000 feet when I am passed by a person on a bicycle supported by about a dozen balloons, from Balloons Are Us, which they keep inflated with their own hot air.

My ocean liner leaves the dock for a cruise, and in the middle of the ocean we encounter a bicycle mounted on a small catamaran. The back wheel of the bicycle operates a treadmill, which turns a small paddle wheel and propels the craft.

Out in the middle of the Sahara Desert, a cloud of dust is approaching. As it nears, I can make out someone on a bicycle with a 55 gallon drum of water strapped to the rear of the bike. As the rider passes, I notice a distant gleam in the rider's eyes, as if to say, today the desert; tomorrow, the entire jungle." I can't resist yelling menacingly out the window, "Beware the Bikers!"

But whoa—I am not a violent man. I was trained at Buckner (Where I also learned to daydream!), and I can't allow a road fantasy to go this far!

Besides the traffic jam seems to have calmed down and so have I. I think we'll make it in time for the Homecoming festivities.

Dr. A. A. Hyden and
Miss Marjorie Barnett Hyden, '56

Marjorie Barnett was a well-loved teacher in the school and later Dean of Girls at Buckner. She married Anglin Hyden, who became our Educational Director, and they both were an integral part of our lives for many years. Then in 1956, they left to go to Mary Hardin Baylor to teach and later to Baylor University, where Dr. Hyden became a Vice President of the college.

They were married in the Home Church with many of the students participating in their wedding. They had loving nicknames for each other, and their romance and happiness was closely watched and appreciated by all the students. Following is a written celebration of their time with us that was presented at their farewell party. There were little boys and girls who acted out the story as the poem was recited to the party goers.

This is the story of Oggie and Red
How they met, and loved, and wed.

"Oggie" better known to her pupils at Buckner Orphans Home as Miss Barnett, was visiting in the little town of Groesbeck, Texas. One day as she was seated at the piano, dressed in a faded robe, there walked into her life a tall young man with a ready grin. Though she was embarrassed, she thought he was very "Puddy" even then.

In time they knew that God above
Had planned this union of two in love.

The chapel at Buckner Orphans Home was a scene of real excitement as the candles and flowers created a perfect atmosphere for a lovely ceremony as this dedicated couple pledged their vows to one another and to God. There were many misty eyes as the choir sang "I Love You Truly."

The Hyden House became a home to all
Where young and old felt welcome to call.

Hospitality became synonymous with the Hyden name as friends soon discovered that not only excellent food, but also finest fellowship and wisest counsel were to be found in the red brick house on the corner. Such specialties as Hydenburgers and Hyden breakfasts became traditional.

While Oggie mothered all the fair lassies,
Anglin was struggling with Seminary classes.

Mrs. Hyden served as Dean of Girls for several years and influenced countless lives as was witnessed recently when a young teacher returning to Buckner quoted some of Mrs. Hyden's teachings as having been guideposts for her life. School work was not easy for Brother Hyden as his time was devoted to multitudinous duties as educational director and counselor.

Party giving is always really quite an art;
The Hydens have planned every sort.

Through the years the Hyden House has been the scene of stork showers, wedding showers, birthday parties, church socials, school functions. New Year, Valentine, Easter, Halloween, Thanksgiving and Christmas—around the calendar; these were festive times for young and old. Invariably someone, regardless of the occasion, would request Marjorie to give her original interpretation of the "Little Red Hen."

The Hyden's pictures have been lots of fun.
They've aimed and clicked at most everyone.

Shutter bugs are fairly common, but not all fans share their hobby with as many as this generous couple does. The Hyden's pictures have served a dual purpose—to entertain as well as to acquaint the people of Texas with the great work of Buckner Orphans Home. Their collection is varied and outstanding, but the one picture most frequently duplicated is that of their favorite model, Mitzie Lee, Marjorie's niece.

An old door closes and a new door appears.
There comes a call of service for future years.

The Hydens have influenced so many young people through the years that it is not unusual to find God opening another door to service with young people for them. We are sure that another Hyden House will be established on the campus of Mary Hardin Baylor where Hydenburgers, Hyden breakfasts and Hyden hospitality will become meaningful words for Baylor students.

Marjorie has two stories that are wonderful to hear, "The Little Red Hen" and the true story of when they were robbed by an armed motorcycle guy, whom they mistook for a student playing a joke on them. Marjorie refused to give him her rings, and laughed and joked with him as if it were all mere play, even when he made them lie down on their faces and tied up their hands. He was very threatening with his gun and very serious. They later decided that he must have mistaken them for a wealthy oil man in Waco.

Bob Newsom, '56

THE PERFECT CRIME BY BILL ADAMS' FRIEND

The summer of 1953 was a great time. I had just completed my freshman year at school, and my seventh year at Buckner. Like most kids there, I had a best friend. Mannie Adams was two years older than I and rather like an older brother. We did everything together; played football, ran track, built a model of the Sea Witch (called it "the boat") from scratch (Mannie drew the plans in study hall), and generally hung around when time allowed. Like most fifteen and seventeen-year-olds though, we had fertile minds.

I lived in Rupard that summer and Mannie lived in the newer Cullom building on the other side of McElroy. Mannie and I built "the boat" in a room on the second floor of Cullom which was not being used as living space, a good place to put our fertile minds to work. I lived on the first floor of Rupard, in the room on the southwest corner of the building with Ed Keathley, Gerald Morris, and Darrel Lewis, affectionately known as "Bird Egg." Mrs. Etheridge was the house mother in charge.

Now Mr. McBride was the Dean of Boys, and it so happened that his office was on the first floor right next to my room. Nothing special about that except Mr. Mac (that's what we called him) kept things in his office that he had confiscated from the boys, things that were not allowed on Campus—which was just about everything that normal fifteen and seventeen-year-olds wanted to have around. Mr. Mac was a great Dean of Boys, but he was also known for his prowess with the belt, and many a boy felt his wrath for some infraction of the rules.

On one of my trips to the office, I noticed that there was a Benjamin Pump Gun leaning against the wall in a corner, something Mr. Mac had obviously confiscated from someone. That caught my eye and like any good friend, I relayed news of my find to Mannie. It wasn't long before we began to think of ways to relieve Mr. Mac of the burden of keeping that pump gun locked up. There were pros and cons in our desire to liberate the gun. Mr. Mac was pretty shrewd and real observant when it came to noticing things missing. We knew if we got caught with the gun, he would recognize it immediately and the jig would be up, along with our hides too. But, not to worry, we figured we could get away with it.

I don't remember how long we thought about it, but the plan went something like this. We would leave the noon meal in Manna Hall early, sprint to Rupard (remember, we were track men), and before everyone else got out (including Mrs. Etheredge) we would get into the office by prying open a screen on a window and climbing in. The rest was easy. I would hand the gun out the window to Mannie. He would put it down his jeans leg (in other words "britches leg it") and we would walk nonchalantly toward Buckner Boule-

vard, cross the road and head for Rockbottom. We didn't plan much beyond that.

It worked perfectly. We were in and out of the office within a few minutes, and heading for the woods, marveling at our audacity and good luck. The rest is history. We shot at vines, trees, rocks, weeds, and squirrel nests to our hearts' content. We even hit some of the things we shot at. But how long can two teenagers occupy themselves in the woods shooting at trees and bushes, especially when hunger sets in? Don't forget, we had left Manna Hall early. Our immediate hunter's and soldier's instincts satisfied, we began to think of the practical problem of where we would hide the gun so it wouldn't be found. Not a good feeling. Stashing it in among our jeans and shirts was out. Too many inquisitive house mothers. Leaving it outside would only ruin it, and someone else might find it. Besides, if Mr. Mac found one of us with it, it would be curtains. There were no good choices. Anyway, our collective conscience was beginning to bother us. After all, we did steal it from the office. The more we thought about it, the more it bothered us. What had seemed like a good deal to begin with now seemed like not such a good deal. After much thought, we came to the same conclusion. We had to return it to the office.

The plan was simple; reverse what we had just done. Except, now we weren't in Manna Hall, it wasn't the noon hour, and there were kids all over the grounds—smart enough to know a "britches legging" when they saw it.

I'm sorry to say that I don't remember how or when we returned the pump gun to the office, but return it we did. To my knowledge, Mr. Mac never missed it. So for Mr. Mac, "That's one on you." On Mr. Mac's side; however, our consciences got the best of us in the end, and we returned the gun without his ever knowing it.

I guess his influence on us was a lot stronger than we realized. He solved the perfect crime without ever even knowing about it. Ring up a big one for the Buckner Home Dean of boys!

Richard Buckner, '57

PARCHED CORN

One of the confections Home kids and a manager's son enjoyed during clear, warm summer days was parched corn. Sometimes we cooked up sugar and syrup in a tin can to mix with the Corn a la Cracker Jax. Last summer my garden corn did not do well and had only a few dry, poorly filled out ears at the end of the summer. I put the kernels in an iron skillet and parched them on the gas range. My spouse, Elizabeth, was amazed at how crunchy, tender and tasty they turned out. Here is the old recipe:

Determine that the ears of corn in the field east of the chain link fence are ripe and not too juicy nor absolutely hard. Do not ask anyone or tell anyone because "stealing" the corn is more fun. Go to the kitchen in Manna Hall and obtain a fresh gallon can from the trash. Clean it on the foot-operated, steam can-cleaning machine. Obtain one or more Home Kids such as Lonnie Duke or Sammy Schwartz by asking a dormitory group mother. (Why couldn't I ask girls from Hardin, Hunt or Crouch?) Kids came because of my access to salt, margarine, sugar and syrup. Climb over the chain link fence (the only reason to think of wearing shoes in summer) and go a few rows into the field of dreams so as not to be seen. Pick more ears than needed and smuggle them back across the fence under shirts (if worn), dropping at least half the ears on the way.

Obtain a clean newspaper, wood and matches. (It is amazing where Home Kids could find wood.) Build a fire on the east side of the stone wall near the chicken pen on "my" lot where mother cannot see from the house. While the wood turns into coals, shuck the corn and remove the kernels to the can. Make a handle out of a coat hanger, punch some holes in the rim with a nail and rock, and attach the handle. Parch the corn, sometimes using a little margarine and keeping the heat just right. Finally, pour it out on the newspaper and add salt. If syrup is to be made, add about half and half white granulated sugar and ribbon cane syrup; a little Karo is sometimes used to keep the candy palatable. Again, using experience, caramelize the sugar, keeping the temperature not too hot or cold, until it will glue the corn together without becoming rock candy. Pour it over the corn and stir with a clean green, peeled stick that has been sterilized briefly in the coals. Cool. Eat with fingers.

Oh, and do not forget to douse the fire and hide the evidence. Then lie back in the pure, green clover while enjoying talking and making a game of finding shapes in the cotton ball clouds, forming and dissolving in the indigo Texas sky.

This is not just a recipe for a confection—it is how to achieve kid Heaven!

THE MORNING MAIL

At the 1998 Northern California Buckner Orphans Home Exes' Reunion, I related the following account of how my family raised most of the ten million dollar annual Buckner Baptist Benevolences' operating expenses, and now I submit these remarks for inclusion with the other written anecdotes.

Most of the operating expenses were covered by checks which were sent in the mail. All campus mail arrived each morning except Sunday at the office under the Chapel. It was therefore necessary for someone to be in the office Saturday mornings as well as on weekdays. Today young parents are very insistent upon having a lot of quality time with their children; my father rarely had any time off except Sundays and vacations, which he did not take in years when demands of time for running the home were severe. If my father went to the office Saturday morning, he usually did not get back until suppertime, and during WW II my mother filled in for him and kept somewhat the same schedule.

By charter, BOH could not operate in debt. Several times when I was a boy walking to or from my house (near the north gate on the drive that went by Pires) to the schools, I was stopped by visitors in cars and asked where the commissary was. One woman had a single can of beans she wanted to give to help feed the orphans; another, a box of toys. Many people left money in their wills to the Home. Some left land and houses; at various times over 10,000 parcels were sold all over the state to meet cash flow needs. All of these gifts were given out of real love and compassion for the children there.

Most of the time my grandfather, Hal, and my father, Robert Cooke, traveled to every Baptist church in the state at least once a year. Every other year, my grandfather got a new Oldsmobile Rocket '98 and my father an '88, and they were always worn out by the trade-in time. These new cars were the only really nice material things we had. Many caring individuals gave sometimes a few, sometimes many dollars, for your sustenance.

Dad and Dada did not say threatening things such as that God was going to take them within eight days unless so much was given. There were no TV appeals, radio solicitations, or mass mailings. There were no endowments, nor investments, or ninety-nine year leases of main campus land to industrial parks. There were no government funds for running adoption services. They did not ask for specific amounts, leaving that to the abilities of the congregations and the touch of the Holy Spirit. They did not even explicitly ask for money. They had faith that Baptists would care.

What my father and grandfather did was describe the various needs in their presentations as offering *opportunities for individuals* to help. About half of all of the churches visited, formed or maintained standing committees to oversee collection of funds at least once a year to send to the Home. Sometimes individuals "sponsored" a child (had them to dinner, took them to outside functions). My mother-in-law, Mary Elizabeth Burnett, at one time sponsored Rena Key, who was in the choir and sang many solos in church. Rena was the older sister of another home student, John Wayne Key, a good friend of mine.

My sweet tooth was reinforced by my dad bringing me a bag of jelly beans after each trip. Sometimes he was gone for a couple of weeks (Texas is a big state and he visited every county seat at one time or another.), and the candy was some compensation for the loneliness I experienced even after he came back home from the war.

A few days after my dad or my grandfather told a church about your needs, *the morning mail arrived*. From a financial standpoint, that is how you got taken care of—by many, many caring individuals, all giving what they could voluntarily, by sending in their checks in the morning mail.

Reading over the above, I can see that it might seem that I am overly concerned about the amount of time my family spent away from me, taking care of raising money. I certainly am not trying to make you feel guilty for the care given you. In raising my daughter Bonnie, I found myself compulsively working when maybe I should have been doing things with her. She, herself, works very hard in trying to get her start as a film editor. Maybe the sins of the fathers are passed down, even unto the fourth generation. What I am really trying to say is how proud I am of my family for doing the work in the way they

did it even though they may not have spent as much time with me as I might have desired.

I doubt if the above scheme would work today; people I know now do not seem to care as much. That is a situation you and I can try to do something about.

An Ex-Buckner Home Girl, '58

When my family arrived at Buckner's gate, we were greeted by Mr. Brashear, who had a gun with him. It was his job to keep undesirables off the campus, and until he found out that we were the new family expected at the Receiving Home, he exhibited a very standoffish, "state-your-business" sort of attitude. He was friendly enough after he found out who we were and referred to himself as "Pop" Brashear, but that first impression made me very cautious around him from that day forward. I warmed up to "Mom" Brashear just fine because she held the key to my heart—and the front door of the Campus Mart.

At the time that my family entered Bucker Orphans Home in 1946, everyone was required to stay at the Receiving Home for ten days before moving onto the main campus in case any child had a communicable disease which would infect the other 600 plus children on campus. Although I was only six years old at the time, my first impression of the Receiving Home was distinct. I remember Mrs. Saddler and Miss Sally with fondness because they took care of us until we could move to the main campus. My family was extremely poor. We had lived in less than habitable housing and were hungry most of the time. The two things that impressed me most were "3 squares a day" and the beautiful honey colored wood floors which shone like a new penny. Mrs. Sadler had runners throughout the house, and she required that we jump from one to the other to save the floors. It was great fun to jump from rug to rug. The challenge was to do it without the rug slipping out from under you on those highly waxed floors. Wood floors were not only pretty, they were fun!

My family left Buckner in 1951, and I returned with my three younger brothers in 1954. Again we stayed ten days at the Receiving Home. This time, as the oldest child of four, my impressions were a little different. Mrs. Sadler and Miss

Sally were still there, but I was required to wash my brothers' clothing and help prepare the meals because I was now fourteen instead of six. The wood floors were still pretty, but they weren't nearly as much fun as when I had been six because I now had to wax them. It's amazing how perceptions changed as I matured. To this day I like the beauty of wood floors; I don't have them because of the work involved in keeping them, but I admire them.

I observed that most of the work was done by Miss Sally and the older children who were staying there, and Mrs. Sadler, who was in charge, did little of the actual work. Although I was sympathetic to Sally and her plight, I didn't ever want to trade places with her. I learned at that time that if you want to work less, be in charge.

One day Mrs. Sadler took my three brothers and me into the sunshine to inspect our hair. I knew she was examining our heads for lice and was insulted that she would even consider the possibility because I equated head lice with filth. I verbally challenged her reason for examining us. She confirmed that she was looking for lice and explained that every child who entered the campus must be thoroughly examined for conditions which might infect the whole group. When my brothers asked what Mrs. Sadler was looking for, to spare their feelings, I told them that she was looking for dandruff. Sometimes it is best to explain why you are doing what you are doing even though you are in charge and cannot explain, and sometimes it is best not to explain if by telling, you hurt people.

In the hospital on campus was a dentist's office, which was equipped with everything but Novacaine. Apparently, dental students from Baylor Dental College came out to practice their skills on the children at Buckner, and there was no budget for Novacaine. As a result if you went to the dentist on campus, he drilled until you could stand the pain no longer and hollered. He then allowed you to rest awhile until you were brave enough for him to drill again. Since I had such rotten teeth, I experienced that pain more than once. As an adult, it was very difficult for me to go to a dentist, but I finally conquered my fear with the help of a very understanding and gentle dentist who used lots of Novacaine.

When I was nine, a revival was held at Buckner, and it was during that time that I made the decision to follow Jesus and become a Christian.

Dr. Hal F. Buckner baptized me, and that will always be a very special event in my life. It dramatically affected the rest of my life. From that point every decision I've ever made has been influenced by the fact that God has His hand on my life. My decision for Christ changed my life.

In Hardin Home there were two matrons whom I'll never forget, Mrs. Brown and Mrs. Zapp, for very different reasons. On the whole I liked Mrs. Brown very much because I felt she was one of the most fair matrons we had, but one thing I totally hated was her requirement that everyone take a big dose of Milk of Magnesia every Saturday night whether we needed it or not. Everyone lined up in the hallway and took that vile medicine which made me wretch just to think of it. She did not intend this as punishment, but to me it seemed that I was being punished. To this day, I won't have Milk of Magnesia in my home, and I certainly never gave it to any of my children.

Mrs. Brown was very inventive when it came to punishment. She had different methods of punishment for different crimes. She had a collection of switches in her broom closet, selected just for switching little legs. Small switches were used for small infractions, but the switches graduated in size according to the seriousness of the crime. The "king size" switch was reserved for major infractions, such as lying.

For ordinary infractions during each week, she put the offender's name on a list, and then every Saturday we gathered in one of the bedrooms where she called the names of those who had disobeyed the rules that week. The offenders were all herded into the space between two of the beds, which we dubbed "the bullpen," and she took each child in turn by one hand and used one of the smaller switches on the child's legs with her other hand. Mrs. Brown was not a very large woman, and the ultimate result was that the child ran circles around her trying to avoid the switch. Mrs. Brown ended up getting very dizzy after switching up to ten girls every Saturday.

Another method she used frequently was having us sit on the wall. This entailed standing with our backs to the wall in the hallway, where on some Saturdays she would have the whole hallway lined with girls. We then had to take one giant step away from the wall and slide down the wall until we formed a lap. We were required to sit there until Mrs. Brown thought we had learned our lesson, which she determined by our contriteness (evidenced by our crying) or when our legs shook so badly we could no longer stand there. The key here was in figuring out how long a time was acceptable to Mrs. Brown before you began to cry. If you cried too quickly, she thought you were not sincere, and you ended up having to stay longer than was comfortable. If you were stubborn and not sincere, then you ended up having to stay longer than was comfortable. If you were stubborn and decided to "show her," you were a big loser here. If you were smart, you cried at just the right moment.

The method Mrs. Brown used for punishing the worst offenses was humiliation. She required the offender to wear a white rag tied around her wrist to the dining hall, where the whole world could see how badly the child had misbehaved. It was my fate to wear the white rag once and that was enough for me. My crime was that I talked at the dining table before prayer (which was a big "no no"), and then lied about it. The girl sitting next to me was talking, and I reminded her, by ducking my head and whispering to her, that she was not supposed to talk. Mrs. Brown noticed her talking, but didn't see me whispering. When Mrs. Brown informed the other girl that she was in trouble for talking, the girl tattled that I had talked also. Mrs. Brown confronted me and I denied talking since I had only whispered in an attempt to save the other girl's hide. By the time Mrs. Brown got me to admit that I had "only whispered," she was so mad she decided I needed the ultimate punishment, a switching with the "king size" switch and wearing a white rag to the dining hall. Fortunately for me it was winter, and I insisted that I was cold and, consequently, kept my coat on during the meal. This hid the rag fairly well. Unfortunately, when my older sister came into the dining hall, I waved at her. She noticed the white rag and pointed it out to everybody. As a result of my acquaintance with Mrs. Brown, I learned the following lessons:

1) Always tell the truth—the sooner the better;
2) Humiliation is too harsh a punishment for a child;
3) Never bring attention to yourself if you have something to hide.

In contrast to Mrs. Brown was Mrs. Zapp, a big, stocky woman of German descent who had a booming voice and tolerated no nonsense. Quite frankly, she scared me out of my wits when I was

six, but as I matured, I grew more comfortable with her. One thing that made me think "her bark was worse than her bite" was her canary. Every morning when Mrs. Zapp uncovered the bird cage, her canary sang a beautiful song as only a canary can sing. I loved to hear that bird, and in my way of thinking, anyone who owned such a beautiful thing couldn't be all bad. The other thing I remember about Mrs. Zapp was that when her telephone rang in her office and she was down the hall, she started shouting at the phone as she ran down the hall, "I'm coming, I'm coming!" To me that was very funny on two levels: seeing a big woman run and knowing that the person on the other end of the ringing phone couldn't even hear her hollering.

One other reason I thought Mrs. Zapp was not all bad was that on Halloween she had a party for us in the attic, a perfect place for a Halloween party. It was sooooo spooooky! The other matrons served us cookies and punch while Mrs. Zapp prepared for her grand entrance. She came in at just the right moment dressed in a sheet hollering "Boo!" in her deep voice. At first, I was thoroughly frightened until I noticed that the ghost was wearing Mrs. Zapp's sensible black oxfords. After she removed the sheet, we all had a great laugh.

My family left Buckner in 1951, just before I promoted to Crouch Home, and returned in 1954. I was placed in Buhrman Home, my favorite place to live on campus because it was convenient to everything and we were treated as young adults. One of the matrons I remember at Buhrman was Mrs. Dorman. I remember her because she was kind to us, and to me in particular. At Christmas when we all went to the auditorium for our Christmas strings, Mrs. Dorman made sure I got a black stuffed dog to put on my bed since I was the only girl in my dorm who did not have a stuffed animal to display on my bed. I was thrilled and made certain she knew how appreciative I was by taking the time to go by her office to tell her how much I appreciated the gifts. Things that don't come easy are more likely to be appreciated.

It was at Buhrman that I was placed in the Open House Room which visitors to the campus viewed. We failed the test, and the girls in my room were swept back upstairs to live because we had embarrassed the "powers that be" with our less than acceptable neatness. At first, I was totally embarrassed about being sent back, but eventually I realized that it was much better to be able to relax than to have all that pressure on me.

At Pender Hall, the two matrons that I remember are Mrs. Cannon and Mrs. Johnson, whom we affectionately referred to as "Mrs. Johnnie." Mrs. Cannon allowed us to watch TV on Sunday night in her room if we had all of our homework done. That was really neat, and she usually provided popcorn, which we really enjoyed. Mrs. Cannon taught me that it's fine to relax, but only after you've finished your work.

She also encouraged me to try out for cheerleader although I was very shy at the time. She bolstered my self-confidence before the tryouts and as I waited for the final results of the vote from the Pep Squad. For the first time in my life, I "went for it" and was amazed that I actually won a spot as a cheerleader. Sometimes the results are worth the risk.

Mrs. Johnnie was memorable because she was so easy going and laughed a lot. She also assigned me the best job I ever had when I was at Buckner.

I think the worst job assignment I remember was having to fill in the holes with sand under the swing sets at Hardin Home when I was six years old. Someone hauled in a dump truck load of sand and dumped it near the swings. It was my job to move that mountain of sand shovelful by shovelful. When I finished that mountain, they brought in another load of sand. My heart sank to my toes. . . . Not another load! Before I finished that load I was rescued by being selected to have my tonsils removed at the campus hospital, along with nineteen other girls and boys with bad tonsils. Some interns at Baylor had asked for volunteers who needed their tonsils removed, and I was happy to volunteer. I had the granddaddy of all sore throats as a result of it, but it was worth it!

Most of the jobs on campus were not chores we were all that excited about being assigned since they usually required hard work—especially as we matured. As a girl on campus, I took my turn doing the usual chores of kitchen duty, which meant that I was part of a team which had to get up at 4:00 A.M. in order to peel enough potatoes to feed between 600 to 1,000 people every day. Sometimes I worked in the laundry, where I was privileged to iron my share of white shirts for every boy on campus to wear on Sunday because I could iron without scorching; or I worked at the mangle where I got to feed sheets into a huge

ironer, or I folded sheets for every child's bed on campus. Other times I waited on tables in Manna Hall for the older boys, whose sole purpose in life seemed to be either to run us to death getting food for them or to make us want to die by embarrassing us to death with their teasing.

One Saturday Mrs. Johnnie called a meeting of the girls in Pender and informed us that some new chores were being assigned to the older girls and asked for a show of hands if we liked children. I raised my hand along with most of the girls in the dorm. She chose other girls for the new assignments of helping at the Sunbeam Home with the children. My heart sank as I imagined that I would be assigned one of the undelightful chores left, which I had already experienced. Imagine my surprise when I was chosen to be a lifeguard. This meant that I got to supervise the girls as they swam on their days at the pool and could teach them to swim when I had time. That began a lifetime of swimming for me and of teaching for twenty years.

Remembering the summer when I was a lifeguard reminded me of the best eating I ever did. On the days when I worked at the pool, I passed the bakery early in the morning when they were baking the bread. Oh, boy! That smell was soooo delicious! Although the bakery was off limits, I occasionally stopped in and got a hot loaf of bread which Mr. Grube split open for me and then poured melted butter into its middle. Umm, ummm! It makes my mouth water to this day to think about that good eating!

There were five teachers who made an impact on my life at Buckner. The first was my second grade teacher whose name I don't recall, which is probably good. The reason she impacted my life was that she gave the girls the big sex talk which consisted of keeping us after school and stationing her husband at the door to keep the boys from peeking at us. After drawing all the shades, she talked to us about how to sit properly with our knees firmly clamped together for modesty, making sure that our underwear never showed. She then approached the delicate subject of using proper foundation garments as we matured, and her Grande Finale was to raise her skirt to show us her slip and girdle. I was shocked that an adult would show us her underwear! If her aim was to get our attention, she succeeded. She was certainly ahead of her time—teaching sex education in the school.

The second teacher I remember was Mrs. Richardson who taught fourth grade. She was a very good teacher, but a strict disciplinarian. If you dared show up in class with gum in your mouth, you had to put the gum on your nose after she had you face the chalkboard on tiptoes so she could draw a circle on the board at just the right height. Your task was to hold the gum on your nose and place your nose in the circle on the board until she told you to stop. You only chewed gum once in her class.

The next teacher I remember was Miss Graves who taught English in High School. She was an ex-Buckner child who had come back to teach after receiving her degree. She opened up worlds to me through great literature, and she increased my vocabulary multiple times over. She was a great teacher, but she didn't last long because some of the boys in class gave her such a hard time. She was one of us, and they didn't respect her authority. What a shame!

Then there was Miss McCullough who taught math in high school. She was probably the best teacher I had in school. When we began to learn algebra, we were so discouraged because the concept was so new and difficult to grasp for some of us. She kept encouraging us by telling us that someday it would make sense if we would just continue to do the exercises. Viola! She was right! One day it was as though blinders had been removed from my eyes and it all made sense. Bless her! It made sense!

The last teacher, who impacted my life in more ways than I can count, was not only my history teacher, but also my coach. It was as coach that Mr. Max Campbell influenced me so strongly. It wasn't his skills in teaching or coaching that impacted me; it was his life! As an ex-Marine, he demanded much from us, but he gave much back to us. He was totally loyal to us, and he taught us discipline which sustains me to this day. His generosity to us was unmatched; I'll always remember the donuts he purchased for the team. More importantly, he tried to set an example for us that we could follow, and he more than succeeded. I watched him struggle to conquer a temper that was almost out of control at times. When his temper finally began to cost the team due to penalties, he decided that he had to control it. At first he tried jumping, and I watched him jump as high as the concrete wall around the gym floor, trying to control his frustration and anger. He finally came up with a solution by holding a towel in his hand at all times. When he got angry or frustrated, he popped that towel, but he controlled his anger in an acceptable manner. By observing Max work through his problem, I learned that anger can be destructive if allowed to take on a life of its own, but it can be controlled if we remain diligent and never give in. This was probably the most valuable lesson I ever learned; behavior patterns can be changed. Thank you, Max!

Today I am the owner of a successful business, and my husband and I own a small apartment complex. We have been married for thirty-six years and raised three wonderful young men who are all college graduates and now have their own families. Buckner Orphans Home/Children's Home was such a large part of my life and affected me in so many ways. I am eternally grateful to Buckner Benevolences and Texas Baptists who cared enough about children to see to it that they were placed in a safe environment whenever families fell apart. I am particularly appreciative to all the people at Buckner who invested their lives in mine. Most of the people at Buckner were there because they wanted to be there, not just because it was a job. That was very apparent by the effort they put into the job.

Thank you all for the part you played in my life.

Frances (Jones) Weber/Saringer, '58

MEMORIES OF LIFE AT BUCKNER:

I remember:
Playing in the big sandbox at Sunbeam Home,
Walking up and down those tiny steps—especially designed for small children,
Sitting in Miss Glover's kindergarten class and wondering if all my teachers would be as wonderful as her,
And always feeling loved, even though I didn't have a real family;
Making that first move to Hardin Home after finishing kindergarten, and
Having Miss Orr as my first dorm mother and feeling that she was a perfect grandmother to all of us.
Looking forward to Christmas and "Buckner Bundles,"

Thinking how strict and mean Miss Zapp was only to realize in my teens that she was really a very good woman,

Standing in front of Miss Zapp in the "Conscience Room" confessing my latest sin or leaning over her bathtub to get a spanking for my most recent transgression,

Having a lot of free time to read, play and let my imagination fly.

We never thought we were missing anything that our children occupy their time with today—TV, videos, computers, etc.

Going to the movie every Saturday night, hating the scary movies, and loving the Shirley Temple and Margaret O'Brien movies.

In our teenage years, looking forward to reel changes when the lights came on and you could turn around and look at the guys.

Worshiping in the chapel every week.

Accepting Christ as an eleven-year-old during a campus revival,

Being privileged to be baptized by Brother Hal. He was getting very elderly and I was in one of the last groups he baptized. I was so tiny that I stood on top of his feet to get my head above the water line.

Having my picture taken many times holding Father Buckner's hand on his statue!

Walking, walking, walking!

Playing baseball and kick ball before school on the playground outside the elementary school.

Many times I started the day with grass stains on my dress! (That must have kindled my interest in sports),

Admiring my teachers; I had a lot of great ones. Their dedication and expectations of us prepared us to go to college.

Assembly programs in the auditorium,

Taking piano lessons from Mrs. Roberts, Miss Blount, and Mrs. Puett,

Getting an early start in loving music and being grateful that my third grade teacher saw my musical potential and recommended me to take piano,

Bonding with all my brothers and sisters as I grew up over an eighteen-year span.

Who else can brag about having such a huge family?

During the summer, eating watermelon brought to our dorms after supper and unloaded on the front lawns.

How we kids loved it and how the dorm mothers dreaded it because so many would wet the bed that night!

Learning to swim in the wonderful campus pool during the summers and

Taking all those Red Cross lessons.

When I was about twelve, I almost drowned and had to be pulled out of the pool.

I wasn't worried about dying as I kept going under, but I was very concerned that I wouldn't get to have fried chicken for lunch!

Finally, getting to be a lifeguard at the pool my last three or four summers at Buckner.

Sunday night fellowships at the Maris Welcome Center,

Saturday afternoon free time at the gym,

Playing basketball in high school,

Roller staking all over the girls' side of the campus, especially loving the ramp outside Manna Hall.

Miss McCullough and her math classes,

Doing homework in Study Hall at the high school,

Getting help from the smart guys in my class,

Waving at my boyfriend across Manna Hall as I left after eating,

Waving again as I got in front of the Chapel!

Getting to dress up in formals for banquets and awards ceremonies.

Making our graduation clothes our senior year in Homemaking Class,

Then getting to show them off with a "style show."

Helping pass out Christmas bundles to the younger children,

The minstrel shows that all the men and older boys starred in. They were delightful. I especially remember how quiet, shy Mr. Grube would come alive during those programs. This event is one of my favorite memories.

The excitement of my senior year and all the activities,

But being scared to face the fact that I'd be leaving the home I had known for over eighteen years.

Now as I look back over my days at Buckner, I realize what a heritage I have! I am grateful to God and to so many faithful, dedicated workers and teachers for the training and opportunities I received throughout those years. I especially am grateful for the religious training as well as a strong academic background. Since Buckner was the only home I ever knew, I am also grateful for the love, kindness, encouragement, and affirmation I received all those years.

God is so good! He placed each of us at Buckner and helped form the enormous family that we all became part of. What a heritage we all share. Let's pass that love and heritage on to others!

Jimmy Sims, '58

My mother and father divorced when I was two. First my father took us; my mother couldn't raise five kids or just didn't want to. I was the fifth and she was only twenty-two. I met her on several occasions when I got older. She contended that our farther had threatened her to the extent that she was afraid to even contact us for twelve or fourteen years.

My father was a contract plumber in Waco, in business with his brother. When they traveled to different towns to work, our father would leave us with a relative somewhere on the way to the other town for a few days, finish the job, and come back to get us. When he worked in town (Waco), we were left in a nursery, The Banjaleer. We stayed there several times; two or three days in a row during the day, but he would always pick us up in the evening.

One day he didn't come for us when it was time for all kids to be gone. Since several of the women who worked there also slept there, they reluctantly kept us overnight several times. Finally, our Aunt Edna from Fort Worth came to get us and took us to Buckner Orphans Home.

When we arrived at Buckner, I remember being fascinated with all the big red brick buildings. Maris Welcome Center had not been built yet. There was the entry gate building which served as a lodging for the gate-keeper and his wife. Cedar bushes grew along the cyclone fence all the way down Buckner Boulevard. We were taken to the largest building which contained the church, an auditorium and the Home offices and told to sit on the curb outside while Aunt Edna and my older sister, Betty Jo, went inside. My older brother, Jerry, kept saying to any adult that came by to look at us, "They are not going to split us up!"

The day was very hot (mid-September). Someone brought us ice-cream on a stick. Jerry would not let us eat the gift, so we just held the sticks and watched the ice cream melt. I was really disappointed. I had never seen an ice-cream on a stick.

Aunt Edna and Betty Jo finally came out. Aunt Edna tearfully kissed us all goodbye and before she left, I heard her telling Sammy not to call Caroline, our younger sister, "Cara-lee-lee." Caroline would get very mad at Sammy when he teased her with the babyish name.

We were then taken to the Receiving Home, a two-story building across Samuell Boulevard from the main campus, where we were all together for about two weeks. I remember a cement water trough structure in the ground. Rumor was that kids had to be dunked (dipped) to clean all the germs off before they were sent to the main campus. I also remember that the Receiving Home had downstairs and upstairs covered porches that went around the building on three sides. There was an old piano on the upstairs porch in the back. A large cat that lived under the building somewhere delighted in walking on the keys of the piano at inopportune times. When this happened, the lady workers would fuss at the cat and shut the keyboard cover. I liked the cat's music so well I would open the cover as soon as I could when no one was around. I also remember liking the indoor bathrooms. We had lived in houses without indoor plumbing. At one of the houses, every time I went out the back door to the outhouse, a large goose would chase me all the way to the small structure, wait for me to come out, and then chase me back to the house. When he caught up with me, he would peck the back of my heels. At another house, a cow in the back yard was my enemy, and harassed me when I went to the out house. Naturally I liked the restrooms at the Receiving Home.

After about two weeks, we were taken to the main campus to live in separate buildings. The Home was set up so that there were five dormitory buildings on one side of the campus for boys, and there were five dormitories on the other side for girls. Kids were housed in different dormitories, and on different floors of the buildings, according to age. Unless siblings were twins of the same sex, they could not live in the same room, even on the same floor. If they were two or three years apart in age, they were not even in the same building. I rarely saw or visited with my two older brothers and saw my sisters even less. The buildings on the boys' side of the campus for six-year-olds to high school seniors started with Pires which was a two story building for boys in grades one and two. From there we would move to Freeland which was a three story building housing grades three to five, starting by grade level on the top floor. McElroy was our next building for grades six and seven. From there we moved to the top floor of Rupard for grades eight and nine. The last building was Cullom for high school boys.

Since Caroline and I were younger than six, we were placed in a special building for preschoolers. I really liked living at the Sunbeam Home building. Within the class that I graduated from high school with, only one other classmate had come to the home before I did. There were from twenty to fifty kids my age at any one time during my sixteen years at Buckner. Even though new kids came throughout the years, and some left us after a few years, some of us stayed until we graduated from Buckner High School.

At the time I was there, the Home consisted of a main campus with many acres of farm land surrounding it. On the main campus were about eighteen to twenty red brick, red roof tiled buildings with two or three floors each. In addition to these buildings, there were other smaller structures for a laundry, Power House (containing a large boiler which produced steam for heating most of the buildings and equipment for campus maintenance), a Manna Hall, church and school. There was also residential housing for families of administrative personnel. The orphanage housed roughly 650 to 750 children from infants to High school seniors, and operated on meager funds. The strict Baptist principle that a kid with an idle mind was the Devil's workshop probably helped the home to be more than 50% self-sufficient. The matrons who were in charge of the kids in the different dormitories were mainly kind Baptist widows, spinsters, or abandoned mothers or wives with no formal training.

Generally, by 6:00 A.M. all 650 kids were up, had made their beds, dressed, formed a line, marched in line to the dinning hall (Manna Hall), sung a hymn, prayed, and eaten. After breakfast, we did chores and then marched to school (after which we did chores again until supper-time), studied, and were in bed by 9:00 or 9:30. On the farmland surrounding the main campus the boys plowed, planted, cultivated and harvested corn,

wheat, sugar cane, and hay. We milked sixty to seventy cows twice daily, killed and butchered hogs and chickens, strung fences, shoveled manure, fed all the livestock, mowed, baled, hauled, and put hay in barns for storage.

On the campus, we raked leaves, mowed, picked up trash, distributed laundry, warehoused commodities, and did maintenance. The girls washed, starched and ironed laundry. They cooked, served meals, washed dishes and floors. Compared to homes for needy children of today, the overhead costs were low.

Boys and girls were strictly segregated. Dean Taylor, and later, Dean McBride lectured my friends and I frequently on the evils of lying, cheating, stealing, and shirking on our jobs. They could be seen protectively patrolling the girls' side of the campus with large flashlights at night. We were occasionally spanked or restricted to our dorms, but the ultimate threat hanging over our heads, especially for crimes of the flesh, was being sent to the dreaded "juvenile detention hall," where large leather straps that brought blood to one's bottom were said to be used. Among the few kids who misbehaved so badly they had to leave the home, I never knew of anyone being sent to the juvenile hall. They either joined the military or went to live with a relative.

When I was in grammar school, there was usually some older, bigger boy that bullied me at different times, but there was no appeal to the authorities. In our code of honor, no crime was so serious as that of being a "tattle-tale." The adult supervisors were very strict, but underneath, it was a "root, hog, or die" world among us boys. Most of us, however, survived and flourished.

During the summer of the year a kid became six before September 1, and ready for first grade, he was moved from the Sunbeam Home to the dormitory buildings; girls to Hardin, boys to Pires. We all took our few belongings and marched from Sunbeam Home around the outer circle road to our buildings. Boys and girls marched together for the last time, and except for school, we rarely were together after that. When we reached the girls' building, we told the girls goodbye, marched off to the boys' building and learned to be boys, not "Sunbeaners." The name, of course, was Sunbeam, but we pronounced it "Sunbean."

We were given beds in a portable building that had been moved to just outside Pires because at that time there were too many boys to house all in the dormitory. I remember only a few bad incidents concerning any of the matrons in the buildings, but one stands out from a time in Pires that really bothered me.

One time our regular matron, whom we all liked, had taken a rare day off. The matron of the first floor, who had a mean reputation, was put in charge of us that day. In Pires there was a large playroom where we took naps after lunch. The mean matron summoned all of us to the playroom and told us to separate into three groups:

1) Those whose parents were both dead ("true orphans," she said).
2) Those with one parent alive.
3) Those whose parents were still alive.

I didn't know whether my parents were dead or alive at the time. I had not even thought about where they were. I assumed they were dead. I headed toward the "true orphans" group. The matron made everyone stop where they were, came to me, grabbed me by the ear and begin admonishing me for moving to the wrong group. She pulled me out by the ear and told me to get with my group. I hurriedly headed for the group with one parent alive, but when I saw the matron heading for me again, I turned and ran to the group with two parents alive. This was the first time I knew for sure that I had a mother and father. This was in 1946. My mother, whom I never knew very well, died in 1999. We had been together a few times, but had never established much of a relationship. I attended her funeral, and felt a tinge of guilt at feeling relieved at finely being an "orphan." My father died in the 50s, but even then I still don't know much about him.

I also remember another bad incident with this same lady. Our matron was gone on some personal business for a few hours. We were in the portable building, "home alone," having a good time jumping from one bed to the other. The mean matron suddenly appeared in the doorway; a shoe, thrown as she was opening the door, hit her hard in the stomach. She hardly even flinched, but she was angry. We were all made to form a line in only our underwear. Then, one at a time, we had to lie face down, and receive five licks. We talked about it with our matron later and all agreed that the mean matron had had just a little bit of a smile as she strapped us. I had been spanked, or whipped several times before, but this was the worst.

However, there were many good times at Pires. We all liked our matron very much, as she was loving, fair and seemed to like her job. One of my good friends of the same age, Darrel Lewis, and I often competed for this matron's favor. Good people somewhere outside the Home often sent used clothing that the matrons distributed to us as needed. After the war the home received a lot of military surplus. Each time our matron would receive the leftovers from what the bigger boys didn't use, we somehow knew and would ask her if any aviator caps had been sent.

One day a box full of the coveted caps had been sent. We could see that nearly all the boys who wanted an aviator cap would get one. As we dug through the box, we found one cap that still had the goggles snapped on. Darrell and I both had told the matron how much we would like to have an aviator cap with goggles. The matron didn't know what to do; we were both begging her for the cap with goggles. She had all the other boys vote on which one of us would get the cap. The vote came out to be a tie. She decided to wait until the next day to decide. That evening when we were all playing Kick-the-Can, Bill Miles fell on the sidewalk while running, skinned his arm and leg really badly, so the matron gave the cap with the goggles to him.

Among the many good times we had while living in Pires, I looked forward most to Christmas and going to the woods. The most memorable Christmas for me was when I had a prayer partially answered; I got a football on my string, but it was stuffed with rags. Our Sunday School teacher was teaching us the value of praying. We were taught that if we thanked God for his love and blessings, and pleaded for forgiveness of our sins, we could ask for anything. These prayer lessons were going on during football season, and I wanted a football very much. Each night I would rush through the necessary part of my prayer and then promise God all kinds of things if He would send me a football for Christmas. I was very excited when the night arrived, and Santa Claus came to the auditorium.

I almost ran over the boy in front of me trying to get back to my room so I could get my football out. At first I was very disappointed. I had gotten a football, but it didn't have a bladder and was stuffed with rags. I was so disappointed with God, I went into my closet almost crying. After a while, still in the closet, God and I had a talk. The football cover had obviously been through several seasons of games played perhaps by some of the best athletes in the world. I felt that some retired professional football player had carefully stuffed the ball and then retied the opening very neatly, as directed by God, just for me. I loved that football after I learned to talk with God.

Another favorite experience while living at Pires was going to the Woods. There was a large wooded acreage west of the campus, across Highway 80 from the dairy. During the summer we were often taken as a group with our matrons to the woods. I looked forward to playing in the woods and eating syrup sandwiches and drinking milk. The sandwiches were made from fresh Buckner Bakery bread with syrup from half-gallon buckets, and the milk came from the Buckner Dairy. We were allowed to run free, explore, climb trees and investigate an old log cabin and several cement bunkers in the woods. The bunkers were about three feet high, completely enclosed, except for an opening large enough for one person to crawl through. We pretended that they were defensive positions from which Southern troops held back thousands of Yankees. Each time we left the woods we would all say together, "Good-by Jackie Woods." This was our name for the Boys' Woods. On a different day the girls would go to a different part of the woods, known as Girls' Woods.

Many of the boys and a few girls acquired nick-names while at Buckner. Actually, I had one and didn't know it. I was called Jimmy by all the adults and kids until I got my other nick-name. But Jimmy was assumed by all to be my real name; it was on all school forms. During my senior year I had to obtain a birth certificate to apply for college entry. With a lot of help from Mr. Perry, our high school principal, I found a birth certificate in Jefferson County, Texas. To my surprise, at eighteen I found out that my real name was James Arthur Sims (with one M) instead of Jimmy Simms with two M's. Also, I found out that my birth date was January 7, instead of the 11th. My brother Sammy still insists that my birth date is the 11th, as our mother had said it was many times.

My other nickname was "Homer." When I was six, my table waiter, a beautiful high school girl named Angie Richardson, called me "Homer Pigeon." In the 40s there was a newspaper cartoon about a pigeon named Homer. He had a feather that came out of the back of his head, curved back and down. It seems that I had a "cowlick" in the back of my hair most of the time. Angie contended that I looked like that cartoon character, so she called me by that name.

The term "table waiter" may need an explanation. When kids grew older, each was given a job or two that they worked at regularly. Among the jobs that many of the older girls did was serving the tables in the Manna Hall. For each of the three meals a day, all the kids six and older marched into Manna hall by age groups and sat on benches that held six to eight kids on each side of long tables. At the head of our table, a girl would sit and eat when she wasn't bringing food in large containers from the kitchen. After the meal we all marched out, at which time the girls would wash our dishes in pans of water carried from the kitchen. After Miss Mamie inspected the tables to be sure everything was clean, the girls were free to go to their dormitory. We called the girl at our table "our waiter."

While I was in Pires, my tonsils were taken out. Each year all six-year-old boys and girls were gathered in the hospital building to have their tonsils removed by Baylor medical students. This served two purposes; the medical students were able to practice surgical skills, and the kids had their tonsils removed. Doctors at that time, believed that tonsils were not needed and should be removed from all kids to prevent future sinus problems.

After two or three years at Pires, I moved to the third floor of Freeland. Each subsequent year I would move down a floor with all my class mates. From Freeland I moved to McElroy and from there to Rupard which was the big boys' building. Before I got to Rupard, Cullom was built for Academy Senior boys, so I finished my last years in Cullom before "I was out the gate in 58," our unofficial class motto.

It was in about fourth or fifth grade that Donald Ray Ritchie acquired a nick name. During a science class, the teacher was describing the babies of the biggest bird in South America, baby Condor Birds. She said they were very ugly, had very long legs, long wings with no feathers, and large mouths. Someone in the class said, "That sounds like Donald Ray." The name stuck. The teacher also told us that when the condor bird grows up, it is the most handsome and largest bird in the sky. Donald Ray got the name

"Condor Bird" and, indeed, did grow up to be the biggest and most handsome guy in our class. Since he is on the alumni association board as chaplain, I sometimes refer to him as Brother Condor, Father Condor, or Reverend Condor. He takes the naming good naturedly and is still a good friend.

At about twelve, I became a member of the field gang. I was destined to work at the dairy farm when I was in high school—my older brothers had worked at the dairy, so I looked forward to becoming old enough to work there. However, until I got old enough for that kind of responsibility, I held many different jobs. One was helping to mow. In the spring and summer by the time we finished mowing the entire campus lawn, it was time to start over again.

This "field-gang" consisted of about 15 to 20 boys with mechanical push mowers that worked very efficiently. Two older boys, who worked at the Power House, were in charge of us. They would have us form a line side by side and push our mower five paces and one step behind the boy in front of us. The older boys took a lot of pride in making sure we were in the right position throughout the mowing. If we looked sloppy while mowing, the other older boys would tease our supervisors about letting the little boys get the best of us. The older boys would follow our line and shout instructions, threats and insults to keep us in order.

While a member of the mowing gang, I learned about the "tunnels." We had heard many stories about the tunnels. There were stories about some boys who had gone into one of the girls' dormitories at night to meet their girlfriends. We also heard stories about boys getting into the commissary through the tunnels. However, we mainly played chase and hide-and-seek in the tunnels. When we were in the ninth grade, several other boys and I would sneak out at night into the tunnels, and go over to the area below the girls' dormitory. There we would sit on the floor of the dark tunnel and listen to girls in the building above us talk. The next day we would tease the girls about what they had talked about. They never found out how we knew about their conversations. Sometimes the girls would accuse each other of telling us about what had been said.

When I was in junior high, I wasn't sure what types of jobs the girls my age had. I just assumed that they were busy scrubbing the hard floors, on their hands and knees, in all the buildings.

Even though we spent a lot of time with our chores, we had plenty of play time. We happily explored the woods, climbed trees, hunted squirrels to keep as pets and foraged for walnuts and pecans. Games were made up, toys were invented. We hunted, killed and cooked rabbits and squirrels; we swam in Bull Pond and the campus swimming pool, shot rocks with homemade squirrel-shooters, and made playful contests out of work.

One game we invented and played during the fall each year was Buster Claim It. During the 40s and 50s, most of the boys had a special pecan they carried in their pocket ready to participate in a game of Buster-Claim-It when challenged by another boy. The competition consisted of squeezing two pecans in the palm of the hand until one of them cracked. The winner was the person whose pecan did not crack and he, therefore, claimed and ate the losing pecan. The game rules were, for the most part, accepted by all. The one challenged got to do the pecan squeezing, unless his hand was sore from too much pecan squeezing. The seam of the pecan could not be placed against the other pecan. If this happened, the squeezer had to give up his pecan—this rule, when broken, usually resulted in an argument, and sometimes a fist-fight. No boy wanted to give up his "Tall," which is what we called our competition pecan. As a form of intimidation, we would rub the meat of a pecan on our Tall and the oil would change the color, making the competition pecan look like it had been in several battles and won.

During this time we also learned from the big boys how to make lead shots for our squirrel-shooters. There were two sets of wide twin flights of stairs leading up to the church. On each step there were three half-inch strips of lead implanted in grooves on each step to provide a non-slip surface. We would remove part of the lead from the steps. Inside one end of each window shade roller was a small metal cup. The metal cup was dug out of the shade roller and the shade was hung back over the window. The shade wouldn't go up or down anymore. The metal cups had three small spikes on the bottom side and could be stuck into a piece of wood.

When the lead and the small metal cups were secured, we would melt the lead in a syrup can over a fire we built by the incinerator. We then carefully tilted the hot can so the melted lead would slowly pour into the cup. We could pop the ready-to-use shot out of the cup when the lead cooled. The cup with the lead, that a small piece of crystal had been embedded into when it was melted, was used in the making of our jerry-rigged radio receiving sets.

The older boys instructed us on how to make a radio receiver. We would construct a small wooden box, with our pocket knife, drill three pairs of holes, insert six small nuts with bolts (the bolts were usually acquired from a piece of furniture—I got mine from the church chairs), and using hay-baling wire (if copper wire could not be found), the bolts were connected. On the top pair of bolts we connected a long piece of baling wire, strung it out the window to a nearby tree for an antenna. Then another piece of wire was connected and attached to the steam-heated radiator in our room for a grounding wire. A large safety pin was attached to one of the middle bolts, and a shade roller cup with lead that had a small piece of crystal embedded into it (when it had been melted and poured), was attached in the middle of the box. An earphone which had been passed down from an older boy (or, if necessary, acquired from an airplane at White Rock Airport during the night) was attached to the bottom set of bolts. When all this engineering was finished, we would set the point of the safety pin on the crystal and could hear several radio stations at one time. Usually, one station could be heard better then the others.

I spent many late night hours with my earphone under my pillow, listening to music and radio plays. The "Big D Jamboree" on Saturday night was one of my favorites. After midnight an English speaking station in Mexico drowned out all the other stations. We laughed at the advertisements from XERF, Del Rio, Texas; such as, small pouches of dirt from the holy land, walk-on-water sandals, and autographed pictures of Christ—suitable for framing. The announcer would spell the address several times during the advertisement, obviously assuming that anyone who would order the goods was not going to be able to spell.

Another yearly event we all looked forward to was Orphans' Day at the State Fair. We would save every penny we could get in anticipation of going to the Fair. During some of the years, a farmer with cotton fields near the Home's land would pay us to pick cotton just before the Fair. I remember the excitement on Fair Day. We would

be loaded onto what we called cattle trucks—one for boys and one for girls. Special sideboards were made at the Farm for the truck-beds. The big boys would get on the truck first and take all the places around the side-boards; the smaller boys in the middle, with standing room only. When the truck would move forward, we would all fall backwards unless we were standing by the side-boards. When the truck stopped, we would all fall forward. The ride was scary, but worth the fright.

Homecoming for the ex-students was another exciting event each year. When we were young, the exes would traditionally throw a handful of change to a group of boys just to watch us scramble and wrestle for the coins. One year James and Orville Griffin charged the exes for parking. The exes knew the boys were not official, but would give them a nickel or dime. The biggest event at Homecoming was the football game. I'm sure the coaches on either team looked forward to this game. The male ex-students would crowd along the sidelines at the line of scrimmage, yelling instructions, admonishing failures, and approving of successes. We usually won the game, probably because the opposing team was so intimidated by the large group of boys yelling on the sidelines.

We spent many hours playing, hunting rabbits and squirrels, and swimming at Bull Pond, the woods, and the farm fields around Buckner. The best hunters among my classmates were Don Ayers, Bill Miles, and Charlie Smith. They had spent much time hunting with some of the older boys like Cotton Barfield, Earl Ray Miles, and Chick Mabry; legendary hunters to us. They were considered sharp-shooters with a squirrel-shooter, could climb any tree with little effort, and seemed to know which brush pile contained a rabbit.

Most boys had home-made squirrel-shooters and a rabbit club for hunting weapons. The shooters were constructed from a carefully selected tree branch that formed a Y. Strips of rubber were cut from an old discarded inner-tube; the tube had to be made of real rubber. At that time manufacturers were just beginning to make tubes of synthetic rubber, which would not stretch on a shooter as well as the real rubber. If a boy could get a rubber inner tube, he would cut strips and use them as trade for many different things that other boys had. A groove was whittled around the two top parts of the Y stalk, and one end of the rubber strips was tied to each top with string that fit into the groove. The other end of the rubber strips were tied to a leather flap for loading a lead-shot, marble, or rock. The leather flap had been the shoe-tongue of an old pair of brogans, which were our standard issue high-top shoes. The rabbit club was made from a table or chair leg, or a modified baseball bat if one was available.

A rabbit hunt consisted of five or more boys (some times up to twenty or thirty). We would spread out about ten yards apart, and advance forward through a field. When a rabbit was spotted, someone would shout out its location and which direction it was running. The nearest boys would throw their club at the running rabbit. Many times an argument over whose club had hit the rabbit would occur. When a rabbit was killed, the successful hunter would cut the rabbit's neck to let the blood out, and then cut a slit through the hind leg so as to hang the rabbit upside down on his belt and continue the hunt. We were very proud when we returned to the campus if we had one or more rabbits hanging from our belt. We also would not send our pants that we had hunted in to the laundry for a long time. These pants had the blood stains from the rabbit on them just below the knee and this was like a badge of hunting skill. I don't know how, but when the pants were sent to the laundry the blood stains were washed out.

When we got back to the campus we would hang the rabbit from a nail on a tree, skin it and remove the intestines, build a fire beside the incinerator and cook the rabbit. We also prepared squirrels the same way. The incinerators were 8 by 8 by 6' concrete trash burning structures, located in several places around the campus. We also boiled corn-on-the-cob in syrup buckets over a fire. Everyone knew that you had to let the water boil over three times before the corn was done. When the corn in the fields was harvested and shucked, we would cook the dried kernels over the fire and call it parched corn.

While in high school, I fulfilled my destiny by working at the dairy farm. Both of my older brothers had worked there. Jerry had spent most of his time at the dairy because he liked it there so much. One of the adult supervisors warned me not to try to hide when the truck would leave to go back to the campus like Jerry would do. It seemed that Jerry would often stay at the dairy when everyone left so he wouldn't have to go to

school. When he did this, they would usually find him later in the day and make him work extra hard, thinking that he wouldn't want to stay again. But, he would rather do all the unwanted chores than go to school. When Jerry left the home (ran away for good), the teachers and other employees at first thought he was just hiding at the dairy somewhere. The dairy farm supervisor told me when I started working there that he tried to tell the other employees that Jerry had left for good.

I didn't see Jerry for three years after he left, until he finally came back for a visit. He was wearing an Army Uniform. I was very proud. He had gone to Tyler and worked on a dairy farm until he was old enough to join the Army. I was fourteen or fifteen years old when he came for the visit. By this time I had already accepted Buckner as my home and knew I was going to stay. I had attempted to leave the home by running away several times when I was even younger, but had always returned within a day or so, because I missed being there, got tired of eating boiled corn, got home-sick or realized that I didn't know where to go after I got four or five miles away from the Home. I usually spent the night in a corn field or an old barn that I was familiar with and then returned to get my punishment. Fortunately most of the time, the matrons and dean were so glad that I was back safe, the punishment wasn't too bad.

When I worked at the dairy, we had three crews of boys. We would rotate so that every other day we would get up at 3:30 or 4:00 A.M. to milk the cows. And every other day we would milk the cows just after school or when athletic practice was over. The cows had to be milked twice a day. The routine was that we would ride in the back of the dairy pick-up to the farm. The pick-up bed was covered with canvas to ward off the cold. When we got to the dairy, if the cows had not come up to the barn, we had to go to one of the partially wooded pastures to drive them to the milk barn. I really hated to go through the cow tunnel under Highway 80 in the dark to get the cows for a morning milking session. Many times there would be a Hobo sleeping in the tunnel (or a scared, lost dog), so the cows would not come through on their own. The thought of what might be in the dark tunnel at night was scary.

When the cows came into the barn, they would immediately go to a row of feeding troughs and put their heads through the head locking apparatus to eat, at which time we would easily lock them in until we were ready to milk them. The cows seemed to know the routine better than we did.

Each cow had a number which was stamped on a two-inch disk that hung on a chain around its neck. A large framed chart hung on the wall in the milking barn with each cow's number, and standard data about each. The chart, also had a girls name beside each number. We often compared a cow's temperament to that of one of the girls at Buckner. (We weren't sensitive to negative chauvinism.) I'll not mention which girl we compared to number 28, Dynamite. This cow was very hard to manage. She would often try to kick us, and generally had a bad temperament. Number 47, named May, was the most gentle cow, and very good looking. We all liked her. She didn't mind if we sat on her back while she grazed or walked to the barn. Because of her amiable nature and good looks, we compared her to Joyce Bangs.

After the cows were all locked into the feeding area, they were released one at a time to enter the milking shoot where a boy would wash their milk bags and udders with a rag and special cleaner. From there they would go into one of the four milking stalls where vacuum cups were attached to their udders. After being milked, they would be released out of the barn. There was a dog in the barn that felt it was his duty to nip at each cow's back leg to get her to exit the barn quickly. (Even, the dog knew not to nip at Dynamite.) We would warm our hands on a cold day by putting them against the warm, milk laden udders. There was also a cat living in the barn. The cat loved for us to turn an udder up and squeeze milk into his face from 15 feet away. We also made a game out of squirting milk from the udders at each other; just like shooting water guns.

The milk was vacuum pumped into about twenty twenty-gallon milk cans. When the milking was finished, we had to wash manure out of the entire barn with a large water hose and push brooms, a dreaded chore. Then the milk cans were loaded onto the pick-up for transport to the Manna Hall kitchen.

Some of the milk was poured into a separator and the cream was kept for making butter. We had no use for the skimmed milk, so it was delivered to the farm and poured into the pigs' feeding troughs.

When we finally delivered the milk to Manna Hall, we would transport it into a large, walk-in refrigerator. When I was a sophomore, I liked Joyce Griffin, a freshman, but I wasn't telling anyone. I wasn't even telling Joyce or most especially her brothers, James and Orville, who were good rabbit and squirrel hunting buddies of mine. I thought Joyce liked me too; it seemed I could detect a special smile when our eyes met in study hall.

During that time, the girls, and sometimes the boys, would call a popular radio station that took song requests to play and dedicate to a selected someone. Someone other than Joyce had called in for the popular song "Sincerely" to be played "for Joyce Griffin to Jimmy Sims." This had embarrassed both of us, but I liked it. It seems that everyone knew we liked each other, but neither of us could make the first advance, so we were not officially "going with" each other.

Once when I had gone inside the refrigerator with a milk can, someone pushed Joyce in with me and shut the door. Alone in the locker, we didn't know what to do except stare at each other until Miss Mamie, who had heard the commotion, opened the door and found us there. When I think about it, I can still hear Miss Mamie yelling at me, and I can also still see the silly grins on the kids' faces who witnessed the event. I was barred from the Manna Hall kitchen, but Joyce's punishment was a lot worse, I guess. She had to continue working in the kitchen with Miss Mamie.

In 1995 Newt Gingrich, a leading U.S. senator, suggested that orphanages be reinvented. He was bitterly criticized. However, if you think of our national epidemic of neglected, abused, and abandoned children, and then consider the thousands of children who lived in orphanages like Buckner and grew up to become contributing members of our society, Gingrich's suggestion may be better than the way we manage unwanted children today.

Karl Fleming, who had grown up in a similar orphanage during the 30s and 40s, wrote an editorial in *Newsweek*, January 30, 1995, a paragraph summing up what he gained from a Methodist orphanage in Raleigh, N.C. This also describes what I feel we gained from having lived at Buckner.

"Into adult life, we carried from the orphanages many valuable tools and lessons. We learned honesty, loyalty, self-discipline, self-sufficiency. We learned to take pride in working hard and doing well even the most menial jobs. We learned to keep our word. We learned fair play and how to work with others. We learned respect for our elders and for rules. We learned good manners, tolerance and generosity. We learned to take our medicine when we did wrong."

Buckner Home was a good place to grow up because we were prepared for adulthood and citizenship. Despite the shortcomings of the Home, living there beat the alternatives. By necessity it was impersonal, and very strict, but we adjusted and generally enjoyed life there. Even when we were outside the home for off-campus activities, such as interscholastic events, we walked with pride and even believed we were superior to the "outside" boys.

Mel Walls, '58

ARRIVAL

We came to the orphanage in October of 1951.

There was an iron gate and a red brick wall, and a quaint little gatehouse that jutted out from the wall and formed a part of it, and when the preacher honked the car horn, an aged man came out of the gatehouse to see what was the matter. We were let in, and drove down a wide boulevard lined with trees, which led us to an inner Circle. Around the Circle there were a good many brick buildings with red tile roofs, all very much alike. The buildings looked outdated even then, and there was an air of stolid indifference to them, as though they had seen many a grave thing happen, but as yet had come to no harm themselves.

In the middle of the Circle was a flagpole, and a flag moving in the breeze, and there was a bronze statue of a man in old-fashioned dress clothing, standing in a statesman's pose.

There were offices below the steps of the great chapel, and while the preacher went in to inquire, we waited, mute and subdued. The place seemed deserted. In all the time that we sat waiting, there was not a soul to be seen.

The preacher returned, and drove us to a

building set far apart from the rest, well away from the campus. It was not much different from the other buildings that we had seen, and it seemed to be as deserted as the others. Eventually though, someone inside was aroused. The preacher unloaded our cardboard boxes onto the steps. Then, his Christian duty done, he wished us well, bade us goodbye, and quickly drove away. It was Quiet Hour, we learned. Our cardboard boxes were allowed inside, but we were relegated to a side porch, and adjured to remain quiet until further notice. There was nothing to do but stand about on the covered porch, and wait in awkward silence.

At long last, other children appeared. Some were newcomers just like ourselves, wearing the same stunned expressions. But there was another—a boy with lank dark hair and red sleepy eyes, and dressed in clothes no better than my own—who turned out to be an orphan of long experience. Shyly, we clustered around him, hoping for answers.

"This is the Receiving Home," said Bill—for it turned out that his given name was Bill.

"All new boys and girls have to stay here for two weeks," he explained, "to see what all diseases they got." Why then was Bill himself at the Receiving Home?

"Worms," Bill said in a matter-of-fact way.

He had been allowed to go home for a three-day visit that summer, and had returned thoroughly infested with hookworms. Undoubtedly, Bill mistook my horrified expression for a look of sympathy.

"I'm used to it by now," he said philosophically. "It happens every time I get to go home." We wanted to know a hundred things, mostly what to expect when we got to the campus. Bill tried his best to tell us, but in the end, he had to give it up. "I can't tell you what it's like," he said. "You got to see it for yourself."

Bill was wiser than he knew. That first supper was a dismal affair. The table was presided over by the withered old couple who ran the Receiving Home, and they seemed to be strongly addicted to silence and dim lights. The table was served by a sullen girl of a nubile age, who then sat down at the table to eat with us. During the entire meal, no words were spoken, except to issue orders to the serving girl, or to correct the manners of the newcomers.

The main foodstuffs were not particularly

appealing, but there was a metal ewer filled with sweet, frothy milk, and there was good bread, different from any that I had ever tasted before. The milk was so cold that the dull, dented sides of the ewer sweated heavily, and the bread was crusty and firm to the tooth. I ignored the other dishes, and made a meal of bread and milk. No one seemed to notice, much less care. Food had been provided, and if I chose not to eat it, no one took issue. Naturally, we were curious about the hostile girl, and once safely away from the ancients, Bill told us about her. "She was going with this boy over in Cullom Building," Bill explained. "One night, they run off together. Now she's got to stay up here at the Receiving Home for a month or two, and she might even get sent away for good."

The whole thing was beyond my comprehension, and I said so. Bill settled a long and thoughtful look upon me, and he sucked at an eyetooth while he reflected, trying to decide whether I was simple, or just plain slow. Then he explained to me exactly why the girl had to stay for a month or two, and what would determine whether she stayed at the orphanage, or was sent away.

"Oh," I said, once I understood. I blushed a deep red, and felt entirely thick.

That first night, we new ones were summoned, one by one, to the living quarters of the ancients. When my turn came, I entered the dim room and saw the old man in his worn robe and slippers, seated in front of a television set. The flickering blue light from the tiny television screen flashed on his skinny white shins. He did not in any way acknowledge my presence. The old woman stood me up before her, and she regarded me impersonally, as though I had been put up for auction. Judging from her expression, any bid she offered would have been a very low one. "Do you have lice?" she asked me.

Even though I hotly denied it, she hung a pair of half-glasses on the end of her nose, and drew my head down. She ran a fine comb through my hair, and held the comb in the light of a lamp, to see for herself. When she finally released me, I stood back, staring hard at her and burning with shame and indignation. Indifferent to my outrage, she looked at me sternly over those little glasses.

"You will behave yourself while you are here," she said. "You will play quietly, and you will come when you are called. You will lie down for

Quiet Hour, whether you sleep or not. Do you understand?"

I was much too full of feeling to say anything at all.

"If I were you," she said, "I would answer 'Yes ma'am.'"

And somehow I managed to do so.

"You can go now," she said. "Send the next one in."

The days at the Receiving Home were long enduring, and each endless hour was very much like the one that had gone before it. Even the time that I slept away was not refreshing, and I awoke feeling sluggish. But neither boredom nor anxiety can completely stop a clock, and the time finally came when we were told to prepare our meager belongings for transport to the main campus.

Once there, my family was sent apart—one brother to this red-tiled building, another to that. Our sister was sent to the Girls' Side, and the youngest of us all to a place called Sunbeam, all the way on the other side of the campus.

I quickly learned that the orphans were regulated by obnoxious noises. A piercing steam whistle woke us up, a grating buzzer demanded that we younger ones go at once to check in with our matrons, and a clanging fire bell summoned us to school. A siren called us to meals. When First Siren called, we formed up in lines in front of our buildings, and when the siren wailed a second time, we stepped off in a designated order, toward the Manna Hall. The youngest ones came to Manna Hall first—apparently on the theory that they were more easily controlled during the long wait for all to arrive. The older ones followed at intervals, so that all across the campus the long lines of orphans moved toward Manna Hall, while the high note of the siren howled, and lingered, and then died away into a drawn-out moan.

That autumn, and on into the early winter, there were great fires in the forests far to the east, and the smoke and ash from those fires drifted scores of miles to where the orphanage was. The days were made a gritty gray, and at night it was so exceedingly dark that all the outside lights on the campus were reduced to little more than dim beacons. A pall settled on the campus. The smoke made morning come late and brought night on early, and when we were called to supper, it was already nearly dark. The orphans formed up in the lowering twilight, and the long lines moved out, converging on the dim lights of Manna Hall like black shadows trudging to the discadent beat of brogan boots.

Inside Manna Hall, the bright lights and the clatter of the taking of the evening meal were jarring, and the gloom outside was deepened by contrast. I decided that this place that I had come to must be hellish indeed, if the sun didn't want to shine on it, and I doubted that the sun would ever come out again.

It did, of course—it always does. I was too young then to realize that everything changes. Since that time, it has been my experience that changes for the worse usually come with a jolt, while changes for the better come a little each day. Time rounds off the sharp edges of the jolts, and in spite of it all, lifts the spirit. But I was very young in those early days, and could not know these things. I only knew that all the days were dark, and all the nights were long, and I wondered what would ever become of me.

I THINK IT WAS CHERRY

I cannot fix the time in my mind but the memory carries with it the blustery feel of one of those dark raw days in the early springtime, when the southerlies blow in strong gusts, but no rain falls from the unbroken black clouds that tumble and turn across the sky. It may have been in 1953, but I can't be sure. It had to have been my Mart Day, though. That much I know, because I distinctly remember that I had an ice cream cone.

I was walking across the campus with my ice cream when my attention was drawn to a matron—whose name shall remain forgotten—standing near the Circle between Rupard and McElroy. She was surrounded by a clutch of urchins, all of whom were pointing to the heavens and urgently commanding her to look! look up there! They were so insistent that I myself felt compelled to look up to see what it was that excited them so.

Up there, just below the troubled clouds, was a military aircraft droning along with one of its starboard engines on fire. The matron, once she saw the item of interest, commenced to dance around in the oddest fashion. She waved her arms about in a most frantic way, and declared repeatedly that somebody ought to do something, or call somebody. I hoped she didn't mean me in particular, because there was nothing I could do

except point and shout, and there was quite enough of that going on at the moment.

The aircraft droned on, apparently oblivious to its plight.

Then the urchins chorused even louder, look! look! and a puff of white burst open behind and below the aircraft, and there was a parachute in the sky, coming down fast. Then there was another, and then another, and before the fourth one opened I saw the man falling through the air—a tiny black figure falling with arms and legs spread wide—and then something streamed out behind him and the parachute snapped open—I swear I heard it pop—and beneath its canopy the man was jerked up short and then he swayed and spun, for all the world like the little lead soldiers we sometimes tied to the toy parachutes that we made of string and red bandannas.

There were seven of them in all, and they came down one above the other like stairsteps. With the strong south wind behind them, they moved horizontally as rapidly as they descended.

The last parachute had no sooner opened than the flaming engine fell away from the aircraft. The remaining engines spooled up with a sound like a hopeless groan, and the aircraft heeled over to the right, and went into a power dive.

The urchins immediately sprang away, running madly for the spot where they reckoned the aircraft would come down, which just happened to be in the same direction as Buckner's front gate. Every orphan they passed along the way—myself included—was swept up in the mindless herd instinct, and soon there was a goodly mob of us charging the front gate.

We did not know where we were going or what we would do when we got there, nonetheless we pelted along in deadly earnest. I did all I could to keep up, but I was handicapped by the ice cream in my hand.

The gatekeeper looked up to see us thundering down on him en masse, and although I cannot say for sure what was in his mind, I think he believed that the long-dreaded Great Escape was underway. He ran out to meet us, arms stretched wide to impede our flight, and the orphans in the lead flowed around him as heedlessly as water slips around a river rock.

Although I doubt that it was actually true, it seems to me now that there was an end to the howling of the engines in those last few seconds before impact, a dreadful pause before the tremendous explosion to come. I do remember that every one of us stopped running when the sound of that explosion hit us. We stood there in the wind and the sudden silence, and we watched, stunned and sober, as the long greasy plume of black smoke rose up into the sky. It was a long way off, and the wind whipped the column of smoke into tatters before it got very high.

Then someone shouted, and pointed up at the parachutes. The mob reversed itself at once, and came pounding back in my direction. I turned to run, but they were upon me before I could get up to speed, and I was very nearly trampled. I think it was then that I lost the last of the ice cream. We streamed back between the dorms and around the high school and up the Boys' Side of the gym, but when we got to the football field, there was Coach Boldin, roaring forth to flank us and turn us to milling. He managed to stop most of us, but a few bolder souls sped on across the gridiron and beyond the dog pens, out into the fields where the parachuting soldiers were just now coming to earth.

Badly winded and with a stitch in my side like you would not believe, I was more than happy to pull up. The football stands were right there, so I sat on the top bleacher and watched it all unfold before me. As I remember, the first soldier managed to clear Highway 80 but the wind was so strong that he could not spill his parachute, and he was dragged through the fields until someone drove out from the barn in a pickup truck and ran the truck over his parachute to collapse it.

The second soldier was not so fortunate. He came down directly on Highway 80, between the power lines, and his parachute dragged him up and over the power lines and dropped him into the barbed wire fence below. Then it tore him loose from the wire. As I recall, this soldier died there in the fields.

The third soldier landed short of the highway, struggled with his parachute, could not spill it, was pulled off his feet, and would have been dragged through the wires himself had a motorist not turned his brand new Henry J automobile off the highway and driven head-on into the billowing silk.

The fourth soldier landed unhurt in the south end of the field. To this day, I feel an affinity for that anonymous soldier, for I saw him take the leap and fall for all those long breathless

seconds before his parachute opened, and I watched as he desperately prepared himself for the jolt of landing, and I cheered when he wrestled the parachute to the ground and finally freed himself from its harness. I could not have been prouder of him if he had been my uncle. The other parachuting soldiers were strung out all the way to Bull Pond. In fact, the story was told that the last soldier out of the aircraft had been crippled by polio, and was in leg braces. Reportedly, he suffered a great anguish all the way down, thinking about what the braces would do to his legs when he hit the ground. He was doubly fortunate that day, for not only did he come to a soft landing in the waters of Bull Pond, but there was a waterlogged boat manned by orphans waiting to rescue him from drowning.

I think only two men died that day—the soldier who fell among the power lines along the highway, and the pilot who stayed with his aircraft until it crashed. One soldier went missing, but he turned up in a hospital, where a good Samaritan had taken him. Some of the parachutes disappeared from the fields where the soldiers landed. One of them was openly displayed on Boys' Side, and Mr. McBride promptly arrived to impound it. It was Government Property, he proclaimed sternly, and the Proper Authorities would soon come looking for it. All other such items were to be turned in immediately, he warned.

Looking thoughtful, the orphans around the confiscated parachute drifted off, and no more parachutes came to light. What happened to them was a great mystery, and remains so to this day. The police came, and the ambulances, and the gawkers, and the military investigators too, I suppose. And the newspaper reporters, of course —disasters draw the press like a carcass draws flies. It seems to me that they talked to a couple of the older orphan boys who had something to do with finding the engine that had fallen away from the burning craft, but that recollection is suspect.

Eventually the officials went away, and once it became clear that the proper authorities were never coming, a surprising array of little souvenirs quietly appeared. Buckles and straps and insignia, silk and cord and other items. Where these trophies came from, and how they were taken, I cannot say, but had they been collected and catalogued, they undoubtedly would have made a small museum for the disaster.

I have tried very hard to recall what flavor of ice cream I had that day but for the life of me, I can't remember. That bothers me. It's the little details that make a memory come to life, and I hate it when one escapes me.

I think it was cherry.

A FIRST TIME FOR EVERYTHING

I wonder what ever happened to John Wayne Key.

John Wayne was a little older than I was. He was on the First Floor of McElroy with Miz Clark for a matron when I was still up on the Second Floor suffering under the tyranny of Prunes Tankersley. John Wayne was a sly one, and wise in the ways of the orphanage. He was the one who taught me how easy it was to steal green onions from Miz Clark's beloved flower beds.

"Just play like we're rasslin'," John Wayne explained. "Then we'll roll over there near the flower beds, where we can grab us a onion." It worked like a charm, too, until the window flew up and Miz Clark yelled out, "John Wayne! You two boys get yourselves in here."

Inside, Prunes Tankersley was waiting with her. Prunes didn't say a word to me, or even bother to look my way, and somehow that made my uneasy sense of foreboding grow stronger.

"John Wayne," Miz Clark said sternly, "I won't abide a thief. Bend over that chair."

She rolled up her sleeves. She brought out a leather strap and took a strong stance. She did everything but spit on her hands, and then—jaws grimly clenched, eyes flashing thunder and lightning—she lit into John Wayne with a fury, and she was so skilled with the leather that she managed to flail at him ten times or more without so much as disturbing the dust on his pants. As soon as he could work himself up to it, John Wayne howled piteously and began to blubber, whereupon Miz Clark dropped the cowhide like it had suddenly become a poison adder. She drew a little gasp, and caught her lower lip between her rather prominent buck teeth. John Wayne stood there snuffling, smearing away his homemade tears with grimy hands, and before long Miz Clark started to sputter around the eyes herself.

"I'd a give you all the onions you wanted, John Wayne," she said brokenly. "All you had to do was ask me."

John Wayne took a deep shuddering breath,

and Miz Clark was overcome. Blinking away the tears, she reached out to pat his shoulder tenderly, and John Wayne— that palpable fraud—just bawled his eyes out.

You may be sure that nothing of this humid scene was lost upon me. Oho, I thought, so that's the way it's done. Nothing to it. Prunes Tankersley reached out for the leather. "Bend over," she said, and I obliged her, smiling confidently to myself, and getting ready to work up the tears.

That woman busted me until the seat of my pants began to smoke, and when she was fully satisfied with the results, she stepped back and regarded me with an expression devoid of anything other than dire promise. "I better not catch you stealing onions again," she said, breathing hard from exertion. "Next time I won't go easy."

In time I moved down to the First Floor, and it was like being released from prison. It didn't take long to learn that Miz Clark was tolerant of almost anything but filth, laziness, and teasing Leland Wells. She was merciless against those who tormented Leland, but for lesser crimes she usually tempered punishment with a small treat of some sort.

Then one day a strange car came around the Circle, and Miz Clark's things were carried out and loaded into the trunk of it. Prunes Tankersley came out to wave cheerily as the car drove away with Miz Clark in the back seat, and then Prunes did the oddest thing. Once the car was well out of sight, she turned her face away, and fled weeping into the building. It was puzzling, and troubling, too, somehow—I would not have thought her capable of such an act. They told us Miz Clark was going away for a rest, but we soon learned that she was sick with cancer. I took it hard, especially when I heard that Prunes Tankersley was moving down to become the new First Floor Matron. She commandeered a number of us First Floor boys to carry her belongings down, but first she sealed up the windows of the matron's room where Miz Clark had contracted cancer, and she burned a massive sulphur candle to purify the air. For days, the infernal stench of that candle clouded the entire First Floor, but modern medical science ought to look into it, because as far as I know, Prunes Tankersley never came down with cancer.

Then the news came that Miz Clark had passed away, and I was among those chosen to attend her funeral.

I was appalled, and somewhat mystified. I

had no idea why I was chosen to go. I had hardly been one of Miz Clark's favorites—I was clean enough, but she suspected me of laziness, and rightly so. I liked Miz Clark, but the thought of going to a funeral made me shudder. There would almost certainly be a dead person in attendance, and I did not approve of that at all.

Get ready, I was told. You're going.

I had dreadful dreams that night.

At least my Sunday suit was presentable. It had only recently returned from the orphanage laundry—it still reeked of naptha, and had those peculiar patches of orange-peel wrinkles that were the hallmark of the orphanage steam press. My necktie was of a style that had enjoyed a mercifully brief period of popularity back in the early Forties. It was an awkward shade of maroon, and was decorated with a handpainted scene that depicted a hunter with his dog, and a terrified pheasant struggling to gain altitude. Most of the gravy stains on the tie were camouflaged among the flaking feathers of that unfortunate bird.

Mr. Browning picked up the funeral party in that old green station wagon—the one that had sides made of genuine wood and peeling varnish—and we drove long miles, into a part of Texas that I had never seen before. The tall pine trees were endless, and the road cut through them in a way that made me think of the way Miz Bearden's clippers cut through the forfeit hair of a runaway boy. We stopped in Athens, and Mr. Browning asked a local if he could tell us a good place to eat. The man frowned deeply, as though he had never given the matter much thought before that moment. He considered, reconsidered, lifted his hat and scratched his half-bald head, and finally directed us to a café half a block away. The meal should have been a treat, but the meat and potatoes were ashes in my mouth. The church could not be far away now, and my appetite succumbed to a rising sense of dread. The country church stood in a small clearing among the pine trees, and we parked in the gravel lot. Mr. Browning ushered us to seats, and I almost stumbled in the aisle, my attention was so riveted on the open coffin that rested among the banks of flowers. My heart raced, my head felt wooden, and my mouth was dry. For the first time in my life, I was in the presence of a dead person.

There was actually little to be seen from our back pew—a suggestion of features among the folds of the satin coverlet, perhaps a hint of stiffly

folded hands, and nothing more. Slowly, I began to calm down. The lady at the piano played an interlude as the last of the latecomers settled in, and then the minister came to the pulpit. When the minister had spoken and the dirges had been sung, the congregation arose to file past the open coffin, and my pulse revved up. Here was that moment I had dreaded most of all. I was about to gaze on the face of the dead.

I took my place in the line, quaking internally. With my heart in my mouth, I passed by the coffin, and saw Miz Clark for the last time.

It was the stillness that struck me. The rouge, the wax, the dressing of the hair which didn't look quite right—the undertaker's art attempted to say it wasn't so. Why, she's only sleeping, his craft insinuated. But the stillness, that absolute stillness that can never be counterfeited so long as a tremor of pulse remains, told me the truth— Miz Clark didn't look to me like she was sleeping.

It looked to me like she was dead.

Once we were back out in the church yard, Mr. Browning moved among the mourners, shaking hands, expressing regret, and introducing us boys. One man reached out his big right hand to me, as he swabbed at his streaming eyes with the handkerchief that he held in his left. "Did you know her, son?" he asked me. His face was distorted with grief, but his strong resemblance to Miz Clark was still unmistakable. "Yes sir," I said. "She was my matron."

"Was she good to you, then?"

"Yes sir," I said. "She was good to everybody."

We didn't go to the graveside service. Mr. Browning made our excuses, citing the long drive that we still had ahead of us. On the way back, I thought of how little I had really known about Miz Clark. She knew the names of all the plants that grew in her flower beds, I remember that much, and she loved miniature paintings. She had half a dozen or more in her room, and she let me admire them on occasion. She had family, too, for there were pictures of them scattered around her room, and I seem to recall someone coming to visit with her at the orphanage. It may have been the man I met at the funeral—the one who had resembled her so closely—but I don't know if he was her son, or her nephew, or her brother.

I think she loved her father, and I think that he loved her. I was once assigned to work for her in those flower beds, and one fine fresh day in the springtime, as we cleaned away the winter debris, she told me something that makes me believe that.

"Finish what you're doing before you start something else," she instructed me, as she paused to lean on the handle of her rake for a moment's rest in the soft spring air. "That way you don't have to pick up anything twice."

Then her gaze seemed to turn inward, and whatever it was that she found among her memories, it made her smile, and the smile became a wide open, sunny grin that made no attempt to conceal her crooked teeth.

"My daddy taught me that when I was just a little girl," she said softly. "Now that man, he was a worker." Few deaths since have affected me as deeply as that first one. I've slipped by the worst ones. It's mostly been a life of light attachments and easy goodbyes, and when somebody died, either I hadn't known them all that long, or I was already long gone.

I almost said "I've been lucky," but sometimes I wonder.

THAT WINNING SEASON

Coach Boldin may not have coined the phrase "intestinal fortitude" himself, but he certainly used it as though he owned it. By "intestinal fortitude," Coach Boldin meant guts, and as far as he was concerned, intestinal fortitude was the defining characteristic of manhood. In his opinion, any shortcoming in man or boy was directly attributable to an inadequate supply of intestinal fortitude.

Coach Boldin knew all there was to know about T-formation football, and he instilled in me a firm belief in the pure genius of that format. To this day, I can't understand that trash the NFL plays on television. But I have lost faith in some of Coach Boldin's other theories.

I guess he was supposed to have "that little talk" with us boys when we got into Junior High. I can see no other explanation for that perplexing lecture he gave us one day in the gym. He seated us in a semi-circle on the basketball court in front of a blackboard that he had set up beneath the basketball net, and on the blackboard he drew a triangle, the apex of which pointed to the floor.

"A man is built like this," he informed us, and the tone of his voice clearly implied that here was a fact of great significance.

Returning to the blackboard, he drew another triangle. This one pointed to the basketball net. "A woman is built like that," he said, and the statement resonated with heavy import.

He gave us a moment to consider these breathtaking revelations, then he tossed the chalk back into the blackboard tray and dusted his hands. "If they weren't built that way," he said flatly, "you would not have been born."

Well. I had never before heard it put just that way. This was heady stuff, quite progressive for that day and time. But since then I have done quite a bit of research on my own, and I'm here to tell you, Coach Boldin greatly over-simplified the matter.

But then, Coach Boldin always did like to keep things simple. That year, our mid-term examination consisted of ten free throws from the foul line of the basketball court. Each shot you made counted ten points, and that was your mid-term grade. I got a big, fat zero—which I considered to be grossly unfair, because it gave me no credit at all for learning that a woman is built like an isosceles triangle.

The greatest thrill of graduating to Junior High School was the chance to play football. Coach held tryouts in the gymnasium. We ran laps and wind sprints in our bare feet on the hardwood floor. We went out for passes, threw the ball, and learned what "skull practice" was. For those of you who don't remember, "skull practice" was an opportunity to doze off while Coach Boldin entertained himself by drawing an incomprehensible series of X's and O's and curvy arrows on the blackboard.

After the trials, Coach Boldin consulted his clipboard, and one by one, he selected the first and second string players, based on their speed, power, and agility. Then he selected the scrubs, based on our ability to fit into the uniforms that he had left over. Oh, I was so proud. Never mind that the uniforms were cast-offs from a by-gone era, when they wore heavy wool jerseys and leather helmets. Coach Boldin issued me pads and pants, cleats and helmet, and a scratchy wool jersey with a number on the back. And a jock strap. With a groin cup. I was so proud.

Once I learned not to put the thigh pads in backwards, I felt as invulnerable as an ancient armored knight. That good feeling stayed with me right up to the first time I tried to block Adrian Godsey.

It happened in my first practice scrimmage.

Adrian Godsey was charging in to make the tackle, and I was foolish enough to interfere with him. Godsey left me crumpled on the turf, with no great inconvenience to himself. I'm not sure he even noticed me. My faith in the padded uniform was shattered, and thereafter I was much more circumspect about throwing myself in front of a determined tackler.

Actually, almost everybody got a uniform of one sort or another. Even Leland Wells got a practice uniform. He didn't suit out for the games, but he scrimmaged with us, and that seemed to satisfy him.

One night, as scrimmage was about to end, Coach Boldin suddenly blew the ball dead. He called some cockamamie foul against the offensive team, and assessed the improbable penalty of thirty-eight yards, which took the ball back to the one-yard line. He paced off the penalty yardage, and placed the ball. Then he yelled to the sideline, calling upon Leland Wells to come into the game as the offensive fullback.

Leland, deeply flustered, fumbled among the loose helmets on the ground, looking for one that might possibly be his. He came loping onto the field, trying to fasten his chin strap. The helmet he had grabbed was several sizes too large, and it kept slipping down over his face.

"Offense, huddle up!"

Leland disappeared into the offensive huddle, and Coach Boldin huddled with them for a moment. Then he came over to the defensive side.

"Defense! Huddle up on me!"

Coach Boldin crouched in the middle of our defensive huddle, his eyes bright with mischief. "Okay, guys," he said. "Leland is coming through their right tackle slot. Let him by, and then chase him all the way to the goal."

Unfortunately, Leland got his signals crossed, and when the ball was snapped, he came right over my position, which was down on the other end of the scrimmage line. I tried to dodge him, but he tripped over my legs. I don't think it mattered, because he didn't even have the ball with him. He had forgotten to take the hand-off.

Coach Boldin's whistle shrieked.

"Offsides, called against the offense!" he cried. "Penalty is half the distance to the goal line, and it's still fourth down."

He marched the ball back to the one-foot line. "Huddle up!"

Coach Boldin came back to the defensive huddle. He looked tickled, as though he could hardly keep from laughing. "Don't fall down in front of him, you guys!" he said. "Get out of his way."

This time, the offensive quarterback grabbed Leland by the back of his jersey, holding him back long enough to stuff the ball into his arms. Then he pushed Leland toward the line of scrimmage. Leland clutched the ball, withdrew as best he could into the safety of his over-sized helmet, and lurched awkwardly up the middle. The defensive players peeled off to either side, launching theatrically ineffective tackles, always missing Leland by ten or twelve feet. Leland shied off from the abortive tackles, wincing and ducking—but he kept on cantering along, plodding desperately for the goal line. He staggered into the end zone, dropped the ball, and embraced an upright of the goal post. He clung to it, wheezing like a broken bellows.

Coach Boldin never tired of telling the story, if Leland was around to hear it. "It was a desperate situation," he would say. "Fourth down, and nearly a hundred yards to go. What else could I do, but call in Leland Wells. Well sir, the first time, he hit that line just the way he lives—hard and fast—but they fouled him. The second time, he broke through the line like a freight train, and I tell you, he was shedding tacklers like a duck sheds rain. He was still picking up speed when he blew by the goal post, and he coasted in somewhere up around the barn."

And folks would goggle at Leland. Oh my! they would say. My goodness! I wish I could have been there to see it.

You could tell it pleased Leland, because he would turn as red as a traffic light, and grin so wide that the corners of his lips touched his brightly glowing ears, and he would wriggle like a puppy.

That first year, I never got to play in a real game unless we were ahead by forty or fifty points, but that suited me fine. I could sit on the bench, and admire the shadow that I cast on the ground, and sneak a wave to Lee Ann Connor, up in the grandstands. I didn't expect much that first year anyway. Next year was good enough for me. I would be an Eighth Grader then—bigger, stronger, faster, and fully prepared to take my place among the stars of the team. By then, God willing, Adrian Godsey would be in High School.

It didn't quite work out the way I planned.

The class behind me was peopled with overgrown young brutes like Don "The Nose" Wallace. Don had a prominent jaw and a prodigious nose, and teeth as tiny as rows of shoe peg corn—when he smiled, his chin and nose would touch. I won't say that Nose Wallace was built like a fireplug. His legs were built like fireplugs; his torso was built more like an oak barrel.

Coach Boldin put Nose Wallace in at the fullback position, and taught him one play, and one play only: Crash through the line, and run over anybody that gets in your way. You couldn't tackle Nose Wallace—all you could do was jump on his back to slow him down, and yell for help.

The nucleus of our team that year was Billy Miles and Bobby Gully. Billy Miles was our quarterback, and his main job was to hit Bobby Gully with a pass. Bobby Gully's hands were as big as baseball mitts, and as sticky as a frog's tongue. Once he had snapped the ball out of the air and turned up the field, Bobby was hard to stop. He never tried to evade tacklers. He chased them, sometimes scaring them right off the field. Bobby Gully was also our place kicker. To the amazement of visiting officials, he kicked barefooted, curling his toes up over his instep to get them out of harm's way, and meeting the football with the ball of his foot. He could put it into the end zone that way.

There were other luminaries on our team that year, only some of whom I can remember. There was Darrell Lewis, who had legs that came up to his armpits. When Darrell Lewis ran, he looked like a crane taking flight, but he sure could cover the territory. There was Gerald Morris, and a kid named Jimmy Meeks, both of them halfbacks who ran as though the police were after them. And Charles Gayle, our defensive safety man, who pounced on a ball-carrier like a cat on a cricket.

Coach Boldin knew he had the makings of a championship team that year, and he wasn't about to let a championship slip by. In the locker room, he chanted his mantra of intestinal fortitude, and on the practice field, he worked us like rented mules. It worked, too. We won game after game, mostly by wide point spreads. There was just one tiny little problem. The orphans played rough, and when we met our opponents on the field, hardly a play ended without the shriek of angry whistles. The red penalty flags fluttered

down like autumn leaves, and many an innocent boy from Away From Here limped off the field bleeding, while the orphans grinned like wolves, and watched him go.

I think Coach Boldin was afraid that his championship team would be disqualified for poor sportsmanship. He railed, and he implored, and he threatened. Time and again, he solemnly assured us that Fair Play and Intestinal Fortitude are so closely akin that they can scarcely be told apart. Our last game of the season was with Farmersville, and it had to be postponed twice because of bad weather. On the day that we finally played them, the sun shined like a copper penny, and it was dreadfully cold. The playing field was frozen as hard as stone.

Dee Roy Stewart hated to play in the cold. "I mean to keep my hands warm, anyway," he said, slipping on a pair of black leather gloves. There was little finesse to the game that day. The players were stiff and awkward, and afraid to slip on the frozen field. It was all flubs and fumbles, and the tackles resembled a crude form of Greco-Roman wrestling. Orphan tempers were short that day, and their play rougher than usual. Whenever there was a pile-up, up from the pile would come an orphan fist—a black-gloved fist, most likely. The fist would come crashing down, and then the outraged whistles would blow and the red flags would fly in the frigid wind. The referee would stalk off the penalty yardage against us, and Coach Boldin would grind his teeth.

We won that final game, something-big to zero. We were the undefeated champions of our conference that year, and everywhere he went, Coach Boldin was glad-handed, and congratulated. On Sunday morning, the preacher announced in church that our beloved Coach Boldin had led our gallant boys to glorious victory, and Coach Boldin fairly glowed with pride.

In fact, Coach Boldin was celebrated so thoroughly that there were those on the team who got their feelings hurt. It didn't suit some of the stars that folks looked over their heads to lionize the coach.

"It ain't fair," grumbled these less than gracious winners. "We win all the games, and he gets all the credit."

Well, maybe so. And rightly so. After all, Coach Boldin had forged a bunch of rough orphans into an effective—if somewhat savage—team. It was he who instilled in us the rudiments of sportsmanship, absolutely forbidding us to kick or bite our opponents on the field. It was he who showed us why it hurt so much when we reversed our thigh pads. The stars of the team had their moments of fleeting glory. A finger-tip pass reception, or a breakaway punt return, and a minor hero was born. But the next week, someone else would make a key interception, or sack the quarterback in the end zone, and a new campus hero would reign. For a week.

Coach Boldin knew that spectacular plays seldom win the game. Games are won by the ordinary plays—well taught, endlessly drilled, and flawlessly executed. Coach Boldin gave a hero his due, but he also took careful note of the player battling it out on the line of scrimmage. He knew who was doing his job, and who just happened to get lucky.

The players on that championship team brought to the field a wealth of raw ability, but it was Coach Boldin who gave us that winning season. More than that, he gave each of us the right forever after to recall those bright autumn days of that year so long ago, and to lay valid claim to our part of the glory.

Why, yes—we old men can truthfully say—I was on the football squad that year.

We were champions, you know.

PRIMITIVE CAMPING

I know people who fancy themselves to be at one with nature. They hike in well-trodden wildernesses, carrying backpacks with internal frames made of exotic metals and filled with dehydrated foods. They spare no expense to save themselves an extra ounce. When they hit the trail, their gear weighs so little that they would probably float off into space if it weren't for their hiking boots, which look like little tugboats with cleated bottoms, and weigh about seven and one half pounds apiece.

At night, these people sleep in complicated tents and plush sleeping bags endorsed by men prominent in the exploring trade. They reconstitute their dissicated dinners, and heat them over the tiny flame of a little stove as intricate as a Swiss watch. This they call "primitive camping."

Ha. Primitive, indeed.

They should have been with me the first year I went to camp with the orphans.

The orphanage leased a section of shoreline along Lake Texhoma. It was a true wilderness in those days, and our camp ground was so far back off the main roads that there wasn't even a fish bait store within miles of the place.

They took us there on that big red tractor-trailer we called the "cattle car." They installed the solid sides on the cattle car when they were hauling orphans, to give us some sparse shelter from wind, sun, and rain. Naturally the Big Boys appropriated the choice places for themselves, and left the rest of us to face the elements. We didn't get rained on that day, but by the time we finally got to the lake, I was nearly cooked from the sun, and it felt like the wind had blown my ears around to the back of my head. The skin on my face was drawn so tight that I could hardly close my eyes.

We put up two or three large canvas tents, none of which was intended to shelter orphans. One was the cook tent, and the others were used to store a large pile of blankets, and what little extra clothing we had brought. For sanitary arrangements, there were the woods and the lake itself. That was the extent of the facilities. Doc Grube cooked over a wood fire, and we washed our dishes in lake water. The pots were carried to the lake, and scoured with sand. When night fell, we went to the tents to draw a blanket, and of course all the little boys thought that the best place to sleep was right down on the shoreline, where the water almost lapped our hands.

I lay there on the shore that first night, and looked up at the stars. Nowhere on earth have I ever found a place where the stars shine so brightly as they do over Texas. It seems to the eye that some hang lower than others do, and the Milky Way glitters abundantly, as though the stars had been sown in the firmament with a single sweep of a mighty Hand, and the majority of the stars had fallen along its arc. I drifted off gently there on the shoreline, with the stars shining down on my face, and the little waves coming ashore to shush me into a sweet sound sleep.

I came awake abruptly and in a state of wild alarm. My heart was pounding urgently and every nerve was ajangle as I tried to recover my senses, and determine the specific cause of my rude arousal.

From somewhere down along the shore, there came muffled shouts of protest, punctuated with certain words that made me wince. It was a good thing for whoever was shouting such things that Prunes Tankersley wasn't there to hear him, that's all I can say.

The shouts and imprecations were overridden by several adolescent voices that chanted cheerily: One . . . two . . . THREE! Then there was a short moment of shocked silence, followed by a sodden splash and a thrashing in the water, and finally a forlorn—and somewhat strangled— wail of despair. The Big Boys who had trapped the little boy in his blankets and thrown him into the lake then fled away into the woods, trailing behind them the echoes of devilish cackling.

An unidentified adult figure emerged from one of the tents, and stumbled groggily down the lakeside, muttering as he went. He dragged the unfortunate boy out of the water by the scruff of his neck, and led him back toward the tents, stopping every few yards to shout impotent threats at the dark and silent woods.

"I mean it, now! You boys better lay down and go to sleep!"

All I heard was the whimpering of the victim, and the sound of lake water dripping from his blanket.

The adult gave the victim a dry blanket and impatiently shooed him away, and went mumbling into the tent. The minute the tent flap dropped, there was a restless, shifting movement all along the shoreline as little boys reconsidered their choices of sleeping arrangements, and began to drift up away from the water.

I moved up closer to the woods myself, resolving to forget about the stars, and to pay more attention to important events that were taking place right here on Earth. I lay on my stomach this time, and heaped up some sand, like a small lunette, and hunkered down behind it. For a long while, I kept a wide-eyed watch for Big Boys, but nothing else happened. Gradually, my head nodded, and nodded again, and then sank onto my arms. In spite of myself, I went back to sleep.

When the next victim began to bleat, I came up out of my blanket at once. All along the shore, I could see little boys popping up into the moonlight, suddenly as alert and interested as so many prairie dogs. And right down there next to the water, four shadows were perfectly visible, swinging an unhappy little boy in the hammock of his blanket. On the count of three, they hurled the blanket and the little boy in it, out into the dark water. They achieved a remarkable distance. This time, Coach Boldin himself came out of the tent.

"All right, you boys!" he shouted sternly at the silent woods. "That's enough of that. Cut the horseplay, and hit the sack."

This elicited no response from the woods.

"I'm not kidding, now," Coach Boldin warned. "I know who you are. I've got all your names."

This elicited a chorus of juvenile snickers and derisive snorts from the deep woods, which I took to be a sign that those concealed therein considered it to be highly unlikely that they would ever be brought to justice. Coach Boldin glared in the direction of the tree line for a minute or two, grumping and grumbling. Then he went back inside, and dropped the tent flap.

That was enough for me. I bunched up my blanket, and joined the throng of little boys shuffling along the beach, headed for the tents. We couldn't get inside, of course, but we could crowd close to the tent walls, and before long, ground space around the outside of the tents was at a premium. The Big Boys were reluctant to abduct anyone in the vicinity of the tents, and there the little boys slept in relative safety.

Had it not been for the Big Boys, camp would have been Paradise. There was minimal interference from the adults, and very few organized activities. We could stay up all night if we wanted to, and get up in the morning when we pleased. If we didn't show up for meals, nobody cared. We swam every day, and never had to comb our hair. There were three aluminum boats, one of them equipped with a balky outboard motor, and every day, a different group was towed out to the islands that lay in the middle of the lake. I was keen to go, because I knew for a fact that most of the islands on this earth abound with lost treasure.

My day finally came. I was in the boat and on my way to the islands, when a sudden storm blew up. The leader of the expedition chose to turn back, and run in ahead of the storm. It was probably wise because we had just enough time to reach the main shore and pull into a small cove before the storm hit us. We beached the boats, and then went back into the water to play in the mini-surf kicked up by the high winds. It was a grand swim, but the storm had cost me the opportunity to search those islands for treasure. To make matters worse, the very next day Joe Powell came back from the islands with an expensive fishing rod—brand new, and complete with a fine reel full of high-test line and a brightly colored artificial lure with treble hooks, just like the ones in the *Field and Stream* magazines. He had dredged it up from beneath the waters just a few yards off the island shoreline.

"It was just lucky I found it," Joe Powell said. "At first I thought it was only a stick, but then I picked it up, and there it was."

I was sick with envy. There was no doubt in my mind that if it hadn't been for that blasted storm, I would have been the one to find that treasure. We spent a week at Lake Texhoma. On the last night, we built a huge bonfire on the sandy shore, and the sparks rose high into the heavens to hide among the stars. When the fire had died down, we covered it with sand, and went away to find our blankets. It was a quiet night, disturbed only by the occasional scream of a marauding Big Boy who had wandered too close to the ashes of the bonfire, and trod upon a buried ember. The little boys in the moonshadow of the tents stirred and shivered at the sounds of the screams. But then, comforted by the snoring of the adults within the tents, they sighed deliciously, and nestling into their blankets, they drifted off again.

The next day, we went back to the orphanage in the cattle truck. It rained on us every mile of the way.

Back in my room, I looked in a mirror for the first time in a week. My skin had been burned repeatedly by sun and wind, and was peeling off in strips, as though from some repulsive disease. My hair looked like the dusty pelt of some untidy burrowing creature. Fat ticks hung from my body like pendants. I looked positively feral.

So when my nature-loving friends regale me with the wonders of primitive camping, and show me their latest camping toy—a titanium toothbrush perhaps, or maybe a pair of Norwegian mesh underwear—I think back on those days and nights on the shore of Lake Texhoma, and I smile wisely.

What do they know about primitive? They have never huddled in the darkness with one thin blanket, and heard the call of Big Boys on the prowl. They have never shivered with dread while the heartrending cries of helpless victims pierced the night. When they have, then they will know what primitive really is.

FOOD

The best part of working in the bakery was the food.

We bakery boys made a brief appearance in the Manna Hall each morning, but we did not eat our breakfast there. We waved away the oranges and the bananas, and smiled as others at the table scrambled for the largess. With a lift of the eyebrow, we disdained the porridges and the dry flakes. Common fodder, suited well enough for others perhaps, but not for the bakery boys.

When the prayer was done, we arose with an easy dignity and strode out. Our work called, and our breakfast awaited us elsewhere. We were the bakery boys.

The bakery was that fragrant shop at one corner of the commissary, just across the street from the Manna Hall kitchen. It was beastly hot inside, and well lit, but the fine-mesh screens on the doors and windows were like one way mirrors. We could see out into the bright sunshine, but it was impossible to see in. Thus we were further set apart from the hoi polloi, and the mystery of our doings was secured.

By the time we had donned the princely raiment of our craft, which consisted of paper caps and long white aprons that came up to our armpits, Doc Grube—master baker and lord of his domain—had the oven going. He laid the bacon—a delicacy unheard of at the Manna Hall tables—into a pan. A single trip on the Ferris wheel of revolving shelves inside the huge and glowing oven, and the bacon was crisped just right. Meanwhile Doc sliced loaves of sturdy orphan bread into slabs precisely two inches thick, which he dipped into a golden mixture of beaten eggs and milk. Carefully, he lifted the slices of soaked bread into a skillet anointed with gently bubbling butter, and when they were crisp and brown on the outside and yet still ever so succulent in the middle, he dusted them generously with a redolent mixture of cinnamon and sugar. There was coffee to go with the French toast—a rich, flavorsome brew. Or better yet, chocolate milk, in profusely sweating quart bottles brought straight in from the arctic lockers of the bottling plant next door.

From time to time, there was ham—always a welcome diversion—and with the ham we had eggs fried in bacon drippings. It was still safe to do that in those distant days. Cholesterol hadn't been invented yet, and nitrates were unknown. Back then, they cured ham and bacon, instead of embalming it. On state occasions, Doc made us biscuits.

We baked cookies, of course—what would Sunday nights have been without peanut butter and orphan cookies? For that matter, what would any story about the orphan days be without some reference to that legendary Sunday supper?

Cookies were a mere sideline, a trifling matter of mixing up dough and stuffing it into the hopper of a palsied machine that rumbled out a sullen rhythm as it cut the cookies and dropped them onto the greased pans—four cookies at a time, two dozen to a pan. The pans took a turn through the oven, and voila! Orphan cookies.

Pies were a different matter. Pies made for a busy time. The giant blending machine made a great whirring while Doc Grube stood by watching closely for that moment when the pastry was mixed to perfection. The pie fillings were stirred in the huge mixing bowls. The crusts had to be rolled and dusted and stretched and fitted to the pie tins and trimmed around the edges with a dull knife.

We made two sorts of pies. One was a gelatinous cream pie hardly worthy of mention, an indifferent affair that was served on Thursday nights as a weak apology for the supper of bread and pallid gravy that accompanied it. But the other pie was a glorious creation. Flaky crusts, top and bottom, embraced a deep rich mixture of apples and sugar, cinnamon and nutmeg. They came out of the oven by the dozens, with the hot juices bubbling out through the slashes that were cut in the top crust to allow the steam to escape. When they had cooled, there was a pie apiece if we wanted one, and we ate them right from the pie pan in which they had baked.

And oh, the lovely bread we made. In those days, the art of baking good bread had fallen upon a Dark Age. The people who dwelt Away From Here demanded "light bread," those dreadful loaves that were turned out of commercial ovens by the millions. An entire loaf of the stuff could be squeezed down to a nasty lump the size of your fist. The slices were limp and airy, and they tore apart like wet toilet paper. The crust was no thicker than a suntan, but it really didn't matter.

Most folks Away From Here either trimmed the crusts from their sandwiches, or they gnawed away "the good part," and threw away the crusts. They didn't care about bread, anyway—it was just something to keep their dirty fingers off the bologna, and the mustard off their hands. The orphanage bakery was an oasis, a rare place where the skill to make a decent loaf was yet extant.

We kneaded the dough and shaped it, and laid the little loaves to rest in greased pans. We put the pans in tall racks, and ran them into the steam cabinet, and tiptoed reverently while the little yeasts worked their magic. Gently, we slipped the risen loaves onto the revolving shelves of the shimmering oven, and closed the oven door behind them.

When the oven door was opened again, the golden loaves poured forth. Here was bread with heft and body, bread worthy of the name. Here was bread to tear apart, to dip in soup or milk. Here was bread to sop in syrup, when nothing else would do.

Here was God's Own Plenty, and the aroma alone was a thing of joy.

When the last loaf was on the cooling rack, we chose one and tore away most of the steaming insides. We slathered the tough crust with rich butter, and we ate it with cold draughts of sweet white milk. Chocolate milk had its place, but with hot bread, white was the milk of choice.

The best part of working in the bakery was the food.

The worst part of working in the bakery was the bakery boys. Gerald Morris and Dee Roy Stewart were a fine pair of merry rogues. Their chief delight was tormenting the little boys who came to the screen door of the bakery to beg for broken cookies.

"Cookie crumbs?" they crooned in beguiling tones. "Why, sure! You stay right there, now. We'll go get you some." And while the expectant gull stood there with his nose pressed into the screen, trying in vain to see inside the bakery shop, Gerald and Dee Roy tiptoed away to fetch the largest bucket they could find, and the little fool outside soon received, not the coveted cookie crumbs, but instead a shocking drench of cold water.

Even little boys are teachable, and a single drenching was usually enough. Thereafter the beggars stayed a respectful distance from that dark and treacherous screen door, and sometimes the bakery boys had to hand out broken cookies for weeks on end, in order to bait their targets back within range of the water bucket. But now and then, a dumb new boy came directly to the bakery door, and when one did, Gerald and Dee Roy crowed with glee.

They dismissed any notion that their playfulness did any lasting damage.

"Learns them a lesson," Gerald said.

Dee Roy agreed.

"Does them good," he asserted. "Smartens them up a little."

Doc Grube smiled indulgently at their high jinks. Doc himself was an accomplished tease, with an inexhaustible repertoire of phrases synonymous with "fat boy." His favorite, though, was "double-bubble." He addressed me thusly a dozen times a day, a practice I considered to be impertinent since he himself was convex in every direction, and from neck to knees, had the figure of a football.

Doc had an instinct for discovering the weaknesses in others. My own flaw was a squeamish imagination—the slightest reference to anything repulsive was likely to turn my stomach. Doc loved to ruin my appetite, and if I hadn't soon conquered my affliction, the man would have starved me to death. Bill Bricker was Doc Grube's protégé, and he was okay. Serious, but good natured about it, he was almost as good a baker as Doc Grube. The bakery was not just Bill Bricker's current job assignment, it was his calling. Doc relied on him a great deal.

I was the pan greaser, which is to say that I carried more responsibility than any other boy in the bakery. If the bread stuck in the pans, I was the one responsible. If the cookies burned on the bottom, it was my fault. If we ran short of eggs, or butter, or flour—or even time, for heaven's sake —I was the one to blame. And if the floor was not swept clean every minute of the day, Doc was likely to comment.

Did I say that baking cookies was a sideline for the bakery? Not for the pan greaser, it wasn't. It was his main reason for living. Doc Grube baked two cookies for every orphan on the campus, plus half again that many to allow for breakage, waste, and pilferage—mostly pilferage. At two dozen cookies to a pan, that worked out to more pans than we had on hand, so as they came out of the oven, I had to clean and grease them again and again, and if a single cookie stuck to the pan, I was made to rue the day.

Dee Roy and Gerald Morris got the exciting jobs. They transported the tall racks of bread and pies through the commissary, down the ramp and across the street and up the other ramp, into the Manna Hall kitchen. It sounds simple enough, but it was nervous work. So many things could go wrong. The wheels of the top-heavy rack could catch at either juncture of ramp and street. Street traffic could suddenly materialize. Little boys could get in the way. The rack could very easily veer off—at that speed, the tiny wheels caused the rack to steer like a rodeo cutting horse. Speed had to be maintained at all cost, for if the heavily laden rack stalled on the up ramp, the pies would surely come sliding out.

Speed, traffic, windage, the force of gravity, the presence of little boys, centrifugal pull, the laws of inertia, and the amount of grease on the bottoms of the pie tins—all these had to be taken into account, if disaster was to be averted. They poised themselves, and when all omens augured well, they launched the rack, and themselves after it. Eyes wide, dirty white aprons streaming out behind them, they dashed madly down the ramp, bellowing out a warning every step of the way. They hit the rougher surface of the street, and struggled to hold the rattling rack on course, while in the rack the pie tins danced and chattered, and made ready to abandon ship. Onto the up ramp, and now they put their backs into it, straining to keep the speed. The rack faltered at the very top, but one last effort, and once again they were safely home.

It was a breathtaking feat. I watched them do it time and again, and fervently hoped that I would never be called upon to try it myself.

Long years have passed since I was a bakery boy. One's horizons broaden, of course, and with them one's gustatory experiences. There was that ancient inn in Cornwall, where the Spanish chef had a remarkable touch with veal. There was the *wiener schnitzel* in Bavaria, the *tortellini* in Italy, the *chiles relleno* in Cancun, the conch fritters in the Caribbean, and the *pollo y langostas de la Catalana* in Baltimore. And then there was that night at Montrachet, in the chateau that stands among the vineyards that produce the finest white burgundy in all the world, where the courses follow one after the other from eight until midnight, and that magnificent wine is poured without reserve.

Wherever I go, wherever I dine, I look first to the bread. Does it have the crust, thick and chewy, that bespeaks a good moist heat in the oven? Is the crumb of the loaf riddled with those irregular caverns that are the product of simple unbleached flour, vivacious yeast, and proper kneading? Is there a heft to the loaf, and a sturdy springiness to the heart of the bread? I point out these things to my fellow diners, whether or not they are truly interested. I know bread, I confide to them. I was once a bakery boy.

THE AFFAIR OF THE BLOODY KNIFE

Were there ever two brothers so different, and so set against one another as Richard and Dee Roy Stewart? Cain and Abel, maybe.

Dee Roy was long in limbs and neck. His face was lean and narrow, and he was fair-headed. He was good natured in a sardonic sort of way, and he loved a rough prank, even if it put his own bones in jeopardy. I remember the day Dee Roy fought George Pitts on the gymnasium basketball court. There were no matrons or coaches in the gym at the time, so the two were free to fight it out. There was no science to it at all—it was all instinct and reflexes and deadly intent—but there was natural grace and style in the way they strived to give hurt to one another, and something chilling in the lack of concern they showed for the hurts that they themselves received.

It was an even match, and they fought until they could fight no more. Then they both withdrew, gingerly disengaging by mutual consent. Nothing was decided—there was no crowing triumph, no humiliating defeat—and as the disappointed crowd turned away, the exhausted combatants staggered off to find their shoes.

When I left the gym, I found myself following Dee Roy, who walked all alone just ahead of me. Not knowing what his mood might be at that moment, and thinking that he could easily turn on me if I said the wrong word, I hung back. But Dee Roy stopped and waited, and when I reluctantly caught up with him, he spoke kindly to me.

Nothing was said about the fight. He said he had a trick that he wanted to show me, something to do with two small coins that he brought out of his pocket. Seemingly unaware that his left eye was rapidly swelling shut, or that a deep cut on his face dripped blood onto the coins in his palm, he went through the trick—which I did not even try to comprehend. His hands shook violently from the combined effects of fatigue and adrenaline, but his voice was steady. He seemed shy, almost self-effacing, and at that moment, very much in need of companionship.

It was the only time I ever saw him act that way. Richard was a well-formed young man—compact and muscled, and dark in both features and mien. He looked angry nearly all of the time. I once saw Richard deliver a kick in the pants to an indiscreet little boy who had made a remark as Richard passed by. The toe of Richard's brogan boot hoisted that kid a good two feet into the air, and when the kid finally came down, he was understandably upset. A matron heard his squalling, and came out to remonstrate with Richard. Richard faced up to her squarely, and said words to this effect, "Either you teach him some respect for the Big Boys, or I will."

Richard appeared to take life very seriously, whereas Dee Roy just wanted to have his rowdy joke. So I have never doubted that it was Dee Roy who came up with the idea of the bloody knife.

. . .

At that time, Cullom Building was governed by an elderly couple. He was a natty little man, with tidy white hair that girdled his head from temple to temple but left his pate bare and shiny. The skin of his face was a pinky white, and it looked as though it had never known the touch of a razor.

She was perhaps six inches taller than he, and had half again his girth. She favored loose dresses, mostly dark ones with white collars, and her mustache was coming along quite nicely. They lived in the matron's apartment in Cullom. There was an office in the front, a bedroom in the back, and a Pullman kitchen from which they often served the boys of Cullom with weak coffee and stale cinnamon buns on Sunday mornings. They were good and decent old people, and they seemed to think that if they were kind and gentle in their dealings with the boys of Cullom, then the boys would be kind and gentle with them. Therefore, I have always believed that they were largely responsible for what occurred the night that Dee Roy visited his brother Richard in Cullom Building.

. . .

Richard and Dee Roy didn't get along at all. They were hardly tender with anyone on this earth, but with one another they became murderous. Although both were eligible to live in Cullom, it was deemed wise to keep them apart, so one of them was always kept back in Rupard Building. In the interest of fairness, they were allowed to switch places every few months.

Still, they were brothers. They wanted to see one another now and then. Thus it was that Dee Roy came over to Cullom that night to visit with Richard, and in the course of the evening, by a most unfortunate happenstance, one of Richard's room mates brought out a Mexican souvenir knife.

Such knives were cheap, gaudy imitations of the famous Bowie knife, and had no useful purpose whatsoever, except for decoration. But the knife certainly looked lethal, and in my imagination, I can see the gleam dawning in Dee Roy's eye as he looked at the knife and realized the possibilities. Richard and his roommates fell in with the plan at once, I have no doubt of that. They probably would not have, if Cullom Building had been ruled with the customary iron fist. But on that night, there was only a mild old man, and his devoted wife—both of whom were pushovers.

So they ripped Dee Roy's white shirt, and stained it liberally with red ink. For effect, they also smeared his belly with the ink, and then they inked the blade of the Mexican knife halfway to the hilt. When all else was ready, they sent out a scout to be sure that the old man was still working at his desk in the office.

Then they launched their mischief.

Dee Roy burst out of the room, and fled screaming down the hall. Richard pursued, eyes madly aflash and bloody knife waving. The co-conspirators—whose part it was to restrain Richard when the proper time came—ran after them, calling upon Richard to desist.

Dee Roy ran straight into the old man's office, beseeching at full voice to be saved from certain death. Richard roared in, trying to corner Dee Roy and finish him off. The co-conspirators rushed in to fall upon Richard according to plan. The old man, horrified by the apparent murder that was unfolding before his very eyes, jumped up from his desk, and began to shout over and over again, "Grab him, boys! Hold him!"

The old man's wife came trundling out to see what on earth was the matter, and the shock of what she saw sent her shrieking back into her bedroom, where she collapsed across the bed.

Attracted by the commotion, the boys of Cullom rushed to the office door, and watched the last few seconds of the melee. By now, the co-conspirators were struggling with Richard down on the floor, while Dee Roy bobbed and jitter-bugged to stay out of the way of the knife, and the old man clutched at his desk for support. He had no voice left for shouting—now it was just a quavering, "Oh my God. Oh my God."

Then Dee Roy started to laugh. He leapt over the pile of boys on the floor, and broke through the gawkers at the door. His co-conspirators sprang up from the floor and followed him,

and their laughter echoed through the halls as they fled back to Richard's room. The door slammed, cutting off the sound of their laughter, and nothing more was heard from them.

The old man leaned over his desk, supporting himself with both hands and gasping raggedly. Slowly, the horror in his eyes faded away—at first to bewilderment, and then to bitter resentment as he realized what these boys had done. Ignoring the boys gathered at his office door, the old man stumbled out of the office, and padded down the hallway to see to his wife. In a little while, he came back to his office and picked up the telephone. Instantly, the boys gathered at the office door scattered.

By the time Mr. McBride arrived, the boys of Cullom were in their proper rooms, and every door was closed. The entire building was very quiet.

Punishment was swift, and harsh beyond all memory. The boys of Cullom were herded together in the parlor, and Mr. McBride—grim, stern, and implacable— explained to them all just how serious an offense had been committed.

"You boys could have caused that old woman to have a heart attack," he said, glaring balefully at the perpetrators from under his beetled black brows.

He pronounced sentence, and executed it on the spot. Later, the boys spoke of the bustings with awe. Those best acquainted with McBride's prowess with the dreaded linoleum paddle agreed that this had indeed been an exceptional performance. "I figured his arm had to give out sooner or later," one of them observed. "But it never did."

I have no memory of the old man and his wife after that night. For all I know, they may have left the orphanage altogether, and I, for one, would not have blamed them in the least.

Soon after the affair of the bloody knife— and quite possibly because of his part in that affair—Dee Roy went away to join the Navy. After boot camp, he came back to the orphanage, looking splendid in his crisp Navy whites. He drew quite a crowd with his stories of boot camp and its hardships, and as you might expect, the worse the hardship, the louder he laughed as he told of it.

Then a touch football game sprang up in the field behind Rupard Building, and in an instant, Dee Roy shucked off his white hat, neckerchief, jumper, and shoes. He rolled up his trouser legs a fold or two, and got right in the game, and that is how I remember him now—bare feet flashing, legs whipping his white Navy trousers as he went out for a pass, reaching out his arms and calling for the ball.

I never saw him again. Richard went in the Marine Corps. I don't know what happened to him after that, but I've heard rumors.

I hope they weren't true.

SUNDAY NIGHT RAIN

There were a great many differences between Here and Away From Here, but none so vast as the rituals of dating. Everywhere else in Texas, nearly every young man had access to a motor vehicle of some description, and when he pulled up out front on Saturday night and honked the horn, a young girl would come cantering across the lawn to meet him, while her mother watched from the open doorway and smiled indulgently. Those lucky young couples who lived Away From Here were allowed to go off alone to hamburger joints, and drive-in movies, and—Lord, help us all—dark and lonely country roads. Some orphans even whispered that Away From Here couples were allowed to dance together, but most of us put little stock in such ridiculous reports. We knew that wickedness abounded Away From Here, but surely not to that extent.

You may be sure that nothing of the sort took place in the orphanage. In the orphanage, even as late as the 1950's, the quaint custom of couples sitting in the parlor was still practiced. The older lads in the orphanage curried and combed themselves on Sunday nights, and attended Vespers voluntarily, because any young man who did so was then permitted to go to the building where his girl resided, and sit with her in the parlor for an hour or so.

Under the vigilant eye of her matron, of course. The matron seated herself in the position that afforded the best view of all present, and although the couples tried to pretend that they were not aware of the matron's presence, they never stopped wishing that she would suddenly disappear in a cloud of smoke. The couples lived for those brief moments when the matron had to leave the parlor for some reason. When she did, each couple would in that next instant turn urgently to one another, and for a small, precious time there would be an intense quietness in the

parlor, broken only by small moist sounds and soft little rustlings.

When the matron had attended to whatever business had called her away, she would hurry back to the parlor door, and she would suddenly spring in, her nose quivering with suspicion, hoping to catch something untoward going on. She seldom did—the orphans were very good at not getting caught.

In fact, the matrons seemed to be much more interested in catching somebody than they were in preventing an impropriety from occurring. Legends grew around the one matron who cut eye holes in her newspaper, so that she could pretend to read, and still keep the couples under surveillance.

And then there was that fellow—I don't remember his name, and wouldn't mention it if I did—who appointed himself guardian of morals on campus. As I recall, he was employed as a laborer up at the barn, so I can't imagine where this busybody got his authority, but no one interfered with him. For all I know, he may have been officially encouraged to continue his Comstockian crusade.

One Sunday night, as the couples sat in the parlor, from outside the window there came a crashing, and a thrashing, and an agonized howling. The boys rushed outside, and there among the branches of a broken tree limb lay the fellow from the barn. He had climbed the tree in order to spy upon the couples inside, and as justice would have it, the limb had given way beneath his weight. To the utter delight of the orphans, his arm had been broken in the tumble.

Now, it may well be that his motives were pure, but in today's more liberated atmosphere, the police undoubtedly would have arrested this man under the Peeping Tom laws, and with any luck at all, he would have been listed forever after as a minor sex offender. Even in those repressed times, a fellow who would carry his zealotry to such absurd lengths was considered to be a little bit . . . quirky.

In the orphanage, change did not come about with any noticeable speed—in all the time that I was there, the weekly menu never varied one whit. But I do confess that other changes did occur, all in their own good time.

For example, television sets had been available on the open market for hardly more than seven years before the orphanage rushed right out to buy a nineteen-inch Muntz. They installed it in a small auditorium in the Education Building, and on Friday nights, we could go there to watch television. The girls could come, too, and — wonder of wonders—couples were allowed to sit together while they watched "The Life of Riley."

Even though their eyes were kept glued to the television screen, the couples paid scant attention to Riley's woes. They were too busy groping. The high-backed pews in the auditorium blocked the view from about the shoulders down, presenting a wealth of sweet opportunities. Hand-holding was virtually undetectable, and for incredibly daring couples, even naughtier events could occur. It must have been a frustrating experience for the matrons. No matter where they sat, or how energetically they twisted and turned, the pews allowed them to see only so much at any one time. When they went on the prowl, their clunky shoes on the wooden floor betrayed them, and if they prowled about in their stockinged feet, their whereabouts were continually reported by discreet coughs and clearings of the throat.

Then the Maris Visitor's Center was officially opened, and the custom of sitting in the parlor on Sunday nights died out. On Sunday evenings, a Social Hour was held at the Maris Center, complete with refreshments, and all the older orphans were invited to attend. Couples sat together at Vespers, and then walked together to the Maris Center. Of course, the matrons stationed themselves at strategic intervals along the way, and patrolled vigilantly, but they could not be in all places at all times. And afterwards the young men escorted their young ladies back to the dormitories, and again the matrons patrolled and prodded, and interrupted as best they could.

Once in a while—but not nearly often enough—it stormed on Sunday nights. On such an occasion, the matrons summarily abandoned their duty. Struggling with their fragile umbrellas, they scurried away for the shelter of the entrance alcoves of the dormitory buildings, driving before them those timid couples who would obey. We who dared straggled along the way, and we kissed in the wind and the rain. The boys opened their coats to protect the girls, and the girls cuddled deliciously close. They lifted their faces to be kissed, and they closed their eyes and gave no thought to the lightning that slashed across the tumbling sky.

When we finally strolled up to the dormitory,

the matrons raged at us from the safety of the alcove, and threatened to take down our names. No one cared. Whatever punishments they meted out would be long forgotten before another storm came on Sunday night.

In fact, it seemed like the perfect time for boldness, so I lifted my girl's chin and kissed her once more, right there in front of the matrons. Ignoring the outraged squawks, I bid that sweet young woman good night, and I walked back to my building through the storm, holding my coat closed tight so that the Sunday night rain could not wash away her fragrance.

THE VALUE OF WATER

James Lundy was small, but he was about as tough as anyone I have ever known. We called him Runt, but he seemed to have it in his mind that he stood six foot seven. He stole a girl from me once. I stole her back again, but through it all, Runt and I stayed friends.

It was Runt who got me to work in the hay fields.

In those days, the orphanage had its own non-commercial radio station—KNER, 88.1 on your FM dial. Charles Gayle and I helped put the station on the air, and we were permanently assigned to work there. The studio was in the balcony of the Chapel, and it was a cool, quiet haven far above the rest of the campus. It was a clean job, perfect for soft hands, and I didn't want to leave it to work in the hay fields. But the station manager had gone away on vacation, and I had to find something to do for those two weeks.

"You can't hide out for very long, and there's worse things than baling hay," Runt said. "At least you'll get some sun. You sure need it."

Runt was wise in all that he said. Nothing attracted the attention of a matron quicker than an idle orphan, and there were already some who resented the easy life I had at the radio station. Naturally, I had done nothing to make them feel any other way, and now that I found myself locked out of that soft berth, I had good reason to think that one or two of the matrons would be delighted to find a suitably nasty job for me.

My relations with the staff—not to mention the orphans—had become increasingly strained. I hated the orphanage, and the orphans, and the staff—and I went to no particular pains to hide my feelings from anybody. I was edgy and restless, continually beset by some ineffable and un-relievable irritability. If only I could put a name to what was troubling me, I thought I might be able to stand it. But I didn't have the right words to say it, not even to myself. So the feeling of discontent just grew worse, and I drifted ever closer to real trouble.

Runt was right. The hay fields were off the campus, and I needed to be out of the way. I could spend most of the day outside the campus fences, except for meals and sleep. The work in the hay fields might be physically taxing, but it required very little in the way of social interaction. I would have plenty of time to brood. So I agreed, and the very next morning, right after breakfast, I met the hay truck behind the Manna Hall kitchen. Runt lifted the galvanized water can down off the truck, and we took it to the icehouse, where we filled it to the top with big chunks of ice. Runt picked up a hose, and ran a little water over the ice.

"The ice will melt down as the day goes on," he said. "We'll have cool water most of the day."

A Black man drove the hay truck for us. In those days, there were two or three Black families who lived in hovels on orphanage property, and they worked year-round in the orphanage farm fields. I had never had much to do with Black folk —I probably hadn't spoken with a dozen Blacks in my entire life. Bear in mind that this was in the mid-Fifties, when segregation was the law throughout the Old South, and racial equality was a dangerous concept. The Greyhound bus station in Dallas still had a "colored" waiting room, and separate-but-unequal water fountains. My racial attitudes were not out of line with the times.

The Black man drove us out into the fields south of the campus, between the Sunbeam Home and Bull Pond. The stubbled fields were dotted with irregularly spaced bales of hay, in long curving rows. The rows faded out of sight into the distance, and there seemed to be thou-sands of bales.

We put the water can in the shade of a tree at the edge of the field, and the Black man drove us to the beginning of an endless row of uncount-able bales of hay.

"Now, you just yell 'ho!' if you want me to stop," the Black man said. He put the truck into its lowest gear, and the truck whined and bucked as it moved slowly up between the rows. We boys moved out among the bales, to fetch them back to the truck.

It was mechanical labor—lift and tote, and swing the bales up to where the stacker on the truckbed could grab them with his hay hook and hoist them aboard. Tiring work, but it required very little mental effort. Soon my mind was adrift, and I was lost in my own stormy thoughts. Then, as I was heaving a bale onto the upper tiers of the growing stack, my foot slipped, and I went down, sprawling over the dropped bale of hay. Runt appeared at my side immediately. "Get up," he said.

He picked up the hay bale I had dropped. "Watch this," he said, trotting forward to catch the truck.

He heaved the hay bale under the truck wheels.

"Ho!" he bellowed to the Black man. The truck bounced over the hay bale, crushing it, and rolled another ten feet before the man braked it to a halt. He put his head out of the window, and looked back to see what was wrong.

"Go ahead," Runt yelled in disgust, waving him on. "It don't matter now."

He turned back to me, and gave me a look full of meaning. "He sleeps at the wheel," he said. "You watch your step. If you go under them tires, you'll be dead."

We went back to picking up the endless bales, and I kept a better part of my mind on what I was doing. It was hot, nasty work. Each time I heaved a bale up onto the truck, the chaff sifted down over me, and soon my nostrils were clogged with the stuff. Heat waves danced all around, so thick that the horizon seemed lost in the haze, and the blistering sun made my skin prickle. The sun climbed swiftly to its zenith, and there it stalled, throbbing down upon us implaca-bly. The truck lumbered on through the heat waves, and the baling wire cut into my hands. I wished that I had thought to bring a pair of gloves. The sun baked my head, and I wished that I had worn a hat. The bales seemed to grow heav-ier and heavier, and I wished I had never let Runt talk me into this. I sweated buckets, but the dry heat sucked away the sweat faster than I could produce it. I began to want water. Then I began to yearn for water.

By the time the truck was loaded, I was des-perate for water. My throat was a husk, and my very soul was sere. We clambered up onto the loaded truck, or stood on its running boards, and the Black man drove slowly out of the scorching heat of the hay field, into the deep shade of the tree where the galvanized can of water waited. We had no dipper, nor a tin cup. Runt wrenched the lid off the water can, and tilted the can to slosh the lid full of cold water. He drank straight from the lid, and when he had had his fill, he passed it on. I watched avidly as the dripping lid was passed from hand to hand, and as it emptied, it was refilled. My throat worked as the water came closer to me, and I reached out, thinking that my turn had come at last, and then the lid was handed . . . to the Black man.

I guess he saw the dismay on my face, because there came to his eye a hint of amusement. He swirled the water lazily, and then he lifted the lid to his lips. His adam's apple bobbled energetically as he drank. Then he handed the lid to me. Potent social currents were suddenly aswirl. A rigid system of caste had been sorely violated. I was an orphan boy, true enough—despised as only the poor can be. He was a poor man, loved only among those of his own kind. But I was white, and he was black, and therefore I held trumps. By all rights, I should have had the lid of water first.

The Black man watched me impassively. The serenity of his features was not disturbed, but his eyes spoke so plainly that it seemed that I could hear the words.

"Don't want to drink after me, do you, boy?" his bland eyes said, but not unkindly. "That's all well and good. But how bad do you want a drink of water? What is that water worth to you?"

I could have dashed the water to the ground, and demanded that the lid be filled afresh. I could have refused to drink at all, and stalked away from the fields. But I chose instead to lift the lid, and I held the Black man's eye until the rim of the lid hid his face from view, and then I closed my eyes, and I drank deeply. The sweet cold water rolled into my mouth, and poured down my chin to my chest, soaking my cheap cotton shirt until it clung to my skin. I drank my fill, and then some more, and every fiber of my being was suddenly made glad, and I could have shouted for joy. Then I lowered the empty lid, and when I could catch my breath again, I handed it back to the Black man.

"Thank you," I said.

You see, I had heard distinctly what the Black man didn't say. If you want something that badly, then you must do whatever it takes to get it.

And I now understood far more than he could have known. His unsaid words had suddenly made something very important become quite clear to me. What I wanted more than anything was not to be poor.

When I came back to the hay fields the next day, I wore a long-sleeved shirt to shed the chaff, and a dirty white sailor hat with the brim turned down, and a pair of mismatched gloves. I worked in the hay fields until the station manager returned, and then I went back to work in the radio station. That was my last summer at the orphanage. After Labor Day, I went Away From Here, and on my seventeenth birthday, I joined the Navy. I had the clothes I wore and a five-dollar bill, but I figured I'd be all right, if I kept in mind the value of water.

AWAY FROM HERE

Before I came to the orphanage, my life had been somewhat unsettled, to say the least. I went to four different schools in the second grade. But still I viewed life as a series of naturally reoccurring events—some exciting, some regrettable, but always fairly predictable. I had never suspected that life could have such sharp divisions, nor such abrupt upheavals.

I had no idea that the day I came in through the wrought iron gates of the front entrance to the orphanage, past the red brick gatehouse that was built right into the brick wall, that I was coming in out of a completely different time zone, known to the orphans as Before I Came Here.

The orphans already in residence Here questioned me closely concerning all that had happened to me Before I Came Here, and they were rather more like a cynical grand jury than they were a sympathetic audience. Any perceived inconsistency was met with derision, and any suspected aggrandizement with scorn. Reports of hardship were dismissed out of hand; they had all known hunger, or deprivation, or rejection of one sort or another.

What they wanted, and what they cross-examined me for until they got it, was a reasonable account of what my life had been like Away From Here. They seemed to thirst for some contact—any contact, even a vicarious one—with Away From Here.

Away From Here was a realm comprised of myth, mystery, and in all but a few instances, memories. Almost every orphan had his own stories to tell about the life he had lived Away From Here, and the fresh ear of a new listener was always welcome. I heard the most appalling things, told matter-of-factly, without self-pity, and often with unconscious black humor—stories of young lives rife with starvation, disaster, poverty, abandonment, murder. Yet, almost every one of those boys spoke wistfully of Away From Here.

For me, Away From Here had little to do with any physical territory that lay beyond the orphanage property lines. I had been moved and removed too many times in my young life to form any lasting attachment to a particular piece of real estate. Away From Here was more of a concept, a way of life that I thought I remembered. Time washed the memories in so many lathers of wishful thinking that eventually the misery faded out of them—Away From Here lost its harsh edge and its hardships, and became a world of imagined bright Christmas Eves, and summer rain running off a porch roof, and a warm bed on a cold night, and supper on the stove.

Actually, Away From Here had never really been that way, but that was how I remembered it, and I wanted to believe that it was still out there somewhere, just waiting for the time when I left Here.

What was Here like? No doubt it was a haven for many, or perhaps for most, of the orphans. But for me, Here was seventeen hundred and eighty-nine sunrises that I didn't want to see, and an equal number of dreaded nightfalls. It was a time of drawing in, and making myself small—a time of being ashamed. In those days, charity carried with it a stigma. I had very little reason to be proud, but I was, and being sent to the orphanage forced me to face the fact that I was poor.

I must have noticed early on in my life that petty authority seldom worked to my advantage, because I have always resented it. Therefore, I found it doubly difficult to get along Here. There were those two different codes of behavior that I had to deal with—the one imposed by the staff, and the other imposed by the orphans. Both of these codes were intentionally vague and ambiguous, and usually diametrically opposed to one another, but both were strictly enforced, most often by a leather strap or the toe of a brogan boot.

I once asked Prunes Tankersley to clarify a point of the matron's law. "I'm not about to tell you every little thing that you can get away with," she snapped at me. "Just behave yourself, or you'll wish you had."

On the other side of that, the orphans abhorred a "goody boy." By definition, a goody boy was one who curried favor with the matrons, one who was "always tryin' to keep hisself out of trouble."

Each matron laid down her own murky law, and the orphans conspired to challenge it. There was no neutral ground. It was as though two warring armies had both sown their own brand of land mines over the same territory. If one side didn't get you, the other one would.

In all fairness, I must admit that Cabbagehead Childress did try to codify the law when she was matron of Rupard. She labored mightily, and brought forth an intricate point system with which to govern our behavior. She wrought a chart of rows and columns, with neatly lettered names, and the days of the week. She composed a list of infractions, and beside each infraction was written its negative value. Ten points off for an unmade bed, fifteen points for an untidy locker, and et cetera, and et cetera. There was a complicated formula for averaging the daily scores, and finally, there was a long list of penalties, based on the weekly score. Eighty-nine percent and below—no movie on Saturday night.

Sixty-five percent and below—a taste of McBride's leather.

Ninety-one percent and above—you were a goody boy. Oh, it was a piece of work, all right, and the day she posted it on the bulletin board in the hall, she was quite full of herself. She had reduced discipline to simple mathematics.

The trouble was, it all began to come unraveled before the day was fully over.

Firstly, her list of infractions was woefully short. She lacked the imagination—and the necessary reams of paper—to list every bit of deviltry that those miscreants could devise. "We're allowed to do that," became the universal protest of the boys in Rupard. "It ain't on the list."

Cabbagehead was kept busy, frantically scribbling addenda to the list of misdemeanors.

Secondly, her negative values and her methods of averaging gave the orphans too much leeway. Dunderheads who couldn't pass eighth grade arithmetic were suddenly capable of calculating averages at the speed of light, and extrapolating those averages into a weekly score, and they would adjust their behavior accordingly. If

James Golden didn't like the movie that was showing on Saturday night, he wouldn't make his bed for a week.

Cabbagehead was continually tinkering with the negative values.

Thirdly, mistakes were bound to happen, therefore erasures were common. Cabbagehead couldn't tell our surreptitious erasures from her own legitimate ones, so she had to keep two sets of books, and when the books didn't agree, we had a valid basis for argument.

Fourth and finally, her ultimate penalty—the leather—came into play much too early. Once a Rupard boy hit that mark of sixty-five points, he was due a busting no matter what else he did, and such an outlawed boy was beyond restraint until the next marking period began. Cabbagehead's point system was a shambles.

McBride finally had to be called in. He held a brief—a very brief—meeting in the parlor of Rupard Building.

"You boys had better settle down, and behave yourselves," he growled. "Or else. Now go back to your rooms."

Cabbagehead continued to natter around with her charts and her lists, but it was so much wasted effort. For all its brevity, McBride's speech had been inspiring, and for many weeks to follow, all our averages hovered around the 90.1 mark.

No doubt the vague system of regulation in the orphanage had evolved in the one way that was best suited for the majority. For me personally, the treacherous path between being a goody boy and getting busted regularly was far too narrow.

For some, there were brief respites from the oppressive Here. On Boy's Saturday, anyone with a dollar to spend could ride that rattly old red school bus into downtown Dallas, and there was a three-day summer vacation for those who had someone to take them. Such excursions quickly taught me that Here could not be left behind temporarily. Here was not a physical place; it was a set of circumstances and a state of mind, neither of which was improved by mere distance.

The only true way to escape was to Leave.

I regarded anyone lucky enough to be Leaving with sharp pangs of envy. I watched them pack their belongings, and tried to think how they must feel. As they sat on their battered suitcases waiting to be taken Away From Here, they already seemed to be remote and out of reach, as though they now rested on the other side of an unfordable river.

They weren't really Here anymore. There was a place waiting for them Away From Here. As soon as I could manage it, it came my time to Leave. I had often imagined how it would feel to walk off that campus for the last time, but as with so many other experiences in my life, the reality was much different from what I had imagined. I had always expected to experience a great joy. What I actually felt was a tremendous relief.

That was forty-four years ago, this past September. Did I ever manage to put Here behind me? It is a question that I tax myself with, now and then. I think so. For the most part. Let me put it this way. By and large, I have led a life that would have caused Prunes Tankersley to gasp, and fumble for her leather strap. I have taken strong drink, and fought in bars. I have squired many a beautiful woman, and raised a champion horse or two. I have crewed more than a few sailing yachts across deep waters, to tropical island anchorages. I have drunk some splendid wines.

In short, it has been a fine life.

I am a gentleman farmer now, retired to the Shenandoah Valley of Virginia with my lovely lady, and my lively young mares. The folks around here treat neighbors like kinfolk. We talk about the weather, and worry about the crops, and we help one another out however we can. I plan to die here.

It could be said, I suppose, that I owe this good life to those early years in the orphanage. And in a way, I might even agree. After all, it was in the orphanage that I learned to live in my imagination. In my own mind, I created a place for myself Away From Here, a place where I belonged, and as soon as they set me free, I set out to find it.

Fifties

The Girl's Choir with Miss Jo and Brother Hal at FBC Corsicana.

The Football Team, 1950; 1st Row: Louis Tate, Lee Roy Mangum, Jerry Joe Nash, Thurman Shurtleff, Cleve Bland, W. L. Smith; 2nd Row: Raymond Tranthan, James Lookadoo, Ira Lee Henslee, Ed Stanley, Corky Cutshall, Charles May, Frankie Hardin; 3rd Row: Billy Houston, Vance Horsley, Willis Grayson, Johnny Ray Taylor, Fon Day, Bobby Baker; 4th Row: Harold Campbell, Ellis Smith, Vernon Horsley, Charlie Corcoran, Robert Bleakley, Carroll Day, Robert McKinney with Coach M. G. Alexander, and Assistant Royce Stephens.

The 1952-1953 Football Team; 1st Row: Rice McLeod, James Lookadoo, W. L. Smith, Robert McKinney, Jack Ballard, Charlie Corcoran, Fon Day; 2nd Row: Thurman Shurtleff, Jerry Joe Nash, Willis Grayson, and James Graves.

Coach Alexander's team on the bus.

The 1952 Basketball Team, c 1952; 1st Row: Horace Mabry, George Phillips, Jerry Fulton, Donald Patterson; 2nd Row: Robert McKinney, James Graves, Jack Ballard, Carroll Day, Fon Day, and Dale Hensley.

The Horsley twins: two great athletes.

The 440 Relay Team: Vance Horsley, Ed Stanley, Willis Grayson, and Vernon Horsley.

182

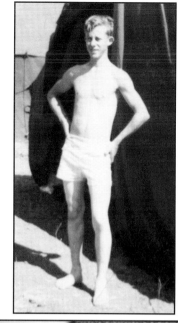

Home Economics Class: Bobbi Richardson, Mary Beth Cutshall, Jane McWhorter, Ophelia Isbel, Sarah Ann Crouch, Rosa Lee Woods, Juanita Graves, Margaret Corcoran, Mary Alpha Gilbert, Ruby Taylor, Maxine Newton, Louise Searcy, and Betty Jean Nelson.

Left:
Cheerleaders Eva Nell Turner, Rena Key, and Ruth Nevil strut their stuff.

Upper right:
Lee Roy Mangum at the Boys' Camp Out, c 50s.

The pool lifeguards: Daisy Morgan, Betty Fern Waller, Elizabeth Atkinson, c 50s.

A classroom at the High School, c 50s.

The best campers with Miss Reeves, Miss Hack, and Daddy Buck.

Billy Dean Richardson mowing the huge lawn, c 50s.

At the Girls' Woods Climbing Trees, 1950.

Top of the hill where the boys hung out: Bobby Baker, Vance Horsley, and Jesse Hardin.

The swim crowd, c 1957.

Raising money for our first annual, class of '50.

Wanda Mae Polk and Dorothy Simmons at the Fair, 50s.

Herman Mangum trying out a trike, 1950.

*John, Tommy, and Harold Vaughan
with their Grandmother, arriving at
Buckner, 1946.*

Robert Bleakley delivering laundry, 1950.

Bobbie Scurlock, Jane McWhorter, and Mary Beth Cutshall at the mop rack, 50s.

Pap Grube, Joe Cline, Billy Ed Taylor, and a young friend behind the Manna Hall.

Mary Turner and Donald Johnson in the cattle truck, our transportation.

Ira Lee Henslee and Norma Lookadoo.

Pete and Harold Campbell, 1950.

Part of the Grammar School Graduation Class of 1946; 1st Row: Kenneth Murray, George Dickey, Donald Johnson, Harold Campbell, Dorothy Thedford, Alice Ann Ward; 2nd Row: Helen Curda, Willie Mae Stringer, Minneola Washburn, Viola Wright, Eva Nell Turner, Dorothy Simmons, Marie Bailey, Peggy Grusendorf, Wanda Mae Polk, Edith Stewart; 3rd Row: Alberta Disch, Wanda Godsey, Katherine Henslee, Frank Powell, A. B. Dunn, Herman Mangum, Ira Lee Henslee, Lee Roy Hutson, Juanita Graves with Bobby Baker in the corner.

Ellis Smith, Helen Curda, and Alice Ward in "All's Well That Ends Well," 1950.

At the top of the hill with Rupard in the background; 1st Row: Vernon Horsley, Donald Johnson, Vance Horsley, Ira Lee Henslee; 2nd Row: Robert Bleakley, Bobby Baker, Harold Campbell, Royce Stephens, Ellis Smith.

Baccalaureate suits sewn by the girls, Willie Mae Stringer, Betty Fern Waller, Mary Beth Cutshall, a teacher, Jane McWhorter, Louise Searcy, and Dorothy Thedford.

Dressed for the Banquet, our first formals: Wanda Mae Polk, Juanita Graves, Jeanette Phillips, Peggy Grusendorf, Katherine Henslee, Rosa Lee Woods, Margaret Corcoran, and Alice Ann Ward.

Graduation in the dresses we've sewn: Jane McWhorter, Mary Beth Cutshall, Eva Nell Turner, and Juanita Graves, 1950.

The Class of 1951 and friends in a formal portrait.

James Graves and Verda Bea Giles, 50s.

Billy Duke, Billy Houston, Rice McLeod, Albert Disch, and Kenneth Murray when they were little boys, c 50s.

Academy Seniors give a program about life at Buckner, 1951.

On the way to the high school, Joan Bye, Wanda Butler, Claudine Fulton, Beulah Sappington, Ruth Nevil, and Ann Curda, 1951.

189

The Buckner Club at Howard Payne College with Miss Sikes, Mr. and Mrs. Gordon Taylor, and Mr and Mrs. Dickey, 1953.

The graduating class of 1952, Kneeling: Edward Stanley, Rice McLeod, Joan Bye, Pete Campbell, Standing: Liz Atkinson, Billie Jean Mabry, Ruth Nevil, Norma Lookadoo, Joy Smith, Daisy Morgan, a friend, Gladys Hall, and Hazel Brown.

Valentine Banquet, c 1954.

Mr. McBride and Mrs. Baird with students on a Bible Trip, 50s.

At the Stadium

The Speech Class relaxing after a performance, 1957.

191

*Mr. Murdock and Mr. McBride
fixing a flat while Gregory Buckner and
Kenneth McKinney look on, 1951.*

*Mel Walls, Don Ritchie, Charles Gayle with
James Lundy in background. A parachute from
the famous plane crash.*

*Earl Ray Miles and a friend
in the Buckner School
Library, 1957.*

The Sixties

"The Christian who is pure and without fault, from God the Father's point of view is the one who takes care of orphans and widows. . . ."

James 12:7a, RSI

"Hal" Harold Golden, '61

At Buckner from 1949-57

When I arrived at Buckner in 1949, my first three years at Pires were spent like most other new kids learning their way through rough and tumble play and being generally observant. I was an extra-ordinarily good kid, who refused to curse, to sneak off campus, to cheat on exams, to sass my matron. I followed Christian doctrine obsessively. I was saved and baptized at eleven and was cloyingly well behaved. I tried to be perfect. At that age I thought that to be perfect, one had to be consistent—unvarying in behavior. Messers McBride's and Grube's hymnals were the whole of my repertoire, and I sang aloud, or whistled those hymns that praised Jesus the live-long day. I read the Bible, tried to interpret it, closed my eyes tightly when I prayed, and tried to envision Jesus.

But when I reached thirteen and moved to McElroy, such behavior had become tedious. Some boy or other was always spoiling for a fight, wanting to invade, trying to take something that one of my brothers had given me, was always making smart cracks; matrons were always looking for someone to "slap around." My matron was one of the least forgiving. Why should I knock myself out for those ingrates?

Temptation to retaliate abounded. It soon became fairly clear that those with elan had the most fun. The "mean" boys—those who sassed the matrons and bullied the little boys and showed a modicum of independence seemed to be getting the most out of life. Originally, they were my antithesis. Suddenly, almost over-night, I was one of them.

I found something else: the lure of the night. It became inescapable. On my bed, chin on my hands clasped on the windowsill, I would stare out onto the campus from my third-floor window. To the west lay the city of Dallas, its night skyline a long, strung-out three-dimensional cluster of Christmas lights. And the girls, having finished washing dishes at Manna Hall, called in lilting sing-song voice to the boys across the forelawn. I heard them with a kind of bitter-sweet ache of a train whistle in the night. Matrons would come in from the evening, their cheeks ruddy, their faces lit from mysterious conversations. There was a deliciousness about the night. I was like a cat, wanting to slink from the purple shadow of one yew tree to the next, to spin and twirl and get crazy under the silver moon glow that lit the whole of the grounds.

I found another boy who also wanted to slip from the choking atmosphere and see what lay outside. Johnny Delaney and I talked about it for a couple of days, then finally laid plans to sneak out. He invited two other boys.

About half an hour after lights out, we slipped on our blue jeans and congregated in the bathroom between bedrooms One and Two. Johnny was the only one still in pajamas. Romantic recollection says that we climbed out of the window and slid down the gutter pipe, but

193

more than likely, we took the back (south) stairs. We had quite an evening laid out: Our destination was the Vocational-Administration Building Auditorium, which had a television. The year before, Mrs. Tankersley, first-floor matron, had owned a set as well, but she had kept careful censure over our viewing habits. We looked forward to watching some of the racier programs she'd never allowed us to tune in.

We used stealth across the great black campus, from tree to tree, bush to bush, crouching low out in the open, till we were at the rear of the building, keeping a vigilant eye out for Mr. Brasher, the night watchman.

The lumber shed, across from the Commissary and water tower, abutted the Administration Building. It was a flimsy, two-story structure covered with thin gauge corrugated aluminum. We crawled and heisted ourselves up until we reached the roof. The Administration window had been left unlocked. The first boy to reach it, pushed it open, effortlessly, and we crawled inside where the TV awaited us.

On the screen, Gorgeous George, a caricature wrestler, clowned his way across the rink. We were too young to know that he was a scam; to us, he was high camp, a real professional with his blond, marcelled hair and barrel chest. Then followed the sophisticated "Tonight Show" with Steve Allen. After the "Million Dollar Showcase" movie began (a boring love story), we reckoned that forty-five minutes in the room was enough. Besides, it was rumored in McElroy that the matrons had midnight bed checks using their flashlights. It behooved us to get back.

It was probably more dumb luck than planning that I lowered myself onto the joist directly under the window without mishap. Johnny Delaney, however, either forgot, or lost his footing. I was clambering between the planks and was only a few feet from the ground when I heard an almighty crashing followed by a heavy thud.

Johnny began an ungodly howling. It was mighty dark, too dark to imagine why he was making so much noise. He was the most boisterous boy in our dormitory. In fact, the whole program had been his suggestion.

I hissed for him to shut up, before Mr. Brasher heard him. But the one boy still in the Administration Building who waited for John to drop onto the metal roof, yelled—yelled—that John had fallen through.

Hundreds of lumber-board-feet, and we had to crawl through them to find Johnny, whose fall was a sheer drop to the ground. We had to drag and thrust and support him through the maze, till we were outside. He was not in shock. His yelling had so been in character, that I couldn't believe he still wasn't playing a prank on us.

How do you take a kid to the hospital at midnight and explain to the awakened nurse, not only had Johnny broken his leg, but also how he'd done it? We tried half a dozen alibis, nonetheless: sleepwalking?—going downstairs for a drink from the water fountain and slipping?—stepping into a puddle of water in the bathroom? . . . We were in trouble, and we knew it. It was tempting to just deposit him at the hospital door and flee into the night.

Johnny's threshold for pain must have been high as the clouds, because he just hobbled along, supported between two other boys, intent on getting proper treatment, hardly crying at all. There was a strange, surreal feeling to all of it. We finally got him across the campus to the hospital . . . a building in silhouette without a single light burning, and pressed the doorbell till Mrs. Dyer arrived to peer through the heavy screen door out at us, still in the process of tightening the belt of her nightgown. We all began talking at once, but she put an end to that by pushing us aside and getting to the root of the issue: Johnny and his broken leg. As she led him inside, she wanted to know what we were doing up at this time of night. Every one of us began to spout our alibis—each a different one.

She told us to get back to our dormitory, and into bed.

Neither honor among thieves nor a code of silence existed at Buckner. When you'd done something wrong, you knew the next voice you heard would be that of either your matron, or the Boys' Dean. And sure enough: On the morrow, following breakfast, the secret of our excursion had been thrown to the winds, and I was called to the Dean's office. En route, many an older boy called to ask me if I'd enjoyed my evening out.

McBride knew everything. I didn't even bother trying to lie. For my punishment, I suffered a "busting," a month-long forfeiture of my weekly nickel and being "campused."

Johnny Delaney, by way of the convoluted logic particular to BOH, was treated with hero status, and as Mrs. Dyer's little darling, had full run of the hospital for six weeks and was fed ice cream daily. Equally annoying, he'd become an unspoken martyr, who, according to Mrs. Dyer, had had the misfortune to fall into bad company.

The most significant outcome of this venture was the beginning of my downfall. Like a girl who has compromised her virtue, I abandoned my self-imposed high morals of trying to be the perfect kid. What was the sense in being perfect, when you've committed a sin? Seemingly, the campus matrons were always waiting to pounce. I was now one of the "mean" boys.

TEACHER PORTRAITS:

MISS BOYD

My first-grade teacher was Miss Boyd— deceased, I believe, c 1956. She was an older woman—a pinched-faced spinster who seemed as much a part of Buckner as the very mortar and bricks of our school building. Her years of experience served her well. There was no indication of being burned out, or of frustration with her lot in life. She was firm without being Teutonic. No child rattled her, nor did I ever experience her taking vindictive pleasure in laying a strap to a mischievous student.

There was something about her that I never experienced in another teacher—her ability to teach the children to sing. She was as methodical in music as she was in teaching basic addition. To this very day (fifty years later) even though I have not heard it sung since, I can recall almost every word of the song, "Texas, My Texas."

It was through her that I learned to read: Our text was DICK AND JANE. Under her tutelage, I learned to write—a torturous, convoluted ordeal. The word that gave me the most grief was 'wind,' and I could not get my fingers to form that letter, "W." Getting my digits to obey the chalk was no less difficult than twisting them into the letter "S." It never seemed to occur to this woman that her students couldn't master the elements of reading and writing. She was staunch and steadfast— never intimate, yet neither was she cold.

Miss Boyd was a dedicated woman who knew her role in life and with her placid disposition, ingrained knowledge into her students through a process gained from experience and dedication. I sincerely lament that she died before I was old enough to appreciate her importance.

MISS HERRING

Mrs. Dale Pingle (nee Herring) was a twenty-four-year-old college graduate when she arrived to teach second grade. I believe that my class in 1950-51, was her first. Not quite beautiful, she had a long-legged, slender femininity about her that lent a swan-like grace. She had a slow, easy smile that bespoke tolerance, and wireless spectacles that bespoke the world of the pedagogue.

She was too young to be cynical, too well bred to demean her little charges and too honest to take umbrage when they attempted to express themselves. She was trusting, yet mature enough to be a disciplinarian. Some months into the school year, she was obliged to whip two of the children for misbehavior. Having made her decision, she placed her arms onto her desk and buried her face so we wouldn't see her crying.

I recall going to her desk to ask her a question, and when she replied frankly, "I don't know," I returned to my desk stricken. For the first time in my life, an adult had confessed not knowing the answer to a question—and was honest enough to admit it.

She loved the world of discovery and invited us to enjoy her experiences. She brought in some little chemical compound known as Magic Rocks that grew into stalagmite-like crystals in every primary and secondary color. When we were especially good, she played an LP disc of Disney's "Cinderella" soundtrack.

One day, she gave each student a tiny birthday candle, then struck a match, held it to my candle and told me to light the child's seated behind me. Within minutes, every candle was lit. "One match . . ." she said, "like a message of goodness, will light up a world of darkness."

After teaching for one more year, she left, and I didn't see her again until one hot summer day two years later, when she pulled up beside Freeland in a pick-up truck. At the wheel was her young husband, Dale (with a dimple in his chin), and in her arms she held her months-old baby daughter—whom I had the pleasure of meeting seventeen years later—a wiry, dark-haired girl who knew very well how to deflect my somewhat cynical, anti-religious prognostications.

There was a flower-like goodness within Mrs. Pingle, an inherent belief in humanity—orphan children notwithstanding; a delicacy that I fully imagine she still retains, even though I haven't seen her for twenty-nine years.

MR. GRUBE

Mr. Grube used to lead the singing at Sunday School when we were little. I remember how we boys giggled when he shifted into another key in the middle of a song, which threw everybody scrambling to get back in tune. He had a really froggy voice, and it must have been his love of singing rather than his expertise that got him his job.

They did do the minstrel shows when I was there. Mr. Grube always had a starring role. I am suddenly reminded of him—the curtain raising with him standing before a pushcart with umbrella, and singing "Peanuts!" An exquisite memory. And he was kind, too. He roasted peanuts, put them into a big cardboard box and set them before a hoard of boys. You didn't see anything but butts and elbows for the next 20 seconds, like piranhas going after fresh meat and leaving the box a ravaged carcass.

After forty years, I will make a confession: I never liked the bakery pies. . .not the lemon, assuredly not the coconut cream and emphatically not the chocolate. After leaving Buckner, it took me years to eat cookies with raisins, after subsisting on those from the bakery. But be sure I ate everything sweet that crossed my path. Not unlike the "doggie in the manger," I might not like something, but I was dog-goned if I'd give it to some other kid just because he coveted it. I was not above doing a little horse trading: maybe that new comic book for my slice of coconut cream.

Ken Norman, '61

SYRUP DECKERS

A syrup container was always on each table in Manna Hall. If children did not like what was being served, they would pour syrup onto their plates and mix in some butter. They would then take a piece of bread and drop it in the syrup-butter mixture. With a fork, the bread would be turned over once in the mixture and then eaten. In sixteen years, I ate hundreds of these "syrup deckers" and liked them all. Jerry Wayne Hayes allegedly ate so many of these over the years, that he became known simply as "Syrup Decker" Hayes.

GETTING EXTRAS AT MANNA HALL

When the whistle blew for meal time, we had to line up, according to height, to go to Manna Hall. As we walked single-file to eat, we would take notice of anyone who was absent (hospital, etc.) and claim their food. For instance, if it were Thursday evening, someone might say, "I said Applegate's pie." If it were Wednesday evening, he might say, "I claim Johnny Ballew's cinnamon roll." Once you "claimed" someone's food, it was never contested. When the waitress brought dessert, you got two pieces of Doc Grube's cherry pie.

CLOTHING STORE

Being limited to only so many purchases at the Clothing Store, we always seemed to come up with a key so that we could make midnight raids and replenish our threads. One night, about ten of us (including Buell Johnson, Bulan Birdsong, James Johnson and Orville Griffin) made a 2:00 A.M. raid. As we were coming back to the dorm, Mr. Byler yelled from across the campus, "Stop!" It appeared that Mr. Byler had a favorable sight angle as we started running toward Cullom. Several of us did stop, but Orville Griffin and Buell Johnson were so fast that they beat Mr. Byler to the dorm and were faking sleep when he made the rounds for bed check. Mr. Byler entered several rooms in Cullom to check for hard-breathing orphans. As he was leaving Buell Johnson's room, he heard a heavy breathing sound. He then pulled the sheets back to find a fully clothed, sweating Buell and said, "Go downstairs, Buell!" Some of us figured that if Orville were involved, Mr. Byler wouldn't be too hard on our rear ends. We were right; when Orville was brought downstairs with the rest of us, we didn't get near as many licks as we probably would have without the gridiron hero in our midst.

CAMPUS MART AND OUR FIVE CENTS WEEKLY ALLOWANCE

At age six through about sixteen (1949 to about 1958), we would line up at about 3:30 P.M. (after two hours of quiet hour for the younger kids) and walk in line to the Campus Mart.

In a hallway behind the mart, a lady behind glass would hand each little orphan one nickel to spend and then check their name off. At 5 cents per week, our allowance came to $2.60 per year.

We would normally make the difficult decision of what we were going to purchase on that long trip to the mart. Some favorite purchases for our nickel at the mart were these: Zeros, Snickers, M&Ms, Milky Ways, any soft drink, three dips of any flavor of ice cream we wanted, and machine malts (which meant chocolate or vanilla coming out of a machine until it would not go any higher).

A trip to the Campus Mart occurred only once each week and was looked upon with much anticipation. We might plan for three days what we were going to buy on our next visit there. Some orphans received money from relatives and would buy a dollar or two worth of candy and soft drinks and go back to their dorms and to a feast with their roommates and selected friends. A favorite was to drink RC Cola with peanuts in the bottle.

Sometime around 1958, the allowances increased to 10 cents for the elementary students, 25 cents for the junior high students and a whopping 40 cents for the high school students. This meant the big boys now had $20.80 per year to spend on soft drinks and candy. This eight-fold increase in our allowance was greatly appreciated.

SELLING CHAIR-BACKS AT THE COTTON BOWL

The Cotton Bowl in the 40s and 50s had only bleacher seats with nothing to lean back against. This meant watching a football game could result in a very long afternoon. In 1958 and continuing until 1961, about ten or fifteen orphans were chosen to rent chair-backs to fans for 50 cents each. These chairbacks would attach to the bleacher boards and were much more comfortable to sit on because you could lean back.

We would have about 250 seats stacked up and would start about one hour before the kick-off and finish at the game's half time. We would stand there for about two hours yelling, "Chair-backs, chair-backs, fifty cents!" After the half, we could go in and watch the second half of the college game or early Dallas Cowboys' games. This was quite a thrill for very sports-oriented orphans. Also the pay was 10 bucks per game so this was about half of our yearly allowance of $20.80.

MAKING MONEY AT HOMECOMING

From about 1953-1957, the eleven to thirteen-year-old orphans really looked forward to

Homecoming. When we got up from "quiet hour" at 3:00 P.M., we would go to the back of the Maris Welcome Center where the ex-students were mulling about visiting with each other. We would walk up to one and ask if they had change for 25 cents (or 50 cents). They would pull out a dollar and give it to us. Then we would go to another alumni and say the same thing. On a good Homecoming, we might get $10-15 dollars. Because the Campus Mart had a lot of five cent items, this was like winning the orphan lottery. This would buy a lot of machine malts and snickers.

EXTENDING OUR DATES

In 1960, we started going to the Dallas Public Schools (Samuell High). We would get friends from Samuell to let us double date with them. Curfew was midnight, which we thought was a little early. We would come in, check in with Mr. Benham, then go to a first story room and crawl out the window to meet the car which had gone out the gates and circled back around outside the gate, just across from Cullom. We would extend the date until about 2:00 A.M. and then sneak back into the dorm through the window. We were never caught doing this.

BASKETBALL GAMES

As eight to ten-year-olds, we would go to watch the high school play basketball games. Among the admired were players like "Flicki" Patterson, "Chicken" Mabry, Clark Watts, Gregory Buckner, etc. We admired the way the huge BUCKNER flap on the back of their jackets bounced up and down. We couldn't wait until the day we would be able to wear that jacket with the BUCKNER flap. We would go back to Freeland and fashion miniature basketball goals out of coat hangers and nets made from torn up T-shirts. Placing these on our doors, we would use a tennis ball for a basketball and get into lay-up lines and act like we were the "big boys!"

ONE OF BUCKNER'S GREATEST ATHLETES

by Vernon Horsley

I read with great interest the article in *Buckner Now* regarding Buckner's greatest athletes. I truly believe that Bob Stokes and Joe Woods were the greatest. However, I want to submit another great to add to that list.

Ken Norman came to Buckner in 1945 at the age of two and left in 1961 after sixteen years. Ken began his career in basketball in the eighth grade and was cut after two games. (Michael Jordan was also cut. . . .) He returned as a 5'11" freshman and led the team in scoring. As a tenth grader, he averaged 20 points a game on the Junior Varsity through five games, and was moved up to Varsity to become the starting center. He led the team in scoring and averaged 16 points in district play. As a 6' 5" junior, he again led his team (and the district) in scoring 474 points, averaging 23 points (18-4 record). He was named the district's MVP (scoring over 30 points on six occasions) and in the last high school game played in the Buckner gym, broke the BOH record with 41 points.

His senior year, Buckner dropped its high school and Ken went to Samuell High School in Dallas. He was All-City and All-Metroplex, scoring 464 points. His team became Samuell's first ever City Champions with a 10-0 record (overall 28-4 record). After high school, over two dozen colleges and universities sought his services. The legendary Henry Iba of Oklahoma State and other coaches from Michigan, TCU, Arkansas, etc., came through the gates of Buckner to court the sixteen-year-old orphan and give him a home.

From Samuell, he went to Lon Morris Junior College and led the Bearcats to 2nd in the nation while scoring 721 points (high game of 44 points). Norman led the team to 31 wins and was named All-Conference and All-Tournament twice. His sophomore year was just as good as the Bearcats had a winning streak of 22 in a row and went 12-0 in conference. Again, he was named All-Conference and the team was ranked number two in the nation most of the season. He finished his two-year junior college career with 1,194 points.

As a junior, Ken chose Texas A&M over Arkansas and promptly helped the Aggies win their first out-right SWC championship in forty-one years. He started every game as a senior and finished as the second leading scorer behind All-American, John Beasley. He averaged 14 points a game, was named to the Houston All-Classic Team and led the team in field goal percentage at 49 percent. Texas A&M coach, Shelby Metcalfe, later said Norman was the best hook shooter he had coached in his twenty-nine years at Texas

A&M. Metcalfe also said about Norman, "Ken has a unique offense of his own. He sort of messes around with the ball. If he gets in the open, you expect a pass. If two or three get on him, you go to the board to rebound because he's going to shoot. And of course he has that great hook if all else fails."

Ken Norman completed his playing career in the Air Force by averaging 25 points a game, winning two World-Wide Armed Forces Championships and being named All-Air Force twice. I know you now agree with me that he also deserves special recognition for his achievement in athletics.

Ken taught in the public schools for 31 years. He was voted "Most-Witty Teacher" in 1994 and was "Teacher of the Year" in 1995. He was voted "Coach of the Year" several times for his district while at Richardson High in the 1970s by the Dallas Morning News. He has now retired from coaching and teaching in public schools, but continues to teach Advanced Placement Economics in a private school, Bishop Lynch High School, and at Richland College. He is a proud grandpa with two grandsons, Randy, Jr., and Reid.

We salute you, Ken Norman, for not only achieving the best in yourself, but also the best for the community around you.

Eugene M. Golden, '64

SUNBEAM HOME

From the age of two and a half until I left the Sunbeam home, some memories stand out in my mind:

The tender hug of a sweet lady who raised up the side of my baby bed and would tell me good night and give me a tender kiss.

The rare occasion of a quarter pint of Carnation Ice Cream given to me by Vera McKee.

The thermometer to check my fever from the unusual end, as I lay on a couch in the lobby with my face covered because people were walking by.

A water hose spraying water as we played out in the street on a hot summer day.

A scary nightmare after looking at a comic book about the ghost rider.

Falling out of the bed onto the floor only to see four beds down from me a rolled up blanket that looked like a man to me. Jumping back in bed, shaking as I covered up my head.

A dream about fire across a fence line. I was on the cool side and even in my little mind, I believed God was telling me to stay on the cool side and not dare climb over the fence.

PIRES

While I was living on the second floor of Pires, Miss Walker and we kids marched in single file as usual to the Manna Hall for supper. When we arrived, there was hard candy in glass containers on the table where we were sitting, but we were told we could not have any until later on that week.

All I knew was that I wanted some of that candy. Oh, it looked so good!

Later that night when everything was quiet, I walked out of the room that I shared with four others into the hall past Miss Walker's room and into another room which joined Miss Walker's. In the dark I found the candy she had confiscated from us in a large open glass jar, just waiting for my little hands to shovel it out into my two top pajama pockets.

As I left the room and was slowly moving back across the hall to my room, Miss Walker was coming out of her room down the hall by her front entrance. Of course she saw me, but I didn't think she could tell who I was since the night lights were dim. She hollered at me, but I didn't stop. I just kept going toward my room and through the other rooms until I came to the bathroom. Then I closed and locked the bathroom stall door. As I was trying to empty my pockets down the commode, Miss Walker told me to open the door. I couldn't get the candy out fast enough to get rid of it because in my greed I had packed the stuff into my pockets like cement.

I opened the door and she grabbed me by the shirt, saying, "What have you done with the candy?" At that she ripped the pockets right off my pajamas, trying to get to the stolen candy.

"Candy, huh? I'll show you," she said as she strong-armed me back to my bed. She threatened to tie me to the bed if I caused anymore trouble. That was enough for me. I went right to sleep till morning. The other boys were delighted with my punishment. I was not allowed to share one piece of the candy she gave out to the other boys later that week.

I never did try to steal any more candy from Miss Walker's room, and she had no trouble keeping me from wandering the halls at night again.

Bobby Davis and I were friends. One night after the lights were out, he showed me that a small bulb, a piece of wire and a small battery would produce light. Well, I thought he was a genius. We hid under the bed cover for some time so no one else could see us experimenting with the light until the battery became too weak to give out light.

In exchange for that interesting experiment with the light, the next day I told Bobby where we could get a pair of roller skates that would fit us. We could put on one skate each and skate out of the Home campus so fast that no one could catch us.

Bobby agreed to my scheme. We each put on one skate and started down Samuell Boulevard toward where Big Town Shopping Center is now. But there were so many potholes in that old road that we had to throw away the skates and walk. We walked until a policeman picked us up. He bought us some candy before taking us back to Buckner. I asked the officer to please tell Miss Walker not to spank us for our little jaunt. He did and, believe it or not, she obeyed him.

CARNETT

My last year at Buckner, we had a gate attendant and night watchman named Mr. Crosby. He was always bragging about all the girl friends he had. He must have been seventy-two years old. He never let up on telling us seniors about the ladies he had met that day outside the campus.

I decided to play a trick on Mr. Crosby. I bought a Beatle wig and since I worked at the laundry, I had access to items of ladies' clothing. So late one night as he was driving around the small circle in his '53 chevy pick up, I jumped out from behind a hedge of cedar bushes, dressed like a woman—wig and short dress—and waved at Mr. Crosby. He saw me and it sounded to me like he floorboarded the truck to get closer to me.

I took off in a hard run—away from Mr. Crosby. After I slightly raised my dress to reveal my legs, I jumped the hedges, for by this time, Mr. Crosby had driven his truck up over the curve near Father Buckner's statue. Mr. Crosby drove round and round trying to catch me, stopping now and then to get his bearings as to where I was. Finally he got out of his truck, trying to shine his flash light to see who I was, but fortunately, I was able to run back to my dorm.

That same evening he was sitting on a bench where he usually sat near the front gate. Once again he was bragging about his adventures, but this time he was talking about a beautiful young girl with fantastic legs and hair. He said that she had been just running loose on the campus that night and though she could run like a deer, she was as lovely as a movie star.

Of course, no one believed him but me.

Miss Mildred McCullough, '41-'64

by Jerre Simmons

AN ENCOMIUM FOR
MILDRED McCULLOUGH

Refrain:
Mildred McCullough, red hair and all,
We learned to love you when we were small.

She came to us in '41 and stayed till '64.
Twenty three years she spent at our Home
Till God said, "Enough, enough, no more!
Pack your bags and leave those orphans alone."

She taught in the Panhandle for two years,
Then came to Buckner to her calling true,
Left us for Plano and Lancaster's dears,
But liked us best of all; that we all knew!

She taught us about Life and all about Math;
Algebra, some Trig and Plane Geometry
So that we could compete on life's hard path
In the very highest levels of society.

She was fun and fair and a little bit stern
While she taught us to have self discipline.
Her goal for life was that we should learn
All the wisdom that the world knew then:

That the shortest distance between two points
Is measured by treading the straightest line,
All about circles and squares and their joints,
How the Pythagorean theory works just fine.

She taught us honesty, morality too,
Hope, love and lots of good patience
Held together with arithmetical glue
And lots of good old common sense.

She was also our teacher of Sunday school
And a favorite elected sponsor of our class,
Who showed us how to live by the golden rule
And cured us of any tendency to sass.

She went with us into the fields of cotton
And what we picked, on scales she weighed;
Loved us though we were sometimes rotten,
And saw that for our work we all got paid.

Then she took us to the Fair to spend that money,
Watched us ride the rides and see the sights,
Held our heads when our tummies felt funny,
And refereed our quarrels and adolescent fights.

She once even coached Girls' Basketball,
And that team toward success she aimed,
But warned them that winning was never all;
What mattered was "how you played the game."

But when all her numbers, she added up whole,
Counted what's wrong and what's right,
While she taught us, our beliefs she helped to
    mold
To keep our morals high and in justice delight.

She took us camping into the woods near,
And when we hungry and thirsty grew,
She fried potatoes on an open camp fire,
And bacon and eggs and other goodies too.

She shared with us her cars, old and new,
On trips to colleges, up mountains, down valleys;
Gave us parties for Sunday School and BTU,
Then taught us games like Streets and Alleys,

Sling a Statue and Knocking on Doors,
How to discover a lucky four leaf clover,
Also Post Office and how to eat Smores,
Even Red Rover, Red Rover, Come Over.

Her love made us stronger than the 100th power
Multiplied by the 100th again and again,
And we loved her more than the 100th power
Multiplied by the 100th again and again.

Final refrain:
Mildred McCullough, we remember you still;
Because you were so good to us, we always will.
[presented by her ex-students in 1994, when she was named "Distinguished Employee of The Year." Ed.]

Sally (Bingham) Hawkins, '66

BUCKNER, THE MEMORIES

Tears were streaming down my face as I slowly drove the streets of Buckner campus for what I knew would be the last time. I carefully looked at each building and well-worn path as I drove, noting the detail of each brick, door, pillar, or roof that my eyes could encompass as I went. And I remembered . . .

He was a giant of a man to my five-year-old eyes as they fastened on the figure at our front door, smiling down at me as I ran to see what he might bring our family. People were always stopping by to bring us food or clothes; he must be one of them! His name was Mr. Carnett, he was from Buckner Orphans' Home, and here to tell us about the new place where we might be going to live! He told us about riding horses, picnics, swimming, playgrounds, and all the food we could eat! It sounded like a great adventure! We had been home from the Lena Pope Home, in Fort Worth, for a short time, but months before, my Dad had left my mother alone with five children, and no means of supporting us. The church had done all they could; the courts were about to do what they felt they needed to do, and Buckner reached out and took all five of us. Two boys, three girls, ages eight to two now had a new place to call home.

I was only five-years-old when I arrived at the Receiving Home at Buckner Orphans Home. In awe I stared at the big red building where we would spend the first ten days of our stay with Buckner. We felt like we'd been given a special prize. At the Receiving Home, I remember swimming in the concrete tank that was on the side of the building, and thinking of how deep it was. Since it was June, we were allowed to go swimming several times; one time I nearly drowned because I couldn't get to the side. Years later, I drove beside that tank, and realized how shallow it was, and thought about how small I had been at that time. I remember taking my first drink of the milk from the dairy and thinking it tasted like it had dirt in it. After drinking it for a while, I wasn't able to remember that first couple of weeks trying to get used to the taste of really fresh milk. I remember thinking the "big girl" who was in the Receiving Home must have been a movie star because I thought she was so pretty. Leota Dancer put stars in my eyes. I always had a special place in my heart reserved especially for her. I still do.

After ten long days (forever for small children), we entered the big campus of Buckner Orphans' Home. Carolyn went to Crouch, Cecil Van went to Pires, I went to Hardin, Brenda Sue and Robert (Bobby), went to the Sunbeam Home. Our adventure had begun. I remember being assigned to a room with five other girls on the second floor—they gave me a closet and told me to put my things away—and realizing that this was "forever." That night I sat in the hall and cried because I wanted my mother to come and get me. I cried and cried, but no one ever came. I finally gave up when the bell rang to get ready

for bed. I wasn't so sure anymore that I wanted this adventure.

Adjustments came with time. Listening to the bells ring in the morning to wake us up, hearing the whistles blow to tell us to come to Manna Hall for a meal, cleaning the dorm after breakfast, taking a required nap after lunch, playing before supper, all these activities were soon an established routine.

Visitors, when they came, would always peer at us during nap-time, and I just wished they would go away. I always felt like I was in a cage for them to look at! Bedtime was 8:00 P.M. at Hardin, summer or winter. Sometimes, we were in bed while the sun was still up. I really didn't like that part. I was used to being able to stay up until I was too tired to keep going! Adjustments, again! While my mother came to visit often in the beginning, as the years went on, she came less and less frequently. Occasionally, my beloved grandmother would send a letter or perhaps a little something, like a new swimsuit or a game. Those came less and less, too, as time moved on. I was always so proud when the matron came to my room on Sunday afternoon and said, "Sally Hawkins, you have a visitor at the Welcome Center." We got to go all the way to the Welcome Center and visit for a short time with a loved one. After a few years, I stopped hearing those words. Then I was truly an orphan; a child without parents.

We made up for our losses by creating our own kind of activities. While at Hardin, I remember we had a matron we didn't particularly care for. (She always made us lean over the bath tub, pull down our pants, and then hit us with the "Bo-Bo Paddle.") One summer evening, when we were feeling particularly frisky, we gathered up a gallon jar of June Bugs and pushed the jar, with the lid off, far into the room of our matron, and ran! We laughed and laughed! It felt good to get even! At Christmas, I remember going to East Texas State University, where the students were so kind to us. I remember "bundles" wrapped in Christmas wrapping paper, and we never could guess what might be in our "bundle." The Christmas Cantatas, with Mr. Grube singing bass, have stayed in my memories as though they happened yesterday. What joyous times we had. Those early musical productions have made me love music even today!

Being in church every time the doors were opened seemed like a lot of church for us back then. I remember when I first could read the signs over the doors in the front of the sanctuary that read, "Be Still and Know That I Am God," and "The Lord Is In His Holy Temple," I felt such fear of God. I knew I was never going to be good enough or still enough to make God like me! And we continued to go to church, because it was a requirement of being a citizen of Buckner. I didn't realize it then, but I'm oh, so grateful now, for the training and experiences we had in the Church at Buckner. Remember the scripture that reads, "Train up a child the way he should go, and when he is old, he will not depart from it." Father Buckner and the leaders of Buckner believed that, and they trained us well. I'm grateful.

With every change in grade, we moved to the next place on campus. Four stops in Hardin, then on to Crouch. With each move, we had additional responsibilities assigned to us. Remember working in the old laundry? We'd go up that circular staircase and iron all day, then deliver those pieces to the correct building! We always wanted to deliver shirts to the Boys' Side. The very thought of walking on the "other" side of the campus was thrilling! Then came the new laundry building across from Hardin. The latest, high-tech laundry facilities, and WE got to use them! Complete with dry cleaning machines! Even today, I fold sheets like they just came out of the Mangle. All that work then created a strong work ethic in each of us!

Remember the assignment sheet? Laundry, Big Kitchen, Little Kitchen, Dishwasher, Mop Girl, Slop Girl, Waitress. And for years and years, the Big Girls singing a hymn before each meal? Every time it rained we sang "There Shall Be Showers Of Blessings!" The cafeteria on the balcony in Manna Hall was for visitors; they shared a meal with us—from above—and looked down on us while we ate. If you were really smart, you'd befriend the kids whose mothers worked in the Cafeteria, so you could go up there with them where all that special food was. You always got something unique by being there, perhaps a coke or an extra slice of cake. Anything different was special!

Homecoming in those days was a real treat, too! I remember cleaning the dorms so returning Exes could stay the night on the first floor of a dorm if they wanted to. We loved to wait on their tables at Homecoming, because they always tipped us, and then we had money to take to the Fair with us.

The Fair! Remember those pennants with Buckner written on them that we wore to tell the ride operators that it was OK to let us on the ride; or if we were lost, that meant we could be easily found. I remember getting into the back of what we called cattle trucks and riding all the way to the Fair Grounds in the back. Many of us were crushed together, standing up while we rode, and singing at the top of our voices! I can remember people staring; I'm sure it was a sight to see, several truck loads of kids singing down the road. I guess the safety rule that required seatbelts was not an issue at that time, because we sure had a good time jolting around as we rode those trucks!

Founder's Day in January was always significant for us. As children, we got new clothes from the Commissary for Founder's Day to wear to church for that special occasion. And it was all to honor Father Buckner. Easter also allowed us to visit the Commissary for new clothes for that favored Sunday service. Starting school each Fall meant another visit to the Commissary for clothes. Those brown oxfords we had to wear during the sixth and seventh grade were an embarrassment to me. I disliked them intensely. I felt like they looked like a boy's shoe, and how would the boys ever notice me, if I were wearing those ugly brown shoes? Ah, just before the teen years! It was my goal in life to race and beat the boys, to play football with them—and be as good as them, or better!

Years and age brought me to higher grades, and the privilege of moving around the campus. Pender, of course, was my goal because that would be the final destination before I got to "Leave for Good." It was what everyone looked forward to; boys and girls alike. That last building before graduation and FREEDOM!

While in the seventh grade, I began a sports life that stayed with me through many, many years. I played basketball, was a cheerleader, played what we called kick-ball (soccer), volleyball, ran track, powder-puff football, soft-ball, tennis, and was the first female lifeguard on campus. I remember the lifeguard time because I quit piano to be a lifeguard. Mrs. Myrna Puett, a dedicated musician, had us practicing all the time. I wish now I had continued my piano studies! I was even in the singing group, the Melodeers! We sang, all over the place, and had a great time! To be a lifeguard, I had to take all the classes and tests with the BOYS! Mr. Hime, several boys, and I were in the class the Red Cross provided. I felt so cool. I could not fail; I had to excel! And I did!

Basketball was probably my all-time favorite. I did very well with softball and volley-ball, enjoyed being a cheerleader (those first blue and gold satin uniforms were the best!), but basketball was my favorite. I played forward for Coach Bertha Wilson. She was a wonderful, caring woman. Through the years of playing basketball, our arch-rival, Duncanville, always won in the Tournaments at the end of the season. While I won a trophy for All-Tourney at the end of my eighth-grade year, we still had our ninth grade year to go. Our ninth grade year was so important to us because it was also the very last ninth grade class for Buckner Orphans Home. After our class, all the Home kids would be going to public schools. So, even while they were planning our Sports Banquet, we decided we had to win this Tournament against Duncanville—for Coach Wilson. Talk about excitement! We began the tournament on a high and it never stopped. Every game I played, my hair was soaked with sweat; anticipation sparked the air, and we advanced in the playoffs. Finally the night came for the last game of the tournament with Duncanville. We ended up playing a second overtime to win against Duncanville, and honoring Coach Wilson for our last Junior High game at Buckner. It was a wonderful, exhilarating feeling, though bittersweet, because there would be no more Junior High at Buckner. I got my second All-Tourney trophy and my letter jacket!

Dating came with High School, and Hunt, Buhrman, and Pender. I remember going to the movies in the auditorium. That same auditorium that held Christmas plays, school plays, and other gatherings that brought Ty Hardin, and that grand old gentleman, Burl Ives, who sang "A Little Bitty Tear Let Me Down." I also remember trying to get out of the light for just a moment for smooching at the corner on those green benches or behind the trees or maybe at Maris Welcome Center in the back because it was always dark and cozy there. And then when they put up the security lights after a man broke into Crouch one night, we thought they were put up so people would be able to see us better, and we rebelled!

We changed boyfriends like we changed socks. While at Buhrman, we would sneak out of the dorm to go to the middle of the campus where Father Buckner's statue resided, and meet the boys who were also sneaking out. It must have been all of 11:00 at night. We would frolic across the middle of the campus; harmless fun, but we

really thought we were doing something exciting. We did that quite a while, until someone snitched. Mrs. England spanked us with a paddle—like the one Don Ritchie made for show one Homecoming—and warned us never to participate in that type of behavior again. We promised to give up night adventures just to get out of her office!

Then on to High School at Samuell we went. It was terrifying to mingle with all those kids we hadn't grown up with, didn't know, and didn't want to know. I did not want to do anything except get back to the campus where we were among "our own." For months, I was too embarrassed to use my meal ticket, because everyone would know I didn't have any money. The "other" kids didn't mind using it though—it saved their money! I finally wised up and figured it out! We still played sports, though not like we had at Buckner. This new school didn't let girls do much outside the school except be cheerleaders or drill team members. Ah, if only we had those days today, we'd be stars again!

I'd had "sponsors" in lieu of parents through the years, but no significant relationship had developed. However, on the night of my ninth grade graduation, I met some friends of another friend's sponsor, C. R. and Millie Crady. They invited me to come live with them at the end of my sophomore year. I was elated . . . leaving for good! My only problem was my little sister and little brother were still at Buckner. I felt so bad about that, but felt so good about leaving. Guilt followed me for years, but the Cradys have turned out to be really good people!

I left Buckner that summer, and even though I was very excited to finally be leaving, it was bittersweet, too, because I was leaving behind the only home I had ever known. Even though I didn't attend many Homecomings in the early days, I was always calling the switchboard to find out about Homecoming and what might be happening. Homecomings came and went, and sometimes, when I wasn't working, I would make it to the revels on Sunday afternoon. I didn't realize then the best part was already over. Until I got heavily involved with the Board of Directors, I didn't really know how much there was to Homecoming. Now that I've been involved for years, I would encourage everyone to become involved. Not everyone has good memories from Buckner. There was a time when it didn't have the best workers, but for the most part, we've all come out with a good work ethic, a caring for family that exceeds our immediate family, and a love for Buckner that is unfathomable to outsiders.

Last year when I entered the campus on Saturday morning for Homecoming, I saw a woman, with a head of gray hair—standing close to the fence, dividing the old campus from the new campus—looking toward the high school and then toward the boys' side of the campus. I paused as I watched from across the campus, because I knew she was remembering days and years gone past. I wished then that I were a painter whose brush could capture that exact moment. It will be forever etched in my mind.

So, as I drove past Manna Hall on Sunday, October 3, 1999, at the end of our annual Homecoming, I realized that I wouldn't see these buildings again. As I slowly drove past the Hospital, I noticed that each end of the building had a stone in place, showing a baby wrapped in swaddling with its hands outstretched. I'd never noticed it before. Now it meant something to me. I looked at trees I'd stood under, windows I'd gone through while I was sneaking in or out, and looked at the place where Father Buckner's statue stood and was grateful that I was a child of this family. Grateful that there was a place like Buckner for a kid like me to go for refuge. I think I've finally figured out what was making me so sad about the buildings being torn down. The Buckner campus that is being torn down was the only home some of us ever knew; the only home we had until we were adults, and losing it is like a little piece of security lost.

We will never stop being "family." There is a special bond that connects all Buckner children, through the years and through the miles. When we see each other, even without the buildings, it will always be like coming home, again.

Sixties

The front steps of Cullom Dorm: Ken Norman, Johnny Huffstutler, and Buck Grayson.

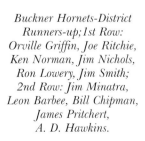

Dennis Tucker working at the dairy.

Ken Norman, a great Sixties athlete.

Buckner Hornets-District Runners-up;1st Row: Orville Griffin, Joe Ritchie, Ken Norman, Jim Nichols, Ron Lowery, Jim Smith; 2nd Row: Jim Minatra, Leon Barbee, Bill Chipman, James Pritchert, A. D. Hawkins.

Loading clothes in the machines.

Working on the tractor.

The Bakery: Ron Lowery, Preston Baxley, Ed Grube.

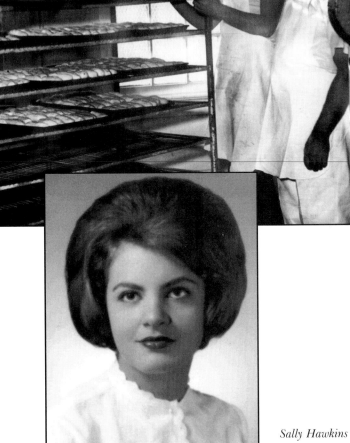

Academy school classroom.

Sally Hawkins

206

Buckner Boxing Club

Academy School Thanksgiving Program, 1968

Inside the gym.

207

The fearful spiral stairway to the old laundry.

The old tree by Hunt Home where we spent many happy hours.

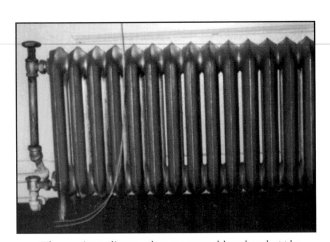

Those noisy radiators where we toasted bread and apples.

Jerry Karlovich, Talent Show practice.

208

The Bakery and Kitchen.

Wayne Hurst and Kathy Sallings, at the "Rec."

Chris Hoyt with clean towels.

Ella Harper, Jeff Capps, Lauren Holloman, and Wanette Holloman, c 68.

The Seventies

"No, I will not abandon you or leave you as orphans
in the storm—I will come to you."

John 14:18, RSI

Brenda (Madkin) Peeples, '70

I was at the Home from the fall of 1966 until I graduated from W. W. Samuell High School in May of 1970.

There are many things I remember about my life at the Home, but my favorite subject is the choir program at the church on campus.

I started singing in choir when Mr. Phil Perrin was our Music Director. He eventually formed a small girls' group, called "The Select Group," to sing in church and at special functions. The group broke up when Mr. Perrin and his family left the Home to work in Kentucky.

Chuck Rednour was the Music director who came next, and shortly after he arrived, he began to play his guitar in church and at choir practice. All of us in the choir thought this was really neat! I expressed an interest in learning to play guitar also, and eventually got my own instrument, which Chuck helped me learn to play for our choir performances.

The first summer Chuck was at Buckner, a group of us kids expressed a desire to go to all the dormitories and tell the kids about our experiences as Christians. This small revival on campus led to the formation of the singing group, The Disciples.

The Disciples sang and gave testimony not only on campus, but also when the choirs went out on church tours. We eventually got to sing at the Houston Astrodome before an Astro's game. We very much enjoyed giving a witness for Christ and for Buckner Home though our music.

The disciples had a sort of "reunion" of their own in 1980. We were invited to sing in church at Homecoming that year. Brother Rednour and quite a few of our group returned, and we had a great time singing together again. Sue, his wife, put together a photo book of our activities and gave each of us our own copy.

Music will always be an important part of my life, and I owe a real debt to Brother Chuck and my experiences in The Disciples.

Anita Lee (Weichert) Muns, '78

LOVE STORY

I lived at the Home from 1976 to 1978 where Joe Wayne Dabbs and I became sweethearts. Joey was in Carnett dorm and I was in Teacherage. Joey was on the basketball team at the home. Two of my friends, Carrie Armstrong and Jean Davis, were at that game and told me that Joey couldn't keep his eyes off me. I did not believe them, but he came right up and asked me if he could walk me to my dorm after the game.

One evening at the recreation center, as I sat down on the bleachers in the gym and reached down to untie my shoes to jump on the trampoline, I heard Joey's voice. I watched as he and one of his dorm mates, Jamie, trotted up and won the

210

court, shooting basket after basket. They caught me watching and started to show off.

Eventually, Joey began teaching me how to turn smoothly on certain moves, but I started goofing off and "crack" went my ankle. Everyone in the gym came running. The coach took me in the van to the hospital off campus. Sure enough, my ankle was broken.

After a trip for X-rays, a cast and crutches, Coach took me to the Home Clinic for a short recuperation time.

The clinic was divided into two sides, boys on one end; girls on the other, with Mrs. Laird in the middle at the nurse's station. I will never forget this beautiful soul. She showed us love when we needed love and when none of us were sure what adult love was.

Joey came by (with permission) every day until I was released to go back to my dorm. We began dating. One night we slipped out for an extra date, got caught and were put on restriction. I was moved over to the Halfway House. I never saw Joey again.

I looked for him off and on for years. I just this year (1999) located him. He said he had thought of me often. Now we are writing and are good friends.

We will always have the memory of the love of first sweethearts, but I also am grateful for the times we shared our pains with each other from before we were at the home. We got each other through a lot as did all of our friends (family) at Buckner. Hopefully someday we can see one another again.

SUNDAYS IN THE DORM

Sundays were pretty quiet around the dorm. The older kids on campus rode the yellow school buses downtown to the Big Baptist Church where W. A. Criswell was pastor. After church we ate Sunday dinner at Manna Hall and then went to our dorms for the rest of the afternoon. We had church that evening in the chapel on campus and headed back to our dorms for chips and sandwiches for supper.

Some of the girls had sponsors or relatives that would pick them up and spend the day with them. One Sunday evening, one of the girls had slipped a pack of Salem cigarettes in and asked two of the other girls and me to meet her in the room after devotions that night.

We tippy-toed down to her room where we all took turns with the one cigarette she had left. Eyes watering and cough choking, we thought we looked so-o-cool! We were too busy noticing our smoke blowing up from our attempts to blow out artfully. We didn't notice anything else. But, while we were showing off to each other, the door flew open and there stood Mr. B.

I immediately tossed the cigarette under the bed.

He said that he had smelled smoke, then asked if we had been smoking.

In spite of the smoke coming up all around us from under the bed where I had tried to hide the evidence, we all tried to look innocent.

He pointed out the smoke curls, and told us that we each had to write a report, thoroughly researched, on the dangers of smoking and turn it in to him the next day.

THE NEW GIRLS ON THE CAMPUS

One very early morning about 2:00 A.M., our house parents knocked on our doors and told us that the Vietnamese dorm (Pires) was on fire. We all gathered on the front lawn and watched firemen running everywhere over the building. The Bickfords told us they had heard there was an electrical fire. They also said some of the Vietnamese girls would be coming to live in our dorm. We all agreed that those girls had already had a bad enough time, being shipped over here to the U.S. when their parents had been killed in the war.

The next morning when we were all lining up to go to Manna Hall, standing in line with us were three of the girls. We all joined hands and formed a circle to thank the Lord they had made it safely out of their dorm and to the U.S. We knew the loneliness of their hearts because we also had no parents at that time.

When we finished, the Vietnamese girls thanked us in their broken English. We accepted each other and came to be friends. We realized we all had a place now where we could feel safe and cared for, and where we could care for each other.

Seventies

The Golden Gloves, 1971.

Girl's track, 1975.

Swimming

*The Manna Hall,
always set for a meal.*

Dr. R. C. Campbell with children, 1972.

*The Dallas Home Academy
School, 1973.*

213

Children ready to travel.

The Bakery was always a favorite place.

Anita Muns and Joe Wayne Dabbs, 1978.

Adults In Our Lives

Brother Hal and Miss Bertha with Bobbi Richardson in font of the chapel, 1951.

Colonel and Mrs. Buckner.

Eunice Work, Housemother, 1928-1944.

Mrs. Jo Shurette at the Centennial Celebration.

Dr. Willie B. Robinson, "Dr. Rob," our dentist, 1930s and 40s.

Mr. and Mrs. G. G. Dickey with 1944 students.

Mildred McCullough and Audra Walker, HS teachers.

Mrs. Lucy Dunn, "Mama Dunn" to all orphans.

Gordon S. Taylor, Dean of Boys and Coach.

Mary McCorkle, Elementary Teacher.

Mr. Ferguson, Farm Boss.

Effie Watkins, Teacher.

216

The famous Redhead Club,
Mabel Wells, Pinky Sikes,
Mildred McCullough,
Dr. and Mrs. Anglin Hyden.

Mr. G. G. Dickey

Colonel Buckner with Jo Ann Nelson and Jane McWhorter.

Mrs. Jean Hack, Miss Reeves, the Hydens.

Our science, reading, and health teacher, 1950.

Miss Chastain, 1950.

Miss Gayle Keeter, Science Teacher and Girls' Basketball Coach.

Ms. Coleman, English Teacher..

Mrs. Gussie Turner and Donald Johnson.

Miss Ophelia Isbel, Home Economics Teacher, 1949-50.

Coach M. L. Greenwood and child.

Miss Fanny Boyd and Mildred McCullough.

Mrs. Helen Roberts, Piano Teacher, 1947-51.

Miss Dora Brady, Dean of Girls with Her Famous Car.

219

Miss Ruth Rouse,
Typing Teacher, 1950.

J. D. Smith,
Farm Hand, 1950.

Miss Swofford,
Elementary Teacher.

Mr. J. V. Browning,
H. S. Principal.

Miss Jean Musick, Elementary Teacher
and Pool Director.

Charles Boldin, High School
Football Coach.

Mr. E. L. Dominy, Elementary Principal.

Frankie Dee Parks and Mr. Browning.

Mr. Tom Arthur Sproles, High School Principal.

Mrs. Ellen Boldin,
High School English and Speech Teacher.

Mr. Mac Alexander, Dean of Boys and Coach,
in front of Pires.

Mrs. Jerre Graves Simmons, English and
Speech,1955-57.

221

Epilogue

The stories in this book are historical, personal recordings of a place and time now alive only in our memories. Each presents the perspective of one individual writer, differing from each other, but also part of a tapestry that will bring to life again a significant yesterday.

Unfortunately, many children arrived at Buckner Home so angry and alarmed at their new circumstances that for a long time they could only lash out at any authority. Others were simply in shock because of the tragedies that had rocked their world. Some few were immediately cognizant that they had found a safe harbor. These fortunate ones had the easiest transition into a new life.

On entry, we all immediately met the inventive, intrepid children who became our friends and whom we now recall with love and a surprising fondness even for those we thought we didn't much like. Unfortunately a roommate that we were not compatible with would not go away, so we had to learn to get along with everyone; not a bad lesson to learn.

Though children were in the majority at the Home, we also encountered there adults who supervised our daily activities. Some of these assumed fearfully mythic proportions for us. They are no longer here to speak in their own defense or explain their actions, but if they were, they might surprise us with reasonable justifications. As a mature Harold Campbell has said, "All the kids thought the matrons were too strict. That's the nature of being a kid."

For one example, Miss Mamie, manager of the Manna Hall, certainly touched all our lives. Some remember her fondly, others not so fondly. However, we all recognize that no matter how harshly we judged her rules and retributions, she was responsible for getting food on the table in the Manna Hall with only a small adult kitchen crew and the older girls. When the whistles blew and the bells rang, the marching lines of exuberant children and teenagers converged on the Manna Hall, and day after day, no matter how many of us there were, we always ate every meal on time. She was responsible for that.

Even then, in spite of her rigid discipline, we all had a grudging admiration for the fierceness of such a woman. She so sought to control the dirt around us that having learned cleanliness from her, we battle it today in our own homes with the same desperately frenzied, but knowledgeable aim that she taught us. We must give her credit for an admirable end product—a squeaky clean kitchen and girls with busy hands—and salute her for withstanding, unmoved, our youthful tempers and tantrums.

Our matrons were on duty day and night, even weekends and holidays. How gratefully they must have welcomed school days after a long summer. What a monumental job they took on, an unattractive mission that could only have been prompted by a desire—which we failed to perceive then—to follow the biblical admonition of service that says "Inasmuch as you have done it unto the least of these, you have done it unto me." We never stopped to consider how difficult their jobs were nor how tiring, but we simply sharpened our negotiation skills as we railed against their attempts to improve our behavior.

The accepted philosophy for bringing up children in most of the early decades of the past century, was based very literally upon the scriptural admonition, "Spare the rod and spoil the child." This philosophy also meant giving out awards and compliments very sparingly and carefully controlling all displays of affection. The greatest worry was that compliments and coddling might make a person too conceited. Humility was admired. No one was concerned with the modern shibboleths of working at building up a child's self image by praise. We thought hard work and strict obedience would eventually produce strong, well adjusted adults.

If we make the mistake of judging events of that past age by today's standards, we do that time and ourselves a disservice. Everyone did things differently then.

Then as now, Buckner was a rescue mission for children, providing a time of stable respite from an untrustworthy world. So many Buckner people gave tirelessly of themselves for us. Another alumni would have a different list of favorite examples, and I must confess that I remember some of those unhappily mentioned in the preceding pages quite differently from the way they are portrayed.

I do remember how the younger girls blossomed under the loving care of Miss Dolly Orr. I remember the kindnesses of Miss Marshall, Miss Ratcliff, and Miss Hardy. I remember Miss Wilson, from Buhrman Hall, whom we called "Miz Willie." When I announced to my friends after college graduation that I was marrying, I was surprised to receive in the mail a white Bible, lovingly inscribed in sprawling script, from "Miz Willie." My wedding day was set on her anniversary date. I carried her Bible in my wedding ceremony and still cherish her kind and meaningful gift.

We cannot mention all those who influenced us by name, but because of the stability we found at Buckner our lives have become human monuments, marking the productive result of the contributions of Father Buckner and all those who dwelt among us.

Though we were for awhile the leftover children, because of those who cared for us, we were not "Oliver Twists," not just orphans adrift in the world, but sheltered on that campus which, as we grew older, became hallowed ground for us.

In fact, though we did not realize it then, for all those years at Buckner, we were "at play in the fields of the Lord."

JERRE SIMMONS

Index